FRENCH
Vocabulary

Third Edition

by

Christopher Kendris

B.S., M.S., M.A., Ph.D.
Diplômé, Faculté des Lettres, Université de Paris
Institut de Phonétique, Paris (en Sorbonne)
Former Chairman
Department of Foreign Languages
Farmingdale High School
Farmingdale, New York

and

Theodore N. Kendris

B.A., Union College
M.A., Northwestern University
Ph.D., Université Laval
Department of Languages and Cultures
Bloomsburg University of Pennsylvania
Bloomsburg, Pennsylvania

BARRON'S EDUCATIONAL SERIES, INC.

To our parish, St. Sophia Greek Orthodox Church
of Albany, New York,
and
to the eternal memory of our beloved
Yolanda Kendris,
who is always by our side.
With love

All inquiries should be addressed to:
Barron's Educational Series, Inc.
250 Wireless Boulevard
Hauppauge, New York 11788
http://www.barronseduc.com

ISBN: 978-0-7641-4770-8

Library of Congress Catalog Card No. 2012932567

PRINTED IN CHINA
9 8 7 6 5 4 3 2 1

CONTENTS

CONTENTS

HOW TO USE THIS BOOK

This book is one of a popular series of handy vocabulary reference guides. It is designed for students, business people, and others who want to "brush up" on their knowledge of French vocabulary in any given subject area. This is not a book of French grammar with exercises and it is not a book of French civilization or culture. It is a book that will help you build, improve, and expand your French vocabulary on many different topics, as you can see in the table of contents. Previous knowledge of French vocabulary has not been taken for granted in these pages.

OVERALL DESIGN

The French vocabulary in this pocket reference book is arranged by topics. Subtopics contain several themes related in thought to the main topic. Under a subtopic you can find many commonly used basic words, phrases, and expressions that are useful in everyday situations. These are valuable not only for students and teachers but also for the general public; for example, travelers in France and other French-speaking countries and regions, persons in the world of business, banking, science and technology, politics, the fine arts, telecommunications, mathematics, the natural sciences, and many others.

The first thing to do is browse through the table of contents. You will find topics of special interest to you because of the wide range of topics. For example, the second chapter is of interest to everyone because it is about people: members of a family, relatives, friends, descriptions of people, personalities, social traits, moods, general human characteristics, basic personal information, parts of the human body, bodily processes and movements, sensory perception, and looking after one's health. If any given topic is of particular interest to you, turn to the page where it begins. We are certain that the section you select will provide you with many interesting and useful basic words, phrases, and expressions.

FEATURES

English words are listed on the left side of the page. French equivalents appear in the middle of the page. Next to the French, you will find abbreviations that indicate gender or part of speech. On the right side of the page you are given sound transcriptions to help you pronounce the French words effectively for communication. The pronunciation guide in the beginning pages of the book introduces you to a simple system of sound transcriptions that we devised.

We sincerely hope that this book will be of some help to you in expanding your knowledge and power of French vocabulary.

Theodore N. Kendris   Christopher Kendris
B.A., M.A., Ph.D.   B.S., M.S., M.A., Ph.D.

PRONUNCIATION GUIDE

The purpose of this guide is to help you pronounce French words as correctly as possible so you can communicate effectively. It is not intended to perfect your pronunciation of French; that is accomplished by imitating correct spoken French.

In French there are several spellings for the same sound; for example, the following spellings are all pronounced *ay*, as in the English word *say*.

et   (j')**ai**   (parl)**é**   (av)**ez**   (all)**er**   (l)**es**

The system of transcription of French sounds used here is English letters in italics. As soon as you catch on to this system, you will find it *ee-zee*. At first, you will have to refer to the list repeatedly until it is fixed in your mind. The sounds are arranged alphabetically in a list in transcription form. This is the easiest way for you to find the transcription quickly as you read the English letters next to the French words.

Consonant sounds are approximately the same in French and English. Any variations in the pronunciation of some French consonants are found in the sound transcriptions. When speaking French, stress is evenly distributed on the vowels but you must raise your voice slightly on the last transcription sound when more than one is in a group; for example, in pronouncing s'il **vous plaît** (please), raise your voice slightly on *pleh* in *seel-voo-pleh*.

There are only four nasal vowel sounds in French. They are expressed in the following catchy phrase, which means *a good white wine*.

un   bon   vin   blanc
UH   *bOH*   *vEH*   *blAH*

A nasal vowel is indicated by two italicized capital letters. How do you nasalize a vowel in French? Instead of letting your breath (air) out of your mouth, you must push it up your nose so that it does not come out of your mouth.

Remember that the two italicized capital letters are nasal vowels. They do not indicate any stress or raising of your voice in pronunciation.

The hyphens in the transcription sounds do not indicate a division of words into syllables. They indicate a separation of the different sounds so you can find them easily in the alphabetical list of italicized transcription letters. Whenever the final consonant of a French word is pronounced and linked, as in a liaison, with the first vowel or silent **h** of the word that follows, this is indicated in the sound transcriptions; for example, normally, **vous** is pronounced *voo*, but in **vous avez** it is pronounced *voo-zavay*.

Transcription letters	Pronounced approximately as in the English word	French word	Sound transcription
a	something like the vowel sound in Tom	**la**	*la*
ah	**ah**!	pas	*pah*
ay	s**ay**	**ai**	*ay*
e	th**e**	**le**	*le*
ee	s**ee**	**ici**	*ee-see*
eh	**e**gg	m**è**re	*mehr*
ew	f**ew**	**lu**	*lew*
ew-ee	**you** **ea**t	**huit**	*ew-eet*
ny	ca**ny**on	monta**gne**	*mOH-ta-ny*
o	als**o**	h**ô**tel	*o-tehl*
oh	**oh**!	ch**ose**	*sh-oh-z*
oo	t**oo**	**ou**	*oo*
or	**or**	p**or**te	*port*
sh	**sh**ip	**ch**ose	*sh-oh-z*
ss	ki**ss**	ce**ss**e	*seh-ss*
u	b**u**n	b**o**nne	*bun*
uh	p**u**dding	p**eux**	*puh*
ur	p**urr**	h**eu**re	*ur*
y	**y**es	jo**y**eux	*zh-wah-yuh*
yay	**yea**	pa**yer**	*pay-yay*
z	**z**ero	**z**éro	*zay-roh*
zh	mea**s**ure	**j**e	*zhe*

NASAL VOWELS

UH	not an English sound, but close to s**ung**	**un**	*UH*
OH	not an English sound, but close to s**ong**	b**on**	*bOH*
EH	not an English sound, but close to s**ang**	**vin**	*vEH*
AH	not an English sound, but close to thr**ong**	bl**anc**	*blAH*

ABBREVIATIONS

adj	adjective	*n*	noun
adv	adverb	*pl*	plural
conj	conjunction	*pol*	polite form
f	feminine	*prep*	preposition
fam	familiar form	*pron*	pronoun
indef	indefinite	*s*	singular
m	masculine	*v*	verb

BASIC INFORMATION

1. ARITHMETIC

a. CARDINAL NUMBERS

zero	zéro	*zay-ro*
one	un	*UH*
	une	*ewn*
two	deux	*duh*
three	trois	*trwah*
four	quatre	*katr*
five	cinq	*sEHk*
six	six	*seess*
seven	sept	*seht*
eight	huit	*ew-eet*
nine	neuf	*nuf*
ten	dix	*dees*
eleven	onze	*OH-z*
twelve	douze	*dooz*
thirteen	treize	*trehz*
fourteen	quatorze	*ka-torz*
fifteen	quinze	*kEHz*
sixteen	seize	*sehz*
seventeen	dix-sept	*dee-seht*
eighteen	dix-huit	*dee-zew-eet*
nineteen	dix-neuf	*deez-nuf*
twenty	vingt	*vEH*
twenty-one	vingt et un	*vEH tay UH*
twenty-two	vingt-deux	*vEH-duh*
twenty-three	vingt-trois	*vEH-trwah*
twenty-four	vingt-quatre	*vEH-katr*
twenty-five	vingt-cinq	*vEH-sEHk*
twenty-six	vingt-six	*vEH-seess*
twenty-seven	vingt-sept	*vEH-seht*
twenty-eight	vingt-huit	*vEH-tew-eet*
twenty-nine	vingt-neuf	*vEH-nuf*
thirty	trente	*trAHt*
thirty-one	trente et un	*trAHt-ay-UH*
thirty-two	trente-deux	*trAHt-duh*
thirty-three	trente-trois	*trAHt-trwah*
. . .		
forty	quarante	*ka-rAHt*
forty-one	quarante et un	*ka-rAHt-ay-UH*
forty-two	quarante-deux	*ka-rAHt-dUH*
forty-three	quarante-trois	*ka-rAHt-trwah*

...

fifty	cinquante	*sEH-k'AHt*
fifty-one	cinquante et un	*sEH-kAHt-ay-UH*
fifty-two	cinquante-deux	*sEH-kAHt-duh*
fifty-three	cinquante-trois	*sEH-kAHt-trwah*

...

sixty	soixante	*swa-sAHt*
sixty-one	soixante et un	*swa-sAHt-ay-UH*

...

seventy	soixante-dix	*swa-sAHt-dees*
seventy-one	soixante et onze	*swa-sAHt-ay-OH-z*
seventy-two	soixante-douze	*swa-sAHt-dooz*

...

eighty	quatre-vingts	*katr-vEH*
eighty-one	quatre-vingt-un	*katr-vEH-UH*

...

ninety	quatre-vingt-dix	*katr-vEH-dees*
ninety-one	quatre-vingt-onze	*katr-vEH-OH-z*

...

one hundred	cent	*sAH*
one hundred and one	cent un	*sAH-UH*
one hundred and two	cent deux	*sAH-duh*

...

two hundred	deux cents	*duh-sAH*
two hundred and one	deux cent un	*duh-sAH-UH*

...

three hundred	trois cents	*trwah-sAH*

...

one thousand	mille	*meel*
one thousand and one	mille un	*meel-UH*

...

two thousand	deux mille	*duh meel*
two thousand and one	deux mille un	*duh meel UH*

...

three thousand	trois mille	*trwah meel*

...

four thousand	quatre mille	*katr meel*

...

one hundred thousand	cent mille	*sAH meel*

...

two hundred thousand	deux cent mille	*duh sAH meel*

...

one million	un million	*UH meel-yOH*
one million and one	un million un	*UH meel-yOH UH*
one million and two	un million deux	*UH meel-yOH duh*
...		
two million	deux millions	*duh meel-yOH*
...		
three million	trois millions	*trwah meel-yOH*
...		
one hundred million	cent millions	*sAH meel-yOH*
...		
one billion	un milliard	*UH meel-yar*
...		
two billion	deux milliards	*duh meel-yar*

b. ORDINAL NUMBERS

first	premier (*adj/m*)	*prem-yay*
	première (*adj/f*)	*prem-yehr*
second	second	*se-gOH*
	seconde	*se-gOH-d (if the 2nd of 2)*
	deuxième	*duhz-yehm (if the 2nd of more than 2)*
third	troisième	*trwahz-yehm*
fourth	quatrième	*katr-yehm*
fifth	cinquième	*sEHk-yehm*
sixth	sixième	*seez-yehm*
seventh	septième	*seht-yehm*
eighth	huitième	*ew-eet-yehm*
ninth	neuvième	*nuhv-yehm*
tenth	dixième	*deez-yehm*
eleventh	onzième	*OHz-yehm*
twelfth	douzième	*dooz-yehm*
thirteenth	treizième	*trehz-yehm*
...		
twenty-third	vingt-troisième	*vEH-trwahz-yehm*
thirty-third	trente-troisième	*trAHt-trwahz-yehm*
forty-third	quarante-troisième	*ka-rAHt-trwahz-yehm*
...		
hundredth	centième	*sAHt-yehm*
...		
thousandth	millième	*meel-yehm*
...		
millionth	millionième	*meel-yun-yehm*
...		
billionth	milliardième	*meel-yard-yehm*

c. FRACTIONS

a (one) half	un demi	*UH dmee*
a (one) third	un tiers	*UH tyehr*
a (one) fourth	un quart	*UH kar*
a (one) fifth	un cinquième	*UH sEHk-yehm*

APPROXIMATE AMOUNTS

about ten	une dizaine	*ewn dee-zehn*
about fifteen	une quinzaine	*ewn kEH-zehn*
about twenty	une vingtaine	*ewn vEH-tehn*
about thirty	une trentaine	*ewn trAH-tehn*
about forty	une quarantaine	*ewn karAH-tehn*
about fifty	une cinquantaine	*ewn sEH-kAH-tehn*
about sixty	une soixantaine	*ewn swa-sAH-tehn*
about a hundred	une centaine	*ewn sAH-tehn*
about a thousand	un millier	*UH meel-yay*

d. TYPES OF NUMBERS

number	chiffre (*m*)	*sheefre*
	nombre (*m*)	*nOH-bre*
	numéro (*m*)	*new-may-ro*
• **number**	numéroter (*v*)	*new-may-rut-ay*
• **numeral**	numéral (*m*)	*new-may-ral*
• **numerical**	numérique (*adj*)	*new-may-reek*
Arabic numerals	chiffres (*m*) arabes	*sheefrez-arab*
binary	binaire (*adj*)	*bee-nehr*
cardinal	cardinal (*adj*)	*kar-dee-nal*
complex	complexe (*adj*)	*kOH-plehks*
digit	chiffre (*m*)	*sheefre*
even	pair (*adj*)	*pehr*
fraction	fraction (*f*)	*fraks-yOH*
• **fractional**	fractionnaire (*adj*)	*fraks-yun-ehr*
imaginary	imaginaire (*adj*)	*ee-ma-zh-ee-nehr*
integer	nombre entier (*m*)	*nOH-bre AHt-yay*
irrational	irrationnel (*adj*)	*ee-ras-yun-ehl*
natural	naturel (*adj*)	*na-tewr-ehl*
negative	négatif (*adj*)	*nay-ga-teef*
odd	impair (*adj*)	*EH-pehr*
ordinal	ordinal (*adj*)	*or-dee-nal*
positive	positif (*adj*)	*pu-see-teef*
prime number	nombre premier (*m*)	*nOH-bre prem-yay*

rational	rationnel (*adj*)	*ras-yun-ehl*
real	réel (*adj*)	*ray-ehl*
reciprocal	réciproque (*adj*)	*ray-see-pruk*
Roman numeral	chiffre (*m*) romain	*sheefre rum-EH*

e. BASIC OPERATIONS

arithmetical operations	opérations fondamentales (*f, pl*)	*up-ay-ras-yOH fOH-da-mAH-tal*
add (on)	ajouter (*v*)	*azh-oo-tay*
• **addition**	addition (*f*)	*a-dee-sy-OH*
• **plus**	plus	*plewss*
	et	*ay*
• **two plus two equals four**	deux et deux font quatre	*duh ay duh fOH katr*
subtract	soustraire (*v*)	*soos-trehr*
• **subtraction**	soustraction (*f*)	*soos-trak-sy-OH*
• **minus**	moins	*mwEH*
• **three minus two equals one**	trois moins deux font un	*trwah mwEH duh fOH UH*
multiply	multiplier (*v*)	*mewl-tee-ply-ay*
• **multiplication**	multiplication (*f*)	*mewl-tee-plee-kas-yOH*
• **multiplication table**	table de multiplication (*f*)	*tabl de mewl-tee-plee-kas-yOH*
• **multiplied by**	multiplié par	*mewl-tee-ply-ay par*
• **three times two equals six**	trois fois deux font six	*trwah fwa duh fOH seess*
divide	diviser (*v*)	*dee-vee-zay*
• **divided by**	divisé par	*dee-vee-zay par*
• **division**	division (*f*)	*dee-vee-zyOH*
• **six divided by three equals two**	six divisés par trois font deux	*seess dee-vee-zay par trwah fOH duh*
raise to a power	élever (*v*) à une puissance	*ayl-vay a ewn pew-ee-sAH-ss*
• **to the power of**	à la puissance de	*a la pew-ee-sAH-ss de*
• **squared**	au carré	*oh ka-ray*
• **cubed**	au cube	*oh kewb*
• **to the fourth power**	à la quatrième puissance	*a la katr-yehm pew-ee-sAH-ss*
• **to the nth power**	à la puissance n	*a la pew-ee-sAH-ss ehn*
• **two squared equals four**	deux au carré égalent quatre	*duh oh ka-ray ay-gal katr*
extract a root	extraire (*v*) la racine	*eks-trehr la ra-seen*
• **square root**	racine au carré	*ra-seen oh ka-ray*
• **cube root**	racine cubique	*ra-seen kew-beek*
• **nth root**	à la racine n	*a la ra-seen ehn*
• **(the) square root of nine is three**	la racine au carré de neuf est trois	*la ra-seen oh ka-ray de nuf eh trwah*

ratio
  • **twelve is to four as nine is to three**

proportion (*f*)
  douze est à quatre comme neuf est à trois

pru-por-syOH
dooz eh ta katr kum nuf eh ta trwah

FOCUS: Arithmetical Operations

Addition—Addition
$2 + 3 = 5$ two plus three equals five   deux et trois font cinq

Subtraction—Soustraction
$9 - 3 = 6$ nine minus three equals six   neuf moins trois font six

Multiplication—Multiplication
$4 \times 2 = 8$ four times two equals eight   quatre fois deux font huit
$4 \cdot 2 = 8$ four multiplied by two equals eight   quatre multipliés par deux égalent huit

Division—Division
$10 \div 2 = 5$ ten divided by two equals five   dix divisés par deux font cinq

Raising to a power—Elévation à une puissance
$3^2 = 9$ three squared (or to the second power) equals nine   trois au carré égalent neuf
$2^3 = 8$ two cubed (or to the third power) equals eight   deux au cube égalent huit
$2^4 = 16$ two to the fourth power equals sixteen   deux à la quatrième égalent seize
x^n x to the nth power   x à la puissance n

Extraction of root—Extraction d'une racine
$\sqrt[2]{4} = 2$ the square root of four is two   la racine carrée de quatre est deux
$\sqrt[3]{27} = 3$ the cube root of twenty-seven is three   la racine cubique de vingt-sept est trois
$\sqrt[n]{x}$ the nth root of x   la racine n de x

Ratio—Proportion
$12 : 4 = 9 : 3$ twelve is to four as nine is to three   douze est à quatre comme neuf est à trois

f. ADDITIONAL MATHEMATICAL CONCEPTS

algebra	algèbre (f)	al-zh-ehbr
• **algebraic**	algébrique (adj)	al-zh-ay-breek
arithmetic	arithmétique (f)	a-reet-may-teek
• **arithmetical**	arithmétique (adj)	a-reet-may-teek
average	moyenne (f)	mwa-yehn
calculate	calculer (v)	kal-kew-lay
• **calculation**	calcul (m)	kal-kewl
constant	constante (f)	kOH-stAHt
count	compter (v)	kOH-tay
• **countable**	comptable (adj)	kOH-tabl
decimal	décimal (adj)	day-see-mal
difference	différence (f)	dee-fay-rAH-ss
equality	égalité (f)	ay-ga-lee-tay
• **equals**	est égal à	eh tay-gal a
• **does not equal**	n'est pas égal à	neh pa-zay-gal a
• **is equivalent to**	est équivalent à	eh tay-kee-val-AH a
• **is greater than**	est supérieur à	eh sew-pay-ry-ur a
• **is less than**	est inférieur à	eh tEH-fay-ry-ur a
• **is similar to**	est pareil à	eh pa-ray a
equation	équation (f)	ay-kwas-yOH
factor	facteur (m)	fak-tur
• **factor**	mettre (v) en facteurs	meht-re AH fak-tur
• **factorization**	mise (f) en facteurs	meez AN fak-tur
factorial	factoriel (adj)	fak-tu-ry-ehl
	factorielle (f)	fak-tu-ry-ehl
function	fonction (f)	fOH-ks-yOH
logarithm	logarithme (m)	lug-a-reet-me
logarithmic	logarithmique (adj)	lug-a-reet-meek
multiple	multiple (m)	mewl-teepl
percent	pour cent	poor sAH
• **percentage**	pourcentage (m)	poor-sAH-tazh
problem	problème (m)	prub-lehm
• **problem to solve**	problème à résoudre	prub-lehm a ray-zoo-dr
product	produit (m)	prud-ew-ee
quotient	quotient (m)	kuss-yAH
set	ensemble (m)	AH-sAH-bl
solution	solution (f)	sul-ew-syOH
• **solve**	résoudre (v)	ray-zoo-dr
statistics	statistique (f)	sta-tees-teek
• **statistical**	statistique (adj)	sta-tees-teek
sum	calcul (m)	kal-kewl
• **sum**	additionner (v)	a-dee-sy-ON-nay
	sommer (v)	sum-ay
symbol	symbole (m)	sEH-bul
variable	variable (f)	var-ya-bl

2. GEOMETRY

a. FIGURES

plane figures	figures planes (*f*)	*feeg-ewr plan*
triangle	triangle (*m*)	*tree-yAH-gl*
• **acute-angled**	acutangle (*adj*)	*akew-tAH-gl*
• **equilateral**	équilatéral (*adj*)	*ay-kew-ee-la-tay-ral*
• **isosceles**	isocèle (*adj*)	*ee-zu-sehl*
• **obtuse-angled**	obtusangle (*adj*)	*up-tew-zAH-gl*
• **right-angled**	rectangle (*adj*)	*rehk-tAH-gl*
• **scalene**	scalène (*adj*)	*ska-lehn*
four-sided figures	figures à quatre côtés	*feeg-ewr a katr ko-tay*
• **parallelogram**	parallélogramme (*m*)	*para-lay-lu-gram*
• **rectangle**	rectangle (*m*)	*rehk-tAH-gl*
• **rhombus**	rhombe (*m*)	*rOH-b*
• **square**	carré (*m*)	*ka-ray*
• **trapezoid**	trapèze (*m*)	*tra-pehz*
n-sided figures	figures à côtés n	*fee-gewr a ko-tay ehn*
• **pentagon**	pentagone (*m*)	*pAH-ta-gun*
• **hexagon**	hexagone (*m*)	*ehg-za-gun*
• **heptagon**	heptagone (*m*)	*eph-ta-gun*
• **octagon**	octogone (*m*)	*uk-tug-un*
• **decagon**	décagone (*m*)	*day-ka-gun*

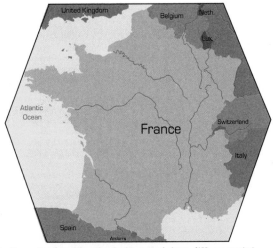

Note: France is often referred to by its general shape, *l'Hexagone (m)*.

FOCUS: Geometrical Figures

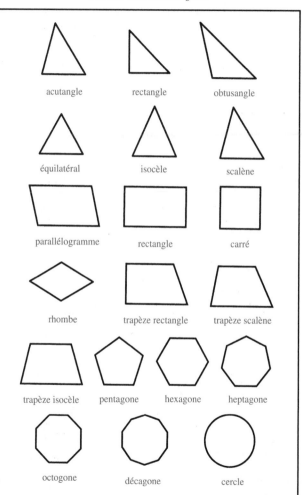

acutangle   rectangle   obtusangle

équilatéral   isocèle   scalène

parallélogramme   rectangle   carré

rhombe   trapèze rectangle   trapèze scalène

trapèze isocèle   pentagone   hexagone   heptagone

octogone   décagone   cercle

FOCUS: Geometrical Solids

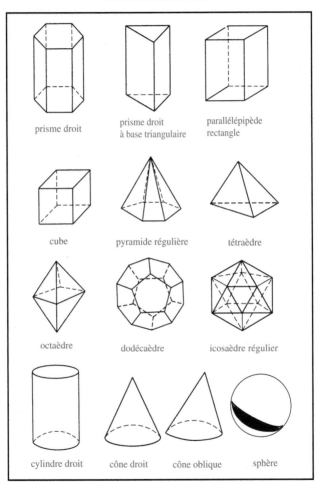

prisme droit

prisme droit
à base triangulaire

parallélépipède
rectangle

cube

pyramide régulière

tétraèdre

octaèdre

dodécaèdre

icosaèdre régulier

cylindre droit

cône droit

cône oblique

sphère

FOCUS: Angles

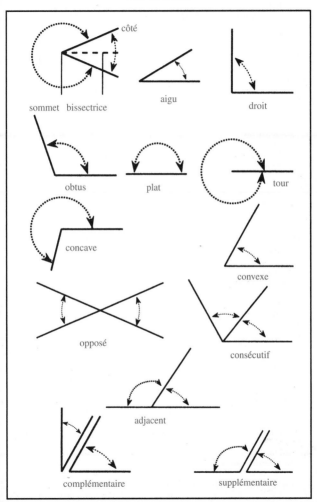

circle	cercle (*m*)	*sehr-kl*
• center	centre (*m*)	*sAH-tr*
• circumference	circonférence (*f*)	*seer-kOH-fay-rAH-ss*
• diameter	diamètre (*m*)	*dya-meh-tr*
• radius	rayon (*m*)	*reh-yOH*
• tangent	tangente (*f*)	*tAH-zh-AHt*
solid figures	figures solides (*f, pl*)	*feeg-ewr sul-eed*
prism	prisme (*m*)	*preesm*
• right prism	prisme droit (*m*)	*preesm drwa*
cube	cube (*m*)	*kewb*
pyramid	pyramide (*f*)	*pee-ra-meed*
polyhedron	polyèdre (*m*)	*pul-yehdr*
• tetrahedron	tétraèdre (*m*)	*tay-tra-ehdr*
• octahedron	octaèdre (*m*)	*uk-ta-ehdr*
• dodecahedron	dodécaèdre (*m*)	*doh-day-ka-ehdr*
• icosahedron	icosaèdre (*m*)	*ee-koh-sa-ehdr*
cylinder	cylindre (*m*)	*see-lEH-dr*
cone	cône (*m*)	*kOHn*
sphere	sphère (*f*)	*sfehr*

b. CONCEPTS

angle	angle (*m*)	*AH-gl*
• acute	aigu (*adj*)	*ay-gew*
• adjacent	adjacent (*adj*)	*ad-zha-sAH*
• bisector	bissectrice (*f*)	*bee-sehk-treess*
• complementary	complémentaire (*adj*)	*kOH-play-mAH-tehr*
• concave	concave (*adj*)	*kOH-kav*
• consecutive	consécutif (*adj*)	*kOH-say-kew-teef*
• convex	convexe (*adj*)	*kOH-vehks*
• obtuse	obtus (*adj*)	*up-tew*
• one turn (360°)	tour (*m*)	*toor*
• opposite	opposé (*adj*)	*up-oh-zay*
• right	droit (*adj*)	*drwa*
• side	côté (*adj*)	*koh-tay*
• straight	droit (*adj*)	*drwa*
• supplementary	supplémentaire (*adj*)	*sew-play-mAH-tehr*
• vertex	sommet (*m*)	*sum-eh*
axis	axe (*m*)	*aks*
coordinate	coordonnée (*f*)	*ku-or-dun-ay*
degree	degré (*m*)	*de-gray*
dimension	dimension (*f*)	*deem-AH-ssyOH*
• two-dimensional (2D)	à deux dimensions (*f, pl*)	*a duh deem-AH-ssyOH*
• three-dimensional (3D)	à trois dimensions (*f, pl*)	*a twa deem-AH-ssyOH*

FOCUS: Lines

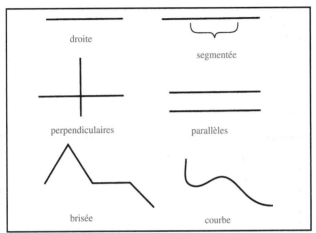

draw	dessiner (*v*)	*day-see-nay*
drawing instruments	instruments de dessin	*EH-strew-mAH de day-sEH*
• **compass**	compas (*m*)	*kOH-pa*
• **eraser**	gomme (*f*)	*gum*
• **pen**	stylo (*m*)	*steel-o*
• **pencil**	crayon (*m*)	*kreh-yOH*
• **protractor**	goniomètre (*m*)	*gun-yu-mehtr*
• **ruler**	règle (*f*)	*rehgl*
• **template**	gabarit (*m*)	*ga-ba-ree*
geometry	géométrie (*f*)	*zhay-u-may-tree*
• **geometrical**	géométrique (*adj*)	*zhay-u-may-treek*
line	ligne (*f*)	*lee-ny*
• **broken**	brisée (*adj*)	*bree-zay*
• **curved**	courbe (*adj*)	*koorb*
• **parallel**	parallèle (*adj*)	*pa-ra-lehl*
• **perpendicular**	perpendiculaire (*adj*)	*pehr-pAH-dee-kew-lehr*
• **segment**	segmentée (*adj*)	*sehg-mAH-tay*
• **straight**	droite (*adj*)	*drwat*
point	point (*m*)	*pwEH*
space	espace (*m*)	*ehs-pas*
trigonometry	trigonométrie (*f*)	*tree-gun-u-may-tree*
• **trigonometric**	trigonométrique (*adj*)	*tree-gun-u-may-treek*
• **cosecant**	cosécante (*f*)	*kus-ay-kAHt*

• **cosine**	cosinus (*m*)	*kus-ee-newss*
• **cotangent**	cotangente (*f*)	*kut-AH-zhAHt*
• **secant**	sécante (*f*)	*say-kAHt*
• **sine**	sinus (*m*)	*see-news*
• **tangent**	tangente (*f*)	*tAH-zhAHt*
vector	vecteur (*m*)	*vehk-tur*

3. QUANTITY AND SPACE

a. WEIGHTS AND MEASURES

area	surface (*f*)	*sewr-fas*
	superficie (*f*)	*sew-pehr-fee-see*
• **hectare**	hectare (*m*)	*ehk-tar*
• **square centimeter**	centimètre carré	*sAH-tee-mehtr ka-ray*
• **square kilometer**	kilomètre carré	*kee-lu-mehtr ka-ray*
• **square meter**	mètre carré	*mehtr ka-ray*
• **square millimeter**	millimètre carré	*meel-ee-mehtr ka-ray*
length	longueur (*f*)	*lOH-gur*
• **centimeter**	centimètre (*m*)	*sAH-tee-mehtr*
• **kilometer**	kilomètre (*m*)	*keel-u-mehtr*
• **meter**	mètre (*m*)	*mehtr*
• **millimeter**	millimètre (m)	*meel-ee-mehtr*
speed	vitesse (*f*)	*vee-tess*
• **per hour**	à l'heure	*a-lur*
• **per minute**	à la minute	*a-la-meen-ewt*
• **per second**	à la seconde	*a-la-se-gOHd*
velocity	vélocité (*f*)	*vay-luss-ee-tay*
volume	volume (*m*)	*vul-ewm*
• **cubic centimeter**	centimètre cubique	*sAH-tee-mehtr kew-beek*
• **cubic kilometer**	kilomètre cubique	*keel-u-mehtr kew-beek*
• **cubic meter**	mètre cubique	*mehtr kew-beek*
• **cubic millimeter**	millimètre cubique	*meel-ee-mehtr kew-beek*
• **liter**	litre (*m*)	*leetr*
• **quart**	quart de gallon	*kar de gal-OH*
weight	poids (*m*)	*pwah*
• **gram**	gramme (*m*)	*gram*
• **hectogram**	hectogramme (*m*)	*ehk-tu-gram*
• **kilogram**	kilogramme (*m*)	*keel-u-gram*
weight (due to gravity)	pesanteur (*f*)	*pe-zAH-tur*

b. WEIGHING AND MEASURING

dense	dense (*adj*)	*dAH-s*
• **density**	densité (*f*)	*dAH-see-tay*
dimension	dimension (*f*)	*dee-mAH-sy-OH*

extension	extension (f)	*ehks-tAH-sy-OH*
heavy	lourd (*adj, m*)	*loor*
	lourde (f)	*loord*
light	léger (*adj, m*)	*lay-zhay*
	légère (f)	*lay-zh-ehr*
long	long (*adj, m*)	*lOH*
	longue (f)	*lOH-g*
mass	masse (f)	*mas*
maximum	maximum (*m*)	*maks-ee-mum*
measure	mesurer (*v*)	*me-zewr-ay*
measuring tape	mètre à ruban	*mehtr a rew-bAH*
medium	moyenne (f)	*mwa-y-ehn*
	moyen (*adj, m*)	*mwa-yEH*
minimum	minimum (*m*)	*mee-nee-mum*
narrow	étroit (*adj, m*)	*ay-trwa*
	étroite (f)	*ay-trwat*
short (thing)	court (*adj, m*)	*koor*
	courte (f)	*koort*
size	grandeur (f)	*grAH-dur*
	mesure (f)	*me-zewr*
	taille (f)	*ta-y*
tall	haut (*adj, m*)	*oh*
	haute (f)	*oh-t*
	grand (*m*)	*grAH*
	grande (f)	*grAH-d*
thick	épais (*adj, m*)	*ay-peh*
	épaisse (f)	*ay-pehs*
thin	maigre (*adj*)	*meh-gr*
	mince (*adj*)	*mEHss*
weigh	peser (*v*)	*pe-zay*
wide	large (*adj*)	*larzh*
• **width**	largeur (f)	*lar-zh-ur*

c. CONCEPTS OF QUANTITY

a lot, much	beaucoup (*adv*)	*bo-koo*
	une grande quantité	*ewn grAH-d kAH-tee-tay*
all, everything	tout (*adj*)	*too*
	toute chose	*toot sh-oh-z*
• **everyone**	tout le monde	*tool mOH-d*
almost, nearly	presque (*adv*)	*prehs-ke*
approximately	à peu près (*adv*)	*a puh preh*
	environ	*AH-vee-rOH*
as much as	tant que	*tAH ke*
	autant que	*oh-tAH ke*
big, large	grand (*adj, m*)	*grAH*
	grande (f)	*grAH-d*

	gros (*adj, m*)	*gro*
	grosse (*f*)	*gros*
• become big	grandir (*v*)	*grAH-deer*
	agrandir (*v*)	*a-grAH-deer*
	grossir (*v*)	*gro-seer*
both	les deux	*lay duh*
	tous (*m*) les deux	*too lay duh*
	toutes (*f*) les deux	*toot lay duh*
capacity	capacité (*f*)	*ka-pa-see-tay*
decrease	diminution (*f*)	*dee-mee-newss-yOH*
• decrease	diminuer (*v*)	*dee-mee-new-ay*
double	double (*adj*)	*doobl*
empty	vide (*adj*)	*veed*
• empty	vider (*v*)	*vee-day*
enough	assez (*adv*)	*a-say*
	suffisant (*adj*)	*sew-fee-zAH*
• be enough	suffire (*v*)	*sew-feer*
	être assez (*v*)	*eh-tre a-say*
entire	entier (*adj*)	*AH-ty-ay*
	entière	*AH-ty-ehr*
every, each	chaque (*adj*)	*shak*
fill	remplir (*v*)	*rAH-pleer*
• full	plein (*adj*)	*plEH*
	pleine	*plehn*
grow	croître (*v*)	*krwa-tr*
• growth	croissance (*f*)	*krwa-sAH-s*
half	demi (*m*)	*de-mee*
	demie (*f*)	*de-mee*
how much (many)	combien (*adv*)	*kOH-byEH*
increase	augmentation (*f*)	*ug-mAH-ta-syOH*
• increase	augmenter (*v*)	*ug-mAH-tay*
less	moins (*adv*)	*mwEH*
little (size)	petit (*adj, m*)	*ptee*
	petite (*f*)	*pteet*
• a little	peu (*adv*), un peu	*puh, UH-puh*
more	plus (*adv*)	*plew, plewss*
no one	personne (*pro*)	*pehr-sun*
nothing	rien (*adv/pro*)	*ryEH*
	nul (*adj/pro, m*)	*newl*
	nulle (*f*)	*newl*
pair	paire (*f*)	*pehr*
part	part (*f*)	*par*
	partie (*f*)	*par-tee*
piece	pièce (*f*)	*pyehs*
portion	morceau (*m*)	*mor-so*
	portion (*f*)	*porsyOH*
quantity	quantité (*f*)	*kAH-tee-tay*
several	plusieurs (*adj/adv*)	*plew-zy-ur*

small	petit (*adj, m*)	*ptee*
	petite (*f*)	*pteet*
• become small	rendre plus petit	*rAH-dr plew ptee*
	rapetisser (*v*)	*rap-tee-say*
some	quelque(*s*) (*adj*)	*kehl-ke*
• some of it, them	en (*pro*)	*AH*
• I have some of it/them.	J'en ai.	*Zh-AH nay*
suffice	suffire (*v*)	*sew-feer*
• sufficient	suffisant (*adj*)	*sew-fee-zAH*
too much	trop (*adv*)	*troh*
triple	triple (*adj*)	*tree-pl*

d. CONCEPTS OF LOCATION

above	au-dessus (*adv*)	*ohd-sew*
	en haut	*AH oh*
across	à travers (*prep*)	*a-tra-vehr*
ahead, forward	avant (*adv*)	*a-vAH*
among	parmi (*prep*)	*parmee (among more than two)*
around	autour de	*oh-toor-de*
away	au loin (*adv*)	*oh-lwEH*
back, backward	en arrière (*adv*)	*AH-na-ree-ehr*
beside, next to	à côté (de) (*prep*)	*a-ko-tay (de)*
between	entre (*prep*)	*AH-tre (between only two)*
beyond	au-delà (de) (*adv/prep*)	*ohd-la (de)*
bottom	fond (*m*)	*fOH*
• at the bottom	au fond	*oh-fOH*
	en bas	*AH-bah*
compass	boussole (*f*)	*boo-sul*
direction	direction (*f*)	*dee-rehk-syOH*
distance	distance (*f*)	*dee-stAH-s*
down	bas (*adv*)	*bah*
	en bas	*AH-bah*
east	est (*m*)	*ehst*
• eastern	oriental (*adj*)	*or-yAH-tal*
• to the east	à l'est	*a-lehst*
edge	bord (*m*)	*bor*
• at the edge of	au bord de	*oh-bor-de*
far	loin (*adv*)	*lwEH*
	lointain (*adj*)	*lwEH-tEH*
fast	vite (*adj/adv*)	*veet*
	rapide	*ra-peed*
from	de (*prep*)	*de*

here	ici *(adv)*	*ee-see*
horizontal	horizontal *(adj)*	*or-ee-zOH-tal*
in	dans *(prep)*	*dAH*
• inside	dedans *(adv)*	*de-dAH*
in front of	devant *(adv/prep)*	*dvAH*
in the middle	au centre	*oh-sAHtr*
	au milieu	*oh-meel-yuh*
left	gauche *(adj)*	*gohsh*
• to the left	à gauche	*a-gohsh*
level	niveau *(m)*	*nee-voh*
near	près (de) *(adv)*	*preh (de)*
north	nord *(m)*	*nor*
• northern	septentrional *(adj)*	*sehp-tAH-tree-yun-al*
• to the north	au nord	*oh-nor*
nowhere	nulle part *(adv)*	*newl-par*
on	sur *(prep)*	*sewr*
outside	dehors *(adv)*	*de-or*
	en dehors *(adv)*	*AN-de-or*
place	endroit *(m)*	*AH-drwa*
	lieu *(m)*	*lyuh*
position	position *(f)*	*pu-zee-syOH*
right	droit *(adj, m)*	*drwa*
	droite *(f)*	*drwat*
• to the right	à droite	*a-drwat*
somewhere	quelque part	*kehl-ke par*
south	sud *(m)*	*sewd*
• southern	méridional *(adj)*	*may-ree-dy-un-al*
• to the south	au sud	*oh-sewd*
there	là *(adv)*	*la*
through	par *(prep)*	*par*
	à travers	*a-tra-vehr*

FOCUS: Compass Points

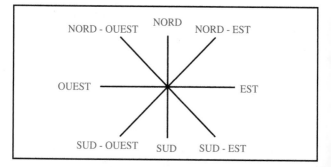

to, at	à (*prep*)	*a*
• to, at someone's place (home)	chez (*prep*)	*shay*
top	sommet (*m*)	*sum-eh*
• at the top	au sommet	*oh-sum-eh*
	en haut	*AH-oh*
toward	vers (*prep*)	*vehr*
under	sous (*prep*)	*soo*
up	haut (*adv*)	*oh*
	en haut	*AH-oh*
vertical	vertical (*adj*)	*vehr-tee-kal*
west	ouest (*m*)	*west*
• western	occidental (*adj*)	*uk-see-dAH-tal*
• to the west	à l'ouest	*al-west*
where	où (*adv*)	*oo*

e. MOVEMENT

arrive	arriver (*v*)	*a-ree-vay*
come	venir (*v*)	*vneer*
Note: **I'm coming!** = J'arrive! (*zha-reev*)		
drive	conduire (*v*)	*kOH-dew-eer*
enter	entrer (*v*)	*AH-tray*
fall	tomber (*v*)	*tOH-bay*
follow	suivre (*v*)	*sew-eevr*
get up, rise	se lever (*v*)	*se-levay*
go	aller (*v*)	*alay*
• go away	s'en aller (*v*)	*sAH-nalay*
• go down, descend	descendre (*v*)	*day-sAH-dr*
• go on foot	aller à pied (*v*)	*alay a pyay*
• go out, exit	sortir (*v*)	*sor-teer*
• go up, climb	monter (*v*)	*mOH-tay*
leave, depart	partir (*v*)	*par-teer*
	quitter (*v*)	*kee-tay*
lie down	se coucher (*v*)	*se-koo-shay*
lift	lever (*v*)	*le-vay*
motion	motion (*f*)	*mo-syOH*
move	bouger (*v*)	*boo-zhay*
	remuer (*v*)	*re-mew-ay*
• move oneself	se déplacer (*v*)	*se-day-pla-say*
	bouger (*v*)	*boo-zhay*
• movement	mouvement (*m*)	*moov-mAH*
pass by	passer (*v*)	*pa-say*
pull	tirer (*v*)	*tee-ray*
put	mettre (*v*)	*meht-re*
	placer (*v*)	*pla-say*
• put down	poser (*v*)	*po-zay*

quickly	vite (*adv*)	*veet*
	rapidement (*adv*)	*ra-peed-mAH*
return	retourner (*v*)	*re-toor-nay*
run	courir (*v*)	*koo-reer*
send	envoyer (*v*)	*AH-vwa-yay*
sit down	s'asseoir (*v*)	*sa-swar*
slow	lent (*adj, m*)	*lAH*
	lente (*f*)	*lAHt*
• **slowly**	lentement (*adv*)	*lAHt-mAH*
stop	arrêter (*v*)	*a-reht-ay*
• **stop oneself**	s'arrêter (*v*)	*sa-reht-ay*
turn	tourner (*v*)	*toor-nay*
walk	marcher (*v*)	*marsh-ay*
	aller (*v*) à pied	*alay a pyay*
• **walk**	promenade (*f*)	*prum-nad*
• **take a walk**	faire (*v*) une promenade	*fehr ewn prum-nad*

4. TIME

a. GENERAL EXPRESSIONS OF TIME

afternoon	après-midi (*m*)	*apreh-mee-dee*
• **in the afternoon**	dans l'après-midi	*dAH lap-reh mee-dee*
	de l'après-midi	*de lap-reh-mee-dee*
• **this afternoon**	cet après-midi	*seht-apreh-mee-dee*
• **tomorrow afternoon**	demain après-midi	*de-mEH apreh-mee-dee*
dawn	aube (*f*)	*ohb*
day	jour (*m*)	*zh-oor*
• **all day**	toute la journée	*toot la zh-oor-nay*
evening	soir (*m*)	*swar*
• **in the evening**	dans le soir	*dAHl-swar*
	du soir	*dew swar*
• **this evening**	ce soir	*se-swar*
• **tomorrow evening**	demain soir	*de-mEH swar*
midnight	minuit (*m*)	*mee-new-ee*
• **at midnight**	à minuit	*a-mee-new-ee*
morning	matin (*m*)	*ma-tEH*
• **in the morning**	dans le matin	*daHl-ma-tEH*
	du matin	*dew-ma-tEH*
• **this morning**	ce matin	*se-ma-tEH*
• **tomorrow morning**	demain matin	*de-mEH ma-tEH*
night	nuit (*f*)	*new-ee*
• **at night**	de nuit	*de-new-ee*
	dans la nuit	*dAH-la-new-ee*

• **last night**	cette nuit	*seht-new-ee (actual night)*
	hier soir	*yehr swar (actual evening)*
• **this night**	cette nuit	*seht new-ee*
• **tomorrow night**	demain pendant la nuit	*de-mEH pAH-dAH la new-ee (actual night)*
	demain soir	*de-mEH swar (actual evening)*
noon	midi (*m*)	*mee-dee*
• **at noon**	à midi	*a-mee-dee*
sunrise	lever (*m*) du soleil	*le-vay dew sul-ay*
sunset	coucher (*m*) du soleil	*koo-shay dew sul-ay*
time (*in general*)	temps (*m*)	*tAH*
• **time** (*hour*)	heure (*f*)	*ur*
• **time** (*as in every time*)	fois (*f*)	*fwa*

> **Time flies!** = Le temps fuit! *le tAH few-ee*
> **at the present time** = à l'heure actuelle *a-lur ak-tew ehl*
> **Once upon a time . . .** = Il était une fois *eel ay-teh tewn fwa*
> **to be on time** = être à l'heure *eh-tre a-lur*

today	aujourd'hui (*adv*)	*oh-zhoor-dew-ee*
tomorrow	demain (*adv*)	*de-mEH*
• **day after tomorrow**	après-demain (*adv*)	*a-pray de-mEH*
• **the next day**	lendemain (*m*)	*lAHd-mEH*

Note: This word is usually used to talk about the following day. *Je suis arrivé à la plage vendredi dernier, mais mes amis ne sont arrivés que le lendemain.* I arrived at the beach last Friday, but my friends didn't arrive until the next day.

tonight	cette nuit	*seht new-ee (actual night)*
	ce soir	*se swar (evening)*
week	semaine (*f*)	*smehn*
• **a week from Tuesday**	mardi en huit	*mar-dee AN ew-eet*
• **in a week**	d'ici une semaine	*dee-see ewn smehn*
• **next week**	la semaine prochaine	*la smehn pro-shehn*
yesterday	hier (*adv*)	*yehr*
• **day before yesterday**	avant-hier (*adv*)	*avAH-tyehr*
• **yesterday afternoon**	hier après-midi	*yehr apreh-mee-dee*
• **yesterday morning**	hier matin	*yehr ma-tEH*

b. TELLING TIME

What time is it?	Quelle heure est-il?	*kehl ur eh-teel*
• It's 1:00.	Il est une heure.	*eel eh-tewn ur*
• It's 2:00.	Il est deux heures.	*eel eh duh-zur*
• It's 3:00.	Il est trois heures.	*eel eh trwa-zur*
• It's exactly 3:00.	Il est trois heures précises.	*eel eh trwa-zur pray-seez*
• It's 3:00 on the dot.	Il est trois heures juste.	*eel eh trwa-zur zh-ewst*
	Il est trois heures pile.	*eel eh trwa-zur peel*
• It's 1:10.	Il est une heure dix.	*eel eh tewn ur dees*
• It's 1:15.	Il est une heure et quart.	*eel eh tewn ur ay-kar*
• It's 4:25.	Il est quatre heures vingt-cinq.	*eel eh katr ur vEH-sEHk*
• It's 3:15.	Il est trois heures et quart.	*eel eh trwa-zur ay kar*
• It's 3:30.	Il est trois heures et demie.	*eel eh trwa-zur ayd-mee*
• It's 2:45.	Il est trois heures moins le quart.	*eel eh trwa-zur mwEH-le kar*
	Il est deux heures quarante-cinq.	*eel eh duh-zur ka-rAHt sEHk*
• It's 5:50.	Il est six heures moins dix.	*eel eh see-zur mwEH dees*

> The 24-hour clock is used throughout France.

Another way to tell time is the official time used by the French government on radio and TV, in railroad and bus stations, and at airports.

- It is the twenty-four-hour system.
- In this system, *quart*, *demi*, *demie*, *moins*, and *et* are not used.
- When you hear or see the stated time, subtract twelve from the number you hear or see. If the number is less than twelve, it is A.M. time, except for *24 heures*, which is midnight; *zéro heure* is also midnight.

EXAMPLES

> *Il est treize heures.* / It is 1:00 P.M.
> *Il est quinze heures.* / It is 3:00 P.M.
> *Il est vingt heures trente.* / It is 8:30 P.M.
> *Il est minuit.* / It is midnight.
> *Il est seize heures trente.* / It is 4:30 P.M.
> *Il est dix-huit heures quinze.* / It is 6:15 P.M.
> *Il est vingt heures quarante-cinq.* / It is 8:45 P.M.
> *Il est vingt-deux heures cinquante.* / It is 10:50 P.M.

The abbreviation for *heure* or *heures* is *h*.

EXAMPLES

> *Il est 20 h. 20.* / It is 8:20 P.M.
> *Il est 15 h. 50.* / It is 3:50 P.M.
> *Il est 23 h. 30.* / It is 11:30 P.M.

• It's 5:00 A.M.	Il est cinq heures.	*eel eh sEH-kur*
• It's 5:00 P.M.	Il est dix-sept heures.	*eel eh dee-seht ur*
• It's 10:00 A.M.	Il est dix heures.	*eel eh dee-zur*
• It's 10:00 P.M.	Il est vingt-deux heures.	*eel eh vEH-duh zur*

At what time?	À quelle heure?	*a kehl ur*
• At 1:00.	À une heure.	*a ewn ur*
• At 2:00.	À deux heures.	*a duh-zur*
• At 3:00.	À trois heures.	*a trwa-zur*

c. UNITS OF TIME

century	siècle (*m*)	*see-ehkl*
day	jour (*m*)	*zhoor*
• daily	quotidien (*adj*)	*kut-ee-dy-EH*
	quotidiennement (*adv*)	*kut-ee-dy-ehn-mAH*
decade	décennie (*f*)	*day-sehn-ee*
hour	heure (*f*)	*ur*
• hourly	à l'heure	*a-lur*
instant	instant (*m*)	*EH-stAH*
millennium	millénaire (*m*)	*meel-ay-nehr*
minute	minute (*f*)	*meen-ewt*
moment	moment (*m*)	*mum-AH*
month	mois (*m*)	*mwa*
• monthly	mensuellement (*adv*)	*mAH-sew-ehl-mAH*
	mensuel (*adj*)	*mAH-sew-ehl*
second	seconde (*f*)	*se-gOHd*
week	semaine (*f*)	*smehn*
• weekly	hebdomadaire (*adj*)	*ehb-dum-ad-ehr*
	hebdomadairement (*adv*)	*ehb-dum-ad-ehr-mAH*
year	an (*m*)	*AH*
	année (*f*)	*a-nay*
• yearly, annually	annuel, annuelle (*adj*)	*a-new-ehl*
	annuellement (*adv*)	*a-new-ehl-mAH*
year two thousand	an (*m*) deux mille	*AH-duh-meel*

d. TIMEPIECES

alarm clock	réveille-matin (*m*)	*ray-veh-y mat-EH*
	réveil (*m*)	*ray-veh-y*
clock	horloge (*f*)	*or-lu-zh*
• atomic clock	horloge (*f*) atomique	*or-lu-zh a-tum-eek*
dial	cadran (*m*)	*ka-drAH*
grandfather clock	horloge à pendule (*f*)	*or-lu-zh a pAH-dewl*
	horloge normande (*f*)	*or-lu-zh nor-mAHd*
hand (of a clock)	aiguille (*f*)	*ayg-ew-ee-y*
watch	montre (*f*)	*mOH-tre*
• The watch is fast.	La montre avance.	*la mOH-tre avAH-s*
• The watch is slow.	La montre retarde.	*la mOH-tre re-tard*
watchband	bracelet (*m*) d'une montre	*bras-leh dewn mOH-tre*
watch battery	pile d'une montre	*peel dewn mOH-tre*
wind	remonter (*v*)	*re-mOH-tay*
wristwatch	bracelet-montre (*m*)	*bras-leh mOH-tre*
	montre (*f*)	*mOH-tre*

e. CONCEPTS OF TIME

after	après (*adv*)	*apreh*
again	encore une fois (*adv*)	*AH-kor ewn fwa*
	de nouveau (*adv*)	*de-noo-voh*
ago	il y a (*adv*)	*eel-yah*
almost never	presque jamais (*adv*)	*prehs-ke zh-a-meh*
already	déjà (*adv*)	*day-zh-a*
always	toujours (*adv*)	*too-zh-oor*
anterior	antérieur(e) (*adj*)	*AH-tay-ree-ur*
as soon as	dès que (*conj*)	*deh-ke*
	aussitôt que (*conj*)	*o-see-toh-ke*
at the same time	en même temps	*AH-mehm-tAH*
	à la fois	*a-la-fwa*
be about to, be on the point/verge of	être sur le point de	*eh-tre sewr le pwEH de*
be on time	être à l'heure	*eh-tre a-lur*
become	devenir (*v*)	*devneer*
before	avant (*adv*)	*avAH*
	auparavant (*adv*)	*o-par-avAH*
begin	commencer (*v*)	*kum-AH-say*
• beginning	commencement (*m*)	*kum-AH-smAH*
	début (*m*)	*day-bew*
brief	bref, brève (*adj, m, f*)	*brehf, brehv*
• briefly	en bref	*AH brehf*
	brièvement (*adv*)	*bree-ehv-mAH*

change	changer (*v*)	*shAH-zh-ay*
continue	continuer (*v*)	*kOH-teen-ew-ay*
• **continually**	continuellement (*adv*)	*kOH-teen-ew-ehl-mAH*
during	pendant (*prep*)	*pAH-dAH*
early	tôt (*adv*)	*toh*
	de bonne heure (*adv*)	*de-bun-ur*
• **be early**	être tôt (*v*)	*eh-tre-toh*
	être de bonne heure (*v*)	*eh-tre de-bun-ur*
end, finish	finir (*v*)	*fee-neer*
• **end**	fin (*f*)	*fEH*
frequent	fréquent(e) (*adj, m, f*)	*fray-kAH(t)*
• **frequently**	fréquemment (*adv*)	*fray-kam-AH*
future	futur (*m*)	*few-tewr*
	avenir (*m*)	*avneer*
happen, occur	se produire (*v*)	*se-pro-dew-eer*
	arriver (*v*)	*a-ree-vay*
immediately	immédiatement (*adv*)	*ee-may-dyat-mAH*
	tout de suite	*tood-sweet*
in an hour's time	dans une heure	*dAH-zewn-ur*
• **in two minutes' time**	dans deux minutes	*dAH duh meen-ewt*
in the meantime	entre-temps (*adv*)	*AH-tre-tAH*
in time	à temps	*a-tAH*
just now	à l'instant	*a-lEH-stAH*
last	durer (*v*)	*dewr-ay*
• **last a long time**	durer longtemps (*v*)	*dew-rayl-OH-t-AH*
• **last a short time**	durer peu de temps (*v*)	*dewr-ay puh de tAH*
last	dernier (*adj, m*)	*dehrn-yay*
	dernière (*f*)	*dehrn-yehr*
	passé(e) (*adj*)	*pah-say*
• **last month**	le mois dernier (passé)	*le mwa dehrn-yay (pah-say)*
• **last year**	l'an dernier (*m*)	*lAH dehrn-yay*
	l'année dernière (*f*)	*la-nay dehrn-yehr*
late	tard	*tar*
	en retard (*adv*)	*AH re-tar*
• **be late**	être tard (en retard)	*eh-tre tar (AH-re-tar)*

Better late than never! Mieux vaut tard que jamais!
myuh voh tar ke zh-a-meh

---

long-term	à long terme	*a-lOH-tehrm*
look forward to	s'attendre à (*v*)	*sat-AH-dre-a*

moment	moment (*m*)	*mum-AH*
• **at the moment**	en ce moment	*AH se mum-AH*
never	jamais (*adv*)	*zh-a-meh*
• **almost never**	presque jamais (*adv*)	*prehs-ke zh-a-meh*
now	maintenant (*adv*)	*mEHt-nAH*
	à présent (*adv*)	*a pray-zAH*
• **for now**	pour le moment	*poorl-mum-AH*
• **from now on**	dès maintenant	*deh mEHt-nAH*
	désormais (*adv*)	*day-zor-meh*
nowadays	de nos jours	*de noh zh-oor*
occasionally	de temps en temps (*adv*)	*de-tAH-zAH-tAH*
often	souvent (*adv*)	*soovAH*
once	une fois	*ewn fwa*
• **once in a while**	de temps à autre	*de tAH za oh-tre*
• **once upon a time**	il était une fois	*eel ay-teh tewn fwa*
only	seulement (*adv*)	*sulmAH*
past	passé (*m*)	*pah-say*
posterior	postérieur(e) (*adj*)	*pus-tay-ree-ur*
present	présent (*m*)	*prayz-AH*
	présent(e) (*adj, m, f*)	*prayz-AH(t)*
	actuel(le) (*adj, m, f*)	*ak-tew-ehl*
• **presently**	actuellement (*adv*)	*ak-tew-ehlm-AH*
	à présent	*a-pray-zAH*
previous	précédent(e) (*adj, m, f*)	*pray-sayd-AH(t)*
	auparavant (*adv*)	*oh-par-avAH*
• **previously**	précédemment (*adv*)	*pray-say-dam-AH*
rare	rare (*adj*)	*rahr*
• **rarely**	rarement (*adv*)	*rahrm-AH*
recent	récent(e) (*adj, m, f*)	*rayss-AH(t)*
• **recently**	récemment (*adv*)	*ray-sam-AH*
regular	régulier (*adj, m*)	*ray-gewl-yay*
	régulière (*f*)	*ray-gewl-yehr*
• **regularly**	régulièrement (*adv*)	*ray-gewl-yehrm-AH*
right away	tout de suite (*adv*)	*tood-sweet*
short-term	à court terme	*a-koor-tehrm*
simultaneous	simultané(e) (*adj, m, f*)	*seem-ewl-ta-nay*
• **simultaneously**	simultanément (*adv*)	*seem-ewl-ta-naym-AH*
since, for	depuis (*prep*)	*de-pew-ee*
• **since Monday**	depuis lundi	*de-pew-ee-lUH-dee*
• **since yesterday**	depuis hier	*de-pew-ee-yehr*
• **for three days**	depuis trois jours	*de-pew-ee trwa zhoor*
slow	lent(e) (*adj, m, f*)	*l-AH-(t)*
• **slowly**	lentement (*adv*)	*l-AH-tem-AH*

soon	bientôt *(adv)*	by-EH toh
• **as soon as**	dès que *(conj)*	deh-ke
	aussitôt que	o-see-toh-ke
• **sooner or later**	tôt ou tard *(adv)*	toh oo tar
spend *(time)*	passer *(v)*	pah-say
spend *(money)*	dépenser *(v)*	daypAH-say
sporadic	sporadique *(adj)*	spu-ra-deek
• **sporadically**	sporadiquement *(adv)*	spu-ra-deek-m-AH
still	encore *(adv)*	AH-kor
	toujours	too-zhoor
take place	avoir lieu	avwar lee-yuh
temporary	temporaire *(adj)*	tAH-pu-rehr
• **temporarily**	temporairement *(adv)*	tAH-pu-rehrm-AH
then	lors	lor
	ensuite *(adv)*	AH-sweet
	alors *(adv)*	a-lor
timetable, schedule	horaire *(m)*	u-rehr
to this day	jusqu'à ce jour *(adv)*	zh-ews-ka-se-zhoor
until	jusque(s) *(prep)*	zh-ews-ke
usually	d'habitude *(adv)*	da-bee-tewd
wait (for)	attendre *(v)*	at-AH-dre
when	quand *(adv)*	k-AH
while	pendant que *(conj)*	p-AH-d-AH-ke
within *(a certain time)*	en *(prep)*	AH
yet	encore *(adv)*	AH-kor

5. DAYS, MONTHS, AND SEASONS

a. DAYS OF THE WEEK

day of the week	jour *(m)* de la semaine	zhoord-la-smehn
• **Monday**	lundi *(m)*	lUH-dee
• **Tuesday**	mardi *(m)*	mar-dee
• **Wednesday**	mercredi *(m)*	mehr-kre-dee
• **Thursday**	jeudi *(m)*	zhuh-dee
• **Friday**	vendredi *(m)*	vAH-dre-dee
• **Saturday**	samedi *(m)*	sam-dee
• **Sunday**	dimanche *(m)*	dee-mAH-sh
• **on Mondays**	le lundi	le-l-UH-dee
• **on Saturdays**	le samedi	le-sam-dee
• **on Sundays**	le dimanche	le-dee-mAH-sh
holiday	un jour férié	UH zhoor fay-ree-ay
weekend	la fin de semaine	laf-EH-de-smehn
	le week-end	le-wee-kehn
What day is it?	Quel jour est-ce?	kehl zhoor eh-ss
• **It's Monday.**	C'est lundi.	say-lUH-dee
workday	un jour de travail	UH zhoor-de-tra-va-y

b. MONTHS OF THE YEAR

month of the year	mois (*m*) de l'année	*mwad-la-nay*
• **January**	janvier (*m*)	*zh-AH-vee-ay*
• **February**	février (*m*)	*fay-vree-ay*
• **March**	mars (*m*)	*marss*
• **April**	avril (*m*)	*avreel*
• **May**	mai (*m*)	*meh*
• **June**	juin (*m*)	*zh-ew-EH*
• **July**	juillet (*m*)	*zh-ew-ee-yay*
• **August**	août (*m*)	*oo (oot)*
• **September**	septembre (*m*)	*sehpt-AH-bre*
• **October**	octobre (*m*)	*uktubre*
• **November**	novembre (*m*)	*nuv-AH-bre*
• **December**	décembre (*m*)	*dayss-AH-bre*
calendar	calendrier (*m*)	*kal-AH-dree-yay*
leap year	une année bissextile	*ewn anay bee-sehks-teel*
monthly	mensuellement (*adv*)	*m-AH-sew-ehlm-AH*
school year	année scolaire	*anay skul-ehr*
What month are we in?	Quel mois sommes-nous?	*kehl mwa sum noo*
What month is it?	Quel mois est-ce?	*kehl mwa eh-ss*
• **It's July.**	C'est juillet.	*say zh-ew-ee-yay*

c. SEASONS

season	saison (*f*)	*sehz-OH*
• **spring**	printemps (*m*)	*preEH-tAH*
• **summer**	été (*m*)	*ay-tay*
• **fall**	automne (*m*)	*oh-tun*
• **winter**	hiver (*m*)	*eev-ehr*

Note: **in the spring** / au printemps (*o prEH-tAH*); **in the summer** / en été (*ahn-ay-tay*); **in the fall** / en automne (*ahn-oh-tun*); **in the winter** / en hiver (*ahn-eev-ehr*)

equinox	équinoxe (*m*)	*ay-kee-nuks*
moon	lune (*f*)	*lewn*
solstice	solstice (*m*)	*sulsteess*
sun	soleil (*m*)	*sul-ay*

d. THE ZODIAC

horoscope	horoscope (*m*)	*u-rus-kup*
zodiac	zodiaque (*m*)	*zud-yak*
• **signs of the zodiac**	signes du zodiaque	*see-ny dew zud-yak*

FOCUS: The Seasons

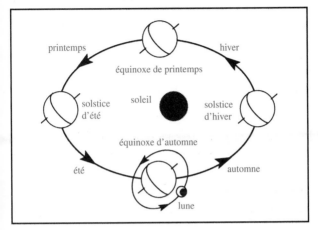

Aries	Bélier (*m*) (*21 mars–20 avril*)	*bayl-yay*
Taurus	Taureau (*m*) (*21 avril–21 mai*)	*toro*
Gemini	Gémeaux (*m, pl*) (*22 mai–21 juin*)	*zhay-mo*
Cancer	Cancer (*m*) (*22 juin–22 juillet*)	*kAH-sehr*
Leo	Lion (*m*) (*23 juillet–23 août*)	*ly-OH*
Virgo	Vierge (*f*) (*24 août–23 septembre*)	*vy-ehrzh*
Libra	Balance (*f*) (*24 septembre–23 octobre*)	*bal-AH-ss*
Scorpio	Scorpion (*m*) (*24 octobre–22 novembre*)	*skor-pyOH*
Sagittarius	Sagittaire (*m*) (*23 novembre–21 décembre*)	*sa-zh-ee-tehr*
Capricorn	Capricorne (*m*) (*22 décembre–20 janvier*)	*kap-ree-korn*

| Aquarius | Verseau (*m*)
(*21 janvier–18 février*) | *vehr-so* |
| Pisces | Poissons
(*m, pl*)
(*19 février–20 mars*) | *pwas-OH* |

e. EXPRESSING THE DATE

| What's today's date? | Quelle est la date aujourd'hui? | *kehl eh la dat oh-zhoor-dew-ee* |

Use the ordinal *premier* (also written as *1er* or *1er*) for the first of each month, and cardinal numbers for the other days.

• It's October first.	C'est le premier octobre.	*seh le prem-yay uktubre*
• It's January second.	C'est le deux janvier.	*seh le duh zh-Ah-vee-ay*
• It's May third.	C'est le trois mai.	*seh le trwa meh*
What year is it?	Quelle année est-ce?	*kehl anay eh-ss*
• It's 2012.	C'est 2012.	*seh duh-meel-dooz*
When were you born?	Quand êtes-vous né? (*m, pol*)	*kAH eht-voo nay*
	Quand êtes-vous née? (*f, pol*)	*kAH eht-voo nay*
	Quand es-tu né (*m, fam*)	*kAH eh-tew nay*
	Quand es-tu née (*f, fam*)	*kAH eh-tew nay*
• I was born in …	Je suis né (*m*)/née (*f*) en …	*zhe sew-ee nay AH*

f. IMPORTANT DATES

the New Year	le Nouvel An	*le noo-vehl AH*
New Year's Day	le Jour de l'An	*le zhoor del AH*
New Year's Eve	la Nuit de la Saint-Sylvestre	*la-new-eed-la-sEH-seel-vestr*
Assumption (August 15, National French holiday)	Assomption (*f*)	*as-OH-psy-OH*
Bastille Day (French national holiday celebrated on July 14)	le quatorze juillet la Fête Nationale	*le ka-torz zh-ew-ee-yay* *la feht nahs-yun-al*
Easter	Pâques (*f, pl*)	*pahk*

Christmas	Noël (m)	*nuh-ehl*
Passover	la Pâque	*la-pahk*
Ramadan	le ramadan	*le-ra-ma-dAH*

6. TALKING ABOUT THE WEATHER

a. GENERAL WEATHER VOCABULARY

air	air (m)	*ehr*
atmosphere	atmosphère (f)	*at-muss-fehr*
• **atmospheric conditions**	conditions atmosphériques (f, pl)	*kOH-dee-sy-OH at-muss-fay-reek*
awful	mauvais (adj)	*muv-eh*
• **be awful (weather)**	faire (v) un temps mauvais	*fehr UH tAH muv-eh*
beautiful	beau (adj)	*bo*
• **be beautiful (weather)**	faire (v) beau temps	*fehr bo tAH*
clear	clair (adj)	*klehr*
• **The sky is clear.**	Le ciel est clair.	*le syehl eh klehr*
climate	climat (m)	*klee-ma*
• **continental**	continental(e) (adj)	*kOH-teen-AH-tal*
• **dry**	sec (adj, m)	*sehk*
	sèche (f)	*seh-sh*
• **humid**	humide (adj)	*ew-meed*
	lourd (adj)	*loor*
	lourde (f)	*loord*
• **Mediterranean**	méditerranéen (adj, m)	*may-dee-tehr-anay-EH*
	méditerranéenne (f)	*may-dee-tehr-anay-ehn*
• **tropical**	tropical(e) (adj, m, f)	*trup-ee-kal*
cloud	nuage (m)	*new-azh*
• **cloudy**	nuageux (adj, m)	*new-azh-uh*
	nuageuse (f)	*new-azh-uhz*
	couvert (adj, m)	*koo-vehr*

---

to be in the clouds (to have one's head in the clouds) = être dans les nuages *eh-tre dAH lay new-azh*

---

cold	froid (m, adj)	*frwa*
• **be cold (weather)**	faire froid	*fehr frwa*
cool	frais (adj)	*freh*
• **be cool (weather)**	faire frais	*fehr freh*

dark	sombre (*adj*)	*sOH-bre*
• It's dark today.	Il fait sombre aujourd'hui.	*eel feh sOH-bre oh-zhoor-dew-ee*
drop (e.g., of rain)	goutte (*f*)	*goot*
fog	brouillard (*m*)	*broo-yar*
• foggy	brumeux (*adj*)	*brewm-uh*
freeze	geler (*v*)	*zhe-lay*
• frozen	gelé(e) (*adj, m, f*)	*zhe-lay*
hail	grêle (*f*)	*grehl*
• hail	grêler (*v*)	*gray-lay*
How's the weather?	Quel temps fait-il?	*kehl tAH feh-teel*
• Its a bit hot.	Il fait un peu chaud.	*eel feh UH puh sho*
It's a bit cold.	Il fait un peu froid.	*eel feh UH puh frwa*
• It's awful.	Il fait un temps affreux.	*eel feh UH tAH af-ruh*
• It's beautiful.	Il fait beau (temps).	*eel feh bo (tAH)*
• It's cloudy.	It fait un temps couvert.	*eel feh UH tAH koo-vehr*
• It's cold.	Il fait froid.	*eel feh frwa*
• It's cool.	Il fait frais.	*eel feh freh*
• It's foul (weather).	Il fait un temps pourri.	*eel feh UH tAH poo-ree*
• It's hot.	Il fait chaud.	*eel feh sho*
• It's humid.	Il fait humide.	*eel feh ew-meed*
• It's mild.	Il fait doux.	*eel feh doo*
• It's muggy.	Il fait un temps lourd.	*eel feh UH tAH loor*
• It's pleasant.	Il fait un temps agréable.	*eel feh UH tAH a-gray-ahble*
• It's raining.	Il pleut.	*eel pluh*

It's raining buckets. = Il pleut à seaux. *eel pluh a so*

• It's snowing.	Il neige.	*eel neh-zh*
• It's sunny.	Il fait (du) soleil.	*eel feh (dew) sul-ay*
• It's thundering.	Il tonne.	*eel tun*
• It's very cold.	Il fait très froid.	*eel feh treh frwa*
• It's very hot.	Il fait très chaud.	*eel feh treh sho*
• It's windy.	Il fait du vent.	*eel feh dew vAH*
• There's lightning.	Il fait des éclairs.	*eel feh day zay-klehr*
humid, damp	humide (*adj*)	*ew-meed*
• be humid	faire humide	*fehr ew-meed*
• humidity	humidité (*f*)	*ew-mee-dee-tay*
hurricane	ouragan (*m*)	*oor-ag-AH*

ice	glace (f)	*glass*
• black ice	verglas (m)	*vehr-glah*
light	lumière (f)	*lew-myehr*
lightning	éclair (m)	*ay-klehr*
	faire (v) des éclairs	*fehr day zay-klehr*
• flash/bolt of lightning	un coup d'éclair	*UH koo day-klehr*
mild	doux (adj, m)	*doo*
	douce (f)	*doos*
• be mild	faire doux	*fehr doo*
moon	lune (f)	*lewn*
mugginess	lourdeur (f)	*loord-ur*
• muggy	lourd (adj, m)	*loor*
	lourde (f)	*loord*
• be muggy	faire un temps lourd	*fehr UH tAH loor*
rain	pluie (f)	*plew-ee*
• rain	pleuvoir (v)	*pluh-vwar*
• It's rainy.	Il fait un temps pluvieux.	*eel feh UH tAH plewv-yuh*
sea	mer (f)	*mehr*
shadow, shade	ombre (f)	*OH-bre*
sky	ciel (m)	*syehl*
snow	neige (f)	*neh-zh*
• snow	neiger (v)	*nay-zh-ay*
star	étoile (f)	*ay-twal*
storm	tempête (f)	*tAH-peht*
sun	soleil (m)	*sul-ay*
thunder, clap of thunder	tonnerre (m)	*tun-ehr*
	coup de tonnerre (m)	*kood-tun-ehr*
• thunder	faire un bruit de tonnerre	*fehr UH brew-ee de tun-ehr*
	tonner	*tun-ay*
tornado	tornade (f)	*tor-nad*
weather	temps (m)	*tAH*
• The weather is beautiful.	Il fait beau temps.	*eel feh bo tAH*

The weather is rotten. = Il fait un temps pourri. *eel feh UH tAH poo-ree*

---

wind	vent (m)	*vAH*
• be windy	faire (v) du vent	*fehr dew vAH*

b. REACTING TO THE WEATHER

be cold	avoir (v) froid	*avwar frwa*
• I am cold.	J'ai froid.	*zh-ay frwa*
be hot	avoir (v) chaud	*avwar sho*
• I am hot.	J'ai chaud.	*zh-ay sho*

have chills	être (*v*) frileux (frileuse)	*eh-tre free-luh (free-luhz)*
I can't stand the cold.	Je ne supporte pas le froid.	*zhen sew-port pahl frwa*
I can't stand the heat.	Je ne supporte pas la chaleur.	*zhen sew-port pah la sha-lur*
I love the cold.	J'aime le froid.	*zh-ehm le frwa*
I love the heat.	J'aime la chaleur.	*zh-ehm la sha-lur*
perspire	transpirer (*v*)	*trAH-spee-ray*
warm up	se chauffer (*v*)	*se-sho-fay*

c. WEATHER-MEASURING INSTRUMENTS AND ACTIVITIES

barometer	baromètre (*m*)	*ba-rum-eht-re*
• **barometric pressure**	pression (*f*) barométrique	*prehs-yOH ba-rum-ay-treek*
Celsius	Celsius	*sehl-see-ews*
Centigrade	centigrade (*adj*)	*sAH-tee-grad*
degree	degré (*m*)	*de-gray*
Fahrenheit	Fahrenheit	*fa-rehn-a-eet*
mercury	mercure (*m*)	*mehr-kewr*
minus	moins (*adv*)	*mwEH*
plus	plus (*adv*)	*plew(s)*
temperature	température (*f*)	*tAH-pay-ra-tewr*
• **high**	élevée (*adj*)	*ayl-vay*
• **low**	basse (*adj*)	*bahs*
• **maximum**	maximum (*adj*)	*mak-see-mum*
• **minimum**	minimum (*adj*)	*mee-nee-mum*
thermometer	thermomètre (*m*)	*tehrm-u-meht-re*
• **boiling point**	point (*m*) d'ébullition	*pwEH day-bewl-ee-syOH*
• **melting point**	point (*m*) de fusion	*pwEH de few-zyOH*
thermostat	thermostat (*m*)	*tehr-mus-ta*
weather forecast	prévision (*f*) scientifique du temps	*pray-veez-yOH syAH-tee-feek dew tAH*
	météo (*f*)	*may-tay-oh*
weather report, bulletin	bulletin (*m*) météorologique	*bewltEH may-tay-u-ru-lu-zh-eek*
zero	zéro (*m*)	*zay-ro*
• **above zero**	dessus zéro	*de-sew zay-ro*
• **below zero**	dessous zéro	*de-soo zay-ro*

7. COLORS

a. BASIC COLORS

What color is it?	De quelle couleur est-ce?	*de kehl koo-lur eh-ss*

It's . . .	C'est . . .	*seh*
• **black**	noir	*nwar*
• **blue**	bleu	*bluh*
• **dark blue**	bleu foncé	*bluh fOH-say*
• **light blue**	bleu clair	*bluh klehr*
• **brown**	brun, marron	*brUH, marOH*
• **gold**	or de couleur	*or-de-koo-lur*
	doré	*du-ray*
• **gray**	gris	*gree*
• **green**	vert	*vehr*
• **orange**	orangé	*or-AH-zh-ay*
	orange (*invariable*)	*or-AN-zh*
• **pink**	rose	*rohz*
• **purple**	violet	*vyuh-leh*
• **red**	rouge	*roozh*
• **silver**	argenté	*ar-zh-AH-tay*
	argent (*invariable*)	*ar-zh-AH*
• **white**	blanc (*m*)	*blAH*
	blanche (*f*)	*blAH-sh*
• **yellow**	jaune	*zh-ohn*

---

to see life through rose-colored glasses = voir la vie en rose *vwar la vee AH rohz*

---

b. DESCRIBING COLORS

bright	éclatant	*ay-klat-AH*
dark	sombre	*sOH-bre*
	foncé	*fOH-say*
dull	terne	*tehrn*
light	clair	*klehr*
lively	vif	*veef*
opaque	opaque	*up-ak*
pale	pâle	*pahl*
pure	pur	*pewr*
transparent	transparent	*tr-AH-spar-AH*
vibrant	vibrant	*veebr-AH*

c. ADDITIONAL VOCABULARY: COLORS

color	couleur (*f*)	*koo-lur*
• **color**	colorer (*v*)	*kul-u-ray*
• **colored**	coloré(e) (*adj, m, f*)	*kul-u-ray*
• **coloring**	colorant (*m*)	*kul-ur-AH*
• **food coloring**	colorant alimentaire	*kul-ur-AH aleem-AH-tehr*

crayon	crayon (*m*) gras	*kreh-y-OH grah*
felt-tip pen	stylo-feutre (*m*)	*stee-loh fuh-tre*
paint	peindre (*v*)	*pEH-dre*
painter	peintre (*m*)	*pEH-tre*
	femme peintre (*f*)	*fam pEH-tre*
pen	stylo (*m*)	*stee-lo*
• **ballpoint**	à bille	*a-bee*
tint	teinte (*f*)	*tEHt*
• **tint**	teindre (*v*)	*tEH-dre*

8. BASIC GRAMMAR

a. GRAMMATICAL TERMS

adjective	adjectif (*m*)	*ad-zh-ehk-teef*
• **demonstrative**	démonstratif (*adj*)	*daym-OH-stra-teef*
• **descriptive**	descriptif (*adj*)	*dehs-kreep-teef*
• **indefinite**	indéfini (*adj*)	*EH-day-fee-nee*
• **interrogative**	interrogatif (*adj*)	*EH-teh-rug-a-teef*
• **possessive**	possessif (*adj*)	*puss-ay-seef*
• **predicate**	attribut (*m*)	*a-tree-bew*
adverb	adverbe (*m*)	*ad-vehrb*
alphabet	alphabet (*m*)	*al-fa-beh*
• **accent**	accent (*m*)	*aks-AH*
• **consonant**	consonne (*f*)	*kOH-sun*
• **letter**	lettre (*f*)	*leht-re*
• **phonetics**	phonétique (*f*)	*fun-ay-teek*
• **pronunciation**	prononciation (*f*)	*prun-OH-syah-sy-OH*
• **vowel**	voyelle (*f*)	*vwa-yehl*
article	article (*m*)	*ar-teekle*
• **definite**	défini (*adj*)	*day-fee-nee*
• **indefinite**	indéfini (*adj*)	*EH-day-fee-nee*
clause	proposition (*f*)	*pru-poh-zee-syOH*
• **main**	principale (*adj*)	*prEH-see-pal*
• **relative**	relative (*adj*)	*re-la-teev*
• **subordinate**	subordonnée (*adj*)	*sew-bor-dun-ay*
comparison	comparaison (*f*)	*kOH-par-ayz-OH*
conjunction	conjonction (*f*)	*kOH-zh-OH-ksyOH*
discourse	discours (*m*)	*dees-koor*
• **direct**	direct (*adj*)	*deer-ehkt*
• **indirect**	indirect (*adj*)	*EH-deer-ehkt*
gender	genre (*m*)	*zh-AH-re*
• **masculine**	masculin (*m*)	*mas-kewl-EH*
• **feminine**	féminin (*m*)	*fay-meen-EH*
grammar	grammaire (*f*)	*gram-ehr*
interrogative	interrogatif (*m*)	*EH-teh-rug-a-teef*

mood	mode (*m*)	*mud*
• **conditional**	conditionnel (*adj*)	*kOH-dee-sy-un-ehl*
• **imperative**	impératif (*adj*)	*EH-pay-ra-teef*
• **indicative**	indicatif (*adj*)	*EH-dee-ka-teef*
• **subjunctive**	subjonctif (*adj*)	*sewb-zh-OH-kteef*
noun	nom (*m*)	*nOH*
number	nombre (*m*)	*nOH-bre*
• **plural**	pluriel (*adj*)	*plew-ry-ehl*
• **singular**	singulier (*adj*)	*sEH-gewl-yay*
object	complément d'objet (*m*)	*kOH-playm-AH dub-zh-eh*
• **direct**	direct (*adj*)	*deer-ehkt*
• **indirect**	indirect (*adj*)	*EH-deer-ehkt*
participle	participe (*m*)	*par-tee-seep*
• **past**	passé (*adj*)	*pah-say*
• **present**	présent (*adj*)	*prayz-AH*
partitive	partitif (*m*)	*par-tee-teef*
person	personne (*f*)	*pehr-sun*
• **first**	première (*adj*)	*prem-yehr*
• **second**	deuxième (*adj*)	*duhz-yehm*
• **third**	troisième (*adj*)	*trwahz-yehm*
predicate	prédicat (*m*)	*pray-dee-ka*
preposition	préposition (*f*)	*pray-poh-zee-sy-OH*
pronoun	pronom (*m*)	*pro-nOH*
• **demonstrative**	démonstratif (*adj*)	*daym-OH-stra-teef*
• **interrogative**	interrogatif (*adj*)	*EH-teh-rug-a-teef*
• **object**	complément d'objet (*m*)	*kOH-playm-AH dub-zh-eh*
• **personal**	personnel (*adj*)	*pehr-sun-ehl*
• **possessive**	possessif (*adj*)	*puss-ay-seef*
• **reflexive**	personnel réfléchi (*adj*)	*pehr-sun-ehl ray-flay-shee*
• **relative**	relatif (*adj*)	*re-la-teef*
• **subject**	sujet (*m*)	*sew-zh-eh*
sentence	phrase (*f*)	*frahz*
• **declarative**	déclarative (*adj*)	*day-klar-a-teev*
• **interrogative**	interrogative (*adj*)	*EH-teh-rug-a-teev*
subject	sujet (*m*)	*sew-zh-eh*
tense	temps (*m*)	*tAH*
• **future**	futur (*m*)	*few-tewr*
• **imperfect**	imparfait (*m*)	*EH-par-feh*
• **past**	passé composé (*m*)	*pah-say kOH-poh-zay*
• **past definite**	passé simple (*m*)	*pah-say sEH-ple*
• **perfect**	parfait (*m*)	*par-feh*
• **pluperfect**	plus-que-parfait (*m*)	*plews-ke-par-feh*
• **present**	présent (*m*)	*prayz-AH*
verb	verbe (*m*)	*vehrb*
• **active**	actif (*adj*)	*ak-teef*

• **conjugation**	conjugaison (*f*)	*kOH-zh-ew-gehz-OH*
• **gerund**	gérondif (*m*)	*zh-ayr-OH-deef*
• **infinitive**	infinitif (*m*)	*EH-fee-nee-teef*
• **intransitive**	intransitif (*adj*)	*EH-tr-AH-see-teef*
• **irregular**	irrégulier (*adj*)	*eer-ray-gewl-yay*
• **modal**	modal (*adj*)	*mud-al*
• **passive**	passif (*adj*)	*pah-seef*
• **reflexive**	pronominal (*adj*)	*pru-num-ee-nal*
• **regular**	régulier (*adj*)	*ray-gewl-yay*
• **transitive**	transitif (*adj*)	*tr-AH-see-teef*

b. DEFINITE ARTICLES

the	le (*m, s*)	*le*
	la (*f, s*)	*la*
	l' (*m/f, s*)	*l*
	les (*m/f, pl*)	*lay*

FOCUS: The Definite Article System

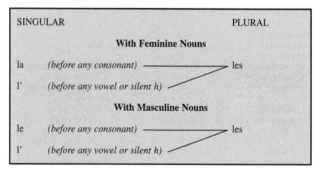

c. INDEFINITE ARTICLES

a, an	un (*m, s*)	*UH*
	une (*f, s*)	*ewn*

FOCUS: The Indefinite Article System

WITH FEMININE NOUNS		WITH MASCULINE NOUNS	
une	*(before any consonant)*	un	*(before any consonant)*
une	*(before any vowel or silent h)*	un	*(before any vowel or silent h)*

d. THE PARTITIVE

some (any)	du (*m, s*)	*dew*
	de l' (*m, s*)	*del*
	de la (*f, s*)	*de la*
	de l' (*f, s*)	*del*
	des (*m/f, pl*)	*day*

FOCUS: The Partitive System

Simple Affirmative

J'ai **du** *café.* / I have some coffee.
J'ai **de la** *viande.* / I have some meat.
J'ai **de** *l'eau.* / I have some water.
J'ai **des** *pâtes.* / I have some pasta.

Simple Negative

Je n'*ai* **pas de** *café.* / I don't have any coffee.
Je n'*ai* **pas de** *viande.* / I don't have any meat.
Je n'*ai* **pas d'**eau. / I don't have any water.
Je n'*ai* **pas de** *pâtes.* / I don't have any pasta.

With an Adjective

J'ai **de jolis** *chapeaux.* / I have some pretty hats.
J'ai **de jolies** *robes.* / I have some pretty dresses.

Note: The plural is rare in the partitive because the partitive is not used for countable things: *des pâtes* / some pasta; *des épinards* / some spinach. When you use *des* with countable things, you are not using the partitive. Instead, you are using the plural indefinite article: *un ami* (a friend) / *des amis* (friends); *une carotte* (a carrot) / *des carottes* (carrots). If the thing you are talking about can be counted individually, you are using the plural indefinite article: *J'ai des bonbons.* / I have some candy. (You can eat a single *bonbon*.)

---

e. DEMONSTRATIVE ADJECTIVES

this, that	ce (*m, s*)	*se*
	cet (*m, s*)	*seht*
	cette (*f, s*)	*seht*
these, those	ces (*m/f, pl*)	*say*

FOCUS: The Demonstrative Adjective System

Ce garçon est beau. / This boy is handsome.
Cet arbre est beau. / This tree is beautiful.
Cette femme est belle. / This woman is beautiful.
Ces hommes sont beaux. / These men are handsome.
Ces livres sont beaux. / These books are beautiful.
Ces dames sont belles. / These ladies are beautiful.

If you wish to make a contrast between "this" and "that" or "these" and "those," add *-ci* (this, these) or *-là* (that, those) to the noun with a hyphen.

Ce garçon-ci est plus fort que ce garçon-là. / This boy is stronger than that boy.

The form *cet* is used in front of a masculine singular noun or adjective beginning with a vowel or silent *h*: *cet arbre, cet homme.*
If there is more than one noun, a demonstrative adjective must be used in front of each noun: *cette dame et ce monsieur.*

---

f. POSSESSIVE ADJECTIVES

my	mon (*m, s*)	*mOH*
	ma (*f, s*)	*ma*
	mes (*m/f, pl*)	*may*
your *(pol)*	votre (*m/f, s*)	*vutr*
	vos (*m/f, pl*)	*vo*
your *(fam)*	ton (*m, s*)	*tOH*
	ta (*f, s*)	*ta*
	tes (*m/f, pl*)	*tay*
his, her	son (*m, s*)	*sOH*
	sa (*f, s*)	*sa*
	ses (*m/f, pl*)	*say*
our	notre (*m/f, s*)	*nutr*
	nos (*m/f, pl*)	*no*
their	leur (*m/f, s*)	*lur*
	leurs (*m/f, pl*)	*lur*

FOCUS: The Possessive Adjective System

MASCULINE

Singular

mon livre/my book
ton stylo/your pen
son ballon/his (her, its)
  balloon
notre parapluie/our umbrella
votre sandwich/your sandwich
leur gâteau/their cake

Plural

mes livres/my books
tes stylos/your pens
ses ballons/his (her, its)
  balloons
nos parapluies/our umbrellas
vos sandwiches/your sandwiches
leurs gâteaux/their cakes

FEMININE

Singular

ma robe/my dress
ta jaquette/your jacket
sa balle/his (her, its) ball
notre maison/our house
votre voiture/your car
leur sœur/their sister

Plural

mes robes/my dresses
tes jaquettes/your jackets
ses balles/his (her, its) balls
nos maisons/our houses
vos voitures/your cars
leurs sœurs/their sisters

---

g. PREPOSITIONS

among	parmi	*par-mee*
at	à	*a*
between	entre	*AH-tre*
for	pour	*poor*
from	de	*de*
in	dans	*dAH*
of	de	*de*
on	sur	*sewr*
to	à	*a*
with	avec	*av-ehk*

FOCUS: Prepositional Contractions

Preposition	Article			Contraction
à *a*	+	le *le*	=	au *oh*
	+	les *lay*	=	aux *oh*
de *de*	+	le *le*	=	du *dew*
	+	les *lay*	=	des *day*

Note: Do not use a contraction for the definite articles *la* and *l'*: à + *la* = à *la*; à + *l'* = à *l'*.

h. SUBJECT PRONOUNS

I	je	*zhe*
you	tu (*s, fam*)	*tew*
you	vous (*s, pol*)	*voo*
he, it	il	*eel*
she, it	elle	*ehl*
one	on (*indef*)	*OH*
we	nous	*noo*
you	vous (*pl*)	*voo*
they	ils (*m*)	*eel*
	elles (*f*)	*ehl*

i. DIRECT OBJECT PRONOUNS

me	me	*me*
you	te (*s, fam*)	*te*
you	vous (*s, pol*)	*voo*
him	le	*le*
her	la	*la*
it	le (*m*)	*le*
	la (*f*)	*la*
us	nous	*noo*
you	vous (*pl*)	*voo*
them	les	*lay*

FOCUS: Direct Object Pronouns

Person	Singular	Plural
1st	*me (m')*/me	*nous*/us
2nd	*te (t')*/you (familiar)	*vous*/you (singular polite or plural)
3rd	*le(l')*/him, it *la (l')*/her, it (person or thing)	*les*/them (persons or things)

j. INDIRECT OBJECT PRONOUNS

to me	me	*me*
to you	te (*s, fam*)	*te*
	vous (*s, pol*)	*voo*
to him/to her	lui	*lew-ee*
to us	nous	*noo*
to you	vous (*pl*)	*voo*
to them	leur	*lur*

Note: For an explanation of French grammar and rules, please consult Barron's *French Now!* fourth edition by Kendris and Kendris or any of the Barron's French grammar books. This book contains basic French vocabulary arranged by topics of general interest to build your word power.

FOCUS: Indirect Object Pronouns

Person	Singular		Plural	
1st	*me (m')*	to me	*nous*	to us
2nd	*te (t')*	to you (familiar)	*vous*	to you (singular polite or plural)
3rd	*lui*	to him, to her	*leur*	to them

k. REFLEXIVE PRONOUNS (ALL BEFORE VERBS)

myself	me	*me*
yourself	te (*s, fam*)	*te*
yourself	vous (*s, pol*)	*voo*
himself/herself/ oneself/itself	se	*se*
ourselves	nous	*noo*
yourselves	vous	*voo*
themselves	se	*se*

FOCUS: Reflexive Pronouns

Person	Singular	Plural
1st	*je me lave*	*nous nous lavons*
2nd	*tu te laves*	*vous vous lavez*
3rd	{ *il se lave* *elle se lave* *on se lave*	{ *ils se lavent* *elles se lavent*

l. DISJUNCTIVE PRONOUNS

FOCUS: Disjunctive Pronouns (as objects of prepositions)

Person	Singular		Plural	
1st	*moi*	me, I	*nous*	us, we
2nd	*toi*	you (familiar)	*vous*	you (formal singular or plural)
3rd	{ *soi* { *lui* { *elle*	oneself him, he her, she	{ *eux* { *elles*	them, they (m.) them, they (f.)

m. DEMONSTRATIVE PRONOUNS

FOCUS: Demonstrative Pronouns

	Singular	**Plural**
Masculine	*celui*/the one	*ceux*/the ones
Feminine	*celle*/the one	*celles*/the ones

n. POSSESSIVE PRONOUNS

FOCUS: Possessive Pronouns

MASCULINE			
	Singular		**Plural**
le mien	mine	*les miens*	mine
le tien	yours (familiar)	*les tiens*	yours (familiar)
le sien	his, hers, its	*les siens*	his, hers, its
le nôtre	ours	*les nôtres*	ours
le vôtre	yours	*les vôtres*	yours
le leur	theirs	*les leurs*	theirs

FEMININE			
	Singular		**Plural**
la mienne	mine	*les miennes*	mine
la tienne	yours (familiar)	*les tiennes*	yours (familiar)
la sienne	his, hers, its	*les siennes*	his, hers, its
la nôtre	ours	*les nôtres*	ours
la vôtre	yours	*les vôtres*	yours
la leur	theirs	*les leurs*	theirs

FOCUS: Word Order of Pronouns in Four Types of Sentences

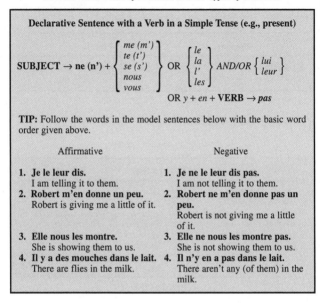

Declarative Sentence with a Verb in a Simple Tense (e.g., present)

$$\text{SUBJECT} \to \textbf{ne (n')} + \begin{Bmatrix} me\ (m') \\ te\ (t') \\ se\ (s') \\ nous \\ vous \end{Bmatrix} \text{OR} \begin{Bmatrix} le \\ la \\ l' \\ les \end{Bmatrix} \text{AND/OR} \begin{Bmatrix} lui \\ leur \end{Bmatrix}$$

$$\text{OR}\ y + en + \textbf{VERB} \to pas$$

TIP: Follow the words in the model sentences below with the basic word order given above.

Affirmative	Negative
1. **Je le leur dis.** I am telling it to them.	1. **Je ne le leur dis pas.** I am not telling it to them.
2. **Robert m'en donne un peu.** Robert is giving me a little of it.	2. **Robert ne m'en donne pas un peu.** Robert is not giving me a little of it.
3. **Elle nous les montre.** She is showing them to us.	3. **Elle ne nous les montre pas.** She is not showing them to us.
4. **Il y a des mouches dans le lait.** There are flies in the milk.	4. **Il n'y en a pas dans le lait.** There aren't any (of them) in the milk.

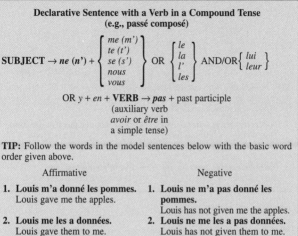

Declarative Sentence with a Verb in a Compound Tense
(e.g., passé composé)

SUBJECT → *ne* (*n'*) + $\left\{\begin{array}{l} me\ (m') \\ te\ (t') \\ se\ (s') \\ nous \\ vous \end{array}\right\}$ OR $\left\{\begin{array}{l} le \\ la \\ l' \\ les \end{array}\right\}$ AND/OR $\left\{\begin{array}{l} lui \\ leur \end{array}\right\}$

OR *y* + *en* + VERB → *pas* + past participle
(auxiliary verb
avoir or *être* in
a simple tense)

TIP: Follow the words in the model sentences below with the basic word order given above.

Affirmative

Negative

1. **Louis m'a donné les pommes.**
   Louis gave me the apples.
2. **Louis me les a données.**
   Louis gave them to me.
3. **Les cerises? Je les leur ai offertes.**
   The cherries? I have offered them to them.

1. **Louis ne m'a pas donné les pommes.**
   Louis has not given me the apples.
2. **Louis ne me les a pas données.**
   Louis has not given them to me.
3. **Les cerises? Je ne les leur ai pas offertes.**
   The cherries? I did not offer them to them.

Note: The preceding direct object pronoun *les cerises* is feminine plural, so the past participle *offertes* is feminine plural.

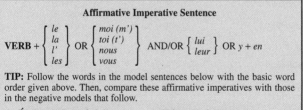

Affirmative Imperative Sentence

VERB + $\left\{\begin{array}{l} le \\ la \\ l' \\ les \end{array}\right\}$ OR $\left\{\begin{array}{l} moi\ (m') \\ toi\ (t') \\ nous \\ vous \end{array}\right\}$ AND/OR $\left\{\begin{array}{l} lui \\ leur \end{array}\right\}$ OR *y* + *en*

TIP: Follow the words in the model sentences below with the basic word order given above. Then, compare these affirmative imperatives with those in the negative models that follow.

1. **Écrivez la lettre à Julie.**
   Write the letter to Julie.
2. **Écrivez-la.**
   Write it.
3. **Écrivez-la-lui**
   Write it to her.

4. **Répondez à la question.**
   Reply to the question.
5. **Répondez-y.**
   Reply to it.
6. **Donnez m'en.**
   Give me some (of it).

Negative Imperative Sentence

$$\text{Ne (N')} + \begin{Bmatrix} me\ (m') \\ te\ (t') \\ nous \\ vous \end{Bmatrix} \text{OR} \begin{Bmatrix} le \\ la \\ l' \\ les \end{Bmatrix} \text{OR} \begin{Bmatrix} lui \\ leur \end{Bmatrix} \text{OR}\ y$$

$$+\ en + \textbf{VERB} \rightarrow pas$$

TIP: Follow the words in the model sentences below with the basic word order given above. Then, compare these negative imperatives with those in the affirmative models on p. 47.

1. **N'écrivez pas la lettre à Julie.**
   Don't write the letter to Julie.
2. **Ne l'écrivez pas.**
   Don't write it.
3. **Ne la lui écrivez pas.**
   Don't write it to her.
4. **Ne répondez pas à la question.**
   Don't reply to the question.
5. **N'y répondez pas.**
   Don't reply to it.
6. **Ne m'en donnez pas.**
   Don't give me any (of it).

---

o. OTHER PRONOUNS

everyone	tout le monde (*m*)	*tool mOHd*
everything	tout (*m*)	*too*
	toute (*f*)	*toot*
no one	personne (*indef*)	*pehr-sun*
one (*in general*)	on (*indef*)	*OH*
others	autrui (*indef*)	*oh-trew-ee*
	les autres	*lay-zoh-tre*
some, of it, of them	en (*before or after a verb*)	*AH*
some (*people*)	des gens	*day zh-AH*
someone	quelqu'un (*m*)	*kehlk-UH*
	quelqu'une (*f*) (rare)	*kehlk-ewn*
something	quelque chose	*kehlke sh-oh-z*

p. CONJUNCTIONS

although	bien que	*byEH-ke*
	quoique	*kwa-ke*
and	et	*ay*
as (since)	comme	*kum*
as if	comme si	*kum-see*
as soon as	dès que	*deh-ke*
	aussitôt que	*oh-see-toh-ke*
because	parce que	*pars-ke*
but	mais	*meh*
even though	même si	*mehm-see*

however	pourtant	*poor-tAH*
	cependant	*se-pAH-dAH*
	toutefois	*toot-fwa*
if	si	*see*
in order that, so that	afin que	*afEH-ke*
	pour que	*poor-ke*
nevertheless	néanmoins	*nay-AH-mwEH*
or	ou	*oo*
provided that	pourvu que	*poor-vew-ke*
since	depuis que	*de-pew-ee-ke*
therefore, consequently	donc	*dOHk*
unless	à moins que	*a-mwEH-ke*
until	jusqu'à ce que	*zn-ews-kas-ke*
when	quand	*kAH*
while, whereas	tandis que	*tAH-dee-ke*

9. REQUESTING INFORMATION

answer	réponse (*f*)	*rayp-OH-s*
• answer	répondre (*v*)	*rayp-OH-dre*
ask (for)	demander (*v*)	*dem-AH-day*
• make a request	faire une demande	*fehr ewn dem-AH-de*
Can you tell	Pourriez-vous me	*poor-ee-ay voom deer*
me . . . ?	dire . . . ? (*pol*)	
	Peux-tu me dire	*puh-tewm deer*
	. . . ? (*fam*)	
How?	Comment?	*kum-AH*
How come?	Mais comment?	*meh kum-AH*
How does one say . . . ? /	Comment dit-on . . . ?	*kum-AH dee-tOH*
How do you say . . . ?		
How much?	Combien?	*kOH-byEH*
I don't understand.	Je ne comprends pas.	*zhen kOH-pr-AH pah*
So?	Et alors?	*ay al-or*
What?	Comment?	*kum-AH*
	Pardon?	*pard-OH*
	Quoi?	*kwah*
What do you call this	Comment appelle-	*kum-AH a-pehl-tOH se-*
(that) in French?	ton ceci (cela) en	*see (sla) AH frAH-seh*
	français?	
What does it mean?	Que veut dire cela?	*ke-vuh-deer-sla*
	Que signifie cela?	*ke-see-ny-ee-fee-sla*
When?	Quand?	*kAH*
Where?	Où?	*oo*
Which (one)?	Lequel? (*m*)	*le-kehl*
	Laquelle? (*f*)	*la-kehl*
Which (ones)?	Lesquels? (*m*)	*lay-kehl*
	Lesquelles? (*f*)	*lay-kehl*
Who?	Qui?	*kee*
Why?	Pourquoi?	*poor-kwa*

PEOPLE

10. FAMILY AND FRIENDS

a. FAMILY MEMBERS

aunt	tante (*f*)	*tAHt*
brother	frère (*m*)	*frehr*
• **brother-in-law**	beau-frère (*m*)	*boh-frehr*
cousin	cousin (*m*)	*koo-zEH*
	cousine (*f*)	*koo-zeen*
dad	papa (*m*)	*pa-pa*
daughter	fille (*f*)	*fee-y*
• **daughter-in-law**	belle-fille (*f*)	*behl-fee-y*
	bru (*f*)	*brew*
family	famille (*f*)	*fa-mee-y*
• **family relationship**	parenté (*f*)	*pa-rAH-tay*
father	père (*m*)	*pehr*
• **father-in-law**	beau-père (*m*)	*boh-pehr*
grandchildren	petits-enfants (*m, f, pl*)	*ptee-zAH-fAH*
grandfather	grand-père (*m*)	*grAH-pehr*
grandmother	grand-mère (*f*)	*grAH-mehr*
husband	mari (*m*)	*ma-ree*
	époux (*m*)	*ay-poo*
mom	maman (*f*)	*ma-mAH*
mother	mère (*f*)	*mehr*
• **mother-in-law**	belle-mère (*f*)	*behl-mehr*
nephew	neveu (*m*)	*ne-vuh*
niece	nièce (*f*)	*nee-ehss*
parents	parents (*m, pl*)	*pa-rAH*
relatives	proches parents (*m, pl*)	*prush parAH*
sister	sœur (*f*)	*sur*
• **sister-in-law**	belle-sœur (*f*)	*behl-sur*
son	fils (*m*)	*fee-ss*
• **son-in-law**	gendre (*m*)	*zh-AH-dre*
twin	jumeau (*m*)	*zh-ew-moh*
	jumelle (*f*)	*zh-ew-mehl*
uncle	oncle (*m*)	*OH-kle*
wife	femme (*f*)	*fam*
	épouse (*f*)	*ay-pooz*

b. FRIENDS

acquaintance	connaissance (f)	kun-eh-sAH-ss
boyfriend	ami (m)	a-mee
	petit ami (m)	ptee-a-mee
chum	copain (m)	kup-EH
	copine (f)	kup-een
colleague, work associate	collègue (m, f)	kul-ehg
enemy	ennemi(e) (m, f)	ehn-mee
fiancé	fiancé (m)	fee-AH-say
fiancée	fiancée (f)	fee-AH-say
friend	ami(e) (m, f)	a-mee
• **become friends**	devenir (v) amis	de-vneer-a-mee
	faire (v) l'amitié	fehr la-mee-tee-ay
• **between friends**	entre amis	AH-tre a-mee
• **break off a friendship**	rompre (v) une amitié	rOHm-pre ewn a-mee-tee-ay
• **close friend**	ami(e) intime (m, f)	a-mee EH-teem
• **dear friend**	cher (chère) ami(e) (m, f)	sh-ehr a-mee
• **family friend**	ami(e) (m, f) de la famille	a-meed la fa-mee-y
• **friendship**	amitié (f)	a-mee-tee-ay
girlfriend	amie (f)	a-mee
	petite amie (f)	ptee-ta-mee
lover	amant (m)	a-mAH
	amante (f)	a-mAH-t
• **love affair**	une liaison	ew-n-lee-yay-zOH

11. DESCRIBING PEOPLE

a. GENDER AND APPEARANCE

attractive	attrayant, beau, bel (adj, m)	a-treh-yAH, boh, behl
	attrayante, belle (f)	a-treh-yAHt, behl
beautiful, handsome	beau (adj, m)	both
	bel (adj, m) (before a vowel or silent h)	behl
	belle (f)	behl
• **beauty**	beauté (f)	boh-tay
big	grand (adj, m)	grAH
	grande (f)	grAHd
• **bigness**	grandeur (f)	grAH-dur
• **become big**	grandir (v)	grAH-deer
blond	blond (m)	blOH
• **blonde**	blonde (f)	blOHd

body	corps (*m*)	*kor*
boy	garçon (*m*)	*gar-sOH*
clean	propre (*adj*)	*pru-pre*
curly-haired	cheveux bouclés	*shvuh boo-klay*
	cheveux frisés	*shvuh free-zay*
dark-haired	cheveux bruns	*shvuh brUH*
dirty	sale (*adj*)	*sal*
elegance	élégance (*f*)	*ay-lay-gAH-ss*
• **elegant**	élégant (*adj, m*)	*ay-lay-gAH*
	élégante (*f*)	*ay-lay-gAH-t*
• **elegantly**	élégamment (*adv*)	*ay-lay-ga-mAH*
• **inelegant**	inélégant (*adj, m*)	*ee-nay-lay-gAH*
	inélégante (*f*)	*ee-nay-lay-gAH-t*
fat	gros (*adj, m*)	*groh*
	grosse (*f*)	*groh-ss*
• **become fat**	grossir (*v*)	*groh-seer*
• **obesity**	obésité (*f*)	*u-bay-zee-tay*
female	femelle (*f*)	*fe-mehl*
• **feminine**	féminin (*adj, m*)	*fay-mee-nEH*
	féminine (*f*)	*fay-mee-neen*
gentleman	monsieur (*m*)	*me-sy-uh*
girl	jeune fille (*f*)	*zh-uhn fee-y*
health	santé (*f*)	*sAH-tay*
• **healthy**	sain (*adj, m*)	*sEH*
	saine (*f*)	*sehn*
	en bonne santé	*AH bun sAH-tay*
height	taille (*f*)	*tah-y*
	stature (*f*)	*sta-tewr*
• **How tall are you?**	Quelle taille avez-vous?	*kehl tah-y avay-voo*
	Combien mesurez-vous?	*kOH-byen me-ze-ray voo*
• **I am . . . tall.**	J'ai la taille . . .	*zh-ay la tah-y*
	Je fais . . . pieds.	*zhe feh . . . pyay*
• **medium (average) height**	la taille moyenne	*la tah-y mwa-y-ehn*
• **short**	petit (*adj, m*)	*ptee*
	petite (*f*)	*pteet*
• **tall**	grand (*adj, m*)	*grAH*
	grande (*f*)	*grAHd*
lady	dame	*dahm*
• **young lady**	demoiselle	*de-mwah-zehl*
large	grand (*adj, m*)	*grAH*
	grande (*f*)	*grAHd*
male	mâle	*mahl*
• **masculine**	masculin	*mas-kew-lEH*
man	homme	*um*
• **young man**	jeune homme	*zh-un um*

physique (appearance)	le physique	*le fee-zeek*
red-haired	roux (*adj, m*)	*roo*
	rousse (*f*)	*roos*
sex	sexe (*m*)	*sehks*
sick	malade (*adj*)	*ma-lahd*
• sickness	maladie (*f*)	*ma-lah-dee*
• become sick	tomber (*v*) malade	*tOH-bay ma-lahd*
small, little	petit (*adj, m*)	*ptee*
	petite (*f*)	*pteet*
strength	force (*f*)	*forss*
• strong	fort (*adj, m*)	*for*
	forte (*f*)	*fort*
ugly	laid (*adj, m*)	*leh*
	laide (*f*)	*lehd*
• ugliness	laideur (*f*)	*lehd-ur*
virile	viril(e) (*adj, m, f*)	*vee-reel*
weak	faible (*adj*)	*feh-ble*
• weakness	faiblesse (*f*)	*feh-bless*
• become weak	s'affaiblir (*v*)	*sa-feh-bleer*
weight	poids (*m*)	*pwah*
• heavy	lourd (*adj, m*)	*loor*
	lourde (*f*)	*loord*
• How much do you weigh?	Combien pesez-vous?	*kOH-byEH pe-zay voo*
• I weigh . . .	Je pèse . . .	*zhe pehz*
• light	léger (*adj, m*)	*lay-zh-ay*
	légère (*f*)	*lay-zh-ehr*
• skinny, thin	maigre (*adj*)	*meh-gr*
• slim, slender	mince	*mEH-ss*
	svelte	*svehlt*
• weigh oneself	se peser (*refl v*)	*se pe-zay*
• become thin	maigrir (*v*)	*meh-greer*
• gain weight	prendre (*v*) du poids	*prAH-dre dew pwah*
• lose weight	perdre (*v*) du poids	*pehr-dre dew pwah*
woman	femme	*fam*

b. CONCEPTS OF AGE

adolescence	adolescence (*f*)	*a-du-leh-sAH-ss*
• adolescent, teenager	adolescent (*m*)	*a-du-leh-sAH*
	adolescente (*f*)	*a-du-leh-sAH-t*
adult	adulte (*m, f*)	*a-dewlt*
age	âge (*m*)	*ah-zh*
baby, child	bébé (*m*)	*bay-bay*
	enfant (*m, f*)	*AH-fAH*
• children	enfants	*AH-fAH*
boy	garçon	*gar-sOH*

elderly person	une personne âgée	*ewn pehr-sun ah-zh-ay*
• have white hair	avoir les cheveux blancs	*a-vwahr lay shvuh blAH*
girl	(jeune) fille	*(zh-un) fee-y*
grow up	grandir (*v*)	*grAH-deer*
old	vieux (*m*)	*vyuh*
	vieil (*m*)	*vy-eh-y*
	vieille (*f*)	*vy-eh-y*
• old age	vieillesse (*f*)	*vyeh-yehss*
• older	plus vieux	*plew vyuh*
• older brother	frère aîné	*frehr eh-nay*
• older sister	sœur aînée	*sur eh-nay*
• How old are you?	Quel âge avez-vous (*pol*)?	*kehl ah-zh a-vay voo*
	Quel âge as-tu (*fam*)?	*kehl ah-zh a tew*
• I am . . . old.	J'ai . . . ans.	*zh-ay AH*
• two-year-old	de deux ans	*de duh zAH*
• three-year-old	de trois ans	*de trwah zAH*
• become old	vieillir (*v*)	*vyeh-yeer*
young	jeune (*adj*)	*zh-un*
• younger	plus jeune	*plew zh-un*
• younger brother	frère cadet	*frehr ka-deh*
• younger sister	sœur cadette	*sur ka-deht*
• youth	jeunesse (*f*)	*zh-un-ehss*
• youthful	juvénile (*adj*)	*zh-ew-vay-neel*
	jeune (*adj*)	*zh-un*

c. MARRIAGE AND THE HUMAN LIFE CYCLE

anniversary	anniversaire (*m*)	*a-nee-vehr-sehr*
• diamond anniversary	noces (*f, pl*) de diamant	*nuss de dya-mAH*
• golden anniversary	noces d'or	*nuss dor*
• silver anniversary	noces d'argent	*nuss dar-zh-AH*
bachelor, unmarried	célibataire	*say-lee-ba-tehr*
birth	naissance (*f*)	*neh-sAH-ss*
• birthday	anniversaire (*m*)	*a-nee-vehr-sehr*
• celebrate one's birthday	fêter (*v*) l'anniversaire	*feh-tay la-nee-vehr-sehr*
• Happy birthday!	Bon anniversaire!	*bun-a-nee-vehr-sehr*
• be born	naître (*v*)	*neh-tre*
• I was born on . . .	Je suis né(e) le . . .	*zhe sew-ee nay le*
bride	mariée (*f*)	*ma-ree-ay*
death	mort (*f*)	*mor*
• die	mourir (*v*)	*moo-reer*

divorce	divorce (m)	*dee-vorss*
• **divorce**	divorcer (v)	*dee-vor-say*
• **divorced**	divorcé (m, adj)	*dee-vor-say*
	divorcée (f)	*dee-vor-say*
engagement	fiançailles (f, pl)	*fee-AH-sa-y*
• **become engaged**	se fiancer (refl v)	*se fee-AH-say*
• **engaged**	fiancé (adj)	*fee-AH-say*
fiancé	fiancé	*fee-AH-say*
fiancée	fiancée	*fee-AH-say*
get used to	s'habituer à (v)	*sa-bee-tew-ay a*
gift	cadeau (m)	*ka-doh*
• **give a gift**	donner (v) un cadeau	*dun-ay UH ka-doh*
go to school	aller (v) à l'école	*alay a lay-kul*
groom (bridegroom)	marié (m)	*ma-ree-ay*
heredity	hérédité (f)	*ay-ray-dee-tay*
• **inherit**	hériter (v)	*ay-ree-tay*
honeymoon	lune (f) de miel	*lewn de mee-ehl*
husband	époux	*ay-poo*
	mari	*ma-ree*
kiss	baiser (m)	*beh-zay*
• **kiss**	embrasser (v)	*AH-bra-say*
life	vie (f)	*vee*
• **live**	vivre (v)	*vee-vre*
love	amour (m)	*a-moor*
• **love**	aimer (v)	*ay-may*
• **fall in love**	tomber (v) amoureux	*tOH-bay a-moo-ruh*
• **in love**	amoureux (adj)	*a-moo-ruh*
marital status	état civil	*ay-ta see-veel*
marriage, matrimony	mariage (m)	*ma-ree-ah-zh*
• **married**	marié(e) (n, adj, m, f)	*ma-ree-ay*
• **marry (someone)**	épouser (v)	*ay-poo-zay*
	se marier (v) avec	*se-ma-ree-ay avehk*
• **unmarried**	célibataire	*say-lee-ba-tehr*
• **newlyweds**	nouveaux-mariés (n, m, pl)	*noo-voh ma-ree-ay*
pregnancy	grossesse (f)	*groh-seh-ss*
• **be pregnant**	être (v) enceinte	*eh-tre AH-sEHt*
• **give birth**	accoucher (v)	*a-koo-shay*
• **have a baby**	avoir (v) un enfant	*avwar UH nAH-fAH*
raise (someone)	élever (v)	*ayl-vay*
reception	réception (f)	*ray-sehp-syOH*
separation	séparation (f)	*say-pa-ra-syOH*
• **separate**	se séparer (v)	*se say-pa-ray*
• **separated**	séparé (adj)	*say-pa-ray*
spouse	époux (m)	*ay-poo*
	épouse (f)	*ay-pooz*

wedding	mariage (*m*)	*ma-ree-ah-zh*
	noce (*f*)	*nuss*
• **wedding invitation**	faire-part de mariage (*m*)	*fehr par de ma-ree-ah-zh*
• **wedding ring**	anneau (*m*) d'alliance	*a-noh da-lee-AH-ss*
	alliance (*f*)	*a-lee-AH-ss*
	anneau (*m*) de mariage	*a-nohd-ma-ree-ah-zh*
widow	veuve	*vuv*
widower	veuf	*vuf*
wife	femme	*fam*
	épouse	*ay-pooz*

d. RELIGION AND RACE

> For nationalities see Section 30.

agnostic	agnostique (*adj/m, f*)	*ag-nus-teek*
archbishop	archevêque	*arsh-vehk*
atheism	athéisme (*m*)	*a-tay-ee-sm*
• **atheist**	athée (*m, f*)	*a-tay*
baptism	baptême (*m*)	*ba-tehm*
belief	croyance (*f*)	*krwah-yAH-ss*
• **believe**	croire (*v*)	*krwar*
• **believe in**	croire (*v*) en	*krwahr AH*
• **believer**	croyant (*m*)	*krwa-yAH*
	croyante (*f*)	*krwa-yAHt*
Bible	Bible (*f*)	*bee-bl*
bishop	évêque	*ay-vehk*
Buddhism	bouddhisme (*m*)	*boo-dees-me*
• **Buddhist**	bouddhiste (*m, f*)	*boo-deest*
catechism	catéchisme (*m*)	*ka-tay-shee-sme*
Catholic	catholique (*adj*)	*ka-tul-eek*
• **Catholicism**	catholicisme (*m*)	*ka-tul-ee-sees-me*
Christian	chrétien (*n, adj, m*)	*kray-tee-yEH*
	chrétienne (*n, adj, f*)	*kray-tee-yehn*
• **Christianity**	christianisme (*m*)	*krees-tee-a-nee-sme*
church	église (*f*)	*ay-gleez*
confirmation	confirmation (*f*)	*kOH-feer-ma-syOH*
faith	foi (*f*)	*fwa*
• **faithful**	fidèle (*adj*)	*fee-dehl*
God	Dieu	*dyuh*
Hebrew, Jewish	hébreu	*ay-bruh*
	juif (*m*)	*zh-ew-eef*
	juive (*f*)	*zh-ew-eev*

human	humain (*m*)	*ew-mEH*
	humaine (*f*)	*ew-mehn*
• human being	être humain (*m*)	*eh-tre ew-mEH*
• humanity	humanité (*f*)	*ew-ma-nee-tay*
Hindu	hindou(e) (*n, m, f*)	*EH-doo*
	hindou(e) (*adj, m, f*)	*EH-doo*
Islamic	islamique (*adj*)	*ee-sla-meek*
Koran	Coran (*m*)	*ko-rAH*
layperson	laïc, laïque (*adj, m, f*)	*la-eek*
• laity, secularism	laïcité (*f*)	*la-ee-see-tay*
Mass	messe (*f*)	*mehss*
minister	ministre (*m*)	*mee-nee-stre*
monk	moine	*mwahn*
mosque	mosquée (*f*)	*mus-kay*
Muslim	musulman (*m*)	*mew-zewl-mAH*
	musulmane (*f*)	*mew-zewl-mahn*
myth	mythe (*m*)	*meet*
nun	religieuse	*re-lee-zh-yuhz*
oriental	oriental(e) (*m, f*)	*or-yAH-tal*
Orthodox	orthodoxe	*or-tud-uks*
pagan	païen (*n/adj, m*)	*pa-yEH*
	païenne (*n, adj, f*)	*pa-yehn*
people	gens (*m & f, pl*)	*zh-AH*
person	personne (*f*)	*pehr-sun*
pray	prier (*v*)	*pree-yay*
• prayer	prière (*f*)	*pree-yehr*
priest	prêtre (*m*)	*preh-tre*
Protestant	protestant (*m*)	*pru-tehs-tAH*
	protestante (*f*)	*pru-tehs-tAHt*
• Protestantism	protestantisme (*m*)	*pru-tehs-tAH-tees-me*
rabbi	rabbin (*m*)	*ra-bEH*
race	race (*f*)	*rass*
religion	religion (*f*)	*re-lee-zh-yOH*
• religious	pieux (*adj, m*)	*pyuh*
	pieuse (*f*)	*pyuhz*
rite	rite (*m*)	*reet*
soul	âme (*f*)	*ahm*
spirit	esprit (*m*)	*ehs-pree*
• spiritual	spirituel(le) (*adj, m, f*)	*spee-ree-tew-ehl*
synagogue	synagogue (*f*)	*see-na-gug*
temple	temple (*m*)	*tAH-ple*
Testament, New	Nouveau Testament (*m*)	*noo-voh tes-tuh-mAH*
Testament, Old	Ancien Testament (*m*)	*AH-syEH tes-tuh-mAH*
Torah	Torah (*f*)	*toh-ra*
western	occidental(e) (*adj, m, f*)	*uks-ee-dAH-tal*

e. CHARACTERISTICS AND SOCIAL TRAITS

active	actif *(adj, m)*	*ak-teef*
	active *(f)*	*ak-teev*
• **activity**	activité *(f)*	*ak-tee-vee-tay*
adapt	adapter *(v)*	*a-dap-tay*
• **adaptable**	adaptable *(adj)*	*a-dap-ta-bl*
affection	affection *(f)*	*a-fehk-syOH*
• **affectionate**	affectueux *(adj, m)*	*a-fehk-tew-uh*
	affectueuse *(f)*	*a-fehk-tew-uhz*
aggressive	agressif *(adj, m)*	*a-greh-seef*
	agressive *(f)*	*a-greh-seev*
• **aggressiveness**	agressivité *(f)*	*a-greh-see-vee-tay*
altruism	altruisme *(m)*	*al-trew-ee-sm*
• **altruistic, altruist**	altruiste *(m/f)*	*al-trew-eest*
ambition	ambition *(f)*	*AH-bee-syOH*
• **ambitious**	ambitieux *(adj, m)*	*AH-bee-syuh*
	ambitieuse *(f)*	*AH-bee-syuhz*
anger	colère *(f)*	*kul-ehr*
• **angry**	en colère	*AH kul-ehr*
	fâché(e) *(adj)*	*fah-shay*
• **become angry**	se fâcher *(v)*	*se fah-shay*
	se mettre en colère	*se meht-r AH kul-ehr*
anxious	anxieux *(adj, m)*	*AH-ksyuh*
	anxieuse *(f)*	*AH-ksyuhz*
• **anxiousness**	anxiété *(f)*	*AH-ksee-ay-tay*
arrogant	arrogant *(adj, m)*	*a-rug-AH*
	arrogante *(f)*	*a-rug-AHt*
art	art *(m)*	*ar*
artistic, talented	artistique *(adj)*	*ar-tees-teek*
astute	astucieux *(adj, m)*	*a-stew-syuh*
	astucieuse *(f)*	*a-stew-syuhz*
• **astuteness**	astuce *(f)*	*a-stewss*
attractive	attrayant, beau, bel *(adj, m)*	*a-treh-yAH, boh, behl*
	attrayante, belle *(f)*	*a-treh-yAHt, behl*
avarice, greed	avarice *(f)*	*a-va-rees*
• **avaricious, greedy**	avare *(adj, n)*	*a-var*
bad, mean	méchant *(adj, m)*	*may-shAH*
	méchante *(f)*	*may-shAHt*
• **meanness**	méchanceté *(f)*	*may-shAH-stay*
brash, bold	effronté(e) *(adj)*	*ay-frOH-tay*
brilliant	brillant(e) *(adj)*	*bree-yAH(t)*
calm	calme *(adj)*	*kalm*
• **calmness**	calme *(m)*	*kalm*
character	caractère *(m)*	*ka-rak-tehr*
• **characteristic**	caractéristique *(adj, n, f)*	*ka-rak-tay-rees-teek*
• **characterize**	caractériser *(v)*	*ka-rak-tay-ree-zay*

conformist	conformiste (m, f)	kOH-form-eest
• nonconformist	non-conformiste (m, f)	nOH-kOH-form-eest
conscience	conscience (f)	kOH-syAH-ss
• conscientious	consciencieux (adj, m)	kOH-syAH-syuh
	consciencieuse (f)	kOH-syAH-syuhz
conservative	conservateur (adj, m)	kOH-sehr-va-tur
	conservatrice (f)	kOH-sehr-va-treess
courage	courage (m)	koo-ra-zh
• courageous	courageux (adj, m)	koo-ra-zh-uh
	courageuse (f)	koo-ra-zh-uhz
courteous	courtois (adj, m)	koor-twa
	courtoise (f)	koor-twaz
• courtesy	courtoisie (f)	koor-twa-zee
• discourteous	discourtois (adj, m)	dees-koor-twa
	discourtoise (f)	dees-koor-twaz
crazy, mad	fou (adj, m)	foo
	fol (adj, m) (before a vowel or silent h)	ful
	folle (f)	ful
• madness	folie (f)	ful-ee
creative	créatif (adj, m)	kray-a-teef
	créative (f)	kray-a-teev
critical	critique (adj)	kree-teek
cry	pleurer (v)	plur-ay
• crying	en larmes	AH larm
cultured	cultivé(e) (adj, m, f)	kewl-tee-vay
curiosity	curiosité (f)	kew-ryo-zee-tay
• curious	curieux (adj, m)	kew-ry-uh
	curieuse (f)	kew-ry-uhz
delicate	délicat(e) (adj, m, f)	day-lee-ka(t)
diligence	diligence (f)	dee-lee-zh-AH-s
• diligent, hardworking	assidu(e) (adj, m, f)	a-see-doo
	travailleur (adj, m)	tra-va-yur
	travailleuse (f)	tra-va-yuhz
diplomatic	diplomatique (adj)	dee-plu-ma-teek
dishonest	malhonnête (adj)	mal-un-eht
• dishonesty	malhonnêteté (f)	mal-un-eht-tay
dynamic	dynamique (adj)	dee-na-meek
eccentric	excentrique (adj)	ehk-sAH-treek
egoism	égoïsme (m)	ay-gu-ees-me
• egoist, egoistic	égoïste (adj)	ay-gu-eest
eloquence	éloquence (f)	ay-luk-AH-s
• eloquent	éloquent(e) (adj, m, f)	ay-luk-AH(t)
energetic	énergique (adj)	ay-nehr-zh-eek
• energy	énergie (f)	ay-nehr-zh-ee
envious	envieux (adj, m)	AH-vyuh
	envieuse (f)	AH-vyuhz
• envy	envie (f)	AH-vee

faithful	fidèle *(adj)*	*fee-dehl*
fascinate	fasciner *(v)*	*fa-see-nay*
• **fascinating**	fascinant(e) *(adj, m, f)*	*fa-see nAH(t)*
• **fascination, attractiveness**	fascination *(f)*	*fa-see-nah-syOH*
fool, clown	bouffon *(m)*	*boo-fOH*
	clown *(m)*	*kloon*
• **foolish, silly**	bête *(adj)*	*beht*
	sot *(adj, m)*	*soh*
	sotte *(f)*	*sut*
friendly	amical(e) *(adj, m, f)*	*a-mee-kal*
	amusant(e) *(adj, m, f)*	*a-mew-zAH(t)*
funny	drôle *(adj)*	*drohl*
	comique *(adj)*	*kum-eek*
	marrant(e) *(adj, m, f)*	*marAH(t)*
fussy	méticuleux *(adj, m)*	*may-tee-kew-luh*
	méticuleuse *(f)*	*may-tee-kew-luhz*
generosity	générosité *(f)*	*zh-ay-nay-roh-zee-tay*
• **generous**	généreux *(adj, m)*	*zh-ay-nay-ruh*
	généreuse *(f)*	*zh-ay-nay-ruhz*
gentle	doux *(adj, m)*	*doo*
	douce *(f)*	*doos*
good, kind	bon *(adj, m)*	*bOH*
	bonne *(f)*	*bun*
• **goodness, kindness**	bonté *(f)*	*bOH-tay*
good (*at something*)	habile *(adj)*	*a-beel*
graceful	gracieux *(adj, m)*	*gra-syuh*
	gracieuse *(f)*	*gra-syuhz*
habit	habitude *(f)*	*a-bee-tewd*
happiness	bonheur *(m)*	*bun-ur*
• **happy**	heureux *(adj, m)*	*ur-uh*
	heureuse *(f)*	*ur-uhz*
	content(e) *(adj, m, f)*	*kOH-tAH(t)*
hate	haine *(f)*	*ehn*
• **hate**	haïr *(v)*	*a-eer*
• **hateful**	détestable *(adj)*	*day-tehs-tabl*
honest	honnête *(adj)*	*un-eht*
• **honesty**	honnêteté *(f)*	*un-eht-tay*
humanitarian	humanitaire *(adj)*	*ew-ma-nee-tehr*
humble	humble *(adj)*	*UH-bl*
• **humility**	humilité *(f)*	*ew-mee-lee-tay*
humor	humour *(m)*	*ew-moor*
• **sense of humor**	sens *(m)* de l'humour	*sAHs de lew-moor*
idealism	idéalisme *(m)*	*ee-day-a-leesm*
• **idealist, idealistic**	idéaliste *(m)*	*ee-day-a-leest*
imagination	imagination *(f)*	*ee-ma-zh-ee-na-syOH*
• **imaginative**	imaginatif *(adj, m)*	*ee-ma-zh-ee-na-teef*
	imaginative *(f)*	*ee-ma-zh-ee-na-teev*

impudence	impudence (f)	EH-pew-dAH-ss
• **impudent**	impudent(e) (adj, m, f)	EH-pew-dAH(t)
impulse	impulsion (f)	EH-pewl-syOH
• **impulsive**	impulsif (adj, m)	EH-pewl-seef
	impulsive (f)	EH-pewl-seev
indecisive	indécis(e) (adj, m, f)	EH-day-see(z)
independent	indépendant(e) (adj, m, f)	EH-day-pAH-dAH(t)
individualist	individualiste (adj)	EH-dee-vee-dew-al-eest
ingenious, clever	ingénieux (adj, m)	EH-zhay-nyuh
	ingénieuse (f)	EH-zhay-nyuhz
• **ingenuity, cleverness**	ingénuité (f)	EH-zhay-new-ee-tay
ingenuous, naive	ingénu(e) (adj, m, f)	EH-zhay-new
	naïf (adj, m)	na-eef
	naïve (f)	na-eev
innocence	innocence (f)	ee-nu-sAH-ss
• **innocent**	innocent(e) (adj, m, f)	ee-nu-sAH(t)
insolence	insolence (f)	EH-sul-AH-ss
• **insolent**	insolent(e) (adj, m, f)	EH-sul-AH(t)
intelligence	intelligence (f)	EH-tay-lee-zh-AH-s
• **intelligent**	intelligent(e) (adj, m, f)	EH-tay-lee-zh-AH(t)
irascible	irascible (adj)	ee-ra-see-bl
irony	ironie (f)	ee-run-ee
• **ironic**	ironique (adj)	ee-run-eek
irritable	irritable (adj)	ee-ree-tabl
jealous	jaloux (adj, m)	zh-a-loo
	jalouse (f)	zh-a-looz
kind	gentil(le) (adj, m, f)	zhAH-tee(y)
laugh	rire (v)	reer
• **laughter**	rire (m)	reer
laziness	paresse (f)	pa-reh-s
• **lazy**	paresseux (adj, m)	pa-reh-suh
	paresseuse (f)	pa-reh-suhz
liberal	libéral(e) (adj, m, f)	lee-bay-ral
lively	vif (adj, m)	veef
	vive (f)	veev
love	amour (m)	a-moor
• **love**	aimer (v)	ay-may
• **lovable**	adorable (adj)	a-du-ra-bl
malicious	malicieux (adj, m)	ma-lee-syuh
	malicieuse (f)	ma-lee-syuhz
mischievous	espiègle (adj, m, f)	ehs-pyegl
miser	avare (adj, m/f)	a-vahr
mood	humeur (f)	ew-mur
• **be in a bad mood**	être de mauvaise humeur	eh-tre de mu-vehz ew-mur

• be in a good mood	être de bonne humeur	*eh-tre de bun ew-mur*
neat	soigné(e) *(adj, m, f)*	*swah-nyay*
nice	sympathique *(adj)*	*sEH-pa-teek*
not nice, odious	antipathique *(adj)*	*AH-tee-pa-teek*
obstinate	obstiné(e) *(adj, m, f)*	*up-stee-nay*
optimism	optimisme *(m)*	*up-tee-mee-sm*
• optimist, optimistic	optimiste *(m/f)*	*up-tee-meest*
original	original(e) *(adj, m, f)*	*o-ree-zh-ee-nal*
patience	patience *(f)*	*pa-sy-AH-s*
• patient	patient(e) *(adj, m, f)*	*pa-sy-AH(t)*
• impatient	impatient(e) *(adj, m, f)*	*EH-pa-sy-AH(t)*
perfection	perfection *(f)*	*pehr-fehk-syOH*
• perfectionist	perfectionniste *(m/f)*	*pehr-fehk-sy-un-eest*
personality	personnalité *(f)*	*pehr-sun-a-lee-tay*
pessimism	pessimisme *(m)*	*pay-see-mee-sm*
• pessimist, pessimistic	pessimiste *(m/f)*	*pay-see-meest*
picky	tatillon *(adj, m)*	*ta-tee-yOH*
	tatillonne *(f)*	*ta-tee-yun*
	difficile *(adj)*	*dee-fee-seel*
pleasant, likeable	aimable *(adj)*	*ay-ma-ble*
	sympathique *(adj)*	*sEH-pa-teek*
• like	aimer *(v)* bien	*ay-may byEH*
polite	poli(e) *(adj, m, f)*	*pu-lee*
poor	pauvre *(adj)*	*poh-vr*
possessive	possessif *(adj, m)*	*pus-ay-seef*
	possessive *(f)*	*pus-ay-seev*
presumptuous	présomptueux *(adj, m)*	*pray-zOH-ptew-uh*
	présomptueuse *(f)*	*pray-zOH-ptew-uhz*
pretentious	prétentieux *(adj, m)*	*pray-tAH-syuh*
	prétentieuse *(f)*	*pray-tAH-syuhz*
proud	fier, fière *(adj, m, f)*	*fyehr*
prudent	prudent *(adj, m)*	*prew-dAH*
	prudente *(f)*	*prew-dAHt*
rebellious	rebelle *(adj, m, f)*	*re-behl*
refined	raffiné(e) *(adj, m, f)*	*ra-fee-nay*
reserved	réservé(e) *(adj, m, f)*	*ray-zehr-vay*
restless	agité(e) *(adj, m, f)*	*a-zh-ee-tay*
rich	riche *(adj, m/f)*	*reesh*
romantic	romantique *(adj)*	*rum-AH-teek*
rough	brut, brute *(adj, m, f)*	*brewt*
rude	impoli(e) *(adj, m, f)*	*EH-pu-lee*
	grossier *(adj, m)*	*groh-sy-ay*
	grossière *(f)*	*groh-sy-ehr*
sad	triste *(adj)*	*treest*
• sadness	tristesse *(f)*	*tree-stehs*
sarcasm	sarcasme *(m)*	*sar-kasm*
• sarcastic	sarcastique *(adj)*	*sar-kas-teek*

seduction	séduction (*f*)	*say-dewk-syOH*
• seductive	séduisant(e) (*adj, m, f*)	*say-dew-ee-zAH(t)*
self-sufficient	indépendant(e) (*adj, m, f*)	*EH-day-pAH-dAH(t)*
sensitive	sensible (*adj*)	*sAH-seebl*
sentimental	sentimental(e) (*adj, m, f*)	*sAH-tee-mAH-tal*
serious	sérieux (*adj, m*)	*say-ryuh*
	sérieuse (*f*)	*say-ryuhz*
shrewd	rusé(e) (*adj, m, f*)	*rew-zay*
• shrewdness	ruse (*f*)	*rewz*
shy	timide (*adj*)	*tee-meed*
simple	simple (*adj*)	*sEH-pl*
sincere	sincère (*adj*)	*sEH-sehr*
• sincerity	sincérité (*f*)	*sEH-say-ree-tay*
sloppy, disorganized	désorganisé(e) (*adj, m, f*)	*day-zor-ga-nee-zay*
	négligé(e) (*adj, m, f*)	*nay-glee-zhay*
smart	intelligent(e) (*adj, m, f*)	*EH-tay-lee-zh-AH(t)*
smile	sourire (*m*)	*soo-reer*
• smile	sourire (*v*)	*soo-reer*
snobbish	hautain (*adj, m*)	*oh-tEH*
	hautaine (*f*)	*oh-tehn*
	snob (*adj*)	*snub*
stingy	radin (*m*)	*rad-EH*
	radine (*f*)	*rad-een*
strong	fort (*adj, m*)	*for*
	forte (*f*)	*fort*
stubborn	entêté (*adj, m*)	*AH-teht-ay*
	entêtée (*adj, f*)	*AH-teht-ay*
	têtu(e) (*adj*)	*teht-ew*
stupid	stupide (*adj*)	*stew-peed*
	bête (*adj*)	*beht*
superstitious	superstitieux (*adj, m*)	*sew-pehr-stee-syuh*
	superstitieuse (*f*)	*sew-pehr-stee-syuhz*
sweet	doux (*adj, m*)	*doo*
	douce (*f*)	*dooss*
traditional	traditionnel(le) (*adj, m, f*)	*tra-dee-sy-un-ehl*
troublemaker	provocateur (*m*)	*pru-vuk-a-tur*
	provocatrice (*f*)	*pru-vuk-a-treess*
vain	vaniteux (*adj, m*)	*va-nee-tuh*
	vaniteuse (*f*)	*va-nee-tuhz*
versatile	versatile (*adj*)	*vehr-sa-teel*
vulnerable	vulnérable (*adj*)	*vewl-nay-rabl*
weak	faible (*adj*)	*fehbl*

well-mannered	bien élevé(e) (adj, m, f)	byEH ayl-vay
willingly	volontiers (adv)	vul-OH-tyay
wisdom	sagesse (f)	sa-zh-ess
• wise	sage (adj)	sa-zh

f. BASIC PERSONAL INFORMATION

> For jobs and professions see Section 38.

address	adresse (f)	a-drehss
• avenue	avenue (f)	av-new
• street	rue (f)	rew
• square	place (f)	plass
• live somewhere	demeurer (v)	de-mur-ay
	habiter (v)	ah-bee-tay
• Where do you live?	Où demeurez-vous (pol)?	oo de-mur-ay voo
	Où demeures-tu (fam)?	oo de-mur tew
• I live on . . . Street.	Je demeure rue . . .	zhe de-mur rew
• house number	numéro de la maison	new-may-roh de la may-zOH
be from	être de	eh-tre de
• city, town	ville (f)	veel
• country	pays (m)	pay-ee
• state	état (m)	ay-ta
• village	village (m)	vee-lazh
career	carrière (f)	ka-ryehr
	profession (f)	pruf-ehs-yOH
date of birth	date (f) de naissance	dat de neh-sAH-ss
education	éducation (f)	ay-dew-ka-syOH
• go to school	aller (v) à l'école	a-lay a lay-kul
• finish school	finir (v) l'école	fee-neer lay-kul
• university degree	licence (f)	lee-sAH-ss
	doctorat (m)	duk-tu-ra
• diploma	diplôme (m)	deep-lohm
• graduate	obtenir un diplôme	up-te-neer UH deep-lohm
• graduate (from university)	obtenir sa licence	up-te-neer sa lee-sAH-ss
	obtenir sa maîtrise	up-te-neer sa meh-treez
	obtenir son doctorat	up-te-neer sOH duk-tu-ra

employment	emploi (*m*)	*AH-plwa*
• **employer**	employeur (*m*)	*AH-plwa-yur*
	employeuse (*f*)	*AH-plwa-yuhz*
• **employee**	employé(e) (*m, f*)	*AH-plwa-yay*
identification	identification (*f*)	*ee-dAH-tee-fee-ka-syOH*
job	travail (*m*)	*tra-va-y*
name	nom (*m*)	*nOH*
• **first name**	prénom (*m*)	*pray-nOH*
• **family name,**	nom (*m*) de famille	*nOH de fa-meey*
surname		
• **be called**	s'appeler (*v*)	*sap-lay*
• **How do you spell**	Comment s'écrit ton	*kum-AH say-kree tOH*
your name?	nom (*fam*)?	*nOH*
	Comment s'écrit	*kum-AH say-kree vutre*
	votre nom (*pol*)?	*nOH*
• **Print your name.**	Ecrire (*v*) en	*ay-kreer AH ka-rak-*
	caractères	*tehr dEH-preem-ree*
	d'imprimerie	
• **What's your name?**	Quel est ton nom	*kehl eh tOH nOH*
	(*fam*)?	
	Quel est votre nom	*kehl eh vutre nOH*
	(*pol*)?	
• **My name is . . .**	Mon nom est . . .	*mOH nOH eh*
	Je m'appelle . . .	*zhe mah-pel*
• **sign**	signer (*v*)	*see-ny-ay*
• **signature**	signature (*f*)	*see-ny-a-tewr*
nationality	nationalité (*f*)	*na-syun-a-lee-tay*
place of birth	lieu (*m*) de	*lyuh de neh-sAH-ss*
	naissance	
place of employment	lieu d'emploi	*lyuh dAH-plwa*
profession	profession (*f*)	*pruf-ehs-yOH*
• **professional**	professionnel (*m*)	*pru-fehs-yun-ehl*
	professionnelle (*f*)	*pru-fehs-yun-ehl*
residence	domicile (*m*)	*dum-ee-seel*
telephone number	numéro (*m*) de	*new-may-ro de tay-lay-*
	téléphone	*fun*
title	titre (*m*)	*teetr*
• **Dr.**	docteur (*m*)	*duktur*
• **Miss, Ms.**	mademoiselle	*mad-mwa-zehl*
• **Mr.**	monsieur	*me-sy-uh*
• **Mrs., Ms.**	madame	*ma-dam*
• **Prof.**	professeur (*m*)	*pruf-ehs-ur*

Note: In general, *docteur* is used for members of the medical profession. Use *madame* or *monsieur* for people who have a doctorate degree.

work	travail (*m*)	*tra-va-y*
• **work**	travailler (*v*)	*tra-va-yay*
• **line of work**	genre de travail	*zh-AH-r de tra-va-y*

12. THE BODY

a. PARTS OF THE BODY

FOCUS: Parts of the Body

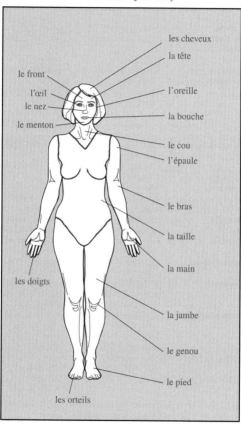

See also Section 40.

ankle	cheville (*f*)	*sh-e-vee-y*
arm	bras (*m*)	*bra*
beard	barbe (*f*)	*barb*
blood	sang (*m*)	*sAH*
body	corps (*m*)	*kor*
bone	os (*m*)	*us*
	les os (*pl*)	*lay zoh*
brain	cerveau (*m*)	*sehr-vo*
breast	sein (*m*)	*sEH*
cheek	joue (*f*)	*zh-oo*
chest	poitrine (*f*)	*pwa-treen*
chin	menton (*m*)	*mAH-tOH*
ear	oreille (*f*)	*u-reh-y*
elbow	coude (*m*)	*kood*
eye	œil (*m*)	*u-y*
	les yeux (*pl*)	*lay zyuh*
eyebrow	sourcil (*m*)	*soor-see*
eyelash	cil (*m*)	*seel*
eyelid	paupière (*f*)	*po-py-ehr*
face	visage (*m*)	*vee-za-zh*
	figure (*f*)	*fee-gewr*
finger	doigt (*m*)	*dwa*
fingernail	ongle (*m*)	*OH-gl*
foot	pied (*m*)	*pyay*
forehead	front (*m*)	*frOH*
hair	cheveux (*m, pl*)	*shvuh*
hand	main (*f*)	*mEH*
head	tête (*f*)	*teht*
heart	cœur (*m*)	*kur*
heel	talon (*m*)	*talOH*
hip	hanche (*f*)	*AH-sh*
index finger	index (*m*)	*EH-dehks*
jaw	mâchoire (*f*)	*mah-sh-war*
knee	genou (*m*)	*zh-noo*
knuckles	les jointures (*f*) des doigts	*lay zh-wEH-tewr day dwa*
	articulations (*f, pl*)	*ar-tee-kyu-la-syOH*
leg	jambe (*f*)	*zh-AH-b*
lip	lèvre (*f*)	*leh-vr*
little finger	petit doigt (*m*)	*ptee dwa*
lung	poumon (*m*)	*poo-mOH*
middle finger	médius (*m*)	*may-dy-ewss*
	majeur (*m*)	*ma-zhur*
moustache	moustache (*f*)	*moos-tash*
mouth	bouche (*f*)	*boosh*
muscle	muscle (*m*)	*mews-kl*
neck	cou (*m*)	*koo*
nose	nez (*m*)	*nay*

nostril	narine (*f*)	*na-reen*
penis	pénis (*m*)	*pay-nees*
ring finger	annulaire (*m*)	*a-new-lehr*
shoulder	épaule (*f*)	*ay-pohl*
sideburns	pattes (*f, pl*)	*paht*
	favoris (*m, pl*)	*fa-vuh-ree*
skin	peau (*f*)	*poh*
stomach	estomac (*m*)	*ehs-tum-a*
thigh	cuisse (*f*)	*kew-ees*
throat	gorge (*f*)	*gor-zh*
thumb	pouce (*m*)	*poos*
toe	orteil (*m*)	*or-teh-y*
tongue	langue (*f*)	*lAH-g*
tooth	dent (*f*)	*dAH*
vagina	vagin (*m*)	*va-zh-EH*
waist	taille (*f*)	*tah-y*
wrist	poignet (*m*)	*pwa-ny-eh*

---

to be at the tip of one's tongue = être sur le bout de la langue *eh-tre sewr le boo de la lAH-g*
to pay through the nose; to pay an arm and a leg = payer un œil *pay-yay UH nu-y*
He (She) is a pain in the neck! = C'est un casse-pieds! *seh tUH kahs-pyay*
Knucklehead! = Tête de nœud! *teht de nuh*

---

b. PHYSICAL STATES AND ACTIVITIES

be cold	avoir (*v*) froid	*avwar frwa*
be hot	avoir (*v*) chaud	*avwar sho*
be tired	être (*v*) fatigué(e)	*eh-tre fa-tee-gay*
breathe	respirer (*v*)	*rehs-pee-ray*
drink	boire (*v*)	*bwar*
eat	manger (*v*)	*mAH-zh-ay*
fall asleep	s'endormir (*v*)	*sAH-dor-meer*
feel bad	se sentir (*v*) mal	*se sAH-teer mal*
	avoir (*v*) mal	*avwar mal*
feel well	se sentir (*v*) bien	*se sAH-teer byEH*
	aller (*v*) bien	*a-lay byEH*
get up	se lever (*v*)	*se le-vay*
go to bed	se coucher (*v*)	*se koo-shay*
hunger	faim (*f*)	*fEH*
• **be hungry**	avoir (*v*) faim	*avwar fEH*
relax	se relaxer (*v*)	*se re-laks-ay*
rest	se reposer (*v*)	*se re-po-zay*
run	courir (*v*)	*koo-reer*

sleep	dormir (v)	*dorm-eer*
• **be sleepy**	avoir (v) sommeil	*avwar sum-ay*
thirst	soif (f)	*swaf*
• **be thirsty**	avoir (v) soif	*avwar swaf*
wake up	se réveiller (v)	*se ray-vay-yay*
walk	marcher (v)	*marshay*
	aller (v) à pied	*alay a pyay*

c. SENSORY PERCEPTION

blind person	aveugle (m/f)	*a-vuh-gl*
• **blindness**	cécité (f)	*say-see-tay*
deaf person	sourd (m)	*soor*
	sourde (f)	*soord*
• **deafness**	surdité (f)	*sewr-dee-tay*
flavor	saveur (f)	*sa-vur*
• **taste**	goûter (v)	*goo-tay*
hear	entendre (v)	*AH-tAH-dr*
• **hearing**	ouïe (f)	*wee*
listen (to)	écouter (v)	*ay-koo-tay*
look	regarder (v)	*re-gar-day*
mute person	muet (m)	*mew-eh*
	muette (f)	*mew-eht*
noise	bruit (m)	*brew-ee*
• **noisy**	bruyant(e) (adj, m, f)	*brew-yAH(t)*
perceive	percevoir (v)	*pehr-se-vwar*
• **perception**	perception (f)	*pehr-sehp-syOH*
see	voir (v)	*vwar*
• **sight**	vision (f)	*vee-zyOH*
	vue (f)	*vew*
sense	sens (m)	*sAH-s*
• **sense, feel**	sentir (v)	*sAH-teer*
smell	odeur (f)	*ud-ur*
	senteur (f)	*sAHt-ur*
• **smell**	sentir (v)	*sAH-teer*
sound	bruit (m)	*brew-ee*
	son (m)	*sOH*
touch	toucher (m)	*too-shay*
• **touch**	toucher (v)	*too-shay*

d. PERSONAL CARE

barber	coiffeur (m)	*kwa-fur*
• **barber shop**	salon (m) de coiffure pour hommes	*salOH de kwa-fewr poor um*
beautician	esthéticien (m)	*ehs-tay-tee-syEH*
	esthéticienne (f)	*ehs-tay-tee-syehn*

brush	brosse (f)	bruss
• brush	se brosser (v)	se bruss-ay
clean	propre (adj)	prup-re
• clean oneself	se débarbouiller (v)	se day-bar-boo-yay
comb	peigne (m)	peh-ny
• comb	se peigner (v)	se peh-ny-ay
curls	boucles (f) de cheveux	book-le de shvuh
	cheveux (m, pl) frisés	shvuh free-zay
• curler	bigoudi (m)	bee-goo-dee
cut one's hair	se faire couper (v) les cheveux	se fehr koo-pay lay sh-vuh
dirty	sale (adj)	sal
dry oneself	se sécher (v)	se say-shay
grooming	toilette (f)	twa-leht
hair spray	laque (f) pour les cheveux	lak poor lay shvuh
	spray (m) pour les cheveux	spreh poor lay shvuh
hairdresser	coiffeur (m)	kwa-fur
	coiffeuse (f)	kwa-fuhz
hygiene	hygiène (f)	ee-zh-y-ehn
• hygienic	hygiénique (adj)	ee-zh-y-ay-neek
makeup	fard (m)	far
	maquillage (m)	mak-ee-y-ah-zh
• put on makeup	se farder (v)	se far-day
	se maquiller (v)	se mak-ee-yay
manicure	soins (m, pl) (esthétiques) des mains	swEH (ehs-tay-teek) day mEH
mascara	mascara (m)	mas-ka-ra
massage	massage (m)	ma-sazh
nail polish	vernis (m) à ongles	vehr-nee a OH-gl
perfume	parfum (m)	par-fUH
• put on perfume	se parfumer (v)	se par-few-may
permanent (wave)	permanente (f)	pehr-ma-nAH-t
razor	rasoir (m)	rahz-war
• electric razor	rasoir électrique (m)	rahz-war ay-lehk-treek
• razor blade	lame (f)	lam
scissors	ciseaux (m)	see-zoh
shampoo	shampooing (m)	sh-AH-pwEH
shave (oneself)	(se) raser (v)	(se) rah-zay
soap	savon (m)	sa-vOH
toothbrush	brosse (f) à dents	bruss a dAH
toothpaste	pâte dentifrice (f)	paht dAH-tee-frees
	dentifrice (m)	dAH-tee-frees

towel, handcloth	serviette de toilette (*f*)	*sehr-vee-y-eht de twa-leht*
wash oneself	se laver (*v*)	*se la-vay*
• **wash one's hair**	se laver les cheveux	*se la-vay lay shvuh*
washcloth	gant (*m*) de bain	*gAHd-bEH*
	gant (*m*) de toilette	*gAHd-twa-leht*

THE PHYSICAL, PLANT, AND ANIMAL WORLDS

13. THE PHYSICAL WORLD

> For signs of the Zodiac, see Section 5.

a. THE UNIVERSE

asteroid	astéroïde (*m*)	*astay-ro-eed*
astronomy	astronomie (*f*)	*as-trun-um-ee*
comet	comète (*f*)	*kum-eht*
cosmos	cosmos (*m*)	*kus-mohs*
dark matter	matière (*f*) noire	*mat-yehr nwar*
eclipse	éclipse (*f*)	*ay-kleeps*
• **lunar eclipse**	éclipse lunaire	*ay-kleeps lew-nehr*
• **solar eclipse**	éclipse solaire	*ay-kleeps sul-ehr*
galaxy	galaxie (*f*)	*ga-lak-see*
gravitation	gravitation (*f*)	*gra-vee-tahs-yOH*
• **gravity**	gravité (*f*)	*gra-vee-tay*
light	lumière (*f*)	*lewm-yehr*
• **infrared light**	lumière infrarouge	*lewm-yehr EH-fra-roozh*
• **ultraviolet light**	lumière ultraviolette	*lewm-yehr ewl-tra-vy-uh-leht*
light year	année (*f*) lumière	*a-nay lewm-yehr*
meteor	météore (*m*)	*may-tay-or*
meteorite	météorite (*f*)	*may-tay-or-eet*
moon	lune (*f*)	*lewn*
• **full moon**	pleine lune	*plehn lewn*
• **moonbeam, ray**	rayon (*m*) de lune	*ray-yOHd lewn*
• **new moon**	nouvelle lune	*noo-vehl lewn*

---

honeymoon = une lune de miel *ewn lewn de mee-ehl*
to be absent-minded = être dans la lune *eh-tre dAH la lewn*

---

orbit	orbite (*f*)	*or-beet*
• **be in orbit**	être (*v*) en orbite	*eh-tre AH nor-beet*
• **put in orbit**	mettre (*v*) en orbite	*mehtr AH nor-beet*
	placer (*v*) sur orbite	*pla-say sewr or-beet*
planet	planète (*f*)	*plan-eht*
• **Earth**	Terre (*f*)	*tehr*
• **Jupiter**	Jupiter (*m*)	*zh-ew-pee-tehr*

• **Mars**	Mars (*m*)	*mars*
• **Mercury**	Mercure (*m*)	*mehr-kewr*
• **Neptune**	Neptune (*m*)	*nehp-tewn*
• **Saturn**	Saturne (*m*)	*sa-tewrn*
• **Uranus**	Uranus (*m*)	*ewr-an-ewss*
• **Venus**	Vénus (*f*)	*vay-newss*
• **Pluto**	Pluton (*m*)	*plewt-OH*

Note: Pluto is no longer considered a planet. It is *une planète naine* (a dwarf planet).

satellite	satellite (*m*)	*sa-tehl-eet*
space	espace (*m*)	*ehs-pas*
• **three-dimensional space**	espace tridimensionnel	*ehs-pas tree-deem-AH-sy-un-ehl*
star	étoile (*f*)	*ay-twal*
sun	soleil (*m*)	*sul-ay*
• **sunlight**	lumière (*f*) solaire	*lewm-yehr sul-ehr*
	lumière du soleil	*lewm-yehr dew sul-ay*
• **sunray**	rayon (*m*) de soleil	*ray-yOHd sul-ay*
• **solar system**	système (*m*) solaire	*sees-tehm sul-ehr*
universe	univers (*m*)	*ew-nee-vehr*
world	monde (*m*)	*mOHd*

b. THE ENVIRONMENT

> See also Section 44.

archipelago	archipel (*m*)	*arsh-ee-pehl*
atmosphere	atmosphère (*f*)	*at-muss-fehr*
• **atmospheric**	atmosphérique (*adj*)	*at-muss-fay-reek*
basin	bassin (*m*)	*bas-EH*
bay	baie (*f*)	*beh*
beach	plage (*f*)	*pla-zh*
channel	chenal (*m*)	*shuh-nal*
cloud	nuage (*m*)	*new-azh*
coast	côte (*f*)	*koht*
continental drift	dérive (*f*) des continents	*day-reev day kOH-teen-AH*
desert	désert (*m*)	*dayz-ehr*
earthquake	tremblement (*m*) de terre	*trAH-ble-mAH de tehr*
	séisme (*m*)	*say-eesm*
environment	environnement (*m*)	*AH-veer-un-mAH*
farmland	terrain (*m*) agricole	*tehr-EH a-gree-kul*
field	champ (*m*)	*shAH*

forest	forêt (*f*)	*for-eh*
glacier	glacier (*m*)	*gla-syay*
grass	herbe (*f*)	*ehrb*
gulf	golfe (*m*)	*gulf*
hill	colline (*f*)	*kul-een*
	coteau (*m*)	*kut-o*
ice	glace (*f*)	*glas*
ice cap	calotte (*f*) glaciaire	*ka-lut gla-see-ayr*
island	île (*f*)	*eel*
lake	lac (*m*)	*lak*
land	terre (*f*)	*tehr*
	terrain (*m*)	*tehr-EH*
landscape	paysage (*m*)	*pay-eez-azh*
lawn	pelouse (*f*)	*pe-looz*
layer	couche (*f*)	*koosh*
mountain	montagne (*f*)	*mOH-ta-ny*
• **mountain chain**	chaîne (*f*) de montagnes	*sh-ehn de mOH-ta-ny*
• **mountainous**	montagneux (*adj, m*)	*mOH-ta-ny-uh*
	montagneuse (*f*)	*mOH-ta-ny-uhz*
• **peak**	sommet (*m*)	*sum-eh*
nature	nature (*f*)	*na-tewr*
• **natural**	naturel(le) (*adj, m, f*)	*na-tewr-ehl*
ocean	océan (*m*)	*us-ay-AH*
• **Antarctic**	Antarctique (*adj*)	*AH-tark-teek*
• **Arctic**	Arctique (*adj*)	*ark-teek*
• **Atlantic**	Atlantique (*adj*)	*atl-AH-teek*
• **Pacific**	Pacifique (*adj*)	*pa-see-feek*
peninsula	péninsule (*f*)	*payn-EH-sewl*
	presqu'île (*f*)	*prehs-keel*
plain	plaine (*f*)	*plehn*
rainforest	forêt (*f*) pluviale	*for-eh plew-vyal*
river (large)	fleuve (*m*)	*fl-uhv*
• **flow**	couler (*v*)	*koo-lay*
• **small river**	rivière (*f*)	*reev-yehr*
rock	roche (*f*)	*rush*
	rocher (*m*)	*rush-ay*
sand	sable (*m*)	*sah-bl*
sea	mer (*f*)	*mehr*
sky	ciel (*m*)	*see-ehl*
stone	pierre (*f*)	*py-ehr*
tide	marée (*f*)	*mar-ay*
• **high tide**	marée haute	*mar-ay oht*
• **low tide**	marée basse	*mar-ay bahss*
valley	vallée (*f*)	*val-ay*
	val (*m*)	*val*
vegetation	végétation (*f*)	*vay-zh-ay-tas-yOH*

volcano	volcan (*m*)	*vulk-AH*
• **eruption**	éruption (*f*)	*ay-rewps-yOH*
• **lava**	lave (*f*)	*lav*
wave	onde (*f*)	*OHd*
	vague (*f*)	*vag*
	flot (*m*)	*floh*
woods	bois (*m, s/pl*)	*bwah*

c. MATTER AND THE ENVIRONMENT

> See also Section 42.

acid	acide (*m*)	*a-seed*
air	air (*m*)	*ehr*
ammonia	ammoniaque (*f*)	*am-un-yak*
atom	atome (*m*)	*a-tohm*
• **charge**	charge (*f*)	*shar-zhe*
• **electron**	électron (*m*)	*ay-lehk-tr-OH*
• **neutrino**	neutrino (*m*)	*nut-ree-no*
• **neutron**	neutron (*m*)	*nuh-tr-OH*
• **nucleus**	noyau (*m*)	*nwa-yoh*
• **proton**	proton (*m*)	*prut-OH*
• **quark**	quark (*m*)	*kwahrk*
bronze	bronze (*m*)	*br-OH-z*
carbon (*element*)	carbone (*m*)	*kar-bun*
chemical	produit (*m*) chimique	*pruhd-wee shee-meek*
chemical	chimique (*adj*)	*shee-meek*
• **chemistry**	chimie (*f*)	*shee-mee*
chemical formula	formule (*f*) chimique	*for-mewl-shee-meek*
chlorine	chlore (*m*)	*klor*
coal	charbon (*m*)	*sharb-OH*
• **coal mine**	mine (*f*) de charbon (*m*)	*meen de sharb-OH*
• **coal mining**	houille (*f*)	*oo-y*
compound	composé (*m*)	*kOH-po-zay*
copper	cuivre (*m*)	*kew-eevr*
cotton	coton (*m*)	*kut-OH*
diesel	gazole (*m*)	*ga-zul*
electrical	électrique (*adj*)	*ay-lehk-treek*
• **electricity**	électricité (*f*)	*ay-lehk-tree-see-tay*
element	élément (*m*)	*ay-laym-AH*
energy	énergie (*f*)	*ay-nehr-zh-ee*
• **fossil**	fossile (*m*)	*fus-eel*
• **nuclear energy**	énergie nucléaire	*ay-nehr-zh-ee new-klay-ehr*

• **radioactive waste**	déchets (*m, pl*) radioactifs	*day-sh-eh rad-yu-ak-teef*
• **solar energy**	énergie solaire	*ay-nehr-zh-ee sul-ehr*
fiber	fibre (*f*)	*fee-br*
fire	feu (*m*)	*fuh*
fuel	carburant (*m*)	*kar-bewr-AH*
	combustible (*m*)	*kOH-bews-teebl*
• **fossil fuel**	combustibles (*m, pl*) fossiles	*kOH-bews-teebl fu-seel*
gas	gaz (*m*)	*gahz*
• **car gas, gasoline, automobile fuel**	essence (*f*)	*ays-AH-s*
• **natural gas**	gaz naturel	*gahz na-tewr-ehl*
gold	or (*m*)	*or*
heat	chaleur (*f*)	*sha-lur*
hydrogen	hydrogène (*m*)	*eed-ru-zh-ehn*
industrial	industriel(le) (*adj, m, f*)	*EH-dews-tree-ehl*
• **industry**	industrie (*f*)	*EH-dews-tree*
iodine	iode (*m*)	*yud*
iron	fer (*m*)	*fehr*
laboratory	laboratoire (*m*)	*la-bor-a-twar*
lead	plomb (*m*)	*plOH*
leather	cuir (*m*)	*kew-eer*
liquid	liquide (*m*)	*lee-keed*
material	matériel (*m*)	*ma-tayr-y-ehl*
matter	matière (*f*)	*mat-yehr*
mercury	mercure (*m*)	*mehr-kewr*
metal	métal (*m*)	*may-tal*
methane	méthane (*m*)	*may-tahn*
microscope	microscope (*m*)	*meek-ru-skup*
mineral	minéral (*m*)	*mee-nay-ral*
molecule	molécule (*f*)	*mul-ay-kewl*
• **model**	modèle (*m*)	*mud-ehl*
• **molecular formula**	formule (*f*) moléculaire	*for-mewl mul-ay-kew-lehr*
• **structure**	structure (*f*)	*strewk-tewr*
natural resources	ressources (*f, pl*) naturelles	*re-soorss na-tewr-ehl*
nitrogen	azote (*m*)	*a-zut*
	nitrogène (*m*)	*neet-ru-zh-ehn*
oil	huile (*f*)	*ew-eel*
organic	organique (*adj*)	*or-gan-eek*
• **inorganic**	inorganique (*adj*)	*een-or-gan-eek*
oxygen	oxygène (*m*)	*uks-ee-zh-ehn*
particle	particule (*f*)	*par-tee-kewl*
petroleum	pétrole (*m*)	*pay-trul*

physical	physique (*adj*)	*fee-zeek*
• **physics**	physique (*f*)	*fee-zeek*
plastic	plastique (*m*)	*plas-teek*
platinum	platine (*m*)	*pla-teen*
pollution	pollution (*f*)	*pul-ews-yOH*
radiation	radiation (*f*)	*ra-dee-ya-syOH*
salt	sel (*m*)	*sehl*
silk	soie (*f*)	*swa*
silver	argent (*m*)	*ar-zh-AH*
smoke	fumée (*f*)	*fewm-ay*
sodium	sodium (*m*)	*sud-yum*
solid	solide (*m*)	*sul-eed*
steel	acier (*m*)	*as-yay*
• **stainless steel**	acier inoxydable	*as-yay een-uks-eed-abl*
stuff	étoffe (*f*)	*ay-tuf*
	tissu (*m*)	*tees-ew*
substance	substance (*f*)	*sewp-st-AH-s*
sulfur	soufre (*m*)	*soof-re*
• **sulfide**	sulfure (*m*)	*sewl-fewr*
• **sulfuric acid**	acide (*m*) sulfurique	*a-seed sewl-fewr-eek*
textile	textile (*m*)	*tehk-steel*
vapor	vapeur (*f*)	*va-pur*
water	eau (*f*)	*oh*
wool	laine (*f*)	*lehn*

d. CHARACTERISTICS OF MATTER

artificial	artificiel (*adj*)	*ar-tee-fee-sy-ehl*
authentic	authentique (*adj*)	*ut-AH-teek*
density	densité (*f*)	*dAH-see-tay*
elastic	élastique (*adj*)	*ay-las-teek*
fake	faux (*adj, m*)	*foh*
	fausse (*f*)	*fohs*
hard	dur (*adj*)	*dewr*
heavy	lourd (*adj*)	*loor*
light	léger (*adj*)	*lay-zh-ay*
malleable	malléable (*adj*)	*mal-ay-abl*
opaque	opaque (*adj*)	*up-ak*
pure	pur (*adj*)	*pewr*
resistant	résistant (*adj*)	*ray-zeest-AH*
robust	robuste (*adj*)	*rub-ewst*
rough	rude (*adj*)	*rewd*
smooth	lisse (*adj*)	*lees*
soft	mou (*adj*)	*moo*
	doux (*adj*)	*doo*
	mœlleux (*adj*)	*mwal-uh*
soluble	soluble (*adj*)	*sul-ew-bl*

stable	stable (*adj*)	*sta-bl*
strong	fort (*adj*)	*for*
synthetic	synthétique (*adj*)	*sEH-tay-teek*
transparent	transparent (*adj*)	*tr-AH-spar-AH*
weak	faible (*adj*)	*feh-bl*

e. GEOGRAPHY

> For names of countries, cities, etc. see Section 30.

Antarctic Circle	Cercle (*m*) antarctique	*sehr-kle AH-tark-teek*
Arctic Circle	Cercle (*m*) arctique	*sehr-kle ark-teek*
area	superficie (*f*)	*sewp-ehr-fee-see*
	surface (*f*)	*sewr-fas*
border	frontière (*f*)	*frOH-ty-ehr*
• **border**	borner (*v*)	*bor-nay*
	toucher (*v*)	*too-shay*
city	ville (*f*)	*veel*
• **capital**	capitale (*f*)	*ka-pee-tal*
continent	continent (*m*)	*kOH-teen-AH*
• **continental**	continental(e) (*adj, m, f*)	*kOH-teen-AH-tal*
country	pays (*m*)	*pay-ee*

> **From what country are you?** = De quel pays êtes-vous? *de kehl pay-ee eht-voo*

equator	équateur (*m*)	*ay-kwa-tur*
geographical	géographique (*adj*)	*zh-ay-u-gra-feek*
• **geography**	géographie (*f*)	*zh-ay-u-gra-fee*
globe	globe (*m*)	*glub*
hemisphere	hémisphère (*m*)	*ay-mees-fehr*
latitude	latitude (*f*)	*la-tee-tewd*
longitude	longitude (*f*)	*lOH-zh-ee-tewd*
locate	localiser (*v*)	*luk-al-ee-zay*
	situer (*v*)	*see-tew-ay*
• **location**	localité (*f*)	*luk-al-ee-tay*
• **be located**	se trouver (*v*)	*se-troo-vay*
map	carte (*f*)	*kart*
map (of city)	plan (*m*)	*plAH*
meridian	méridien (*m*)	*may-reed-y-EH*
• **prime meridian**	méridien origine	*may-reed-y-EH or-ee-zh-een*
nation	nation (*f*)	*nahs-y-OH*
• **national**	national(e) (*adj, m, f*)	*nahs-yun-al*

Regions of France

IMPORTANT FRENCH-SPEAKING POPULATIONS

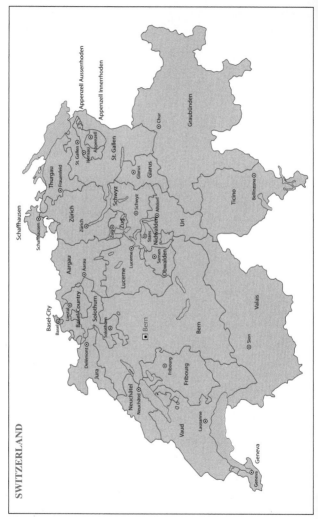

SWITZERLAND

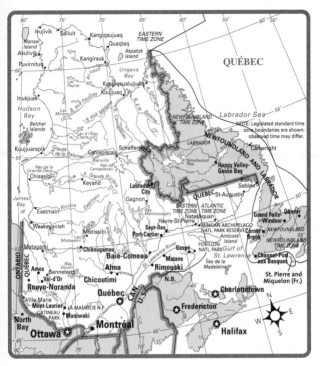

pole	pôle (*m*)	*pohl*
• **North Pole**	Pôle Nord	*pohl nor*
• **South Pole**	Pôle Sud	*pohl sewd*
province	province (*f*)	*pruv-EH-s*
region	région (*f*)	*ray-zh-y-OH*
state	état (*m*)	*ay-ta*
territory	territoire (*m*)	*tehr-eet-war*
time zone	fuseau (*m*) horaire	*few-zoh u-rehr*
tropic	tropique (*m*)	*trup-eek*
• **Tropic of Cancer**	Tropique du Cancer	*trup-eek dew kAH-sehr*
• **Tropic of Capricorn**	Tropique du Capricorne	*trup-eek dew ka-pree-korn*
• **tropical**	tropique (*adj*)	*trup-eek*
zenith	zénith (*m*)	*zay-neet*
zone	zone (*f*)	*zohn*

14. PLANTS

a. GENERAL VOCABULARY

agriculture	agriculture (*f*)	*a-gree-kewl-tewr*
bloom	fleurir (*v*)	*flur-eer*
botanical	botanique (*adj*)	*but-a-neek*
• **botany**	botanique (*f*)	*but-a-neek*
branch	branche (*f*)	*brAHsh*
bud	bourgeon (*m*)	*boor-zh-OH*
• **bud**	bourgeonner (*v*)	*boor-zh-un-ay*
bulb	bulbe (*m*)	*bewlb*
cell	cellule (*f*)	*sehl-ewl*
• **membrane**	membrane (*f*)	*mAH-bran*
• **nucleus**	noyau (*m*)	*nwah-yo*
chlorophyll	chlorophylle (*f*)	*klu-ru-feel*
cultivate	cultiver (*v*)	*kewl-tee-vay*
• **cultivation**	culture (*f*)	*kewl-tewr*
dig	creuser (*v*)	*kruh-zay*
flower	fleurir (*v*)	*flur-eer*
foliage	feuillage (*m*)	*fuh-ya-zh*
gather, reap	récolter (*v*)	*ray-kul-tay*
	cueillir (*v*)	*kuh-yeer*
grain, wheat	froment (*m*)	*frum-AH*
	blé (*m*)	*blay*
greenhouse	serre (*f*)	*sehr*
hedge	haie (*f*)	*eh*
horticulture	horticulture (*f*)	*or-tee-kewl-tewr*
leaf	feuille (*f*)	*fuh-y*
organism	organisme (*m*)	*or-gan-ee-sm*
photosynthesis	photosynthèse (*f*)	*fu-tus-EH-tehz*

plant	plante (*f*)	*pl-AH-t*
• plant	planter (*v*)	*pl-AH-tay*
pollen	pollen (*m*)	*pul-AH*
reproduce	reproduire (*v*)	*re-prud-ew-eer*
• reproduction	reproduction (*f*)	*re-prud-ewks-y-OH*
ripe	mûr(e) (*adj, m, f*)	*mewr*
root	racine (*f*)	*ra-seen*
rotten	pourri(e) (*adj, m, f*)	*poor-ee*
sap	sève (*f*)	*seh-v*
seed	semence (*f*)	*sem-AH-s*
• seed	semer (*v*)	*se-may*
species	espèce (*f*)	*ehs-pehs*
stem	tige (*f*)	*tee-zh*
transplantation	transplantation (*f*)	*tr-AH-spl-AH-tahs-y-OH*
• transplant	transplanter (*v*)	*tr-AH-spl-AH-tay*
trunk	tronc (*m*)	*tr-OH*
water	arroser (*v*)	*a-ro-zay*

b. FLOWERS

carnation	œillet (*m*)	*uh-yeh*
cyclamen	cyclamen (*m*)	*seek-la-men*
dahlia	dahlia (*m*)	*dal-ya*
daisy	marguerite (*f*)	*mar-ge-reet*
flower	fleur (*f*)	*flur*
• bouquet of flowers	botte (*f*) de fleurs	*but de flur*
• flower bed	parterre (*m*) de fleurs	*par-tehr de flur*
• wildflower	fleur sauvage	*flur so-va-zh*
• wilted flower	fleur (*f*) fanée	*flur fan-ay*
geranium	géranium (*m*)	*zh-ay-ra-ny-um*
gladiolus	glaïeul (*m*)	*gla-yul*
lily	lis/lys (*m*)	*lees*
orchid	orchidée (*f*)	*or-kee-day*
petal	pétale (*m*)	*pay-tal*
petunia	pétunia (*m*)	*pay-tewn-ya*
pick flowers	cueillir (*v*) des fleurs	*kuh-yeer day flur*
poppy	pavot (*m*)	*pa-vo*
	coquelicot (*m*)	*kuk-lee-ko*
rose	rose (*f*)	*rohz*
thorn	épine (*f*)	*ay-peen*
tulip	tulipe (*f*)	*tew-leep*
violet	violette (*f*)	*vyu-leht*

c. TREES

| beech tree | hêtre (*m*) | *eh-tr* |
| chestnut tree | châtaignier (*m*) | *sha-tay-ny-ay* |

cypress tree	cyprès (*m*)	*see-preh*
fir tree	sapin (*m*)	*sap-EH*
fruit tree	fruitier (*m*)	*frew-eet-yay*
• **apple tree**	pommier (*m*)	*pum-yay*
• **cherry tree**	cerisier (*m*)	*se-reez-yay*
• **fig tree**	figuier (*m*)	*feeg-yay*
• **lemon tree**	citronnier (*m*)	*see-trun-yay*
• **olive tree**	olivier (*m*)	*ul-eev-yay*
• **orange tree**	oranger (*m*)	*or-AH-zh-ay*
• **peach tree**	pêcher (*m*)	*pay-shay*
• **pear tree**	poirier (*m*)	*pwa-ree-yay*
• **walnut tree**	noyer (*m*)	*nwa-yay*
maple tree	érable (*m*)	*ay-ra-ble*
oak tree	chêne (*m*)	*sh-ehn*
palm tree	palmier (*m*)	*palm-yay*
pine tree	pin (*m*)	*pEH*
poplar tree	peuplier (*m*)	*puh-plee-yay*
tree	arbre (*m*)	*ar-br*

d. FRUITS

apple	pomme (*f*)	*pum*
apricot	abricot (*m*)	*a-bree-ko*
banana	banane (*f*)	*ba-nan*
cherry	cerise (*f*)	*sreez*
chestnut	marron (*m*)	*mar-OH*
	châtaigne (*f*)	*sha-teh-ny*
citrus	agrumes (*m, pl*)	*ag-rewm*
• **citric**	citrique (*adj*)	*see-treek*
date	datte (*f*)	*dat*
fig	figue (*f*)	*feeg*
fruit	fruit (*m*)	*frew-ee*
grapefruit	pamplemousse (*m/f*)	*pAH-ple-mooss*
grape	raisin (*m*)	*rehz-EH*
lemon	citron (*m*)	*seetr-OH*
lime	citron (*m*) vert	*seetr-OH vehr*
mandarin orange	mandarine (*f*)	*mAH-da-reen*
melon	melon (*m*)	*mel-OH*
olive	olive (*f*)	*ul-eev*
orange	orange (*f*)	*or-AH-zh*
peach	pêche (*f*)	*peh-sh*
pear	poire (*f*)	*pwar*
pineapple	ananas (*m*)	*a-na-nas*
plum	prune (*f*)	*prewn*
prune	pruneau (*m*)	*prew-no*
raisin	raisin (*m*) sec	*rehz-EH sehk*
raspberry	framboise (*f*)	*fr-AH-bwaz*
strawberry	fraise (*f*)	*frehz*

tomato	tomate (*f*)	*tum-at*
walnut	noix (*f*)	*nawh*
watermelon	pastèque (*f*)	*pas-tehk*
	melon (*m*) d'eau	*mel-OH doh*

e. VEGETABLES AND HERBS

artichoke	artichaut (*m*)	*ar-tee-sh-o*
asparagus	asperge (*f*)	*as-pehr-zh*
basil	basilic (*m*)	*ba-zee-leek*
bean	haricot (*m*)	*aree-ko*
	fèves (*f*) de haricot	*fehv de aree-ko*
beet	betterave (*f*)	*beht-rav*
broccoli	brocoli (*m*)	*bruk-u-lee*
cabbage	chou (*m*)	*shoo*
carrot	carotte (*f*)	*ka-rut*
cauliflower	chou-fleur (*m*) (*pl,* choux-fleurs)	*shoo-flur*
celery	céleri (*m*)	*sehl-ree*
corn	maïs (*m*)	*ma-ees*
cucumber	concombre (*m*)	*kOH-kOH-br*
eggplant	aubergine (*f*)	*o-behr-zh-een*
fennel	fenouil (*m*)	*fe-noo-y*
garden	jardin (*m*)	*zh-ard-EH*
• **vegetable garden**	potager (*m*)	*pu-ta-zh-ay*
garlic	ail (*m*)	*ah-y*
grass	herbe (*f*)	*ehrb*
green bean	haricot (*m*) vert	*aree-ko veh-r*
green pepper	poivron (*m*) vert	*pwa-vrOH veh-r*
herbs	les fines herbes (*f, pl*)	*lay feen-zehrb*
lentil	lentille (*f*)	*l-AH-tee-y*
lettuce	laitue (*f*)	*lay-tew*
lima bean	fève (*f*)	*fehv*
mint	menthe (*f*)	*m-AH-t*
mushroom	champignon (*m*)	*sh-AH-pee-ny-OH*
onion	oignon (*m*)	*u-ny-OH*
parsley	persil (*m*)	*pehr-see*
pea	(petits) pois (*m*)	*(ptee) pwa*
potato	pomme (*f*) de terre	*pum de tehr*
pumpkin	citrouille (*f*)	*see-troo-y*
radish	radis (*m*)	*ra-dee*
rosemary	romarin (*m*)	*rum-ar-EH*
spinach	épinards (*m, pl*)	*ay-pee-nar*
string bean	haricot vert (*m*)	*aree-ko vehr*
vegetable	légume (*m*)	*layg-ewm*
zucchini	courgette (*f*)	*koor-zh-eht*

15. THE ANIMAL WORLD

a. **ANIMALS**

animal	animal (*m*)	*a-nee-mal*
bat	chauve-souris (*f*)	*sh-ohv-soo-ree*
	pipistrelle (*f*)	*pee-pee-strehl*
bear	ours (*m*)	*oors*
beast	bête (*f*)	*beht*
buffalo	buffle (*m*)	*bew-fl*
bull	taureau (*m*)	*tor-o*
camel	chameau (*m*)	*sha-mo*
cat	chat (*m*)	*sha*
	chatte (*f*)	*shat*
• **meow**	miauler (*v*)	*mee-yo-lay*
cow	vache (*f*)	*vash*
deer	cerf (*m*)	*sehr*
dog	chien (*m*)	*sh-y-EH*
	chienne (*f*)	*sh-y-ehn*
• **bark**	aboyer (*v*)	*a-bwa-yay*
donkey	âne (*m*)	*ahn*
elephant	éléphant (*m*)	*ay-layf-AH*
farm	ferme (*f*)	*fehrm*
• **barn**	grange (*f*)	*gr-AH-zh*
• **farmer**	fermier (*m*)	*fehrm-yay*
	fermière (*f*)	*fehrm-yehr*
• **fence**	clôture (*f*)	*klo-tewr*
	barrière (*f*)	*bar-yehr*
fox	renard (*m*)	*re-nar*
giraffe	girafe (*f*)	*zh-ee-raf*
goat	chèvre (*f*)	*sh-ehvre*
groundhog	marmotte (*f*) (d'Amérique)	*mahr-muht (dah-may-reek)*
hare	lièvre (*m*)	*lee-ehvre*
hippopotamus	hippopotame (*m*)	*ee-pu-pu-tam*
horse	cheval (*m*)	*shval*
• **neigh**	hennir (*v*)	*ehn-eer*
human	humain (*adj, m*)	*ew-mEH*
	humaine (*adj, f*)	*ew-mehn*
human being	être (*m*)	*eh-tr*
	être (*m*) humain	*eh-tr ew-mEH*
hunter	chasseur (*m*)	*sha-sur*
	chasseuse (*f*)	*sha-suhz*
• **hunting**	chasse (*f*)	*shass*
hyena	hyène (*f*)	*yehn*
lamb	agneau (*m*)	*a-ny-o*
leopard	léopard (*m*)	*lay-up-ar*
lion	lion (*m*)	*lee-y-OH*
• **roar**	rugir (*v*)	*rew-zh-eer*

mammal	mammifère (*m*)	*ma-mee-fehr*
mole	taupe (*f*)	*tohp*
monkey	singe (*m*)	*sEH-zh*
moose	orignal (*m*)	*uh-ree-nyal*
mouse	souris (*f*)	*soo-ree*
mule	mulet (*m*)	*mew-leh*
ox	bœuf (*m*)	*buhf*
	bœufs (*pl*)	*buh*
paw	patte (*f*)	*pat*
pet	animal (*m*) domestique	*a-nee-mal dum-ehs-teek*
pig	cochon (*m*)	*ku-sh-OH*
pony	poney (*m*)	*pun-eh*
primate	primate (*m*)	*pree-mat*
rabbit	lapin (*m*)	*lap-EH*
rat	rat (*m*)	*ra*
rhinoceros	rhinocéros (*m*)	*reen-u-say-rus*
sheep	mouton (*m*)	*moot-OH*
• bleat	bêler (*v*)	*bay-lay*

---

to stand in line, to line up, queue up = faire la queue *fehr la kuh*

---

tail	queue (*f*)	*kuh*
tiger	tigre (*m*)	*teeg-re*
vertebrate	vertébré(e) (*adj, m, f*)	*vehr-tay-bray*
• invertebrate	invertébré(e) (*adj, m, f*)	*EH-vehr-tay-bray*
wild animal	animal sauvage (*m*)	*a-nee-mal so-va-zh*
wolf	loup (*m*)	*loo*
	louve (*f*)	*loov*
• howl	hurler (*v*)	*ewr-lay*
zebra	zèbre (*m*)	*zeh-bre*
zoo	zoo (*m*)	*zoh-oh*
	jardin zoologique (*m*)	*zh-ard-EH zu-ul-uzh-eek*
• zoological	zoologique (*adj*)	*zu-ul-uzh-eek*
• zoology	zoologie (*f*)	*zu-ul-uzh-ee*

b. BIRDS AND FOWL

albatross	albatros (*m*)	*al-ba-tros*
beak	bec (*m*)	*behk*
bird	oiseau (*m*)	*wa-zoh*
blackbird	merle (*m*)	*mehrl*
chick	poussin (*m*)	*poos-EH*
chicken	poule (*f*)	*pool*
	poulet (*m*)	*pool-eh*

crow	corbeau (*m*)	*kor-bo*
dove	colombe (*f*)	*kul-OH-b*
duck	canard (*m*)	*kan-ar*
eagle	aigle (*m*)	*ehg-l*
falcon	faucon (*m*)	*fo-kOH*
feather	plume (*f*)	*plewm*
goose	oie (*f*)	*wa*
hen	poule (*f*)	*pool*
nightingale	rossignol (*m*)	*rus-ee-ny-ul*
ostrich	autruche (*f*)	*oh-trew-sh*
owl	hibou (*m*)	*ee-boo*
	chouette (*f*)	*sh-wet*
parakeet	perruche (*f*)	*pay-rew-sh*
parrot	perroquet (*m*)	*pehr-uk-eh*
pelican	pélican (*m*)	*pay-leek-AH*
penguin	manchot (*m*)	*mAH-shoh*
pigeon	pigeon (*m*)	*pee-zh-OH*

> **to be the fool in an affair** = être le pigeon dans une affaire *eh-tr le pee-zh-OH d-AH zewn a-fehr*

robin	rouge-gorge (*m*)	*roo-zhe gor-zhe*
rooster	coq (*m*)	*kuk*
seagull	mouette (*f*)	*mweht*
sparrow	moineau (*m*)	*mwa-no*
	piaf (*m*)	*pyaf*
stork	cigogne (*f*)	*see-gu-ny*
swallow	hirondelle (*f*)	*eer-OH-dehl*
swan	cygne (*m*)	*see-ny*
turkey	dinde (*f*)	*dEH-d*
wing	aile (*f*)	*ehl*

c. FISH, REPTILES, AMPHIBIANS, AND MARINE ANIMALS

catfish	poisson-chat (*m*)	*pwas-OH-sha*
codfish	morue (*f*)	*mor-ew*
crocodile	crocodile (*m*)	*kru-ku-deel*
dolphin	dauphin (*m*)	*dof-EH*
eel	anguille (*f*)	*AH-gee-y*
fish	poisson (*m*)	*pwas-OH*
• **fin**	nageoire (*f*)	*na-zh-war*
• **fish**	pêcher (*v*)	*pay-shay*
	aller (*v*) à la pêche	*a-lay a la peh-sh*
• **fishbone**	arête (*f*)	*ar-eht*
• **fisherman**	pêcheur (*m*)	*peh-sh-ur*
	pêcheuse (*f*)	*peh-sh-uhz*

• fishing	pêche (f)	peh-sh
• fishing rod	canne (f) à pêche	kan a peh-sh
• hook	hameçon (m)	ams-OH
frog	grenouille (f)	gre-noo-y
goldfish	poisson rouge (m)	pwas-OH roo-zh
octopus	pieuvre (f)	pee-yuv-re
	poulpe (m)	poolp
porpoise	marsouin (m)	mar-swEH
reptile	reptile (m)	rehp-teel
salamander	salamandre (f)	sa-la-mAH-dr
sardine	sardine (f)	sar-deen
seal	phoque (m)	fuk
snake	serpent (m)	sehrp-AH
sole fish	sole (f)	sul
swordfish	espadon (m)	ehs-pad-OH
toad	crapaud (m)	kra-po
trout	truite (f)	trew-eet
tuna	thon (m)	tOH
turtle	tortue (f)	tor-tew
whale	baleine (f)	bal-ehn

d. INSECTS AND OTHER INVERTEBRATES

ant	fourmi (f)	foor-mee
bed bug	punaise (f)	pew-nehz
bee	abeille (f)	a-beh-y
butterfly	papillon (m)	pa-pee-y-OH
caterpillar	chenille (f)	she-nee-y
cockroach	blatte (f)	blat
	cafard (m)	ka-far
flea	puce (f)	pewss
fly	mouche (f)	moosh
insect	insecte (m)	EH-sehkt
louse	pou (m) (pl, poux)	poo
maggot	asticot (m)	as-tee-ko
metamorphosis	métamorphose (f)	may-ta-mor-foz
mosquito	moustique (m)	moos-teek
moth	papillon (m)	pa-pee-y-OH
	(nocturne)	(nuk-turn)
organism	organisme (m)	organ-ees-me
scorpion	scorpion (m)	shor-py-OH
silkworm	ver (m) à soie	vehr a swa
spider	araignée (f)	ar-ay-ny-ay
termite	termite (m)	tehr-meet
tick	tique (f)	teek
wasp	guêpe (f)	gehp
worm	ver (m)	vehr

COMMUNICATING, FEELING, AND THINKING

16. BASIC SOCIAL EXPRESSIONS

a. GREETINGS AND FAREWELLS

Farewell!	Adieu!	*ad-yuh*
Good afternoon!	Bonjour!	*bOH-zhoor*
Good evening!	Bonsoir!	*bOH-swar*
Good morning!	Bonjour!	*bOH-zhoor*
Good night!	Bonsoir!	*bOH-swar*
	Bonne nuit! (*when going to bed*)	*bun new-ee*
Good-bye!	Au revoir!	*or-vwar*
greet	saluer (*v*)	*sal-ew-ay*
• **greeting**	salut (*m*)	*sal-ew*
	salutation (*f*)	*sal-ew-tas-y-OH*
Hello!	Bonjour! (*during daytime*)	*bOH-zhoor*
	Bonsoir! (*during evening hours*)	*bOH-swar*
Hi!	Salut!	*sal-ew*
How are you?	Comment allez-vous? (*pol*)	*kum-AH tal-ay voo*
	Comment vas-tu? (*fam*)	*kum-AH va-tew*
How's it going?	Comment ça va?	*kum-AH sa-va*
	Ça va?	*sa-va*
• **Bad(ly)!**	Mal!	*mal*
• **Fine!**	Bien!	*byEH*
• **Not bad!**	Pas mal!	*pah mal*
• **Quite well!**	Très bien!	*treh byEH*
• **So, so!**	Comme-ci, comme-ça!	*kum-see kum-sa*
• **Very well!**	Très bien!	*treh byEH*
Please give my regards/greetings to . . .	Mon bon souvenir à . . .	*mOH bOH soov-neer a*
See you!	Salut!	*sal-ew*
• **See you later!**	À tout à l'heure!	*a-too-ta-lur*
• **See you soon!**	À bientôt!	*a-byEH-toh*
• **See you Sunday!**	À dimanche!	*a-deem-AH-sh*
shake hands	serrer (*v*) la main à quelqu'un	*sehr-ay lam-EH a kehlk-UH*
	donner (*v*) la main à quelqu'un	*dun-ay lam-EH a kehlk-UH*
• **handshake**	poignée de main (*f*)	*pwa-ny-ayd-mEH*

b. FORMS OF ADDRESS AND INTRODUCTIONS

A pleasure!	C'est un plaisir!	*seht-UH-play-zeer*
• The pleasure is mine!	C'est mon plaisir!	*sehm-OH play-zeer*
acquaintance	connaissance (*f*)	*kun-eh-SAH-s*
Allow me to introduce myself.	Permettez-moi de me présenter.	*pehrm-eht-ay-mwa dem prayz-AH-tay*
Allow me to introduce you to . . .	Permettez-moi de vous présenter à . . .	*pehrm-eht-ay-mwa de voo-prayz-AH-tay a*
be seated	s'asseoir (*v*)	*sas-war*
• Be seated, please.	Asseyez-vous, s'il vous plaît. (*pol*)	*ass-ay-yay-voo seel-voo-pleh*
	Assieds-toi, s'il te plaît. (*fam*)	*ass-yay-twa seel-te-pleh*
be on a first-name basis	tutoyer (*v*)	*tew-twa-yay*
be on a formal basis	vouvoyer (*v*)	*voo-vwa-yay*
business card	carte (*f*) de visite	*kart de vee-zeet*
calling card	carte (*f*) de visite	*kart de vee-zeet*
Come in!	Entrez! (*pol*)	*AH-tray*
	Entre! (*fam*)	*AH-tre*
• enter (into)	entrer (*v*) (dans)	*AH-tray (dAH)*
Delighted!	Heureux! (*m*)	*ur-uh*
	Heureuse! (*f*)	*ur-uhz*
Happy to make your acquaintance!	Heureux(-euse) de faire votre connaissance! (*pol*)	*ur-uh(-uhz) de fehr vut-re kun-eh-sAH-s*
	Heureux(-euse) de faire ta connaissance! (*fam*)	*ur-uh(-uhz) de fehr ta kun-eh-sAH-s*
introduce someone	présenter (*v*) quelqu'un	*prayz-AH-tay kehl-kUH*
• introduction	présentation (*f*)	*prayz-AH-tas-y-OH*
know someone	connaître quelqu'un	*kun-eht-re kehl-kUH*
Let me introduce you to . . .	Je vous présente à . . . (*pol*)	*zhe-voo-prayz-AH-t a*
	Je te présente à . . . (*fam*)	*zh-te-prayz-AH-t a*
meet, run into someone	rencontrer (*v*)	*rAH-kOH-tray*
	pour la première fois (*for the first time*)	*poor la prem-yehr fwa*
title	titre (*m*)	*tee-tre*
• Dr. (*M.D. degree*)	docteur (*m*)	*duk-tur*
	docteure (*f*)	*duk-tur*

• Dr. (*Ph.D. degree*)	docteur (*m*)	*duk-tur*
• Miss, Ms.	mademoiselle	*mad-mwa-zehl*
• Mr.	monsieur	*me-sy-uh*
• Mrs.	madame	*ma-dahm*
What's your name?	Comment vous appelez-vous? (*pol*)	*kum-AH voo-zap-lay-voo*
	Comment t'appelles-tu? (*fam*)	*kum-AH tap-ehl-tew*
• My name is . . .	Je m'appelle . . .	*zhem-ap-ehl*
• I'm . . .	Je suis . . .	*zhe-swee*

c. COURTESY

Best wishes!	Meilleurs vœux!	*meh-y-ur vuh*
Bless you! (*after a sneeze*)	À vos souhaits! (*pol*)	*a-vo-sw-eh*
	À tes souhaits! (*fam*)	*a-tay-sw-eh*
Cheers!	À votre santé!	*a vut-re sAH-tay*
	À la vôtre!	*a-la-voh-tre*
Congratulations!	Félicitations!	*fay-lee-see-tas-y-OH*
Don't mention it!	De rien!	*der-yEH*
	Il n'y a pas de quoi!	*eel-ny-a-pahd-kwa*
Enjoy your meal!	Bon appétit!	*bun-apay-tee*
Excuse me!	Excusez-moi! (*pol*)	*ehks-kew-zay-mwa*
	Excuse-moi! (*fam*)	*ehks-kewz-mwa*
	Pardonnez-moi! (*pol*)	*par-dun-ay-mwa*
	Pardonne-moi! (*fam*)	*par-dun-mwa*
Good luck!	Bonne chance!	*bun-sh-AH-s*
Happy Easter!	Joyeuses Pâques!	*zh-wah-yuh-z pahk*
Happy New Year!	Bonne (et heureuse) année!	*bun (ay ur-uhz) a-nay*
Have a good vacation!	Bonnes vacances!	*bun vak-AH-s*
Have a good time!	Amusez-vous bien! (*pol*)	*a-mew-zay-voo byEH*
	Amuse-toi bien! (*fam*)	*a-mewz-twa byEH*
Have a good trip!	Bon voyage!	*bOH vwa-ya-zh*
Happy birthday!	Bon anniversaire!	*bun a-nee-vehr-sehr*
Many thanks!	Merci mille fois!	*mehr-see meel fwa*
	Merci infiniment!	*mehr-see EH-fee-neem-AH*
May I come in?	Puis-je entrer?	*pew-ee-zh AH-tray*
May I help you?	Vous désirez?	*voo day-zee-ray*
	Puis-je vous aider?	*pew-ee-zh voo-zay-day*
Merry Christmas!	Joyeux Noël!	*zh-wa-yuh nu-ehl*
No!	Non!	*nOH*
OK!	D'accord!	*dak-or*
	Entendu!	*AH-t-AH-dew*
Please!	S'il vous plaît! (*pol*)	*seel-voo-pleh*
	S'il te plaît! (*fam*)	*seel-te-pleh*

Season's Greetings	Meilleurs vœux	*meh-y-ur vuh*
Thank you!	Merci!	*mehr-see*
Yes!	Oui!	*wee*
You're welcome!	Je vous en prie! (*pol*)	*zhe-vooz-AH-pree*
	Je t'en prie! (*fam*)	*zh-tAH-pree*
	De rien!	*dur-yEH*
	Il n'y a pas de quoi!	*eel-nya-pad-kwa*

17. SPEAKING AND TALKING

a. SPEECH ACTIVITIES AND TYPES

advice	conseil (*m*)	*k-OH-say*
• **advise**	conseiller (*v*)	*k-OH-say-yay*
allude	faire (*v*) allusion	*fehr al-ewz-y-OH*
analogy	analogie (*f*)	*a-na-luzh-ee*
announce	annoncer (*v*)	*an-OH-say*
• **announcement**	annonce (*f*)	*an-OH-s*
answer	réponse (*f*)	*rayp-OH-s*
• **answer**	répondre (*v*)	*rayp-OH-dre*
argue	se disputer (*v*)	*se dees-pew-tay*
• **argument**	dispute (*f*)	*dees-pewt*
	argument (*m*)	*ar-gewm-AH*
articulate	articuler (*v*)	*ar-tee-kew-lay*
ask	demander (*v*)	*dem-AH-day*
ask to do (*something*)	demander (*v*) de faire quelque chose	*dem-AH-dayd fehr kehlke sh-oh-z*
blog	blog (*m*)	*bluhg*
call	appeler (*v*)	*aplay*
change subject	changer (*v*) de sujet	*sh-AH-zh-ayd sew-zh-eh*
chat	causer (*v*)	*ko-zay*
communicate	communiquer (*v*)	*kum-ewn-ee-kay*
• **communication**	communication (*f*)	*kum-ewn-ee-kas-y-OH*
compare	comparer (*v*)	*k-OH-pa-ray*
• **comparison**	comparaison (*f*)	*k-OH-par-ehz-OH*
conclude	conclure (*v*)	*k-OH-klewr*
• **conclusion**	conclusion (*f*)	*k-OH-klewz-y-OH*
congratulate	féliciter (*v*)	*fay-lee-see-tay*
conversation	conversation (*f*)	*k-OH-vehr-sas-y-OH*
debate	débat (*m*)	*day-ba*
• **debate**	débattre (*v*)	*day-bat-re*
declare	déclarer (*v*)	*day-klar-ay*
deny	nier (*v*)	*nee-yay*
describe	décrire (*v*)	*day-kreer*
• **description**	description (*f*)	*dehs-kreeps-y-OH*
dictate	dicter (*v*)	*deek-tay*
digress	faire (*v*) une digression	*fehr ewn deeg-rays-y-OH*

discuss	discuter (v)	dees-kew-tay
• discussion	discussion (f)	dees-kews-y-OH
emphasis	accent (m)	aks-AH
• emphasize	mettre (v) l'accent sur	meht-re laks-AH sewr
excuse	excuse (f)	ehks-kewz
• excuse oneself	s'excuser (v)	sehks-kew-zay
explain	expliquer (v)	ehks-plee-kay
• explanation	explication (f)	ehks-plee-kahs-y-OH
express	exprimer (v)	ehks-pree-may
• express oneself	s'exprimer (v)	sehks-pree-may
• expression	expression (f)	ehks-prehs-y-OH
figure of speech	figure (f) de rhétorique	feeg-ewr de ray-tor-eek
• allegory	allégorie (f)	al-ay-gor-ee
• literal	litéral(e) (adj, m, f)	lee-tay-ral
• metaphor	métaphore (f)	may-ta-for
• symbol	symbole (m)	s-EH-bul
gossip	bavardage (m)	ba-var-dazh
	potins (m, pl)	put-EH
• gossip	potiner (v)	put-een-ay
hesitation	hésitation (f)	ay-zee-tahs-y-OH
• hesitate	hésiter (v)	ay-zee-tay
identify	identifier (v)	eed-AH-teef-yay
indicate, point out	indiquer (v)	EH-dee-kay
• indication	indication (f)	EH-dee-kahs-y-OH
inform	informer (v)	EH-form-ay
	faire savoir (v)	fehr savwar
interrupt	interrompre (v)	EH-tayr-OH-pre
• interruption	interruption (f)	EH-tayr-ewps-y-OH
invite	inviter (v)	EH-vee-tay
jest	plaisanter (v)	plehz-AH-tay
joke	plaisanterie (f)	plehz-AH-tree
	blague (f)	blag
• tell a joke	raconter (v) une plaisanterie	rak-OH-tay ewn plehz-AH-tree
keep quiet	se taire (v)	se-tehr
lecture	conférence (f)	kOH-fayr-AH-s
• lecture	donner (v) une conférence	dun-ay ewn kOH-fayr-AH-s
lie	mensonge (m)	m-AH-s-OH-zh
• lie	mentir (v)	m-AH-teer
• liar	menteur (m)	m-AH-tur
	menteuse (f)	mAH-tuhz
listen to	écouter (v)	ay-koo-tay
malign, speak badly	diffamer (v)	deef-a-may
mean	signifier (v)	see-ny-eef-yay
	vouloir dire (v)	vool-war deer
• meaning	signification (f)	see-ny-ee-fee-kas-y-OH
	sens (m)	sAHs

mention	mentionner (v)	mAH-sy-un-ay
	faire (v) mention de	fehr mAH-syOH de
mumble	grommeler (v)	grum-lay
murmur	murmurer (v)	mewr-mew-ray
nag	harceler (v)	ar-se-lay
offend	offenser (v)	uf-AH-say
oral	oral(e) (adj, m, f)	or-al
• orally	oralement (adv)	or-alm-AH
order	ordre (m)	or-dre
• order	ordonner (v)	or-dun-ay
• order (food)	commander (v)	kum-AH-day
outspokenly	franchement (adv)	frAH-sh-mAH
praise	louer (v)	lway
pray	prier (v)	pree-yay
• prayer	prière (f)	pree-yehr
preach	prêcher (v)	pray-shay
• sermon	sermon (m)	sehrm-OH
promise	promesse (f)	prum-ehs
• promise	promettre (v)	prum-eh-tre
pronounce	prononcer (v)	prun-OH-say
• pronunciation	prononciation (f)	prun-OH-see-yas-yOH
propose	proposer (v)	prup-OH-zay
recommend	recommander (v)	re-kum-AH-day
relate	raconter (v)	rak-OH-tay
repeat	répéter (v)	ray-pay-tay
• repetition	répétition (f)	ray-pay-tees-y-OH
report	compte rendu (m)	kOHt-rAH-dew
• report	faire (v) un compte rendu	fehr UH kOHt-rAH-dew
	faire (v) un rapport sur	fehr UH ra-por sewr
reproach	reprocher (v)	re-prush-ay
request	demande (f)	dem-AH-d
• request	demander (v)	dem-AH-day
rhetoric	rhétorique (f)	ray-tor-eek
• rhetorical	rhétorique (adj)	ray-tor-eek
• rhetorical question	question (f) rhétorique	kehst-yOH ray-tor-eek
rumor	bruit (m)	brew-ee
• Rumor has it that . . .	Le bruit court que . . .	le brew-ee koor ke
say, tell	dire (v)	deer
shout, yell	cri (m)	kree
• shout, yell	crier (v)	kree-yay
Shut up!	Ferme-la!	ferm-la
	Tais-toi!	teh-twa
silence	silence (m)	seel-AHs
• silent	silencieux(-euse) (adj, m, f)	seel-AHs-yuh(-yuhz)

speak, talk	parler (v)	*par-lay*
• **speech, talk**	discours (m)	*dees-koor*
state	affirmer (v)	*a-feerm-ay*
• **statement**	affirmation (f)	*a-feerm-as-y-OH*
story	conte (m)	*kOHt*
	histoire (f)	*ees-twar*
• **tell** (*a story*)	conter (v)	*kOH-tay*
	raconter (v) une histoire	*rakOH-tay ewn ees-twar*
suggest	suggérer (v)	*sewg-zh-ay-ray*
summarize	résumer (v)	*ray-zewm-ay*
• **summary**	sommaire (m)	*sum-ehr*
	résumé (m)	*ray-zewm-ay*
swear (*e.g., in court*)	jurer (v)	*zh-ew-ray*
• (*e.g., profanity*)	dire (v) des jurons	*deer day zh-ewr-OH*
thank	remercier (v)	*re-mehr-see-yay*
threat	menace (f)	*me-nas*
• **threaten**	menacer (v)	*me-nas-ay*
toast	toast (m)	*tost*
• **toast**	porter (v) un toast	*por-tay UH tost*
translate	traduire (v)	*trad-ew-eer*
• **translation**	traduction (f)	*trad-ewks-yOH*
vocabulary	vocabulaire (m)	*vu-ka-bew-lehr*
warn	avertir (v)	*a-vehr-teer*
	prévenir (v)	*pray-vneer*
• **warning**	avertissement (m)	*a-vehr-tees-mAH*
whisper	chuchoter (v)	*shew-shut-ay*
word	mot (m) (*written*)	*mOH*
	parole (f) (*spoken*)	*pa-rul*
yawn	bâillement (m)	*bah-y-mAH*
• **yawn**	bâiller (v)	*bah-yay*

b. USEFUL EXPRESSIONS

Actually	Effectivement (*adv*)	*ay-fehk-teev-mAH*
As a matter of fact	En fait	*AH-feht*
Briefly	En bref	*AH-brehf*
By the way	À propos	*a-pro-po*
Go ahead!	Allez-y! (*pol*)	*a-lay-zee*
	Vas-y! (*fam*)	*va-zee*
How do you say . . . in French?	Comment dit-on . . . en français?	*kum-AH deet-OH . . . AH frAH-seh*
I don't understand!	Je ne comprends pas!	*zhen-kOH-prAH-pah*
I'm sure that	Je suis sûr(e) (m, f) que	*zhe swee sewr ke*
	Je suis certain(e) (m, f) que	*zhe swee sehr-tEH (sehr-ten) ke*
In short	En somme	*AH sum*

Isn't it so?	N'est-ce pas?	*nehs-pah*
It seems that	Il semble que	*eel sAH-bl ke*
It's necessary that	Il faut que	*eel foh ke*
	Il est nécessaire que	*eel eh nay-say-sehr ke*
It's not true!	Ce n'est pas vrai!	*se-neh-pah vreh*
It's obvious that	Il est évident que	*eel eh tay-veed-AH ke*
It's true!	C'est vrai!	*seh vreh*
Listen	Écoutez (*pol*)	*ay-koo-tay*
	Écoute (*fam*)	*ay-koot*
Now	Maintenant	*mEHt-nAH*
What was I saying?	Qu'est-ce que je disais?	*kehs-ke zhe dee-zeh*
Who knows?	Qui sait?	*kee seh*

FOCUS: Some Common Gestures

> In common speech situations, French people gesticulate (make gestures) quite noticeably. They also tend to touch each other much more upon greeting each other.

Are you crazy?	Êtes-vous (*pol*) fou (*m*)/folle (*f*)?	*eht-voo foo (ful)*
	Es-tu (*fam*) fou (*m*)/folle (*f*)?	*eh-tew foo (ful)*

Come here!	Venez (*pol*) ici!	*vnay-zee-see*
	Viens (*fam*) ici!	*vy-EH-zee-see*

Hello (*pol*)!	Bonjour! (*during daytime*)	*bOH-zhoor*
	Bonsoir! (*during evening hours*) (see also 16a)	*bOH-swar*

Hi (*fam*)!	Salut!	*sal-ew*

Let me introduce you to . . .	Je vous (*pol*) présente à . . .	*zhe voo prayz-AH-t a . . .*
	Je te (*fam*) présente à . . .	*zh-te prayz-AH-t a . . .*

No way!	Pas de moyen!	*pahd-mwa-yEH*
	Pas possible!	*pah pus-eebl*
	Pas question!	*pah-kehst-yOH*

It's very good!	C'est très bon!	*seh treh bOH*

18. THE TELEPHONE

a. TELEPHONES AND ACCESSORIES

answering machine	répondeur (*m*) téléphonique	*rayp-OH-dur tay-lay-fun-eek*
	téléphone-répondeur (*m*)	*tay-lay-fun rayp-OH-dur*
cable	câble (*m*) téléphonique	*kah-bl tay-lay-fun-eek*
caller ID	afficheur (*m*)	*a-feesh-ur*
cell phone	téléphone (*m*) cellulaire	*tay-lay-fun sehl-yew-lehr*
	portable (*m*)	*por-ta-ble*
fax machine	télécopieur (*m*)	*tay-lay-kup-yur*
intercom	interphone (*m*)	*EH-tehr-fun*
optic fiber	fibre (*f*) optique	*feebr-up-teek*
pager	pager (*m*)	*pa-zh-ur*
receiver (*handset*)	combiné (*m*)	*kOH-bee-nay*
• **earphone**	écouteur (*m*)	*ay-koot-ur*
telecommunication	télécommunication (*f*)	*tay-lay-kum-ew-nee-kas-yOH*
• **telecommunications satellite**	satellite (*m*) de télécommunications	*sat-eh-leet de tay-lay-kum-ew-nee-kas-yOH*
telephone	téléphone (*m*)	*tay-lay-fun*
	appareil (*m*) téléphonique	*a-pa-ray tay-lay-fun-eek*

• cellular phone	téléphone (m) cellulaire	*tay-lay-fun-sehl-yew-lehr*
	téléphone (m) portable portable (m)	*tay-lay-fun por-ta-ble por-ta-ble*
• cordless phone	téléphone (m) sans fil	*tay-lay-fun-sAH-feel*
• outlet (*phone*)	prise (f)	*preez*
• pay phone	téléphone (m) public	*tay-lay-fun pew-bleek*
• phone book	annuaire (m) téléphonique	*a-new-ehr tay-lay-fun-eek*
	Bottin (m)	*but-EH*
• phone booth	cabine (f) téléphonique	*ka-been tay-lay-fun-eek*
• plug	fiche (f) téléphonique	*feesh tay-lay-fun-eek*
• portable phone	téléphone (m) portatif	*tay-lay-fun por-ta-teef*
• telephone	téléphoner (v)	*tay-lay-fun-ay*
telephone credit card	télécarte (f)	*tay-lay-kart*
yellow pages	pages (f, pl) jaunes	*pazh zh-ohn*

b. USING THE TELEPHONE

answer	répondre (v)	*rayp-OH-dre*
• pick up (the phone)	décrocher (v)	*day-krush-ay*
area code	code (m) régional	*kud ray-zh-un-al*
call collect	téléphoner (v) en P.C.V.	*tay-lay-fun-ay AH pay-say-vay*
dial	composer le numéro	*kOH-poh-zayl new-may-roh*
• direct dialing	téléphoner en direct	*tay-lay-fun-ay AH dee-rehkt*
fax	télécopie (f)	*tay-lay-kup-ee*
	fax (m)	*fahks*
hands free	mains (f, pl) libres	*mEH lee-bre*
hang up	raccrocher (v)	*rak-rush-ay*
information	renseignement (m)	*rAH-seh-ny-mAH*
long-distance call	appel (m) interurbain	*ap-ehl EHt-ur-ur-bEH*
make a call	faire (v) un appel téléphonique	*fehr UH nap-ehl tay-lay-fun-eek*
• Hello!	Allô!	*a-loh*
• Is . . . in?	Est-ce que . . . est là?	*ehs-ke eh la*
• This is . . .	Ici . . .	*ee-see*
• Who's speaking?	Qui parle?	*kee parl*
	Qui est à l'appareil?	*kee-yeht a la-pa-ray*
• Wrong number!	Mauvais numéro!	*muv-eh new-may-roh*
message	message (m)	*may-sa-zh*
operator	téléphoniste (m/f)	*tay-lay-fun-eest*
• switchboard operator	standardiste (m/f)	*stAH-dard-eest*

phone	téléphoner (*v*)	*tay-lay-fun-ay*
phone bill	facture (*f*)	*fak-tewr*
phone call	appel (*m*) téléphonique	*ap-ehl tay-lay-fun-eek*
phone line	ligne (*f*) téléphonique	*lee-ny tay-lay-fun-eek*
• **busy (line)**	occupée (*adj*)	*uk-ew-pay*
• **free (line)**	libre (*adj*)	*lee-bre*
phone number	numéro (*m*) de téléphone	*new-may-rohd tay-lay-fun*
ring (*phone*)	sonner (*v*)	*sun-ay*
telex	télex (*m*)	*tay-lehks*
text	texto (*m*)	*tehks-toh*
• **SMS**	SMS (*m*)	*ess-em-ess*
• **to send a text**	envoyer (*v*) un texto	*EH-vwa-yay UH tehks-toh*

For information on computer terminology, see Section 42.

---

19. LETTER WRITING

a. FORMAL SALUTATIONS/CLOSINGS

Cordially yours	Salutations amicales	*sa-lew-tas-yOH ah-mee-kahl*
Dear Sir	Monsieur	*me-sy-uh*
Dear Madam	Madame	*ma-dahm*
To whom it may concern	À qui de droit	*a-kee de drwa*
Yours truly	Veuillez agréer mes salutations distinguées	*vuy-yay a-gray-ay may sa-lew-tas-yOH deest-EH-gay*
Please accept	Veuillez accepter	*vuh-yay ak-sehp-tay*
	Veuillez agréer	*vuh-yay a-gray-ay*

b. FAMILIAR SALUTATIONS/CLOSINGS

Dear	Cher (*adj/m*); (*pl*, Chers)	*sh-ehr*
	Chère (*f*); (*pl*, Chères)	*sh-ehr*
Yours	Bien à toi	*byEH a twa*
Greetings	Sincères salutations	*sEH-sehr sa-lew-tas-yOH*
Affectionately	Affectueusement (*adv*)	*a-fehk-tew-uhz-mAH*
Give my regards to	Un bon souvenir à	*UH bOH soo-vneer a*
A kiss	baiser (*m*), bise (*f*)	*bay-zay, beez*
• **love and kisses**	grosses bises (*f, pl*)	*gros-beez*

c. PARTS OF A LETTER/PUNCTUATION

body	contenu (*m*)	*kOH-te-new*
	corps (*m*)	*kor*
closing	formule (*f*) de politesse	*for-mewl de pu-lee-tehss*
	salutation (*f*) (finale)	*sa-lew-tas-yOH (fee-nal)*
date	date (*f*)	*dat*
heading	l'en-tête (*f*)	*lAH-teht*
	vedette (*f*)	*ve-deht*
place	lieu (*m*)	*ly-uh*
punctuation	ponctuation (*f*)	*pOHk-tew-as-yOH*
• **accent**	accent (*m*)	*aks-AH*
• **apostrophe**	apostrophe (*f*)	*a-pus-truf*
• **asterisk**	astérisque (*m*)	*as-tay-reesk*
• **bracket**	crochet (*m*)	*krush-eh*
• **capital letter**	lettre (*f*) majuscule	*leht-re ma-zh-ews-kewl*
• **colon**	deux points (*m, pl*)	*duh pwEH*
• **comma**	virgule (*f*)	*veerg-ewl*
• **exclamation point**	point (*m*) d'exclamation	*pwEH dehks-kla-mas-yOH*
• **hyphen**	tiret (*m*)	*teer-eh*
	trait (*m*) d'union	*trehd-ew-ny-OH*
• **italics**	en italique (*m*)	*AH nee-ta-leek*
• **parenthesis**	parenthèse (*f*)	*par-AH-tehz*
in parenthesis	entre parenthèses	*AH-tre par-AH-tehz*
• **period**	point (*m*)	*pwEH*
• **question mark**	point (*m*) d'interrogation	*pwEH-dEH-tay-rug-as-yOH*
• **quotation mark**	guillemet (*m*)	*gee-y-meh*
• **semicolon**	point (*m*) virgule (*f*)	*pwEH veerg-ewl*
• **small letter**	lettre (*f*) minuscule	*leht-re meen-ews-kewl*
• **square bracket**	crochet (*m*)	*krush-eh*
• **underlining**	soulignement (*m*)	*soo-lee-ny-mAH*
salutation	formule (*f*) initiale	*for-mew-lee-nees-yal*
sentence	phrase (*f*)	*frahz*
signature	signature (*f*)	*see-ny-a-tewr*
• **sign**	signer (*v*)	*see-ny-ay*
spelling	orthographe (*f*)	*or-tug-raf*
text	texte (*m*)	*tehkst*
• **abbreviation**	abréviation (*f*)	*ab-rayv-y-as-yOH*
• **letter** (*of the alphabet*)	lettre (*f*)	*leht-re*
• **line**	ligne (*f*)	*lee-ny*
• **margin**	marge (*f*)	*mar-zh*
• **P. S.**	P. S.	*pay-ehs*
	post-scriptum (*m*)	*pust-skreep-tum*

• **paragraph**	paragraphe (*m*)	*pa-ra-graf*
• **phrase**	phrase (*f*)	*frahz*
word	mot (*m*)	*moh*

d. WRITING MATERIALS AND ACCESSORIES

adhesive tape	ruban (*m*) adhésif	*rewbAH ad-ay-zeef*
computer keyboard	clavier (*m*) d'ordinateur	*klav-yay dor-dee-na-tur*
envelope	enveloppe (*f*)	*AH-vlup*
eraser	gomme (*f*)	*gum*
glue	colle (*f*)	*kul*
ink	encre (*f*)	*AH-kre*
letter	lettre (*f*)	*leht-re*
letterhead	papier (*m*) à en-tête	*pap-yay a AH-teht*
marker	marqueur (*m*)	*mark-ur*
	crayon-feutre (*m*)	*kray-yOH fuh-tr*
pad	bloc-notes (*m*)	*bluk nut*
page	page (*f*)	*pazh*
paper	papier (*m*)	*pap-yay*
paper clip	trombone (*m*)	*trOH-bun*
pen	stylo (*m*)	*stee-loh*
• **ballpoint pen**	stylo (*m*) à bille	*stee-loh a bee-y*
• **felt-tip pen**	stylo-feutre (*m*)	*stee-loh fuh-tr*
pencil	crayon (*m*)	*kray-yOH*
printer	imprimante (*f*)	*EHpreem-AHt*
ruler	règle (*f*)	*reh-gle*
scissors	ciseaux (*m, pl*)	*see-zoh*
staple	agrafe (*f*)	*ag-raf*
• **stapler**	agrafeuse (*f*)	*ag-gra-fuhz*
string	ficelle (*f*)	*fee-sehl*
toner	toner (*m*)	*tu-nehr*
typewriter	machine (*f*) à écrire	*ma-sheen a ay-kreer*
• **carriage**	chariot (*m*)	*shar-ee-oh*
• **keyboard**	clavier (*m*)	*klav-yay*
• **tab**	tabulateur (*m*)	*ta-bew-la-tur*
• **type**	taper (*v*) (à la machine)	*ta-pay (a la ma-sheen)*

e. AT THE POST OFFICE

abroad	à l'étranger	*al-ay-trAH-zh-ay*
address	adresse (*f*)	*ad-rehs*
• **return address**	adresse (*f*) de l'expéditeur	*ad-rehs de lehks-pay-dee-tur*
addressee	destinataire (*m*)	*day-steen-a-tehr*
airmail	par avion	*par av-yOH*

FOCUS: Letters

Formal

Lieu et date	Paris, le premier (ler) juin 20 . . .
Destinataire	M. Charles DURAND, Directeur Institut de Beauté 52, Square Henri Delormel 75014 Paris
Formule (Salutation) initiale	Monsieur le Directeur,
le contenu (le corps)	Veuillez m'envoyer . . . .
Formule (Salutation) finale	Veuillez agréer, Monsieur, l'expression de mes sentiments distingués.
Signature	_____
	Monique PAULY 29, rue des Jardins 75008 Paris

Familiar

Paris, le 2 juin 20 . . .

Chers amis,
   J'écris ces quelques mots pour . . . .
. . . .

                                 Grosses bises,
                                 Dominique

announcement	faire-part (m)	fehr par
• **wedding announcement**	faire-part (m) de mariage	fehr par de ma-ree-ah-zh
business letter	lettre (f) commerciale	leht-re kum-ehrs-yal
clerk	commis (m)	kum-ee
	employé(e) (m, f)	AH-plwa-yay
clerk's window	guichet (m)	geesh-eh
correspondence	correspondance (f)	kor-ehs-pOH-dAH-ss
• **envelope**	enveloppe (f)	AH-vlup
general delivery	poste (f) restante	pust rehstAHt
invitation	invitation (f)	EH-veet-as-yOH
letter carrier	facteur (m)	fak-tur
	factrice (f)	fak-treess
mail	courrier (m)	koor-yay
	poste (f)	pust
• **mail**	mettre (v) une lettre à la poste	meht-re ewn leht-re a la pust
mail delivery	distribution (f) du courrier	dees-tree-bews-yOH dew koor-yay
mailbox (slot)	boîte (f) à lettres	bwat a leht-re
money order	mandat (m) postal	mAHda pus-tal
package	colis (m)	kul-ee
	paquet (m)	pa-kay
post office	bureau (m) de poste	bew-rohd pust
post office box	boîte (f) postale	bwat pus-tal
	case (f) postale	kahz pus-tal
postage	affranchissement (m)	a-frAH-shees-mAH
postal code	code (m) postal	kud pus-tal
postal rate	tarif (m)	tar-eef
postcard	carte (f) postale	kart pus-tal
printed matter	imprimés (m, pl)	EH-pree-may
receive	recevoir (v)	res-vwar
registered letter	lettre (f) recommandée	leht-re re-kum-AH-day
reply	réponse (f)	raypOHs
• **reply**	répondre (v)	rayp-OH-dre
send	expédier (v)	ehks-payd-yay
	envoyer (v)	AH-vwa-yay
sender	expéditeur (m)	ehks-pay-dee-tur
special delivery	expédition (f) express	ehks-payd-ees-yOH ehks-press
stamp (postage)	timbre-poste (m)	tEH-bre pust
wait (for)	attendre (v)	at-AH-dre
write	écrire (v)	ay-kreer

20. THE MEDIA

a. PRINT MEDIA

advertising	publicité (*f*)	*pew-blee-see-tay*
appendix	appendice (*m*)	*ap-AH-deess*
atlas	atlas (*m*)	*at-lahss*
author	auteur (*m*)	*oh-tur*
	auteure (*f*)	*oh-tur*
book	livre (*m*)	*leev-re*
comic book	magazine (*m*) de	*ma-ga-zeen de bAHd*
	bandes dessinées	*day-see-nay*
comic strip	bande (*f*) dessinée	*bAHd day-see-nay*
cover	couverture (*f*)	*koo-vehr-tewr*
essay	essai (*m*)	*ay-seh*
fiction	ouvrage (*m*) de	*oov-ra-zh de feeks-yOH*
	fiction	
• **nonfiction**	ouvrage (*m*)	*oov-ra-zh nOH*
	non romanesque	*rum-an-esk*
• **science fiction**	science-fiction (*f*)	*syAHs-feeks-yOH*
index	index (*m*)	*EH-dehks*
magazine	magazine (*m*)	*ma-ga-zeen*
	revue (*f*)	*re-vew*
newspaper	journal (*m*)	*zh-oor-nal*
• **article**	article (*m*)	*ar-teekl*
• **criticism**	critique (*f*)	*kree-teek*
• **daily newspaper**	quotidien (*m*)	*kut-eed-y-EH*
• **editor (writing)**	rédacteur (*m*)	*ray-dak-tur*
	rédactrice (*f*)	*ray-dak-treess*
• **editor (correcting)**	correcteur (*m*)	*kur-ehk-tur*
	correctrice (*f*)	*kur-ehk-treess*
• **editorial**	éditorial (*m*)	*ay-dee-tor-yal*
• **front page**	la une (*f*)	*la-ewn*
	première page (*f*)	*prem-yehr pazh*
• **heading**	rubrique (*f*)	*rew-breek*
• **headline**	manchette (*f*)	*mAH-sh-eht*
• **illustration**	illustration (*f*)	*eel-ew-stras-yOH*
• **interview**	interview (*f*)	*EH-tehr-vew*
• **journalist**	journaliste (*m/f*)	*zh-oor-nal-eest*
• **news**	actualités (*f*)	*ak-tew-a-leet-ay*
• **obituary**	notice (*f*)	*nut-eess*
	nécrologique	*nay-kru-lu-zheek*
	nécrologie (*f*)	*nay-kru-lu-zhee*
• **photo**	photo(graphie) (*f*)	*fu-tu(graf-ee)*
• **reader**	lecteur (*m*)	*lehk-tur*
	lectrice (*f*)	*lehk-treess*
• **reporter**	reporter (*m/f*)	*re-port-ehr*
	journaliste (*m/f*)	*zh-oor-nal-eest*

• **review**	critique (*f*)	*kree-teek*
• **weekly periodical**	hebdomadaire (*adj/n, m, f*)	*ehb-dum-a-dehr*
note	note (*f*)	*nut*
• **footnote**	note (*f*) en bas de page	*nut-AH-bahd-pazh*
novel	roman (*m*)	*rum-AH*
• **adventure**	d'aventure	*dav-AH-tewr*
• **best-seller**	best-seller (*m*)	*behst-sehl-ur*
• **mystery**	policier (*adj*)	*pul-ees-yay*
• **plot**	intrigue (*f*)	*EH-treeg*
• **romance**	d'amour	*da-moor*
page	page (*f*)	*pazh*
pamphlet, brochure	dépliant (*m*)	*day-plee-yAH*
	brochure (*f*)	*brush-ewr*
play	pièce (*f*) de théâtre	*pee-ehss de tay-ah-tre*
• **comedy**	comédie (*f*)	*kum-ay-dee*
• **drama**	drame (*m*)	*drahm*
• **musical**	comédie (*f*) musicale	*kum-ay-dee mew-zeek-al*
• **tragedy**	tragédie (*f*)	*tra-zh-ay-dee*
pocket book/paperback	livre (*m*) de poche	*leev-re de push*
poem	poème (*m*)	*pu-ehm*
poetry	poésie (*f*)	*pu-ay-zee*
printing	imprimerie (*f*)	*EH-preem-ree*
• **editor (correcting)**	correcteur (*m*)	*kur-ehk-tur*
• **editor (writing)**	rédacteur (*m*)	*ray-dak-tur*
• **print**	imprimer (*v*)	*EH-preem-ay*
• **printing, typography**	typographie (*f*)	*teep-ug-raf-ee*
• **printing edition (in publishing)**	tirage (*m*)	*tee-ra-zh*
• **proofreader**	correcteur (*m*)	*kur-ehk-tur*
publish	publier (*v*)	*pew-blee-yay*
• **publisher**	éditeur (*m*)	*ay-deet-ur*
• **publishing house**	maison (*f*) d'édition	*meh-zOH day-dee-syOH*
read	lire (*v*)	*leer*
reference book	ouvrage (*m*) de référence	*oov-ra-zh de ray-fayr-AH-s*
• **definition**	définition (*f*)	*day-fee-nees-yOH*
• **dictionary**	dictionnaire (*m*)	*deek-see-yun-ehr*
entry (dictionary)	entrée (*f*)	*AH-tray*
• **encyclopedia**	encyclopédie (*f*)	*AH-see-klup-ay-dee*
entry (encyclopedia)	article (*m*)	*ar-teekle*
science fiction	science-fiction (*f*)	*syAHs-feeks-yOH*
short story	conte (*m*)	*kOHt*
	nouvelle (*f*)	*noo-vehl*

table of contents	table (*f*) des matières	*tabl day mat-yehr*
text	texte (*m*)	*tehkst*
title	titre (*m*)	*teet-re*
turn pages, leaf through	tourner (*v*) les pages	*toor-nay lay pahzh*
	feuilleter (*v*)	*fuh-y-tay*
write	écrire (*v*)	*ay-kreer*

b. ELECTRONIC MEDIA

antenna	antenne (*f*)	*AH-tehn*
audio-visual equipment	appareils (*m, pl*) audio-visuels	*a-pa-reh-y ohd-hyu vee-zew-ehl*
• **compact disc**	disque compact (*m*)	*deesk-kOH-pakt*
• **DVD**	D.V.D. (*m*)	*day-vay-day*
• **headphones**	casque (*m*) (à écouteurs)	*kask (a-ay-koo-tur)*
• **loudspeaker**	haut-parleur (*m*)	*oh-par-lur*
• **microphone**	microphone (*m*)	*meek-ruf-un*
• **play a record**	passer un disque	*pah-say UH deesk*
• **receiver, tuner**	dispositif (*m*) d'accord	*dees-poh-zee-teef dak-or*
• **record**	disque (*m*)	*deesk*
	enregistrer (*v*)	*AH-re-zh-ees-tray*
• **record player**	tourne-disque (*m*)	*toorn-deesk*
• **speaker**	caisse (*f*) acoustique	*kehs-akoos-teek*
	baffle (*m*)	*bah-fle*
• **stereo**	stéréo(phonique) (*adj*)	*stay-ray-u-(fun-eek)*
	chaîne-stéréo (*f*)	*shen-stay-ray-o*
• **tape**	bande (*f*) magnétique	*bAHd ma-ny-ay-teek*
bluetooth	technologie (*f*) bluetooth	*tehk-nu-lu-zhee blew-tewth*
program	programme (*m*)	*prug-ram*
	émission (*f*)	*ay-mees-yOH*
projector	projecteur (*m*)	*pruzh-ehk-tur*
radio	radio (*f*)	*rad-yo*
• **car radio**	autoradio (*m*)	*u-tu-rad-yo*
• **listen to**	écouter (*v*)	*ay-koo-tay*
• **news report**	nouvelles (*f, pl*)	*noo-vehl*
• **newscast**	informations (*f, pl*)	*EH-for-ma-syOH*
	les infos (*f, pl*)	*layz-EH-foh*
• **portable radio**	radio portative (*f*)	*rad-yo port-a-teev*
• **satellite radio**	radio (*f*) (par) satellite	*rad-yo (par) sa-tay-leet*
• **station**	station (*f*) de radio	*stas-yOH-de-rad-yo*
show	émission (*f*)	*ay-mee-syOH*
spam	spam (*m*)	*spahm*
	pourriel (*m*)	*poo-ree-yehl*

television	télévision (*f*)	*tay-lay-veez-yOH*
• **cable television**	télévision (*f*) par câble	*tay-lay-veez-yOH par kahbl*
• **channel**	canal (*m*)	*ka-nal*
	chaîne (*f*)	*sh-ehn*
• **closed circuit**	circuit fermé (*m*)	*seer-kew-ee fehrm-ay*
• **commercial**	publicité (*f*)	*pew-blee-see-tay*
• **documentary**	documentaire (*m*)	*duk-ewm-AH-tehr*
• **interview**	interview (*f*)	*EH-tehr-vew*
• **look at, watch**	regarder (*v*)	*re-gar-day*
• **network**	réseau (*m*)	*ray-zoh*
• **news report**	actualités (*f*)	*ak-tew-a-leet-ay*
• **newscast**	journal (*m*) télévisé	*zh-oor-nal tay-lay-vee-zay*
• **on the air**	à l'antenne	*a-lAH-tehn*
• **remote control**	télécommande (*f*)	*tay-lay-kum-AH-d*
• **satellite television**	télévision (*f*) par satellite	*tay-lay-veez-yOH par sa-tay-leet*
• **series**	série (*f*) télévisée	*say-ree tay-lay-veez-ay*
• **soap opera**	feuilleton (*m*)	*fuh-ye-tOH*
	soap (*m*)	*sohp*
• **television set**	téléviseur (*m*)	*tay-lay-veez-ur*
• **transmission**	émission (*f*)	*ay-mees-yOH*
• **TV**	télé (*f*)	*tay-lay*
• **TV movie**	téléfilm (*m*)	*tay-lay feelm*
	magnétoscope (*m*)	*man-yay-tus-kup*
	VCR (*m*)	*vay-say-ehr*
• **VHS/SECAM/TV**	VHS/SECAM/TV (*m*)	*vay-ash-ehs say-kahm tay-vay*
• **video game**	jeu-vidéo (*m*)	*zh-uh vee-day-o*
• **videorock**	vidéorock (*m*)	*vee-day-o ruk*
• **volume control**	réglage (*m*) de volume	*ray-glazh de vul-ewm*
text	texto (*m*)	*tehk-stoh*
turn off	éteindre (*v*)	*ayt-EH-dre*
turn on	allumer (*v*)	*al-ew-may*
walkie-talkie	talkie-walkie (*m*)	*tuk-ee-wuk-ee*
website	site (*m*) web	*seet wehb*

21. FEELINGS

a. MOODS/ATTITUDES/EMOTIONS

affection	affection (*f*)	*af-ehks-yOH*
agree	être (*v*) d'accord	*eh-tre dak-or*
anger	colère (*f*)	*kul-ehr*
• **angry**	fâché(e) (*adj, m, f*)	*fah-shay*

anxiety, anxiousness	anxiété (*f*)	*AHks-yay-tay*
• **anxious**	anxieux (*adj, m*)	*AHks-yuh*
	anxieuse (*adj, f*)	*AHks-yuhz*
assure	assurer (*v*)	*a-sewr-ay*
attitude	attitude (*f*)	*a-tee-tewd*

FOCUS: Colloquial Expressions

Here are a few idioms dealing with ways of expressing displeasure:

Come on!	Allons donc!	*al-OH dOH*
Cut it out!	Arrêtez!	*a-reht-ay*
Darn it!	Zut!	*zewt*
"dirty word"	"mot grossier" (*m*)	*moh gros-yay*
Get lost!	Allez-vous en!	*a-lay-vooz-AH*
	Va-t'en!	*va-tAH*
No way!	Pas question!	*pah-kehst-yOH*
Shut up!	Ferme-la!	*ferm-la*
Yuch!	Berk! pouah!	*berk/pwa*

---

be able to	pouvoir (*v*)	*poo-vwar*
be down	avoir (*v*) le cafard	*avwar le ka-far*
be up	être (*v*) remonté(e)	*eh-tre rem-OH-tay*
	être (*v*) heureux / heureuse	*eh-tre ur-uh / ur-uz*
bore	ennuyer (*v*)	*AH-new-ee-yay*
• **become bored**	s'ennuyer (*v*)	*sAH-new-ee-yay*
• **feel bored**	crever (*v*) d'ennui	*kre-vay dAH-new-ee*
• **boredom**	ennui (*m*)	*AH-new-ee*
complain	se plaindre (*v*)	*se-plEH-dre*
• **complaint**	plainte (*f*)	*plEHt*
cry (weep)	pleurer (*v*)	*plur-ay*
• **tears**	larmes (*f*)	*larm*
depressed	déprimé(e) (*adj, m, f*)	*day-preem-ay*
• **depression**	dépression (*f*)	*day-prays-yOH*
desperate	désespéré(e) (*adj, m, f*)	*dayz-ehs-pay-ray*
• **desperation**	désespoir (*m*)	*dayz-ehs-pwar*
disagree	être (*v*) en désaccord	*eh-tre AH day-za-kor*
• **disagreement**	désaccord (*m*)	*day-za-kor*
• **be against**	être (*v*) contre	*eh-tre kOHtre*
disappoint	décevoir (*v*)	*day-svwar*
• **disappointed**	déçu(e) (*adj/m, f*)	*dayss-ew*
disappointment	déception (*f*)	*day-sehp-syOH*

dissatisfaction	insatisfaction (*f*)	*EH-sa-tees-faks-yOH*
	mécontentement (*m*)	*may-kOH-tAHt-mAH*
• **dissatisfied**	insatisfait(e) (*adj, m, f*)	*EH-sa-tees-feh(t)*
	mécontent(e) (*adj, m, f*)	*may-kOH-tAH(t)*
encourage	encourager (*v*)	*AH-koor-azh-ay*
• **encouragement**	encouragement (*m*)	*AH-koor-azh-mAH*
faith, trust	confiance (*f*)	*kOH-fy-AH-s*
• **trust**	avoir (*v*) confiance en	*avwar kOH-fy-AH-s AH*
fear	peur (*f*)	*pur*
• **be afraid**	avoir (*v*) peur	*avwar pur*
feel	sentir (*v*)	*sAH-teer*
• **feel like**	avoir (*v*) envie de	*avwar AH-vee-de*
flatter	flatter (*v*)	*flat-ay*
• **flattery**	flatterie (*f*)	*flat-ree*
fun, enjoyment	amusement (*m*)	*a-mewz-mAH*
• **have fun, enjoy oneself**	s'amuser (*v*)	*sa-mewz-ay*
happiness	bonheur (*m*)	*bun-ur*
• **happy**	heureux (*adj, m*)	*ur-uh*
	heureuse (*adj, f*)	*ur-uz*
	content(e) (*adj, m, f*)	*kOHt-AH(t)*
have reason to be worried	avoir de quoi s'inquiéter	*avward-kwa-sank-ee-ay-tay*
have to, must	devoir (*v*)	*de-vwar*
hope	espoir (*m*)	*ehs-pwar*
• **hope**	espérer (*v*)	*ehs-pay-ray*
indifference	indifférence (*f*)	*EH-dee-fay-rAH-s*
• **indifferent**	indifférent(e) (*adj, m, f*)	*EH-dee-fay-rAH(t)*
joy	joie (*f*)	*zh-wa*
laugh	rire (*v*)	*reer*
• **laughter**	rire (*m*)	*reer*
• **to laugh halfheartedly, reluctantly**	rire (*v*) jaune, rire (*v*) à contrecoeur	*reer-zh-ohn, reer-a-kOH-tre-kur*
matter	importer (*v*)	*EH-por-tay*
mood	humeur (*f*)	*ew-mur*
• **in a bad mood**	de mauvaise humeur	*de muv-ehz ew-mur*
• **in a good mood**	de bonne humeur	*de bun ew-mur*
need	besoin (*m*)	*be-zwEH*
• **need**	avoir (*v*) besoin de	*avwar be-zwEH de*

patience	patience (*f*)	*pas-yAHs*
• **have patience**	avoir (*v*) de la patience	*avwar-dla-pas-yAHs*
relief	soulagement (*m*)	*sool-azh-mAH*
• **sigh of relief**	soupir (*m*) de soulagement	*soo-peer de sool-azh-mAH*
sad	triste (*adj*)	*treest*
• **sadness**	tristesse (*f*)	*treest-ehs*
satisfaction	satisfaction (*f*)	*sa-tees-faks-yOH*
• **satisfied**	satisfait(e) (*adj, m, f*)	*sa-tees-feh(t)*
shame	honte (*f*)	*OHt*
• **be ashamed**	avoir (*v*) honte	*avwar OHt*
smile	sourire (*v & n, m*)	*soo-reer*
sorrow	chagrin (*m*)	*shag-rEH*
surprise	surprise (*f*)	*sewr-preez*
• **surprise**	surprendre (*v*)	*sewr-prAH-dre*
• **surprised**	surpris(e) (*adj, m, f*)	*sewr-pree(z)*
sympathy	compassion (*f*)	*kOH-pahs-yOH*
• **sympathetic**	compatissant(e) (*adj, m, f*)	*kOH-pa-tees-AH(t)*
thankfulness	gratitude (*f*)	*gra-tee-tewd*
	reconnaissance (*f*)	*re-kun-ehs-AH-s*
• **thankful**	reconnaissant(e) (*adj, m, f*)	*re-kun-ehs-AH(t)*
• **thank**	remercier (*v*)	*re-mehr-see-yay*
tolerance	tolérance (*f*)	*tul-ay-rAHs*
• **tolerate**	tolérer (*v*)	*tul-ay-ray*
want to	vouloir (*v*)	*vool-war*
	désirer (*v*)	*day-zee-ray*

b. LIKES AND DISLIKES

accept	accepter (*v*)	*aks-ehp-tay*
• **acceptable**	acceptable (*adj*)	*aks-ehp-ta-ble*
• **unacceptable**	inacceptable (*adj*)	*een-aks-ehp-ta-ble*
approval	approbation (*f*)	*ap-rub-ahs-yOH*
• **approve**	approuver (*v*)	*ap-roov-ay*
be fond of	avoir (*v*) une passion pour	*avwar ewn pahs-yOH poor*
	aimer (*v*) beaucoup	*ay-may bo-koo*
detest	détester (*v*)	*day-tehst-ay*
disgust	dégoût (*m*)	*day-goo*
• **disgusted**	dégoûté(e) (*adj, m, f*)	*day-goo-tay*
hate	haïr (*v*)	*a-eer*
• **hatred**	haine (*f*)	*ehn*

I can't stand him (her)!	Je ne peux pas le (la) supporter!	zhen puh pahl(la) sew-por-tay
kiss	embrasser (v)	AH-bra-say
like	aimer (v) bien	ay-may byEH
• liking (taste)	penchant (m)	pAH-shAH
	goût (m)	goo
• dislike (not to like)	ne pas aimer (v)	ne-pah-zay-may
love	amour (m)	a-moor
• love	aimer (v)	ay-may
mediocre	médiocre (adj)	mayd-y-uk-re
pleasant	agréable (adj)	a-gray-abl
• unpleasant	désagréable (adj)	dayz-a-gray-abl
prefer	préférer (v)	pray-fay-ray
Too bad!	Dommage!	dum-azh

c. EXPRESSING EMOTIONS

Are you joking?	Vous plaisantez? (pol)	voo-pleh-zAH-tay
	Tu plaisantes? (fam)	tew-pleh-zAHt
Be careful!	Attention!	atAHs-yOH
Enough!	Assez!	a-say
Fortunately!	Heureusement! (adv)	ur-uhz-mAH
Good heavens!/Oh my!	Oh! là! là!	oh-la-la
I don't believe it!	Je ne le crois pas!	zhen le krwah pah
I don't feel like . . .	Je n'ai pas envie de . . .	zhen ay pah AH-vee de . . .
I wish! (If only . . . !)	Si seulement . . . !	see sulmAH
I'm serious!	Je suis sérieux (m) (sérieuse) (f)	zhe swee say-ry-uh (say-ry-uhz)
I'm sorry!	Je regrette!	zher-greht
	Je suis désolé!	zhe swee day-zo-lay
Impossible!	Pas possible!	pah-pus-eebl
It doesn't matter!	Peu importe!	puh EH-port
My God!	Mon Dieu!	mOH dy-uh
Poor man!	Pauvre homme!	poh-vr um
Poor woman!	Pauvre femme!	poh-vr fahm
Quiet!	Silence!	seel-AHs
Really?	Vraiment?	vrehm-AH
Keep quiet!	Taisez-vous!	teh-zay-voo
	Tais-toi! (fam)	teh-twa
Thank goodness!	Grâce à Dieu!	grahss a dy-uh
	Dieu merci!	dy-uh mehr-see
Ugh!	Pouah!	pwa
Unbelievable!	Incroyable!	EH-krwa-yabl
Unfortunately!	Malheureusement!	mal-ur-uhz-mAH

What a bore!	Quel raseur! (*m*)	*kehl rahz-ur*
	Quelle raseuse! (*f*)	*kehl rahz-uhz*
	Quelle barbe!	*kehl barb*

22. THINKING

a. DESCRIBING THOUGHT

complicated	compliqué(e) (*adj, m, f*)	*kOH-plee-kay*
concept	concept (*m*)	*kOH-sehpt*
conscience	conscience (*f*)	*kOH-sy-AHs*
conscientious	consciencieux (*adj, m*)	*kOH-sy-AHs-yuh*
	consciencieuse (*f*)	*kOH-sy-AHs-yuhz*
difficult	difficile (*adj*)	*dee-fee-seel*
doubt	doute (*m*)	*doot*
easy	facile (*adj*)	*fa-seel*
existence	existence (*f*)	*ehg-zees-tAHs*
hypothesis	hypothèse (*f*)	*ee-pu-tehz*
idea	idée (*f*)	*ee-day*
ignorant	ignorant(e) (*adj, m, f*)	*ee-ny-or-AH(t)*
imagination	imagination (*f*)	*ee-ma-zh-ee-nas-yOH*
interesting	intéressant(e) (*adj, m, f*)	*EH-tay-rehs-AH(t)*
judgment	jugement (*m*)	*zh-ew-zh-mAH*
justice	justice (*f*)	*zh-ewss-teess*
knowledge	connaissance (*f*)	*kun-ehs-AHs*
	savoir (*m*)	*sav-war*
knowledgeable	connaisseur (*adj, m*)	*kun-ehs-ur*
	connaisseuse (*f*)	*kun-ehs-uhz*
mind	esprit (*m*)	*ehs-pree*
opinion	opinion (*f*)	*up-ee-ny-OH*
• in my opinion	à mon avis (*m*)	*a-mOH-nah-vee*
problem	problème (*m*)	*prub-lehm*
• No problem!	Pas de problème!	*pahd-prub-lehm*
reason	raison (*f*)	*reh-zOH*
simple	simple (*adj*)	*sEH-pl*
thought	pensée (*f*)	*pAH-say*
wisdom	sagesse (*f*)	*sa-zh-ehs*

b. BASIC THOUGHT PROCESSES

agree	être (*v*) d'accord	*eh-tre dak-or*
be interested in	s'intéresser (*v*) à	*sEH-tay-ray-say a*
be right	avoir (*v*) raison	*avwar rehz-OH*
be wrong	avoir (*v*) tort	*avwar tor*
believe	croire (*v*)	*krwar*

convince	convaincre (*v*)	*kOH-vEH-kre*
demonstrate	démontrer (*v*)	*day-mOH-tray*
doubt	douter (*v*)	*doo-tay*
forget	oublier (*v*)	*oobl-yay*
imagine	imaginer (*v*)	*ee-ma-zh-een-ay*
know (a fact)	savoir (*v*)	*sav-war*
know (a person)	connaître (*v*)	*kun-eht-re*
learn	apprendre (*v*)	*ap-rAH-dre*
persuade	persuader (*v*)	*pehr-sew-a-day*
	convaincre (*v*)	*kOH-vEH-kre*
reason	raisonner (*v*)	*reh-zun-ay*
reflect	réfléchir (*v*)	*ray-flay-sheer*
remember	se rappeler (*v*)	*se-rap-lay*
	se souvenir de	*se-soov-neer de*
study	étudier (*v*)	*ay-tewd-yay*
think	penser (*v*)	*pAH-say*
understand	comprendre (*v*)	*kOH-prAH-dre*
• **What do you think?**	Qu'en pensez-vous? (*pol*)	*kAH-pAH-say-voo*
	Qu'en penses-tu? (*fam*)	*kAH-pAH-s tew*

DAILY LIFE

23. AT HOME

a. PARTS OF THE HOUSE

attic	grenier (*m*)	*gren-yay*
basement	sous-sol (*m*)	*soo-sul*
bathtub	baignoire (*f*)	*beh-ny-war*
ceiling	plafond (*m*)	*plafOH*
chimney	cheminée (*f*)	*shmeen-ay*
corridor	couloir (*m*)	*kool-war*
door	porte (*f*)	*port*
doorbell	sonnette (*f*)	*sun-eht*
entrance	entrée (*m*)	*AHtray*
faucet	robinet (*m*)	*rub-een-ay*
fireplace	cheminée (*f*)	*shmee-nay*
floor	plancher (*m*)	*plAH-shay*
	parquet (*m*)	*par-kay*
floor (*level*)	étage (*m*)	*ay-ta-zh*
• **first floor** (U.S.)	rez-de-chaussée (*m*)	*ray-de-show-say*
• **second floor** (U.S.)	premier étage (*m*)	*prem-yayr-ay-ta-zh*
garage	garage (*m*)	*gar-azh*
garden	jardin (*m*)	*zh-ard-EH*
ground floor	rez-de-chaussée (*m*)	*rayd-sh-oh-say*
house	maison (*f*)	*meh-zOH*
mailbox	boîte (*f*) à lettres	*bwat-a-leht-re*
porch	porche (*m*)	*porsh*
	véranda (*f*)	*vay-rAH-da*
roof	toit (*m*)	*twa*
shelf	étagère (*f*)	*ay-ta-zy-ehr*
shower	douche (*f*)	*doosh*
sink	évier (*m*)	*ayv-yay*
	lavabo (*m*) (*in a bathroom*)	*la-va-boh*
stairs	escalier (*m*)	*ehs-kal-yay*
switch	interrupteur (*m*)	*EH-tehr-ewp-tur*
terrace	terrasse (*f*)	*tehr-ahs*
threshold	seuil (*m*)	*soy*
wall	mur (*m*)	*mewr*
window	fenêtre (*f*)	*fneht-re*
window sill	rebord (*m*) de la fenêtre	*re-bor-dla-fneht-re*

b. ROOMS

bathroom	salle (*f*) de bains	*sal de bEH*
bedroom	chambre (*f*) à coucher	*shAH-br a koo-shay*
closet	penderie (*f*)	*pAH-de-ree*
	placard (*m*)	*plak-ar*
dining room	salle (*f*) à manger	*sal a mAHzh-ay*
kitchen	cuisine (*f*)	*kew-ee-zeen*
living room	salon (*m*)	*salOH*
	salle (*f*) de séjour	*sal de say-zh-oor*
room	pièce (*f*)	*py-ehs*
wine cellar	cave (*f*) à vin	*kav a vEH*

c. FURNITURE AND DECORATION

armchair	fauteuil (*m*)	*foh-tuh-y*
bed	lit (*m*)	*lee*
bedside table	table (*f*) de chevet	*ta-bl de sh-veh*
	table (*f*) de nuit	*ta-bl-de-new-ee*
bookcase	bibliothèque (*f*)	*beeb-lee-yut-ehk*
bookshelf	étagère (*f*) à livres	*ay-ta-zh-er a leevr*
carpet, rug	tapis (*m*)	*ta-pee*
chair	chaise (*f*)	*sh-ehz*
chest of drawers, dresser	commode (*f*)	*kum-ud*
curtains	rideaux (*m*)	*reed-oh*
decorating	décoration (*f*)	*day-kor-as-yOH*
drawer	tiroir (*m*)	*teer-war*
furniture	meuble (*m*)	*muh-bl*
lamp	lampe (*f*)	*lAHp*
mirror	miroir (*m*)	*meer-war*
painting	tableau (*m*)	*tab-loh*
sofa	canapé (*m*)	*ka-na-pay*
	sofa (*m*)	*soh-fah*
stool	tabouret (*m*)	*tab-oor-eh*
table	table (*f*)	*tabl*
wall-to-wall carpeting	moquette (*f*)	*muk-eht*
writing desk	secrétaire (*m*)	*sek-ray-tehr*

d. APPLIANCES AND COMMON HOUSEHOLD ITEMS

bag	sac (*m*)	*sak*
• **shopping bag**	sac à provisions	*sak-a-pru-veez-yOH*
basket	corbeille (*f*)	*kor-bay*
	panier (*m*)	*pan-yay*
bedspread	couvre-lit (*m*)	*koo-vre-lee*

blanket	couverture (*f*)	*koov-ehr-tewr*
bottle	bouteille (*f*)	*boo-tay*
box	boîte (*f*)	*bwat*
broom	balai (*m*)	*bal-eh*
clothes hanger	cintre (*m*)	*sEH-tre*
coffee machine	cafetière (*f*) électrique	*kaf-tyehr ay-lehk-treek*
	percolateur (*m*)	*pehrk-u-la-tur*
coffee pot	cafetière (*f*)	*kaf-tyehr*
cup	tasse (*f*)	*tas*
dishwasher	lave-vaisselle (*m*)	*lav-veh-sehl*
dryer	sèche-linge (*m*)	*sesh-lEH-zh*
	sécheuse (*f*)	*say-sh-uhz*
fork	fourchette (*f*)	*foorsh-eht*
freezer	congélateur (*m*)	*kOHzh-ay-la-tur*
glass (*drinking*)	verre (*m*)	*vehr*
kettle	bouilloire (*f*)	*boo-y-war*
key	clef (*f*)	*klay*
knife	couteau (*m*)	*koo-toh*
• **blade**	lame (*f*)	*lahm*
• **handle**	manche (*m*)	*mAH-sh*
ladle	louche (*f*)	*loosh*
lid	couvercle (*m*)	*koov-ehr-kl*
microwave oven	four (*m*) à micro-ondes (*f, pl*)	*foor a meek-ro-OHd*
mug	chope (*f*)	*shuhp*
napkin	serviette (*f*)	*sehrv-yeht*
oven	four (*m*)	*foor*
pail	seau (*m*)	*soh*
pan	casserole (*f*)	*kas-rul*
	sauteuse (*f*)	*soh-tuhz*
pillow	oreiller (*m*)	*or-ay-yay*
pillowcase	taie (*f*) d'oreiller	*teh dor-ay-yay*
plate	assiette (*f*)	*as-yeht*
pot	faitout (*m*)	*feh-too*
	marmite (*f*)	*mar-meet*
pots and pans	batterie (*f*) de cuisine	*bat-ree de kew-ee-zeen*
radio	radio (*f*)	*rad-yo*
refrigerator	frigo (*m*)	*free-go*
	réfrigérateur (*m*)	*ray-free-zh-ay-ra-tur*
saucer	soucoupe (*f*)	*soo-koop*
sewing machine	machine (*f*) à coudre	*ma-sheen-a-kood-re*
sheet (*bed*)	drap (*m*)	*dra*
spoon	cuiller (*f*)	*kew-ee-yehr*
• **tablespoon**	cuiller (*f*) à soupe	*kew-ee-yehr-a-soop*
• **teaspoon**	cuiller (*f*) à café	*kew-ee-yehr-a-ka-fay*

stove	cuisinière (*f*)	*kew-ee-zeen-yehr*
• **electric**	électrique	*ay-lekh-treek*
• **gas**	à gaz	*a gaz*
tablecloth	nappe (*f*)	*nap*
tableware	ustensiles (*m, pl*) à table	*ewst-AH-seel-a-tabl*
teapot	théière (*f*)	*tay-yehr*
television set	téléviseur (*m*)	*tay-lay-veez-ur*
toaster	grille-pain (*m*)	*gree-y pEH*
tools	outils (*m, pl*)	*oo-tee*
trash can	poubelle (*f*)	*poo-bell*
tray	plateau (*m*) à servir	*pla-toh a sehr-veer*
vacuum cleaner	aspirateur (*m*)	*as-pee-ra-tur*
washing machine	lave-linge (*m*)	*lav-lEH-zh*
	machine (*f*) à laver	*ma-sheen a la-vay*
wastebasket	corbeille (*f*) à papier	*kor-bay a pap-yay*

e. SERVICES

air conditioning	climatisation (*f*)	*klee-ma-tee-zass-yOH*
• **air conditioner**	climatiseur (*m*)	*klee-ma-tee-zuhr*
electricity	électricité (*f*)	*ay-lehk-tree-see-tay*
furnace	chaudière (*f*)	*sh-ohd-yehr*
gas	gaz (*m*)	*gaz*
heating	chauffage (*m*)	*sh-oh-fazh*
• **central heating**	chauffage (*m*) central	*sh-oh-fazh sAH-tral*
light, power	éclairage (*m*)	*ay-klehr-azh*
telephone	téléphone (*m*)	*tay-lay-fun*
water	eau (*f*)	*oh*

f. ADDITIONAL HOUSEHOLD VOCABULARY

at home	à la maison	*a-la-mehz-OH*
	chez soi	*shay-swa*
build	construire (*v*)	*kOH-strew-eer*
buy	acheter (*v*)	*ash-tay*
clean	nettoyer (*v*)	*neht-wa-yay*
clear the table	desservir (*v*) la table	*day-sehr-veer la ta-bl*
	débarasser (*v*) la table	*day-ba-rah-say la ta-bl*
fix, do it yourself	bricoler (*v*)	*bree-ku-lay*
live (in)	habiter (*v*)	*a-bee-tay*
make the bed	faire (*v*) le lit	*fehr le lee*
move (*out of a house*)	déménager (*v*)	*day-may-na-zh-ay*
paint	peindre (*v*)	*pEH-dr*
put a room in order	mettre (*v*) une pièce en ordre	*meh-tr ewn py-ehs AH-nor-dr*
restore	restaurer (*v*)	*re-sto-ray*
sell	vendre (*v*)	*vAH-dr*

set the table	mettre (v) le couvert	*meh-tr le koo-vehr*
wash	laver (v)	*la-vay*
• wash the clothes	faire (v) la lessive	*fehr la less-eev*
• wash the dishes	faire (v) la vaisselle	*fehr la veh-sehl*

g. LIVING IN AN APARTMENT

apartment	appartement (m)	*a-par-tem-AH*
apartment building	immeuble (m)	*eem-uh-bl*
building	édifice (m)	*ay-dee-feess*
condominium	immeuble (m) en copropriété (f)	*eem-uh-bl AH ko-pro-pree-ay-tay*
elevator	ascenseur (m)	*ass-AH-sur*
ground floor	rez-de-chaussée (m)	*rayd-sh-oh-say*
landlord	propriétaire (m/f)	*prup-pree-yay-tehr*
lease	bail (m)	*ba-y*
rent	loyer (m)	*lwa-yay*
• rent	louer (v)	*lway*
superintendent (*of apartment building*)	concierge (m/f)	*kOH-see-ehr-zh*
tenant	locataire (m/f)	*luk-a-tehr*

24. EATING AND DRINKING

a. MEALS

breakfast	petit déjeuner (m)	*ptee day-zh-un-ay*
dinner	dîner (m)	*dee-nay*
food	nourriture (f)	*noo-ree-tewr*
lunch	déjeuner (m)	*day-zh-un-ay*
meal	repas (m)	*re-pah*
snack	casse-croûte (m)	*kass-kroot*
	goûter (m)	*goo-tay*

b. PREPARATION

broiled, grilled	grillé(e) (adj, m, f)	*gree-yay*
cooking, cuisine	cuisine (f)	*kew-ee-zeen*
marinated	mariné(e) (adj, m, f)	*ma-ree-nay*
medium	à point	*a-pwEH*
rare	saignant(e) (adj, m, f)	*seh-ny-AH(t)*
roast	rôti(e) (adj, m, f)	*roh-tee*
well-done	bien cuit(e) (adj, m, f)	*byEH kwee(t)*
with sauce (gravy)	au jus	*oh-zh-ew*

c. MEAT AND POULTRY

bacon	bacon (*m*)	*bay-kun*
beef	bœuf (*m*)	*buhf*
chicken	poulet (*m*)	*poo-leh*
cold cuts	viandes (*f, pl*) froides	*vee-y-AHd frwahd*
duck	canard (*m*)	*kan-ar*
ham	jambon (*m*)	*zh-AH-bOH*
lamb	agneau (*m*)	*a-ny-oh*
liver	foie (*m*)	*fwa*
meat	viande (*f*)	*vee-y-AHd*
pork	porc (*m*)	*por*
poultry	volaille (*f*)	*vul-ah-yuh*
salami	salami (*m*)	*sa-la-mee*
sausage	saucisse (*f*)	*so-seess*
turkey	dinde (*f*)	*dEH-d*
veal	veau (*m*)	*voh*

d. FISH, SEAFOOD, AND SHELLFISH

anchovy	anchois (*m*)	*AH-sh-wa*
clam	palourde (*f*)	*pa-loord*
cod	morue (*f*)	*mu-rew*
dried cod	merluche (*f*)	*mehr-lewsh*
eel	anguille (*f*)	*AH-gee-y*
fish	poisson (*m*)	*pwassOH*
herring	hareng (*m*)	*ar-AH*
lobster	homard (*m*)	*um-ar*
	langouste (*f*)	*lAH-goost*
mussels	moules (*f, pl*)	*mool*
oyster	huître (*f*)	*ew-eet-re*
prawn	langoustine (*f*)	*lAH-goos-teen*
	crevette (*f*)	*kre-veht*
salmon	saumon (*m*)	*so-mOH*
sardine	sardine (*f*)	*sar-deen*
seafood	fruits de mer (*m, pl*)	*frew-eed-mehr*
shellfish	crustacés (*m, pl*)	*krew-sta-say*
shrimp	crevette (*f*)	*kre-veht*
sole	sole (*f*)	*sul*
squid	calmar (*m*)	*kal-mar*
trout	truite (*f*)	*trew-eet*
tuna	thon (*m*)	*tOH*

e. VEGETABLES

artichoke	artichaut (*m*)	*ar-tee-sh-oh*
asparagus	asperge (*f*)	*as-pehr-zh*

bean	fève (*f*)	*fehv*
	haricot (*m*)	*a-ree-koh*
beet	betterave (*f*)	*beht-rav*
broccoli	brocoli (*m*)	*bruk-ul-ee*
cabbage	chou (*m*)	*shoo*
carrot	carotte (*f*)	*kar-ut*
cauliflower	chou-fleur (*m*)	*shoo-flur*
celery	céleri (*m*)	*sehl-ree*
cucumber	concombre (*m*)	*kOH-kOH-br*
eggplant	aubergine (*f*)	*oh-behr-zh-een*
lettuce	laitue (*f*)	*leht-ew*
mushroom	champignon (*m*)	*shAH-pee-ny-OH*
olive	olive (*f*)	*ul-eev*
onion	oignon (*m*)	*u-ny-OH*
peas	pois (*m*); petits pois (*m*, *pl*)	*pwa; ptee pwa*
potato	pomme (*f*) de terre	*pum-de-tehr*
potato salad	salade (*f*) de pommes de terre	*sa-lad-de-pum-de-tehr*
spinach	épinards (*m*, *pl*)	*ay-pee-nar*
string bean	haricot vert (*m*)	*a-ree-koh-vehr*
vegetables	légumes (*m*, *pl*)	*lay-gewn*

f. FRUITS

apple	pomme (*f*)	*pum*
apricot	abricot (*m*)	*a-bree-ko*
banana	banane (*f*)	*ba-nan*
blueberry	myrtille (*f*)	*meer-tee-y*
	bleuet (*m*) (Québec)	*bluh-eh*
cherry	cerise (*f*)	*sreez*
citrus fruit	agrumes (*m*, *pl*)	*a-grewm*
date	datte (*f*)	*daht*
fig	figue (*f*)	*feeg*
fruit	fruit (*m*)	*frew-ee*
grapefruit	pamplemousse (*m/f*)	*pAH-ple-mooss*
grapes	raisins (*m*, *pl*)	*reh-zEH*
lemon	citron (*m*)	*seet-rOH*
mandarin orange	mandarine (*f*)	*mAH-da-reen*
melon	melon (*m*)	*mel-OH*
orange	orange (*f*)	*or-AH-zh*
peach	pêche (*f*)	*peh-sh*
peanut	arachide (*f*)	*a-rash-eed*
	cacahouète (*f*) ·	*ka-ka-weht*
pineapple	ananas (*m*)	*a-na-nass*
plum	prune (*f*)	*prewn*
prune	pruneau (*m*)	*prewn-oh*

raisin	raisin sec (*m*)	*reh-zEH sehk*
raspberry	framboise (*f*)	*frAH-bwahz*
strawberry	fraise (*f*)	*frehz*
tomato	tomate (*f*)	*tum-at*
walnut	noix (*f*)	*nwa*
watermelon	pastèque (*f*)	*pas-tehk*
	melon (*m*) d'eau	*mel-OH doh*

g. MEAL AND MENU COMPONENTS

aperitif	apéritif (*m*)	*a-pay-ree-teef*
appetizer	hors-d'œuvre variés (*m, pl*)	*or-duh-vre va-ree-yay*
broth	bouillon (*m*)	*boo-yOH*
cake	gâteau (*m*)	*gah-toh*
cutlet	côtelette (*f*)	*koht-leht*
dessert	dessert (*m*)	*day-sehr*
dumpling	boulette (*f*)	*boo-leht*
filet	filet (*m*)	*fee-leh*
fish stew	bouillabaisse (*f*)	*boo-ya-behss*
French fries	frites (*f, pl*)	*freet*
fruit tartlet	tartelette (*f*) aux fruits	*tart-leht oh frew-ee*
garlic	ail (*m*)	*a-y*
• **clove of garlic**	gousse (*f*) d'ail	*gooss da-y*
menu	carte (*f*)	*kart*
	menu (*m*)	*me-new*
of the day	du jour	*dew zh-oor*
pancake	crêpe (*f*)	*krehp*
pasta	pâtes (*f, pl*)	*paht*
pie	tarte (*f*)	*tart*
• **apple**	aux pommes	*oh pum*
• **cherry**	aux cerises	*oh sreez*
• **chocolate**	au chocolat	*oh sh-uk-ul-a*
• **peach**	aux pêches	*oh peh-sh*
quiche	quiche (*f*)	*keesh*
• **cheese**	au fromage	*oh frum-azh*
• **ham**	au jambon	*oh zh-AH-bOH*
rice with vegetables	riz (*m*) aux légumes	*ree oh layg-ewm*
roast beef	rosbif (*m*)	*rohs-beef*
salad	salade (*f*)	*sa-lad*
sandwich	sandwich (*m*)	*sAHd-weesh*
• **cheese**	au fromage	*oh frum-azh*
• **ham**	au jambon	*oh zh-AH-bOH*
sherbet	sorbet (*m*)	*sor-beh*
snails	escargots (*m, pl*)	*ehs-kar-go*

soup	soupe (f)	soop
	potage (m)	pu-tazh
• fish	au poisson	oh pwass-OH
• onion	à l'oignon	al-u-ny-OH
• thick puree	purée	pew-ray
steak	bifteck (m)	beef-tehk

h. DAIRY PRODUCTS, EGGS, AND RELATED FOODS

butter	beurre (m)	bur
cheese	fromage (m)	frum-azh
• grated	râpé	rah-pay
• melted	fondu	fOHdew
• puffed	soufflé	soo-flay

FOCUS: A Few Popular French Cheeses

brie (m)	*bree*	gruyère (m)	*grew-yehr*
camembert (m)	*kamAH-behr*	port-salut (m)	*pohr-sa-lew*
cantal (m)	*kAH-tal*	reblochon (m)	*re-blu-shOH*
chèvre (m)	*sh-ehv-re*	roquefort (m)	*ruk-for*

cream	crème (f)	krehm
• whipped	crème Chantilly	krehm shAH-tee-yee
dairy product	produit (m) laitier	prud-ew-ee leht-yay
egg	œuf (m)	uhf
• two eggs	deux œufs	duh-zuh
• fried (sunny side up)	sur le plat	sewr le pla
• hard-boiled	dur	dewr
• omelette	omelette (f)	um-leht
• cheese	au fromage	oh frum-azh
• ham	au jambon	oh zhAH-bOH
• whipped cream	omelette mousseline	um-leht moos-leen
• poached	poché	pu-shay
• soft-boiled	à la coque	a la kuk
• stuffed	œuf dur farci	uhf dewr far-see
ice cream	glace (f)	glass
	crème (f) glacée	krehm gla-say
• cone	cornet (m)	kor-neh
• chocolate	au chocolat	oh shuk-ul-a
• strawberry	aux fraises	oh frehz
• vanilla	à la vanille	a la van-ee-y
milk	lait (m)	leh
• buttermilk	babeurre (m)	ba-bur
	lait de beurre	lehd-bur
• skimmed	écrémé	ay-kray-may

pudding	crème (*f*)	*krehm*
• **caramel**	au caramel	*oh ka-ra-mehl*
• **coffee**	au café	*oh ka-fay*
• **custard**	flan	*flAH*
• **rice**	de riz	*de ree*
• **tapioca**	tapioca au lait	*ta-pee-uk-a oh leh*
yogurt	yaourt (*m*)	*ya-oor(t)*

i. GRAINS AND GRAIN PRODUCTS

barley	orge (*f*)	*or-zh*
bread	pain (*m*)	*pEH*

FOCUS: French Breads

breads	les pains (*m*)	*lay pEH*
brioche	brioche (*f*)	*bree-yush*
croissant	croissant (*m*)	*krwasAH*
double roll	petit pain (*m*) double	*ptee pEH doobl*
gingerbread	pain (*m*) d'épices	*pEH day-peess*
long loaf of bread	pain (*m*) long	*pEH lOH*
long stick of bread	baguette (*f*)	*bag-eht*
	flûte (*f*)	*flewt*
pretzel	bretzel (*m*)	*bred-zehl*
pumpernickel	pain (*m*) noir	*pEH nwar*
roll	petit pain (*m*) chapelet	*ptee pEH shap-leh*
round bread	pain (*m*) rond	*pEH rOH*
rusk (Melba toast)	biscotte (*f*)	*beess-kut*
rye and wheat bread	pain (*m*) de campagne	*pEHd-kAH-pan-y*
rye bread	pain (*m*) au seigle	*pEH oh sehgl*
small round loaf of bread	petite boule (*f*)	*pteet bool*
whole wheat bread	pain (*m*) complet	*pEH kOH-pleh*

cookie	sablé (*m*)	*sa-blay*
	petit-beurre (*m*)	*ptee-bur*
	gâteau sec (*m*)	*gah-toh sehk*
	biscuit (*m*)	*bee-skwee*
corn	maïs (*m*)	*ma-eess*
crouton	croûton (*m*)	*kroot-OH*
crumb	miette (*f*)	*mee-yet*
crust	croûte (*f*)	*kroot*
flour	farine (*f*)	*fa-reen*
oat	avoine (*f*)	*av-wan*

FOCUS: French Pastries

pastries	pâtisseries (f)	*pah-teess-ree*
cheesecake	gâteau (m) au fromage	*gah-toh oh frum-azh*
coconut macaroon	macaron (m)	*ma-karOH*
cream cake (pie)	gâteau (m) à la crème	*gah-toh a la krehm*
cream puff	chou (m) à la crème	*shoo a la krehm*
creamed horn	cornet (m) feuilleté à la crème	*korn-eh fu-y-tay a la krehm*
eclair	éclair (m)	*ay-klehr*
fruit flan	flan (m) aux fruits	*flAH oh frew-ee*
icing, iced, glazed	glacé(e) (adj)	*gla-say*
jelly roll	roulé (m)	*roo-lay*
meringue	meringue (f)	*me-rEHg*
napoleon	millefeuille (m)	*meel-fu-y*
slice of cream cake	tranche (f) de gâteau à la crème	*trAHsh de gah-toh a la krehm*
tartlet	tartelette (f)	*tart-leht*
wafer	gaufrette (f)	*go-freht*
waffle	gaufre (f)	*go-fr*

pastry	pâtisserie (f)	*pah-tee-sree*
rice	riz (m)	*ree*
wheat	blé (m)	*blay*

j. CONDIMENTS AND SPICES

basil	basilic (m)	*ba-zee-leek*
garlic	ail (m)	*a-y*
herb	herbe (f)	*ehrb*
honey	miel (m)	*mee-yehl*
horseradish sauce	sauce (f) au raifort	*sohs-oh-reh-for*
jam (*preserves*)	confiture (f)	*kOH-fee-tewr*
jelly	gelée (f)	*zh-lay*
marmalade	confiture(f) d'oranges	*kOH-fee-tewr dor-AH-zh*
	marmalade (f) d'oranges	*mahr-ma-lahd dor-AH-zh*
mint	menthe (f)	*mAHt*
oil	huile (f)	*ew-eel*
parsley	persil (m)	*pehr-see*
pepper	poivre (m)	*pwa-vre*
rosemary	romarin (m)	*rum-ar-EH*
salt	sel (m)	*sehl*

spice	épice (*f*)	*ay-peess*
sugar	sucre (*m*)	*sew-kre*
vinegar	vinaigre (*m*)	*veen-ehg-re*

k. DRINKS

alcoholic beverage	boisson (*f*) alcoolique (adj)	*bwass-OH al-ku-(u)-leek*
beer	bière (*f*)	*bee-yehr*
chamomile	camomille (*f*)	*ka-mum-eel*
coffee	café (*m*)	*kafay*
• black	noir	*nwar*
• light (half-and-half)	au lait	*oh-leh*
• with cream	café-crème	*kafay-krehm*
drink	boisson (*f*)	*bwass-OH*
juice	jus (*m*)	*zh-ew*
liqueur	liqueur (*f*)	*lee-kur*
mineral water	eau (*f*) minérale	*oh mee-nay-ral*
soft drink	gazeuse (*f*)	*gaz-uhz*
tea	thé (*m*)	*tay*
water	eau (*f*)	*oh*
wine	vin (*m*)	*vEH*

l. AT THE TABLE

bottle	bouteille (*f*)	*boo-tay*
bowl	bol (*m*)	*bul*
	assiette (*f*) creuse	*ass-ee-yeht kruhz*
cup	tasse (*f*)	*tass*
fork	fourchette (*f*)	*foorsh-eht*
glass (drinking)	verre (*m*)	*vehr*
knife	couteau (*m*)	*koo-toh*
napkin	serviette (*f*)	*sehr-vee-yeht*
plate	assiette (*f*)	*ass-ee-yeht*
saucer	soucoupe (*f*)	*soo-koop*
spoon	cuiller (*f*)	*kew-ee-yehr*
	cuillère (*f*)	*kew-ee-yehr*
table	table (*f*)	*ta-bl*
tablecloth	nappe (*f*)	*nap*
tableware	ustensiles (*m, pl*) de table	*ewst-AH-seel de ta-bl*
	couvert (*m*)	*koo-vehr*
teaspoon	cuiller (*f*) à café	*kew-ee-yehr a kafay*
toothpick	cure-dent (*m*)	*kewr-dAH*
tray (serving)	plateau (*m*) à servir	*pla-toh a sehr-veer*
wineglass	verre (*m*) à vin	*vehr a vEH*

| Cheers! | À votre santé! | *a-vutr-sAH-tay* |
| Enjoy your meal! | Bon appétit! | *bun-a-pay-tee* |

m. DINING OUT

bartender	barman (*m*)	*bar-man*
bill, check	addition (*f*)	*a-dee-syOH*
cafeteria	restaurant (*m*) self-service	*rehs-tor-AH sehlf-sehr-veess*
	cafétéria (*f*)	*ka-fay-tay-rya*
cover charge	couvert (*m*)	*koo-vehr*
fast food	fast-food (*m*)	*fahst-food*
fixed price	prix (*m*) fixe	*pree-feeks*
pizza parlor	pizzeria (*f*)	*peed-zayr-ya*
price	prix (*m*)	*pree*
reservation	réservation (*f*)	*ray-zehr-vas-yOH*
• **reserved**	réservé(e) (*adj, m, f*)	*ray-zehr-vay*
restaurant	restaurant (*m*)	*rehs-tor-AH*
• **informal restaurant**	bistro, bistrot (*m*)	*bee-stro*
server	serveur (*m*)	*sehr-vur*
	serveuse (*f*)	*sehr-vuhz*
service	service (*m*)	*sehr-veess*
snack bar	buffet (*m*)	*bew-feh*
take-out	à emporter (*v*)	*a-AH-por-tay*
tip	pourboire (*m*)	*poor-bwar*
• **tip**	donner (*v*) un pourboire	*dun-ay UH poor-bwar*

n. BUYING FOOD AND DRINK

bakery	boulangerie (*f*)	*bool-AH-zh-ree*
butcher (shop)	boucherie (*f*)	*boosh-ree*
dairy	laiterie (*f*)	*leht-ree*
delicatessen	épicerie (*f*) fine	*ay-peess-ree feen*
fish store	poissonnerie (*f*)	*pwa-sun-ree*
fruit market	marché (*m*) aux fruits	*marsh-ay oh frew-ee*
grocery store	épicerie (*f*)	*ay-peess-ree*
market	marché (*m*)	*marsh-ay*
pastry shop	pâtisserie (*f*)	*pah-tee-sree*
supermarket	supermarché (*m*)	*sew-pehr-marsh-ay*
vegetable market	marché (*m*) aux légumes	*marsh-ay oh layg-ewm*

o. FOOD AND DRINK: ACTIVITIES

add up the bill	faire (*v*) l'addition	*fehr la-dee-syOH*
be hungry	avoir (*v*) faim	*avwar fEH*
be thirsty	avoir (*v*) soif	*avwar swaf*
clear the table	desservir (*v*) la table	*day-sehr-veer la ta-ble*
	débarrasser (*v*) la table	*day-ba-rah-say la ta-bl*
cook	cuire (*v*)	*kew-eer*
	faire (*v*) la cuisine	*fehr la kew-ee-zeen*
	cuisiner (*v*)	*kew-eez-ee-nay*
cost	coûter (*v*)	*koo-tay*
cut	couper (*v*)	*koo-pay*
drink	boire (*v*)	*bwar*
eat	manger (*v*)	*mAH-zh-ay*
have a snack	prendre (*v*) un goûter	*prAH-dre UH goo-tay*
have dinner	dîner (*v*)	*dee-nay*
have lunch	déjeuner (*v*)	*day-zh-un-ay*
order	commander (*v*)	*kumAH-day*
peel	éplucher (*v*)	*ay-plew-shay*
pour	verser (*v*)	*vehr-say*
serve	servir (*v*)	*sehr-veer*
set the table	mettre (*v*) la table	*meht-re la ta-ble*
shop for food	faire (*v*) les courses	*fehr lay koorss*
slice	trancher (*v*)	*trAH-shay*
take out (food to go)	emporter (*v*)	*AH-por-tay*
toast	griller (*v*)	*gree-yay*
weigh	peser (*v*)	*pe-zay*

p. DESCRIBING FOOD AND DRINK

appetizing	appétissant(e) (*adj, m, f*)	*a-pay-tee-sAH(t)*
bad	mauvais(e) (*adj*)	*muv-eh(z)*
baked	au four	*oh-foor*
bitter	amer, amère (*adj, m, f*)	*a-mehr*
cheap	bon marché	*bOH marsh-ay*
cold	froid(e) (*adj, m, f*)	*frwa(d)*
expensive	cher, chère (*adj, m, f*)	*sh-ehr*
	coûteux(-euse) (*adj, m, f*)	*koo-tuh(-tuhz)*
fried	frit(e) (*adj*)	*free(t)*
good	bon (*adj, m*)	*bOH*
	bonne (*f*)	*bun*
hot	chaud(e) (*adj, m, f*)	*sh-oh(d)*
mild	pas très épicé(e)	*pa tray-zay-pee-say*

salty	salé(e) (*adj, m, f*)	*sal-ay*
sour	aigre (*adj*)	*eh-gr*
spicy	épicé(e) (*adj, m, f*)	*ay-pee-say*
sweet	doux (*adj, m*)	*doo*
	douce (*f*)	*dooss*
tasty	savoureux(-euse)	*sa-voor-uh(-uhz)*
	(*adj, m, f*)	
with ice	avec glaçons (*m, pl*)	*a-vehk glasOH*

25. SHOPPING AND ERRANDS

a. **GENERAL VOCABULARY**

bag (*shopping*)	sac (*m*) à provisions	*sak a pru-veez-yOH*
become	devenir (*v*)	*de-vneer*
bill (*from cash register*)	fiche (*f*) de caisse (*f*)	*feesh de kehss*
• **bill** (*invoice*)	facture (*f*)	*fak-tewr*
bring	apporter (*v*)	*a-port-ay*
buy	acheter (*v*)	*ash-tay*
cash register	caisse (*f*)	*kehss*
• **cashier**	caissier (*m*)	*kehs-yay*
	caissière (*f*)	*kehs-yehr*
change (*money*)	monnaie (*f*)	*mun-eh*
• **change**	changer (*v*)	*sh-AH-zh-ay*
cost	coût (*m*)	*koo*
	prix (*m*)	*pree*
• **cost**	coûter (*v*)	*koo-tay*
• **How much does it cost?**	Ça coûte combien?	*sa koot kOH-byEH*
• **How much does it come to?**	Ça fait combien?	*sa feh kOH-byEH*
• **How much is it?**	C'est combien?	*seh kOH-byEH*

It costs an arm and a leg! = Cela coûte les yeux de la tête (*lit.*, It costs both eyes from the head)! *sla koot lay-zyuhd la teht*

---

counter	comptoir (*m*)	*kOHtwar*
customer	client(e) (*m, f*)	*klee-yAH(t)*
department (*of a store*)	rayon (*m*)	*ray-yOH*
entrance	entrée (*f*)	*AHtray*
exchange	échanger (*v*)	*ay-shAHzh-ay*
exit	sortie (*f*)	*sor-tee*
gift	cadeau (*m*)	*ka-doh*
lack	manquer (à) (*v*)	*mAH-kay (a)*
look for something	chercher (*v*)	*sh-ehr-shay*
package	colis (*m*)	*kul-ee*
	paquet (*m*)	*pa-kay*

pay	payer (v)	pay-yay
• cash	en espèces	AH-nehs-pehss
• with a check	par chèque	par sh-ehk
• credit card	carte (f) de crédit	kart de kray-dee
price	prix (m)	pree
• discount	rabais (m)	ra-beh
	remise (f)	re-meez
• expensive	cher, chère (adj, m, f)	sh-ehr
	coûteux(-euse) (adj, m, f)	koo-tuh(-tuhz)
• fixed price	prix (m) fixe	pree-feeks
• inexpensive	bon marché	bOH marsh-ay
• price tag, label	étiquette (f)	ay-tee-keht
• reduced price	prix (m) réduit	pree ray-dew-ee
purchase	achat (m)	a-sha
	acheter (v)	ash-tay
receipt	reçu (m)	res-ew
refund	rembourser (v)	rAH-boor-say
	rendre (v)	rAH-dr
sale	vente (f)	vAHt
• for sale	à vendre (v)	a-vAH-dr
• on sale	en vente (f)	AH vAHt
• sales (lower prices)	soldes (m, pl)	sohld
• sell	vendre (v)	vAH-dre
shop	boutique (f)	boo-teek
• shop	faire (v) des achats (m, pl)	fehr day za-sha
	faire (v) des emplettes (f, pl)	fehr day zAH-pleht
	faire (v) du shopping (m)	fehr dew shup-een
shopping mall	centre (m) commercial	sAH-tre-kum-ehrs-yal
	grande surface (f)	grAHd-sewr-fahs
spend (money)	dépenser (v)	day-pAH-say
store	magasin (m)	ma-gaz-EH
• closed	fermé (adj)	fehr-may
• deparment store	grand magasin (m)	grAH ma-gaz-EH
• open	ouvert (adj)	oo-vehr
• store clerk	employé(e) (m, f)	AH-plwa-yay
• store hours	heures (f, pl)	ur
• opening hours	heures d'ouverture (f)	ur doov-ehr-tewr
• closing time	heure de fermeture (f)	ur de fehrm-tewr
• store/shop window	vitrine (f)	vee-treen
take	prendre (v)	prAH-dr
• take back (return an item)	rendre (v)	rAH-dr

b. HARDWARE

battery	pile (f)	peel
cable	câble (m)	kah-ble
clamp	serre-joint (m)	sehr-zhwEH
drill	foreuse (f)	for-uhz
	perceuse (f)	pehr-suhz
electrical	électrique (adj)	ay-lehk-treek
file	lime (f)	leem
flashlight	lampe (f) de poche	lAHp de pu-sh
fuse	fusible (m)	few-zee-bl
	plomb (m) fusible	plOH few-zee-bl
hammer	marteau (m)	mar-toh
hardware store	quincaillerie (f)	kEH-kah-y-ree
insulation	isolant (m)	ee-zul-AH
ladder	échelle (f)	ay-shell
lawnmower	tondeuse (f)	tOH-duhz
light bulb	ampoule (f)	AH-pool
• fluorescent	fluorescent(e) (adj, m, f)	flew-or-ay-sAH(t)
• neon	au néon	oh-nay-OH
masking tape	papier (m) cache	pap-yay kash
mechanical	mécanique (adj)	may-kan-eek
nail	clou (m)	kloo
outlet	prise (f)	preez
pick	pic (m)	peek
	pioche (f)	pee-yush
plane	rabot (m)	ra-boh
pliers	pince (f)	pEHss
plug	fiche (f) de prise (f) de courant	feesh de preez de koor-AH
plumbing	plomberie (f)	plOHbree
punch	poinçon (m)	pwEH-sOH
rake	râteau (m)	rah-toh
saw	scie (f)	see
screw	vis (f)	veess
screwdriver	tournevis (m)	toorn-veess
shovel	pelle (f)	pehl
tool	outil (m)	oo-tee
transformer	transformateur (m)	trAHs-form-at-ur
wire	fil (m) métallique	feel may-ta-leek
wrench, adjustable	clé (f) anglaise	klay AH-glehz

c. STATIONERY

adhesive tape	ruban (m) adhésif	rewbAH ad-ay-zeef
ballpoint pen	stylo (m) à bille	stee-lo a bee-y
briefcase	serviette (f)	sehr-vee-yeht

envelope	enveloppe (*f*)	*AHvlup*
marker	marqueur (*m*)	*mark-ur*
paper	papier (*m*)	*pap-yay*
pen	stylo (*m*)	*stee-lo*
pencil	crayon (*m*)	*kreh-yOH*
sheet (*of paper*)	feuille (*f*) de papier (*m*)	*fuh-y de pap-yay*
staple	agrafe (*f*)	*ag-raf*
stapler	agrafeuse (*f*)	*ag-ra-fuhz*
stationery store	papeterie (*f*)	*pap-tree*
string	ficelle (*f*)	*fee-sehl*
writing/note pad	bloc-notes (*m*)	*bluk-nut*

d. PHOTO/CAMERA

camera	appareil (*m*) photo	*a-pa-reh-y foto*
• **movie camera**	caméra (*f*)	*ka-may-ra*
• **video camera**	caméra (*f*) vidéo	*ka-may-ra vee-day-o*
camera shop	magasin (*m*) de photo	*ma-gaz-EH de foto*
digital camera	appareil (*m*) photo numérique	*a-pa-reh-y foto new-may-reek*
film	film (*m*)	*feelm*
• **roll of film**	rouleau (*m*) de film	*roo-lohd feelm*
	rouleau (*m*) de pellicule (*f*)	*roo-lohd pay-leek-ewl*
	pellicule (*f*)	*pay-leek-ewl*
flash	flash (*m*)	*flash*
lens	objectif (*m*)	*ub-zh-ek-teef*
light bulb	ampoule (*f*)	*AH-pool*
memory card	carte (*f*) d'extension mémoire	*kart deks-tEH-syOH may-mwar*
photo, picture	photo(graphie) (*f*)	*foto(gra-fee)*
• **clear (picture)**	photo (*f*) nette	*foto neht*
• **out of focus**	photo (*f*) floue	*foto floo*
• **color (picture)**	en couleur (*f*)	*AH koo-lur*
• **focus**	mettre (*v*) au point	*meht-r oh pwEH*
• **in black and white**	en noir et blanc	*AH nwar ay blAH*
• **take a picture**	prendre (*v*) une photo	*prAH-dr ewn foto*
• **The picture turned out badly.**	La photo a mal réussi.	*la foto a mal ray-ew-see*
• **The picture turned out well.**	La photo a bien réussi.	*la foto a byEH ray-ew-see*

screen	écran (*m*)	*ay-krAH*
slide	diapositive (*f*)	*dya-po-zee-teev*
zoom	zoom (*m*)	*zoom*

e. TOBACCO

card	carte (*f*)	*kart*
cigar	cigare (*m*)	*see-gar*
cigarette	cigarette (*f*)	*see-gar-eht*
lighter	briquet (*m*)	*breek-eh*
matches	allumettes (*f*)	*a-lew-meht*
pipe	pipe (*f*)	*peep*
smoke shop	bureau (*m*) de tabac	*bew-rohd ta-ba*
tobacco	tabac (*m*)	*ta-ba*
tobacconist	buraliste (*m, f*)	*bewr-al-eest*

f. COSMETICS/TOILETRIES

bath oil	huile (*f*) de bain	*ew-eeld bEH*
blade	lame (*f*)	*lam*
brush	brosse (*f*)	*bruss*
cologne	eau (*f*) de cologne	*ohd ku-lu-ny*
comb	peigne (*m*)	*peh-ny*
cosmetics/perfume shop	parfumerie (*f*)	*par-fewm-ree*
cream	crème (*f*)	*krehm*
curler	bigoudi (*m*)	*bee-goo-dee*
deodorant	déodorant (*m*)	*day-ud-u-rAH*
electric razor	rasoir (*m*) électrique	*rahz-war ay-lehk-treek*
face powder	poudre (*f*)	*pood-re*
hair dryer	séchoir (*m*) à cheveux	*say-sh-war a sh-vuh*
lipstick	rouge (*m*) à lèvres	*roo-zh a leh-vre*
lotion	lotion (*f*)	*loh-syOH*
make-up	maquillage (*m*)	*ma-kee-ya-zh*
mascara	mascara (*m*)	*mah-ska-ra*
nail polish	vernis (*m*) à ongles	*vehr-nee a OHgle*
perfume	parfum (*m*)	*parfUH*
razor	rasoir (*m*)	*rahz-war*
shampoo	shampooing (*m*)	*sh-AH-pwEH*
shaving cream	crème (*f*) à raser	*krehm a rah-zay*
	mousse (*f*) à raser	*mooss a rah-zay*
soap	savon (*m*)	*savOH*
talcum powder	talc (*m*)	*tal-k*

g. LAUNDRY

button	bouton (m)	bootOH
clean	propre (adj)	prup-r
clothes	vêtements (m, pl)	veht-mAH
• clothes basket	panier (m) à linge	pan-yay a lEHzh
• clothespin	pince (f) à linge	pEHss a lEHzh
dirty	sale (adj)	sal
dry cleaning	nettoyage (m) à sec	neht-wa-ya-zh a sehk
hole	trou (m)	troo
iron	fer (m) à repasser	fehr a re-pah-say
• iron	repasser (v)	re-pah-say
laundry	linge (m)	lEHzh
	lessive (f)	leh-seev
mend	raccommoder (v)	ra-kum-ud-ay
pocket	poche (f)	pu-sh
sew	coudre (v)	koo-dr
sleeve	manche (f)	mAHsh
soap powder	lessive (f) en poudre	leh-seev AH poo-dr
spot, stain	tache (f)	tash
starch	amidon (m)	a-meed-OH
stitch	point (m)	pwEH
wash	laver (v)	la-vay
• washable	lavable (adj)	la-va-bl
zipper	fermeture (f) à glissière	fehrm-tewr a gleess-yehr
	fermeture (f) éclair	fehrm-tewr ay-klehr

h. PHARMACY/DRUGSTORE

adhesive strip	sparadrap (m)	spa-ra-dra
antibiotic	antibiotique (m)	AH-tee-byu-teek
antidepressant	antidépresseur (m)	AH-tee-day-press-ur
antihistamine	antihistaminique (m)	AH-tee-heess-ta-mee-neek
aspirin	aspirine (f)	as-pee-reen
bandage	pansement (m)	pAHs-mAH
cortisone	cortisone (f)	kor-tee-zun
drugstore/pharmacy	pharmacie (f)	farma-see
injection	injection (f)	EH-zh-ehks-yOH
	piqûre (f)	peek-ewr
insulin	insuline (f)	EH-sewl-een
medicine	médicament (m)	may-deek-am-AH
ointment	pommade (f)	pum-ad
penicillin	pénicilline (f)	pay-nee-see-leen
pharmaceutical drug	médicament (m)	may-deek-am-AH
pharmacist	pharmacien (m)	farm-ass-yEH
	pharmacienne (f)	farm-ass-yehn

pill	pilule (*f*)	*peel-ewl*
powder	poudre (*f*)	*poo-dre*
prescription	ordonnance (*f*)	*or-dun-AH-ss*
shot	piqûre (*f*)	*peek-ewr*
sodium bicarbonate	bicarbonate (*m*) de soude (*f*)	*bee-kar-bun-at de sood*
sodium citrate	citrate (*m*) de soude (*f*)	*see-trat de sood*
syrup	sirop (*m*)	*see-roh*
tablet	comprimé (*m*)	*kOHpree-may*
thermometer	thermomètre (*m*)	*tehr-mum-eht-re*
tissue	mouchoir (*m*) de papier (*m*)	*moosh-war de pap-yay*
toothbrush	brosse (*f*) à dents	*bruss a dAH*
toothpaste	dentifrice (*m*)	*dAHtee-freess*
vaccine	vaccin (*m*)	*vahk-sEH*
vitamin	vitamine (*f*)	*vee-ta-meen*

i. JEWELRY

artificial	artificiel(le) (*adj, m, f*)	*ar-tee-fee-sy-ehl*
bracelet	bracelet (*m*)	*bras-leh*
brooch	broche (*f*)	*brush*
carat	carat (*m*)	*ka-ra*
chain	chaîne (*f*)	*sh-ehn*
diamond	diamant (*m*)	*dy-am-AH*
earring	boucle (*f*) d'oreille (*f*)	*book-l dor-ay*
emerald	émeraude (*f*)	*ehm-rohd*
false	faux (*adj, m*)	*foh*
	fausse (*f*)	*foh-ss*
fix, repair	ajuster (*v*)	*a-zh-ew-stay*
	réparer (*v*)	*ray-pa-ray*
gold	or (*m*)	*or*
jewel	bijou (*m*)	*bee-zh-oo*
jewelry store	bijouterie (*f*)	*bee-zh-oo-tree*
	joaillerie (*f*)	*zh-u-ah-y-ree*
necklace	collier (*m*)	*kul-yay*
opal	opale (*f*)	*up-al*
pearl	perle (*f*)	*pehrl*
precious	précieux (*adj, m*)	*pray-sy-uh*
	précieuse (*f*)	*pray-sy-uhz*
ring	bague (*f*)	*bag*
	anneau (*m*)	*an-oh*
ruby	rubis (*m*)	*rew-bee*
sapphire	saphir (*m*)	*sa-feer*
silver	argent (*m*)	*ar-zh-AH*
topaz	topaze (*f*)	*tup-ahz*

watch	montre (f)	mOH-tr
• alarm clock	réveille-matin (m)	ray-veh-y-matEH
• clock	horloge (f)	or-lu-zh
• dial	cadran (m)	kad-rAH
• hand	aiguille (f)	ehg-ew-ee-y
• spring	ressort (m)	re-sor
• watchband	bracelet (m) d'une montre	bra-sleh dewn mOHtr
• wind	remonter (v)	re-mOH-tay
• wristwatch	bracelet-montre (m)	bra-sleh-mOHtr
	montre-bracelet (f)	mOHtr bra-sleh

j. MUSIC

cassette	cassette (f)	kaseht
CD	CD (m)	say-day
classical music	musique (f) classique	mew-zeek kla-seek
compact disc	disque compact (m)	deesk-kOH-pakt
composer	compositeur (m)	kOH-po-zeet-ur
	compositrice (f)	kOH-po-zeet-reess
dance music	musique (f) de danse (f)	mew-zeek de dAHs
download	télécharger (v)	tay-lay-shahr-zhay
jazz	jazz (m)	dzh-ahz
music	musique (f)	mew-zeek
rap	rap (m)	rahp
record	disque (m)	deesk
rock music	musique (f) rock	mew-zeek ruk
singer	chanteur (m)	shAHtur
	chanteuse (f)	shAHtuhz
song	chanson (f)	shAH-sOH

k. CLOTHING

bathing suit	maillot (m) de bain (m)	ma-yod bEH
belt	ceinture (f)	sEH-tewr
blouse	chemisier (m)	sh-em-eez-yay
bra	soutien-gorge (m)	soot-y-EH gohr-zh
cardigan	cardigan (m)	kahr-dee-gAH
clothing	habillement (m)	ab-ee-y-mAH
	vêtements (m, pl)	veht-mAH
coat	manteau (m)	mAH-toh
• fur coat	manteau (m) de fourrure	mAH-toh de foor-ewr
dress	robe (f)	rub
dressing room	cabine (f) d'essayage	ka-been dess-ay-azh
fashion	mode (f)	mud
glove	gant (m)	gAH

handkerchief	mouchoir (*m*)	*moosh-war*
hat	chapeau (*m*)	*sha-poh*
jacket	veste (*f*)	*vehst*
	veston (*m*)	*vehstOH*
men's shop/clothing	magasin (*m*) d'habillement masculin	*ma-gaz-EH dab-ee-y-mAH mas-kewl-EH*
miniskirt	minijupe (*f*)	*mee-nee-zh-ewp*
pajamas	pyjama (*m*)	*pee-zha-ma*
pants	pantalon (*m*)	*pAH-tal-OH*
raincoat	imperméable (*m*)	*EH-pehr-may-abl*
scarf	écharpe (*f*)	*ay-sharp*
shirt	chemise (*f*)	*shmeez*
size, fit	taille (*f*)	*ta-y*
	mesure (*f*)	*me-zewr*
skirt	jupe (*f*)	*zh-ewp*
slip	jupon (*m*)	*zh-ewp-OH*
	fond (*m*) de robe	*fOH de rub*
	combinaison (*f*)	*kOH-been-ehzOH*
smock	blouse (*f*)	*blooz*
suit	costume (*m*)	*kus-tewm*
	complet (*m*)	*kOHpleh*
suit jacket	veste (*f*)	*vehst*
	veston (*m*)	*vehstOH*
sweater	tricot (*m*)	*tree-koh*
	sweater (*m*)	*sweht-ehr*
	pull-over (*m*)	*pewl-uv-ehr*
tailored suit (*woman's*)	tailleur (*m*)	*ta-y-ur*
T-shirt	T-shirt (*m*)	*tee-sh-ehrt*
tie	cravate (*f*)	*kra-vat*
underpants, panties	slip (*m*)	*sleep*
underwear	sous-vêtements (*m, pl*)	*soo-veht-mAH*
vest	gilet (*m*)	*zh-ee-leh*
windbreaker	blouson (*m*)	*blooz-OH*
women's shop/clothing	magasin (*m*) d'habillement féminin	*ma-gaz-EH dab-ee-y-mAH fay-meen-EH*

l. DESCRIBING CLOTHING

For colors, see Section 7.

beautiful	beau (*m*)	*boh*
	bel (*m, s*) (before a vowel or silent *h*)	*behl*
	belle (*f, s, pl*)	*behl*

big	grand	*grAH*
	grande *(f)*	*grAHd*
cotton	coton *(m)*	*kutOH*
elegant	élégant(e)	*ay-lay-gAH(t)*
fabric	tissu *(m)*	*teess-ew*
in the latest	à-la-mode	*a-la-mud*
style/fashion	au dernier cri	*oh dehrn-yay kree*
leather	cuir *(m)*	*kew-eer*
loose	vague *(adj)*	*vag*
	non-ajusté(e) *(adj, m, f)*	*nOH a-zh-ew-stay*
	ample *(adj)*	*AHpl*
nylon	nylon *(m)*	*neelOH*
polyester	polyester *(m)*	*pu-lee-ehs-tehr*
silk	en soie *(f)*	*AHswa*
small	petit(e) *(adj, m, f)*	*ptee(t)*
striped	rayé(e) *(adj, m, f)*	*ray-yay*
This looks bad on me.	Ceci ne me va pas bien.	*se-see nem va pah byEH*
This looks nice on me.	Ceci me va bien.	*se-see me va byEH*
tight	serré(e) *(adj, m, f)*	*sehr-ay*
ugly	laid(e) *(adj, m, f)*	*leh(d)*
wool	en laine *(f)*	*AH lehn*

m. CLOTHING: ACTIVITIES

get dressed	s'habiller *(v)*	*sa-bee-yay*
lengthen	faire *(v)* allonger *(v)*	*fehr al-OH-zh-ay*
let out	faire *(v)* élargir *(v)*	*fehr ay-lar-zh-eer*
put on	(se) mettre *(v)*	*(se) meht-r*
shorten	raccourcir *(v)*	*ra-koor-seer*
shrink	rétrécir *(v)*	*ray-tray-seer*
take in	reprendre *(v)*	*re-prAH-dr*
take off	enlever *(v)*	*AH-lvay*
try on	essayer *(v)*	*ay-say-yay*
undress	se déshabiller *(v)*	*se day-za-bee-yay*
wear	porter *(v)*	*por-tay*

n. SHOES

boot	botte *(f)*	*but*
pair	paire *(f)*	*pehr*
shoe	chaussure *(f)*	*sh-oh-sewr*
shoe horn	chausse-pied *(m)*	*sh-ohss-pyay*
shoe repair store	cordonnerie *(f)*	*kor-dun-ree*
shoe store	magasin *(m)* de chaussures *(f)*	*ma-gaz-EH de sh-oh-sewr*

shoelace	lacet (*m*)	*la-seh*
size (*of shoe*)	pointure (*f*)	*pwEH-tewr*
slipper	pantoufle (*f*)	*pAH-too-fle*
	chausson (*m*)	*sh-oh-sOH*
sock	chaussette (*f*)	*sh-oh-seht*
stocking	bas (*m*)	*bah*

o. BOOKS

book	livre (*m*)	*lee-vr*
best-seller	best-seller (*m*)	*behst-sehl-ehr*
bookstore	librairie (*f*)	*lee-breh-ree*
book of adventure	livre (*m*) d'aventure (*f*)	*lee-vr dav-AH-tewr*
comic book	magazine (*m*) de bandes dessinées	*ma-gaz-een de bAHd day-seen-ay*
cookbook	livre (*m*) de cuisine	*lee-vr de kew-ee-zeen*
dictionary	dictionnaire (*m*)	*deek-see-yun-ehr*
encyclopedia	encyclopédie (*f*)	*AH-see-klup-ay-dee*
guidebook	guide (*m*)	*geed*
magazine	magazine (*m*)	*ma-gaz-een*
	revue (*f*)	*re-vew*
mystery novel	roman (*m*) policier	*rumAH pul-eess-yay*
newspaper	journal (*m*)	*zh-oor-nal*
novel	roman (*m*)	*rumAH*
poetry	poésie (*f*)	*pu-ay-zee*
reference book	ouvrage (*m*) de référence (*f*)	*oov-ra-zh de ray-fayr-AH-s*
romance book	livre (*m*) d'amour	*lee-vr dahm-oor*
science-fiction book	livre (*m*) de science-fiction	*lee-vr de see-AH-s-feeks-yOH*
technical book	livre (*m*) de technologie (*f*)	*lee-vr de tehk-nu-lu-zh-ee*
textbook	livre (*m*) de classe (*f*)	*lee-vr de klahs*
	livre (*m*) d'étude (*f*)	*lee-vr day-tewd*

26. BANKING AND COMMERCE

> For numerical concepts, see Section 1.

account	compte (*m*)	*kOHt*
• **ATM**	guichet (*m*) automatique	*kee-sheh u-tum-a-teek*
• **close an account**	arrêter (*v*) un compte	*ar-eh-tay UH kOHt*
	clore (*v*) un compte	*klor UH kOHt*

• debit card	carte (*f*) de retrait	*kart de re-treh*
• open an account	ouvrir (*v*) un compte	*oov-reer UH kOHt*
bank	banque (*f*)	*bAHk*
• head office	siège (*m*) social	*see-yeh-zh suss-yahl*
• work in a bank	travailler (*v*) dans une banque	*tra-va-yay dAH zewn bAHk*
bank book	carnet (*m*) de banque	*kar-neh de bAHk*
bank draft	traite (*f*) bancaire	*treht bAH-kehr*
bank rate	taux (*m*) bancaire	*toh bAH-kehr*
• fixed	fixe (*adj*)	*feeks*
• variable	variable (*adj*)	*va-ree-abl*
bill, banknote	billet (*m*) de banque	*bee-yeh de bAHk*
• dollar	dollar (*m*)	*dul-ar*
• large bill	gros billet (*m*)	*groh bee-yeh*
• small bill	petit billet (*m*)	*ptee bee-yeh*
bond	obligation (*f*)	*ub-lee-gas-yOH*
budget	budget (*m*)	*bewd-zh-eh*
cash	en espèces	*AH-nehs-pehs*
• cash a check	toucher (*v*) un chèque	*too-shay UH sh-ehk*
• cash register	caisse (*f*)	*kehss*
cashier, teller	caissier (*m*)	*kehs-yay*
	caissière (*f*)	*kehs-yehr*
check	chèque (*m*)	*sh-ehk*
• checkbook	carnet (*m*) de chèques	*kar-neh de sh-ehk*
cost of living	coût (*m*) de la vie	*koo de la vee*
credit	crédit (*m*)	*kray-dee*
• credit card	carte (*f*) de crédit	*kart de kray-dee*
currency	billets (*m*) de banque	*bee-yeh de bAHk*
	monnaie (*f*) fiduciaire	*mun-eh fee-dew-see-yehr*
current account	compte (*m*) courant	*kOHt koor-AH*
customer	client(e) (*m*, *f*)	*klee-yAH(t)*
debit	débit (*m*)	*day-bee*
debt	dette (*f*)	*deht*
deposit	versement (*m*)	*vehrs-mAH*
• deposit	verser (*v*) une somme au compte	*vehr-say ewn sum oh kOHt*
deposit slip	fiche (*f*) de versement	*feesh de vehrs-mAH*
employee	employé(e) (*m*, *f*)	*AH-plwa-yay*
endorse	endosser (*v*)	*AH-doh-say*
• endorsement	endossement (*m*)	*AH-dohs-mAH*
	endos (*m*)	*AH-doh*
euro	euro (*m*)	*uh-ro*
Eurocurrency	eurodevise (*f*)	*uh-rod-veez*
Eurodollar	eurodollar (*m*)	*uh-ro-du-lar*

exchange	change (*m*)	*shAH-zh*
• exchange	changer (*v*)	*shAH-zh-ay*
• exchange rate	taux (*m*) du change	*toh dew shAH-zh*
expiry (date)	échéance (*f*)	*ay-shay-AH-s*
income	revenu (*m*)	*rev-new*
insurance	assurance (*f*)	*as-ew-rAHs*
interest	intérêt (*m*)	*EH-tay-reh*
• interest rate	taux (*m*) d'intérêt	*toh dEH-tay-reh*
invest	investir (*v*)	*EH-vehs-teer*
• investment	investissement (*m*)	*EH-vehs-tees-mAH*
line	queue (*f*)	*kuh*
• line up	faire (*v*) la queue	*fehr la kuh*
loan	prêt (*m*)	*preh*
• get a loan	obtenir (*v*) un prêt	*up-te-neer UH preh*
loose change	monnaie (*f*)	*mun-eh*
manager	directeur(-trice) (*m, f*)	*dee-rehk-tur(-trice)*
money	argent (*m*)	*ar-zh-AH*
money order	mandat (*m*) de paiement (*m*)	*mAHda de peh-mAH*
mortgage	hypothèque (*f*)	*ee-pu-tehk*
pay	payer (*v*)	*pay-yay*
• pay off	acquitter (*v*)	*a-kee-tay*
• payment	paiement (*m*)	*peh-mAH*
postdate	postdater (*v*)	*pust-da-tay*
receipt	reçu (*m*)	*res-ew*
	acquit (*m*)	*a-kee*
safe	coffre-fort (*m*)	*kuf-re-for*
• safe deposit box	coffre (*m*) (de sécurité)	*kuf-re (de say-kew-ree-tay)*
salary	salaire (*m*)	*sal-ehr*
save	économiser (*v*)	*ay-kun-um-ee-zay*
	épargner (*v*)	*ay-parn-yay*
• savings	épargne (*f*)	*ay-parn-y*
sign	signer (*v*)	*seen-yay*
• signature	signature (*f*)	*seen-ya-tewr*
stock, share	action (*f*)	*aks-yOH*
• stock market/exchange	Bourse (*f*)	*boorss*
teller's window	guichet (*m*)	*geesh-eh*
traveler's check	chèque (*m*) de voyage	*sh-ehk de vwa-ya-zh*
withdraw	prélever (*v*)	*prayl-vay*
• withdrawal	prélèvement (*m*)	*pray-lehv-mAH*
• withdrawal slip	fiche (*f*) de prélèvement (*m*)	*feesh de pray-lehv-mAH*

27. GAMES AND HOBBIES

a. **GAMES AND HOBBIES**

bingo	bingo (*m*)	*been-go*
• **bingo card**	fiche (*f*)	*feesh*
billiards, to play	jouer (*v*) au billard (*m*)	*zh-oo-ay oh bee-yar*
• **billiard ball**	bille (*f*)	*bee-y*
• **billiard table**	table (*f*) de billard (*m*)	*ta-bl de bee-yar*
• **cue**	queue (*f*) de billard (*m*)	*kuh de bee-yar*
• **cushion**	bande (*f*)	*bAHd*
• **pocket**	poche (*f*)	*puhsh*
checkers (to play)	jouer (*v*) aux dames	*zh-oo-ay oh dahm*
• **checkerboard**	damier (*m*)	*dahm-yay*
• **checker piece**	pion (*m*)	*pee-yOH*
chess (to play)	jouer (*v*) aux échecs	*zh-oo-ay oh zay-sh-ehk*
• **bishop**	fou (*m*)	*foo*
• **checkmate**	échec et mat (*m*)	*ay-shek-ay-maht*
• **chessboard**	échiquier (*m*)	*ay-sheek-yay*
• **king**	roi (*m*)	*rwa*
• **knight**	cavalier (*m*)	*ka-val-yay*
• **pawn**	pion (*m*)	*pee-yOH*
• **queen**	dame (*f*)	*dahm*
• **rook**	tour (*f*)	*toor*
coin	monnaie (*f*)	*mun-eh*
• **coin collecting**	numismatique (*f*)	*new-mees-ma-teek*
dice, to play	jouer (*v*) aux dés (*m, pl*)	*zh-oo-ay oh day*
game	jeu (*m*)	*zh-uh*
	partie (*f*)	*par-tee*
hobby	passe-temps (*m*)	*pahs-tAH*
play cards	jouer (*v*) aux cartes (*f, pl*)	*zh-oo-ay oh kart*
• **ace**	as (*m*)	*ahss*
• **ace of spades**	as (*m*) de pique (*f*)	*ahss de peek*
• **clubs**	trèfle (*m*)	*treh-fl*
• **diamonds**	carreau (*m*)	*kar-oh*
• **hearts**	cœur (*m*)	*kur*
• **joker**	joker (*m*)	*zh-uk-ur*
• **king**	roi (*m*)	*rwa*
• **queen**	reine (*f*)	*rehn*
	dame (*f*)	*dahm*
• **spades**	pique (*f*)	*peek*
• **tarot**	tarot (*m*)	*tar-oh*
stamp (postage)	timbre-poste (*m*)	*tEHbr-pust*
• **stamp collecting**	collection (*f*) de timbres	*kul-ehks-yOH de tEHbr*
	philatélie (*f*)	*feel-ah-tay-lee*

b. SPORTS, PHYSICAL FITNESS, AND MARTIAL ARTS

aikido	aïkido (m)	ah-y-keedoh
amateur	amateur (m)	a-ma-tur
athlete	athlète (m/f)	at-leht
ball	balle (f)	bal
• catch	attraper (v)	a-trap-ay
• hit	battre (v)	bat-r
• kick	donner (v) un coup de pied	dun-ay UH kood pee-yay
• pass	passer (v)	pah-say
• throw	lancer (v)	lAH-say
baseball	base-ball (m)	behz-bol
• ball	balle (f)	bal
• base	base (f)	bahz
	but (m)	bew(t)
• bat	batte (f)	bat
• batter	batteur (m)	ba-tur
• catcher's mask	masque (m) du receveur	mask dew re-se-vur
• foul line	ligne (f) de jeu	lee-ny de juh
• glove	gant (m)	gAH
• home plate	plaque (f)	plahk
• out	retrait (m)	ruh-treh
• pitcher	lanceur (m)	lAH-sur
• run	point (m)	pwEH
basketball	basket(-ball) (m)	bas-keht(-bol)
• ball	ballon (m) de basket	ba-lOH de bas-keht
• basket	panier (m)	pan-yay
bicycle racing	courses (f) cyclistes	koorss see-kleest
body building	culturisme (m)	kewl-tewr-ees-me
• weight lifting	haltérophilie (f)	al-tay-ru-feel-ee
bowling	bowling (m)	bul-een-y
• bowl	jouer (v) au bowling (m)	zh-oo-ay oh bul-een-y
• bowling alley	piste (f)	peest
• bowling ball	boule (f)	bool
• bowling pin	quille (f)	kee-y
boxing	boxe (f)	buks
• boxing glove	gant (m) de boxe	gAH de buks
• boxing ring	ring (m)	ree-ny
• ropes	cordes (f, pl)	kord
car racing	course (f) automobile	koorss oh-tum-u-beel
coach	entraîneur (m/f)	AH-trehn-ur
competition	concours (m)	kOHkoor
fencing	escrime (f)	ehs-kreem
• fence	faire (v) de l'escrime	fehr de lehs-kreem
• French foil	fleuret (m) français	flur-eh frAHseh

• **mask**	masque (*m*)	*mask*
• **On guard!**	En garde! (*f*)	*AH gard*
• **saber**	sabre (*m*) d'escrime (*f*)	*sah-br dehs-kreem*
• **Touché!**	Touché!	*too-shay*
field	champ (*m*)	*shAH*
football	football (*m*) américain	*foot-bohl a-may-reek-EH*
game, match	jeu (*m*)	*zh-uh*
	match (*m*)	*mat-sh*
	partie (*f*)	*par-tee*
goal	but (*m*)	*bew(t)*
• **goalie**	gardien(-ienne) (*m, f*) de but	*gard-yEH(-yehn) de bew(t)*
golf (to play)	jouer (*v*) au golf (*m*)	*zh-oo-ay oh gulf*
gymnasium	gymnase (*m*)	*zh-eem-nahz*
• **work out**	faire (*v*) de l'exercice	*fehr de lehg-zehr-seess*
gymnastics	gymnastique (*f*)	*zh-eem-nas-teek*
helmet	casque (*m*)	*kask*
hockey (ice)	hockey (*m*) sur glace	*uk-eh sewr glahss*
• **hockey player**	joueur(-euse) (*m, f*) de hockey	*zh-oo-ur(-uhz) de uk-eh*
• **hockey stick**	crosse (*f*)	*kruss*
	stick (*m*)	*steek*
• **puck**	palet (*m*)	*pal-eh*
	puck (*m*)	*puk*
• **rink**	patinoire (*f*)	*pa-tee-nwar*
• **skate**	patin (*m*) à glace	*patEH a glahss*
	patiner (*v*)	*pa-tee-nay*
jog	faire (*v*) du jogging (*m*)	*fehr dew dzh-ug-een*
• **jogging**	jogging (*m*)	*dzhug-een*
judo	judo (*m*)	*zh-ew-doh*
karate	karaté (*m*)	*ka-ra-tay*
mountain climbing	alpinisme (*m*)	*alp-een-ees-me*
• **knapsack**	sac (*m*) à dos (*m*)	*sak a doh*
• **mountain boot**	chaussure(*f*) d'escalade (*f*)	*sho-sewr dehs-ka-lad*
• **rope**	corde (*f*) d'alpinisme (*m*)	*kord dalp-een-ees-me*
• **snow goggles**	lunettes (*f, pl*) de glacier (*m*)	*lew-neht de glas-yay*
net	but (*m*)	*bew(t)*
penalty	pénalité (*f*)	*pay-nal-ee-tay*
play	jeu (*m*)	*zh-uh*
• **player**	joueur (*m*)	*zh-oo-ur*
	joueuse (*f*)	*zh-oo-uhz*
point	marque (*f*)	*mark*

professional	professionel(-elle) (m, f)	pruf-ehs-ee-yun-ehl
race	course (f)	koorss
• **horse racing**	course (f) au galop	koorss oh gal-oh
	courses (f) de chevaux	koorss de shvoh
referee	arbitre (m/f)	ar-beet-r
run	courir (v)	koo-reer
score	marque (f)	mark
• **draw, tie**	match (m) nul	mat-sh newl
• **draw**	terminer (v) à match nul	tehr-mee-nay a mat-sh newl
	terminer (v) à égalité	tehr-mee-nay a ay-gal-ee-tay
• **lose**	perdre (v)	pehr-dr
• **loss**	perte (f)	pehrt
• **win**	gain (m)	gEH
	gagner (v)	gan-yay
skate	patiner (v)	pa-teen-ay
• **to ice skate**	patiner (v) sur glace	pa-teen-ay sewr glahss
• **to roller skate**	patiner (v) à roulettes	pa-teen-ay a roo-leht
skateboard	skateboard (m)	skayt-bohrd
	planche (f) à roulettes	plAHsh a roo-let
ski	skier (v)	skee-yay
	faire (v) du ski	fehr dew skee
• **cross-country skiing**	ski (m) de fond	skeed-fOH
• **downhill skiing**	ski (m) alpin	skee-alpEH
• **ski**	ski (m)	skee
• **skier**	skieur (m)	skee-ur
	skieuse (f)	skee-uhz
• **water skiing**	ski (m) nautique	skee noh-teek
snowboarding	surf (m) des neiges	suhrf day nezh
soccer	foot (m)	foot
• **play soccer**	jouer (v) au foot	zh-oo-ay oh foot
• **soccer ball**	ballon (m)	balOH
sport	sport (m)	spor
• **practice a sport**	faire (v) du sport (m)	fehr dew spor
• **sports fan**	fan (m)	fahn
	fanatique (m/f) du sport	fan-a-teek dew spor
	enthousiaste (m/f) du sport	AH-too-zee-ast dew spor
stadium	stade (m)	stad
swim	nager (v)	na-zh-ay
• **swimming**	natation (f)	na-tas-yOH
• **swimming pool**	piscine (f)	pee-seen

team	équipe (*f*)	*ay-keep*
tennis (*to play*)	jouer (*v*) au tennis	*zh-oo-ay oh tehn-eess*
• racket	raquette (*f*)	*ra-reht*
ticket	billet (*m*)	*bee-yeh*
	ticket (*m*)	*teek-eh*
track	piste (*f*)	*peest*
volleyball	volley-ball (*m*)	*vul-eh-bol*
water polo	water-polo (*m*)	*wa-tehr-pu-loh*
wrestling	lutte (*f*)	*lewt*

28. THE ARTS

a. CINEMA

actor	acteur (*m*)	*ak-tur*
actress	actrice (*f*)	*ak-treess*
aisle	allée (*f*)	*alay*
box office	guichet (*m*)	*geesh-eh*
cinema	cinéma (*m*)	*see-nay-ma*
	ciné (*m*)	*see-nay*
lobby	foyer (*m*)	*fwa-yay*
movie, film	film (*m*)	*feelm*
• make a movie	tourner (*v*) un film	*toor-nay UH feelm*
• premiere showing	première (*f*)	*prem-yehr re-prayz-*
	représentation (*f*)	*AH-tas-yOH*
• three-D goggles	lunettes (*f, pl*) 3D	*lew-neht trwah-day*
• three-D movie	film (*m*) en relief	*feelm AH ruh-lyef*
movie director	réalisateur (*m*)	*ray-al-eez-at-ur*
	metteur (*m*) en	*meht-ur AH sehn*
	scène (*f*)	
movies	cinéma (*m*)	*see-nay-ma*
row	rang (*m*)	*rAH*
screen	écran (*m*)	*ay-krAH*
seat	place (*f*)	*plass*
	siège (*f*)	*see-yeh-zh*
soundtrack	bande (*f*) sonore	*bAHd sun-or*

b. ART/SCULPTURE/ARCHITECTURE

architecture	architecture (*f*)	*arsh-ee-tehk-tewr*
• blueprint	bleu (*m*)	*bluh*
art	art (*m*)	*ar*
artist	artiste (*m/f*)	*ar-teest*
brush	pinceau (*m*)	*pEHsoh*
easel, tripod	chevalet (*m*)	*sh-val-eh*
exhibition	exposition (*f*)	*ehks-poh-zees-yOH*
fresco painting	fresque (*f*)	*frehsk*
masterpiece	chef (*m*) d'œuvre (*f*)	*shay duv-re*

paint	peindre (*v*)	*pEH-dr*
• **painter**	peintre (*m/f*)	*pEH-tr*
	artiste-peintre (*m/f*)	*ar-teest pEH-tr*
• **painting**	peinture (*f*)	*pEH-tewr*
	tableau (*m*)	*tab-loh*
palette	palette (*f*)	*pal-eht*
pastel	pastel (*m*)	*pas-tehl*
portrait	portrait (*m*)	*port-reh*
sculpt	sculpter (*v*)	*skewl-tay*
• **sculptor**	sculpteur (*m*)	*skewl-tur*
• **sculptress**	femme sculpteur (*f*)	*fahm skewl-tur*
• **sculpture**	sculpture (*f*)	*skewl-tewr*
watercolor	aquarelle (*f*)	*ak-wa-rehl*

c. MUSIC/DANCE

accordion	accordéon (*m*)	*ak-or-day-OH*
ballet	ballet (*m*)	*bal-eh*
brass instruments	cuivres (*m, pl*)	*kew-eevre*
• **horn**	cor (*m*)	*kor*
• **trombone**	trombone (*m*)	*trOH-bun*
• **trumpet**	trompette (*f*)	*trOH-peht*
• **tuba**	tuba (*m*)	*tew-ba*
classical music	musique (*f*) classique	*mew-zeek kla-seek*
composer	compositeur (*m*)	*kOH-po-zee-tur*
	compositrice (*f*)	*kOH-po-zee-treess*
• **composition**	composition (*f*)	*kOH-po-zees-yOH*
concert	concert (*m*)	*kOH-sehr*
dance	bal (*m*)	*bal*
• **dance**	danser (*v*)	*dAH-say*
• **dancer**	danseur (*m*)	*dAH-sur*
	danseuse (*f*)	*dAH-suhz*
folk music	musique (*f*) folklorique	*mew-zeek fulk-lur-eek*
guitar	guitare (*f*)	*geet-ar*
• **guitarist**	guitariste (*m, f*)	*geet-ar-eest*
harmony	harmonie (*f*)	*arm-un-ee*
harp	harpe (*f*)	*arp*
hip-hop	hip-hop (*m*)	*eep-ohp*
instrument	instrument (*m*)	*EH-strew-mAH*
• **play an instrument**	jouer (*v*) de (du, de l', de la)	*zh-oo-ay de (dew, del, de la)*
jazz	jazz (*m*)	*dzh-ahz*
keyboard instruments	instruments (*m/pl*) à clavier (*m*)	*EH-strew-mAH a klav-yay*
• **grand piano**	piano (*m*) à queue (*f*)	*pee-yan-oh a kuh*
• **harpsichord**	clavecin (*m*)	*klav-sEH*

• organ	orgue (m)	org
• pianist	pianiste (m, f)	pee-yan-eest
• piano	piano (m)	pee-yan-oh
• synthesizer	synthétiseur (m)	sEH-tay-teez-ur
• upright piano	piano (m) droit	pee-yan-oh drwa
light music	musique (f) légère	mew-zeek lay-zh-ehr
mandolin	mandoline (f)	mAH-dul-een
music	musique (f)	mew-zeek
• musician	musicien (m)	mew-zees-yEH
	musicienne (f)	mew-zees-yehn
note	note (f)	nut
opera	opéra (m)	up-ay-ra
orchestra	orchestre (m)	or-kehs-tre
orchestra conductor	chef (m) d'orchestre (m)	sh-ehf dor-kehs-tre
percussion	instruments (m, pl)	EH-strew-mAH a pehr-
instruments	à percussion (f)	kewss-yOH
• bass drum	grosse caisse (f)	groh-ss kehss
• cymbals	cymbales (f, pl)	sEH-bal
• drum	tambour (m)	tAH-boor
• set of drums	batterie (f)	bat-ree
• timpani	timbales (f, pl)	tEH-bal
player	joueur (m)	zh-oo-ur
	joueuse (f)	zh-oo-uhz
rap	rap (m)	rap
reggae	reggae (m)	reh-gay
rhythm	rythme (m)	reet-me
show	spectacle (m)	spehk-takl
song	chanson (f)	shAH-sOH
• sing	chanter (v)	shAH-tay
• singer	chanteur (m)	shAH-tur
	chanteuse (f)	shAH-tuhz
stringed instruments	instruments (m, pl)	EH-strewm-AH a kord
	à cordes (f)	
• bow	archet (m) de violon (m)	arsh-eh de vee-yulOH
• cello	violoncelle (m)	vee-yulOH-sehl
• double bass	contrebasse (f)	kOH-tre-bahss
• string	corde (f)	kord
• viola	viole (f)	vee-yul
• violin	violon (m)	vee-yulOH
• violinist	violoniste (m, f)	vee-yul-un-eest
symphony	symphonie (f)	sEH-fun-ee
wind instruments	instruments (m, pl)	EH-strew-mAH a vAH
	à vent (f)	
• bagpipes	cornemuse (f)	korn-mewz
• bassoon	basson (m)	bahsOH
• clarinet	clarinette (f)	kla-reen-eht
• flute	flûte (f)	flewt

| • oboe | hautbois (*m*) | *oh-bwah* |
| • saxophone | saxophone (*m*) | *saks-uf-un* |

d. LITERATURE

appendix	appendice (*m*)	*ap-EH-deess*
autobiography	autobiographie (*f*)	*ut-ub-yug-ra-fee*
biography	biographie (*f*)	*bee-yug-ra-fee*
chapter	chapitre (*m*)	*sh-ap-eet-re*
character (*in a novel, play*)	personnage (*m*)	*pehr-sun-azh*
criticism	critique (*f*)	*kree-teek*
fable	fable (*f*)	*fah-bl*
fairy tale	conte (*m*) de fées (*f*)	*kOHt de fay*
fiction	livre (*m*) de fiction (*f*)	*lee-vre de feeks-yOH*
genre	genre (*m*)	*zh-AH-re*
graphic novel	bande (*f*) dessinée	*bAHd day-see-nay*
literature	littérature (*f*)	*lee-tay-ra-tewr*
myth	mythe (*m*)	*meet*
mythology	mythologie (*f*)	*meet-ul-u-zh-ee*
novel	roman (*m*)	*rumAH*

National Library of France, Paris—La bibliothèque nationale de France, Paris

plot	intrigue (*f*)	*EH-treeg*
poet	poète (*m*)	*pu-eht*
	poétesse (*f*)	*pu-ay-tess*
poetry	poésie (*f*)	*pu-ay-zee*
preface	préface (*f*)	*pray-fass*
rhetoric	rhétorique (*f*)	*ray-tu-reek*
short story	conte (*m*)	*kOHt*
	nouvelle (*f*)	*noo-vehl*

style	style (*m*)	*steel*
theme	thème (*m*)	*tehm*
work (*literary*)	ouvrage (*m*)	*oov-razh*
writer	écrivain (*m*)	*ay-kreev-EH*
	écrivaine (*f*)	*ay-kreev-ehn*

e. THEATER

act	acte (*m*)	*akt*
• act	jouer (*v*) dans une pièce	*zh-oo-ay dAH zewn pee-yehs*
applause	applaudissement (*m*)	*ap-loh-dees-mAH*
• applaud	applaudir (*v*)	*ap-loh-deer*
audience	spectateurs (*m, pl*)	*spehk-ta-tur*
	public (*m*)	*pew-bleek*
comedian	acteur(-trice) (*m, f*) comique	*ak-tur(-treess) kum-eek*
comedy	comédie (*f*)	*kum-ay-dee*
curtain	rideau (*m*) de scène (*f*)	*reed-oh de sehn*
drama	drame (*m*)	*drahm*
hero	héros (*m*)	*ay-roh*
heroine	héroïne (*f*)	*ay-ru-een*
intermission	entracte (*m*)	*AH-trakt*
mime	mime (*m, f*)	*meem*
pantomime	pantomime (*f*)	*pAH-tum-eem*
play	pièce (*f*) de théâtre (*m*)	*pee-yehs de tay-ah-tr*
playwright	dramaturge (*m, f*)	*dra-ma-tewr-zh*
	auteur (*m*) dramatique	*oh-tur dra-ma-teek*
	auteure (*f*) dramatique	*oh-tur dra-ma-teek*
plot	intrigue (*f*)	*EH-treeg*
production	mise (*f*) en scène (*f*)	*meez-AH-sehn*
program	programme (*m*)	*prug-ram*
rehearsal	répétition (*f*)	*ray-pay-tee-syOH*
scene	scène (*f*)	*sehn*
scenery	décor (*m*)	*day-kor*
stage	scène (*f*)	*sehn*
theater	théâtre (*m*)	*tay-ah-tr*
tragedy	tragédie (*f*)	*tra-zh-ay-dee*

29. HOLIDAYS AND GOING OUT

a. HOLIDAYS/SPECIAL OCCASIONS

All Saints' Day	La Toussaint	*lah too-sEH*
anniversary	anniversaire (*m*)	*a-nee-vehr-sehr*
Bastille Day (July 14)	La Prise de la Bastille	*la preez dla bastee-y*
	le quatorze juillet	*le ka-torz zh-ew-ee-yay*

birthday	anniversaire (m) de naissance (f)	a-nee-vehr-sehr de neh-sAHss
Christmas	Noël (m)	nu-ehl
Easter	Pâques (f, pl)	pahk
engagement	fiançailles (f, pl)	fee-yAH-sah-y
Feast of the Assumption (Aug. 15)	Assomption (f)	a-sOH-ps-yOH
French National Holiday (July 14)	la Fête Nationale (le Quatorze Juillet)	la feht nas-yun-al le ka-torz zh-ew-ee-yay
holiday (official)	jour (m) férié	zh-oor fay-ree-yay
holidays	jours (m, pl) de fête (f)	zh-oor de feht
name day	fête (f)	feht
New Year's Day	le Jour de l'An (m)	le zh-oor de lAH
New Year's Eve	la Nuit de la Saint-Sylvestre	la-new-eed-la-sEH-seel-vestr
Passover	Pâque (f)	pahk
picnic	pique-nique (m)	peek-neek
Ramadan	ramadan (m)	ra-ma-dAH
Rosh Hashana	Roch ha-Shana (m)	rush ha-shah-nah
vacation	vacances (f, pl)	va-kAH-ss
wedding	mariage (m)	mar-ee-yazh
	noces (f, pl)	nuss

b. GOING OUT

dance	bal (m)	bal
• dance	danser (v)	dAH-say
disco	discothèque (f)	dees-kut-ehk
go out	sortir (v)	sor-teer
have fun	s'amuser (v)	sam-ew-zay
nightclub	boîte (f) de nuit	bwat de-new-ee
party	fête (f)	feht
remain	rester (v)	rehs-tay
return	retourner (v)	re-toor-nay
	revenir (v)	rev-neer
visit (friends, relatives)	rendre (v) visite à	rAH-dr vee-zeet a

c. SPECIAL GREETINGS

Best wishes!	Meilleurs vœux! (m, pl)	meh-yur vuh
Compliments!	Mes compliments! (m, pl)	may kOH-pleem-AH
Congratulations!	Félicitations! (f, pl)	fay-lee-see-tas-yOH
Happy Birthday!	Bon anniversaire! (m)	bun-a-nee-vehr-sehr

Happy Easter!	Bonnes Pâques! (*f*, *pl*) *or* Joyeuses Pâques!	*bun pahk* *zh-wah-yuh-z pahk*
Happy New Year!	Bonne année! (*f*)	*bun-a-nay*
	Heureuse année! (*f*)	*ur-uhz a-nay*
Have a good vacation!	Bonnes vacances! (*f*, *pl*)	*bun va-kAh-ss*
Have a nice day!	Bonne journée! (*f*)	*bun-zh-oor-nay*
Have fun!	Amusez-vous! (*pol*)	*a-mew-zay voo*
	Amuse-toi! (*fam*)	*a-mewz twa*
Merry Christmas!	Joyeux Noël (*m*)	*zh-wa-yuh nu-ehl*

TRAVEL

30. CHOOSING A DESTINATION

> For more related vocabulary, see Section 13.

a. AT THE TRAVEL AGENCY/ON LINE

abroad	à l'étranger	*al-ay-trAH-zh-ay*
brochure	brochure (*f*)	*brush-ewr*
charter flight	vol (*m*) charter	*vul shar-tehr*
city	ville (*f*)	*veel*
• **capital city**	capitale (*f*)	*kap-ee-tal*
class	classe (*f*)	*klahss*
• **business class**	classe (*f*) affaires	*klahss uh-fehr*
• **first class**	première classe (*f*)	*prem-yehr klahss*
• **economy class**	classe (*f*) touriste	*klahss tooreest*
continent	continent (*m*)	*kOH-teen-AH*
country	pays (*m*)	*peh-ee*
downtown	en ville	*AH veel*
	centre-ville (*m*)	*sAH-tre veel*
excursion	excursion (*f*)	*ehks-kewrs-yOH*
insurance	assurance (*f*)	*ass-ewr-AHss*
nation	nation (*f*)	*nahss-yOH*
outskirts, suburbs	environs (*m, pl*)	*AH-veerOH*
	banlieue (*f*)	*bAHl-yuh*
see	voir (*v*)	*vwar*
ticket	billet (*m*)	*bee-yeh*
• **by boat**	en bateau (*m*)	*AH ba-toh*
• **by plane**	en avion (*m*)	*AH nav-yOH*
• **by train**	par le train	*parl trEH*
• **buy a ticket**	acheter (*v*) un billet	*ash-tay UH bee-yeh*
• **one-way ticket**	aller-simple (*m*)	*ah-lay sEHpl*
• **round-trip ticket**	aller-retour (*m*)	*alay retoor*
tour	voyage (*m*) organisé	*vwa-yazh organ-ee-zay*
tour bus	autocar (*m*) de tourisme	*u-toh-kar de toor-eesm*
	autocar (*m*) d'excursion	*u-toh-kar dehks-kewrs-yOH*
tour guide	guide (*m, f*)	*geed*
tourist	touriste (*m, f*)	*toor-eest*
travel	voyager (*v*)	*vwa-ya-zh-ay*
• **travel agency**	agence (*f*) de voyages	*azh-AH-ss de vwa-ya-zh*

trip, journey	voyage (m)	*vwa-ya-zh*
• **Have a nice trip!**	Bon voyage!	*bOH vwa-ya-zh*
• **take a trip**	faire (v) un voyage	*fehr UH vwa-ya-zh*
visit	visiter (v)	*vee-zee-tay*
world	monde (m)	*mOHd*

b. COUNTRIES AND CONTINENTS

Africa	Afrique (f)	*af-reek*
Algeria	Algérie (f)	*al-zh-ay-ree*
America	Amérique (f)	*a-may-reek*
• **Latin America**	Amérique (f) latine	*a-may-reek la-teen*
• **North America**	Amérique (f) du Nord	*a-may-reek dew nor*
• **South America**	Amérique (f) du Sud	*a-may-reek dew sewd*
Asia	Asie (f)	*a-zee*
Australia	Australie (f)	*us-tra-lee*
Austria	Autriche (f)	*oh-treesh*
Belgium	Belgique (f)	*behl-zh-eek*
Brazil	Brésil (m)	*bray-zeel*
Canada	Canada (m)	*ka-na-da*
• **Alberta**	Alberta (f)	*al-behr-ta*
• **British Columbia**	Colombie (f) Britannique	*kuh-lOH-bee bree-tah-neek*
• **Manitoba**	Manitoba (m)	*ma-nee-toh-ba*
• **Newfoundland**	Terre-Neuve (f)	*tehr-nuv*
• **New Brunswick**	Nouveau-Brunswick (m)	*noo-voh brUH-zweek*
• **Nova Scotia**	Nouvelle-Écosse (f)	*noo-vehl ay-kuss*
• **Ontario**	Ontario (m)	*ohn-ta-ree-yo*
• **Prince Edward Island**	Île-du-Prince-Édouard (f)	*eel dew prEHss ay-dwar*
• **Quebec**	Québec (m)	*kay-behk*
• **Saskatchewan**	Saskatchewan (m)	*sahss-kah-tsheh-wahn*
Central America	Amérique (f) centrale	*a-may-reek sAH-tral*
China	Chine (f)	*sheen*
Denmark	Danemark (m)	*dahn-mark*
Egypt	Egypte (f)	*ay-zh-eept*
England	Angleterre (f)	*AH-gle-tehr*
Europe	Europe (f)	*ur-up*
France	France (f)	*frAHs*
• **French Polynesia**	Polynésie (f) française	*puh-lee-nay-zee frAH-sehz*
Germany	Allemagne (f)	*al-ma-ny*
Greece	Grèce (f)	*greh-ss*
Haiti	Haïti (m)	*ah-ee-tee*
Holland	Hollande (f)	*ul-AHd*

India	Inde (*f*)	*EHd*
Ireland	Irlande (*f*)	*eer-lAHd*
Israel	Israël (*m*)	*ees-ra-ehl*
Italy	Italie (*f*)	*ee-ta-lee*
Japan	Japon (*m*)	*zh-ap-OH*
Luxembourg	Luxembourg (*m*)	*lewx-AH-boor*
Mexico	Mexique (*m*)	*mehk-seek*
New Zealand	Nouvelle-Zélande (*f*)	*noo-vehl zayl-AHd*
Norway	Norvège (*f*)	*nor-veh-zh*
Poland	Pologne (*f*)	*pu-lu-ny*
Portugal	Portugal (*m*)	*por-tew-gal*
Russia	Russie (*f*)	*rew-see*
Spain	Espagne (*f*)	*ehs-pa-ny*
Sweden	Suède (*f*)	*sew-ed*
Switzerland	Suisse (*f*)	*sweess*
Thailand	Thaïlande (*f*)	*tah-y-lAHd*
United States of America	États-Unis (*m, pl*) d'Amérique	*ay-ta-zew-nee da-may-reek*

c. A FEW CITIES

Algiers	Alger	*al-zh-ay*
Barcelona	Barcelone	*bar-se-lun*
Beijing/Peking	Béjing/Pékin	*bay-zheen/pay-keen*
Berlin	Berlin	*behrlEH*
Florence	Florence	*flu-rAH-ss*
Frankfurt	Francfort	*frAH-for*
London	Londres	*loH-dre*
Marseilles	Marseille	*mar-seh-y*
Milan	Milan	*meel-AH*
Montreal	Montréal	*mOH-ray-al*
Moscow	Moscou	*mus-koo*
Naples	Naples	*nap-le*
Paris	Paris	*pah-ree*
Rome	Rome	*rum*
Venice	Venise	*vneez*

to go to + country	aller (*v*) + prep. + country	
• to go to France	aller (*v*) en France	*a-lay AH frAHs*
to go to + city	aller (*v*) + à + city	
• to go to Paris	aller (*v*) à Paris	*a-lay a pah-ree*

Iceland
Islande

Sweden
Suède

Norway
Norvège

Denmark
Danemark

Ireland
Irlande

United Kingdom
Royaume-Uni

Neth.
Pays-Bas

Bel.
Belgique

Lux.
Luxembourg

Germany
Allemagne

Po
Po

Czech Rep.
République tchèque

Sl
Sl

F r a n c e
France

Switz.
Suisse

Austria
Autriche

Hu
Hor

Slovenia
Slovénie

Croatia
Croatie

Bosnie-
Herzégovine

Portugal
Portugal

S p a i n
Espagne

Andorra
Andorre

Italy
Italie

Mont.
Monté-négro

Morocco
Maroc

Tunisia
Tunisie

A l g e r i a
Algérie

Libya
Libye

0	210	420 Miles
0	210	420 KM

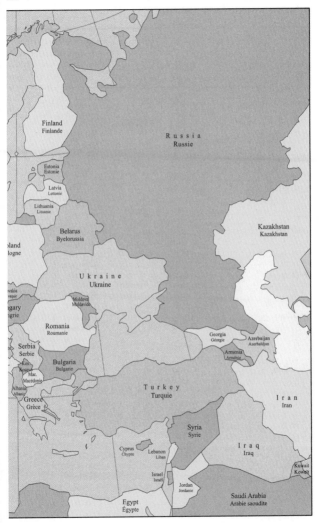

Finland
Finlande

R u s s i a
Russie

Estonia
Estonie

Latvia
Lettonie

Lithuania
Lituanie

Kazakhstan
Kazakhstan

Belarus
Byelorussia

Poland
Pologne

Ukraine
Ukraine

Slovakia
Slovaquie

Hungary
Hongrie

Moldova
Moldavie

Romania
Roumanie

Serbia
Serbie

Georgia
Géorgie

Azerbaijan
Azerbaïdjan

Kos.
Kosovo

Armenia
Arménie

Mac.
Macédonie

Bulgaria
Bulgarie

Albania
Albanie

Greece
Grèce

T u r k e y
Turquie

I r a n
Iran

Syria
Syrie

Cyprus
Chypre

Lebanon
Liban

I r a q
Iraq

Kuwait
Koweït

Israel
Israël

Jordan
Jordanie

Saudi Arabia
Arabie saoudite

Egypt
Égypte

d. NATIONALITIES AND LANGUAGES

> Gender has not been provided for the names of languages, which are invariably masculine in French. Pronunciation has not been provided for the names of languages when it is the same as that of the masculine form of the nationality.

American	Américain (*m*)	*a-may-reekEH*
	Américaine (*f*)	*a-may-reek-ehn*
	(*languages:* **English** anglais;	*AH-gleh;*
	American américain)	*a-may-reekEH*
Arab	Arabe (*m, f*)	*a-rab*
	(*language:* **Arabic** arabe)	
Australian	Australien (*m*)	*us-tral-yEH*
	Australienne (*f*)	*us-tral-yehn*
	(*language:* **English** anglais)	
Austrian	Autrichien (*m*)	*oh-treesh-yEH*
	Autrichienne (*f*)	*oh-treesh-yehn*
	(*language:* **German** allemand)	*almAH*
Belgian	Belge (*m, f*)	*behl-zh*
	(*languages:* **French** français;	*frAH-seh*
	Flemish flamand)	*fla-mAH*
Brazilian	Brésilien (*m*)	*bray-zeel-yEH*
	Brésilienne (*f*)	*bray-zeel-yehn*
	(*language:* **Portuguese** portugais)	*por-tew-geh*
Canadian	Canadien (*m*)	*kan-ad-yEH*
	Canadienne (*f*)	*kan-ad-yehn*
	(*languages:* **English** anglais;	*AH-gleh*
	French français)	*frAH-seh*
Chinese	Chinois (*m*)	*sheen-wa*
	Chinoise (*f*)	*sheen-waz*
	(*language:* **Chinese** chinois)	
Danish	Danois (*m*)	*dan-wa*
	Danoise (*f*)	*dan-waz*
	(*language:* **Danish** danois)	

Dutch	Hollandais (*m*)	*ul-AH-deh*
	Hollandaise (*f*)	*ul-AH-dehz*
	(*language:* **Dutch** hollandais)	
English	Anglais (*m*)	*AH-gleh*
	Anglaise (*f*)	*AH-glehz*
	(*language:* **English** anglais)	
French	Français (*m*)	*frAH-seh*
	Française (*f*)	*frAH-sehz*
	(*language:* **French** français)	
German	Allemand (*m*)	*al-mAH*
	Allemande (*f*)	*al-mAHd*
	(*language:* **German** allemand)	
Greek	Grec (*m*)	*grehk*
	Grecque (*f*)	*grehk*
	(*language:* **Greek** grec)	
Haitian	Haïtien (*m*)	*ah-yee-syEH*
	Haïtienne (*f*)	*ah-yee-syehn*
	(*languages:* **French** français; **Creole** créole)	
Irish	Irlandais (*m*)	*eer-lAH-deh*
	Irlandaise (*f*)	*eer-lAH-dehz*
	(*languages:* **English** anglais;	*AH-gleh*
	Gaelic gaélique)	*ga-ay-leek*
Israeli	Israélite (*m, f*)	*ees-ra-ay-leet*
	(*languages:* **Hebrew** hébreu;	*ay-bruh*
	Arabic arabe;	*a-rab*
	English anglais)	*AH-gleh*
Italian	Italien (*m*)	*ee-ta-lee-yEH*
	Italienne (*f*)	*ee-ta-lee-yehn*
	(*language:* **Italian** italien)	
Japanese	Japonais (*m*)	*zh-ap-un-eh*
	Japonaise (*f*)	*zh-ap-un-ehz*
	(*language:* **Japanese** japonais)	
Norwegian	Norvégien (*m*)	*nor-vay-zh-yEH*
	Norvégienne (*f*)	*nor-vay-zh-yehn*
	(*language:* **Norwegian** norvégien)	

Polish	Polonais (*m*)	*pul-un-eh*
	Polonaise (*f*)	*pul-un-ehz*
	(*language:* **Polish** polonais)	
Portuguese	Portugais (*m*)	*por-tew-geh*
	Portugaise (*f*)	*por-tew-gehz*
	(*language:* **Portuguese** portugais)	
Russian	Russe (*m, f*)	*rewss*
	(*language:* **Russian** russe)	
Spanish	Espagnol (*m*)	*ehs-pan-yul*
	Espagnole (*f*)	*ehs-pan-yul*
	(*language:* **Spanish** espagnol)	
Swede	Suédois (*m*)	*sew-ay-dwa*
	Suédoise (*f*)	*sew-ay-dwaz*
	(*language:* **Swedish** suédois)	
Swiss	Suisse (*m, f*)	*sweess*
	(*languages:* **French** français;	*FrAH-seh*
	German allemand;	*al-MAH*
	Italian italien)	*ee-ta-lee-yEH*

31. PACKING AND GOING THROUGH CUSTOMS

baggage, luggage	bagages (*m, pl*)	*ba-ga-zh*
• **hand luggage**	bagages (*m, pl*) à main	*ba-ga-zh a mEH*
border	frontière (*f*)	*frOHt-yehr*
carry	porter (*v*)	*por-tay*
carry-on baggage	bagages (*m, pl*) à main	*ba-ga-zh a mEH*
customs	douane (*f*)	*dwan*
• **customs officer**	douanier (-ère) (*m, f*)	*dwan-yay*
declare	déclarer (*v*)	*day-kla-ray*
• **nothing to declare**	rien à déclarer	*ree-yEH a day-kla-ray*
• **something to declare**	quelque chose (*pron*) à déclarer	*kehl-ke sh-oh-z a day-kla-ray*
documents	documents (*m, pl*)	*duk-ewm-AH*
duty tax	tarif (*m*) douanier	*tar-eef dwan-yay*
• **pay customs/duty**	payer (*v*) les droits de douane	*pay-ay lay drwa de dwan*
foreign currency	monnaie (*f*) étrangère	*mun-eh ay-trAH-zh-ehr*
foreigner	étranger (*m*)	*ay-trAH-zh-ay*
	étrangère (*f*)	*ay-trAH-zh-ehr*

form (*to fill out*)	formule (*f*)	*form-ewl*
identification (*paper*)	carte (*f*) d'identité	*kart deed-AH-tee-tay*
import	importer (*v*)	*EH-por-tay*
knapsack	sac (*m*) à dos	*sak a doh*
overnight bag	sac (*m*) de voyage	*sak de vwa-ya-zh*
pack (one's bags/luggage)	faire (*v*) les bagages	*fehr lay ba-ga-zh*
passport	passeport (*m*)	*pahs-por*
passport control	contrôle (*m*) de passeports	*kOH-trohl de pahs-por*
suitcase, piece of luggage	valise (*f*)	*val-eez*
tariff	tarif (*m*)	*tar-eef*
visa	visa (*m*)	*vee-za*
weight	poids (*m*)	*pwa*
• **heavy**	lourd(e) (*adj, m, f*)	*loor(d)*
• **light**	léger (*adj, m*)	*lay-zh-ay*
	légère (*f*)	*lay-zh-ehr*
• **maximum**	maximum (*m*)	*maks-ee-mum*

32. TRAVELING BY AIR

a. IN THE TERMINAL

airline	ligne (*f*) aérienne	*lee-ny a-ayr-yehn*
airport	aéroport (*m*)	*a-ay-rup-or*
arrival	arrivée (*f*)	*a-ree-vay*
baggage claim	délivrance (*f*) des bagages	*day-leev-rAH-s day ba-ga-zh*
connection	correspondance (*f*)	*kor-ehsp-OH-dAH-s*
departure	départ (*m*)	*day-par*
economy class	classe (*f*) touriste	*klahss toor-eest*
e-ticket (electronic ticket)	billet (*m*) électronique	*bee-yeh ay-lek-truh-neek*
flight	vol (*m*)	*vul*
first class	première classe (*f*)	*prem-yehr klahss*
gate	porte (*f*)	*port*
go on board	monter (*v*) à bord	*mOHtay a bor*
• **boarding**	embarquement (*m*)	*AH-bark-mAH*
• **boarding pass**	carte (*f*) d'embarquement	*kart dAH-bark-mAH*
information desk	bureau (*m*) de renseignements	*bew-roh de rAH-seh-ny-mAH*
lost and found	objets (*m, pl*) perdus	*ub-zh-eh pehr-dew*
no smoking	défense de fumer	*dayf-AHs de few-may*
porter	porteur (*m*)	*por-tur*
reservation	réservation (*f*)	*ray-zehr-vas-yOH*

security	contrôle (*m*) de sécurité	*kOH-trohl de say-kew-ree-tay*
terminal	terminal (*m*)	*tehr-meen-al*
	aérogare (*f*)	*ah-ehr-oh-gahr*
ticket	billet (*m*)	*bee-yeh*
ticket window	guichet (*m*)	*geesh-eh*
waiting room	salle (*f*) d'attente (*f*)	*sal dat-AHt*

b. FLIGHT INFORMATION

canceled flight	vol (*m*) annulé	*vul an-ew-lay*
early	tôt (*adv*)	*toh*
	en avance	*AH-nav-AH-s*
late	en retard	*AH re-tar*
on time	à l'heure	*al-ur*

c. ON THE PLANE

airplane	avion (*m*)	*av-yOH*
aisle	passage (*m*)	*pahs-azh*
	allée (*f*)	*alay*
cabin	cabine (*f*)	*kabeen*
co-pilot	copilote (*m, f*)	*kup-ee-lut*
crew	équipage (*m*)	*ay-keepa-zh*
emergency exit	sortie (*f*) de secours	*sorteed sekoor*
flight attendant	hôtesse (*f*) de l'air	*oh-tehss de lehr*
	steward (*m*)	*stew-ar*
headphones	casque (*m*) d'écoute	*kask-day-koot*
land	atterrir (*v*)	*a-tay-reer*
• landing	atterrissage (*m*)	*a-tay-rees-azh*
lifejacket	gilet (*m*) de sauvetage	*zh-ee-leh de sohv-tazh*
passenger	passager (*m*)	*pah-sa-zh-ay*
	passagère (*f*)	*pah-sa-zh-ehr*
runway	piste (*f*)	*peest*
seat	siège (*m*)	*see-yeh-zh*
• aisle	côté (*m*) allée	*koh-tay ah-lay*
• window	côté (*m*) fenêtre	*koh-tay fneh-tre*
	côté (*m*) hublot	*koh-tay hew-bloh*
seat belt	ceinture (*f*) de sécurité	*sEH-tewr de say-kew-ree-tay*
• buckle up, fasten	boucler (*v*)	*boo-klay*
sit down	s'asseoir (*v*)	*sa-swar*
takeoff	décollage (*m*)	*day-kul-azh*
take off	décoller (*v*)	*day-kul-ay*
toilet	toilettes (*f, pl*)	*twa-leht*
tray	plateau (*m*)	*pla-toh*

turbulence	turbulence (*f*)	*tewr-bewlAHss*
wheel, landing gear	train (*m*) d'atterrissage	*trEH da-tay-rees-azh*
window	hublot (*m*)	*ew-bloh*
wing	aile (*f*)	*ehl*

33. ON THE ROAD

a. **VEHICLES**

ambulance	ambulance (*f*)	*AHbewlAHss*
automobile	automobile (*f*)	*oh-tum-u-beel*
	auto (*f*)	*oh-toh*
bicycle	bicyclette (*f*)	*bee-see-kleht*
• **bike**	vélo (*m*)	*vay-loh*
• **brake**	frein (*m*)	*frEH*
• **chain guard**	couvre-chaîne (*m*)	*koov-re sh-ehn*
• **handlebar**	guidon (*m*)	*geed-OH*
• **pedal**	pédale (*f*)	*pay-dal*
• **seat**	selle (*f*)	*sehl*
• **spoke**	rayon (*m*)	*reh-yOH*
• **tire**	pneu (*m*)	*pnuh*
bus	autobus (*m*)	*u-toh-bewss*
• **streetcar**	tram (*m*)	*tram*
	tramway (*m*)	*tram-weh*
• **trolley**	trolley (*m*)	*trul-eh*
car	auto (*f*)	*u-toh*
	voiture (*f*)	*vwa-tewr*
• **convertible**	décapotable (*f*)	*day-ka-puh-tabl*
• **rental car**	voiture (*f*) de location	*vwa-tewr de luk-as-yOH*
• **sport utility vehicle**	véhicule (*m*) sport utilitaire	*vay-ee-kewl-spor ew-teelee-tehr*
• **sports car**	voiture (*f*) de sport	*vwa-tewr de spor*
compact car	voiture (*f*) compacte	*vwa-tewr kOHpakt*
minivan	fourgonnette (*f*)	*foor-gun-eht*
motorcycle	motocyclette (*f*)	*mu-tu-see-kleht*
	moto (*f*)	*mut-oh*
• **driver**	motocycliste (*m, f*)	*mu-tu-see-kleest*
• **moped**	Mobylette (*f*)	*mu-bee-leht*
• **scooter**	scooter (*m*)	*skoot-ehr*
station wagon	break (*m*)	*breh-k*
SUV	SUV (*m*)	*ehss-yew-vay*
	véhicule (*m*) sport utilitaire	*vay-ee-kewl sport ew-tee-lee-tehr*
taxi	taxi (*m*)	*tak-see*
trailer	remorque (*f*)	*re-mork*

truck	camion (m)	kam-yOH
• dump	camion-benne (m)	kam-yOH behn
• fire	fourgon-pompe (m)	foorgOH-pOHp
• garbage	de collecte	de-kul-ehkt
• pickup	camionnette (f)	kam-yun-eht
• tanker	camion-citerne (m)	kam-yOH-see-tehrn
• tow	dépanneuse (f)	day-pan-uhz
• tractor	camion-tracteur (m)	kam-yOH-trak-tur
• transport	des marchandises	day marsh-AH-deez
van	fourgon (m)	foorgOH
• passenger van	fourgon automobile	foorgOH u-tum-u-beel
vehicle	véhicule (m)	vay-ee-kewl

b. DRIVING: PEOPLE AND DOCUMENTS

driver (of a car)	chauffeur (m)	shoh-fur
	automobiliste (m, f)	oh-tum-u-beel-eest
• to drive	conduire (v)	kOH-dew-eer
driver's license	permis (m) de conduire	pehr-mee de kOH-dew-eer
insurance card	carte (f) d'assurance	kart das-ewr-AH-s
ownership papers	documents (m) de propriété	duk-ewm-AH de prup-ree-yay-tay
passenger	passager (m)	pah-sa-zh-ay
	passagère (f)	pah-sa-zh-ehr
pedestrian	piéton (m)	pee-yay-tOH
	piétonne (f)	pee-yay-tun
police	police (f)	pul-eess
• highway police	agent (m) de police routier	azh-AHd pul-eess root-yay
• police officer	agent (m) de police	azh-AHd pul-eess
	policier (m)	pul-ees-yay
	femme (f) policier	fahm-pul-ees-yay
• traffic police	agent (m) de patrouille	azh-AHd pa-troo-y
registration papers	carte (f) grise	kart greez
road map	carte (f) routière	kart root-yehr

c. DRIVING

accident	accident (m)	ak-seed-AH
back up	reculer (v)	re-kew-lay
brake	freiner (v)	fray-nay
break down	tomber (v) en panne	tOH-bay AH-pahn
breakdown	panne (f)	pahn

bridge	pont (*m*)	*pOH*
corner (street)	coin (*m*) de la rue	*kwEHd la rew*
curve	courbe (*f*)	*koorb*
	virage (*m*)	*vee-razh*
distance	distance (*f*)	*deest-AH-s*
drive	conduire (*v*)	*kOH-dew-eer*
fine, ticket	contravention (*f*)	*kOH-trav-AH-syOH*
gas station	station-service (*f*)	*stas-yOH-sehr-veess*
• **check the oil**	vérifier (*v*) l'huile	*vay-reef-yay lew-eel*
• **fill up**	faire (*v*) le plein	*fehr le plEH*
• **fix**	réparer (*v*)	*ray-pa-ray*
• **gas**	essence (*f*)	*ay-sAH-ss*
• **mechanic**	mécanicien (*m*)	*may-ka-nees-yEH*
	mécanicienne (*f*)	*may-ka-nees-yehn*
• **self-service**	self-service (*m*)	*sehlf-sehr-veess*
• **tools**	outils (*m, pl*)	*oo-tee*
• **unleaded gas**	essence (*f*) sans plomb	*ay-sAH-ss sAH-plOH*
gears (change)	changer (*v*) de vitesse (*f*)	*sh-AH-zh-ay de veet-ehss*
go forward	avancer (*v*)	*av-AH-say*
highway	autoroute (*f*)	*u-toh-root*
intersection	carrefour (*m*)	*kar-foor*
	croisement (*m*)	*krwaz-mAH*
lane (traffic)	voie (*f*)	*vwa*
park	stationner (*v*)	*stas-yun-ay*
• **parking**	stationnement (*m*)	*stas-yun-mAH*
• **public parking**	stationnement (*m*) public	*stas-yun-mAH pew-bleek*
pass	dépasser (*v*)	*day-pah-say*
pedestrian crossing	passage (*m*) pour piétons	*pahs-azh poor pee-yay-tOH*
	passage (*m*) piétonnier	*pahs-azh pee-yay-tun-yay*
	passage (*m*) clouté	*pahs-azh kloo-tay*
ramp	rampe (*f*)	*rAHp*
	bretelle (*f*) d'accès	*bruh-tel-da-kseh*
road	chemin (*m*)	*sh-mEH*
	route (*f*)	*root*
rush hour	les heures (*f, pl*) d'affluence	*lay-zur daf-lew-AH-s*
	les heures (*f, pl*) de pointe	*lay-zur de pwEHt*
speed	vitesse (*f*)	*veet-ehs*
• **slow down**	ralentir (*v*)	*ral-AH-teer*
• **speed up**	accélérer (*v*)	*aks-ay-lay-ray*
start (car)	mettre (*v*) en marche	*meht-re AH marsh*
	démarrer (*v*)	*day-ma-ray*

toll booth	poste (*m*) de péage	*pust de pay-azh*
traffic	circulation (*f*)	*seer-kew-las-yOH*
• **traffic jam**	embouteillage (*m*)	*AHboo-teh-yazh*
	bouchon (*m*)	*boo-shOH*
traffic lights	les feux (*m, pl*)	*lay fuh*
traffic signal	feu (*m*) de signalisation	*fuh de seen-yal-eez-a-syOH*
tunnel	tunnel (*m*)	*tew-nehl*
turn	virer (*v*)	*vee-ray*
• **(to the) left**	à gauche	*a goh-sh*
• **(to the) right**	à droite	*a drwat*

d. ROAD SIGNS

Bicycle Lane	Piste cyclable	*peest seek-la-ble*
Emergency Lane	Piste d'urgence	*peest dewr-zh-AH-s*
Intersection	Carrefour	*kar-foor*
Level Crossing	Passage à niveau	*pahs-azh a neev-oh*
Merge	Confluence	*kOH-flew-AH-s*
No Entry	Défense d'entrer	*dayf-AH-s dAH-tray*
	Entrée interdite	*AH-tray EH-tehr-deet*
No Left Turn	Virage à gauche interdit	*veer-azh a goh-sh EH-tehr-dee*
No Parking	Stationnement interdit	*stas-yun-mAH EH-tehr-dee*
No Passing	Interdiction de dépasser	*EH-tehr-deeks-yOH de day-pah-say*
No Right Turn	Virage à droite interdit	*veer-azh a drwat EH-tehr-dee*
No Stopping	Arrêt interdit	*a-reh EH-tehr-dee*
No Thoroughfare	Circulation interdite	*seer-kew-las-yOH EH-tehr-deet*
No U-Turn	Demi-tour (*m*) interdit	*dmee-toor-EH-tehr-dee*
One Way	Sens unique	*sAHs ew-neek*
Passing Lane	Voie (*f*) de dépassement	*vwa de day-pahss-mAH*
Road Work (in Progress)	Travaux	*tra-voh*
Slippery When Wet	Chaussée glissante	*sho-say glees-AHt*
Speed Limit	Vitesse maximum	*veet-ehs mak-see-mum*
	Limitation (*f*) de vitesse	*lee-mee-ta-syOH de veet-ehs*
Stop	Arrêt	*a-reh*
	Stop	*stup*
Toll	Péage	*pay-azh*
Tow-Away Zone	Zone de remorquage	*zohn de re-mork-azh*
Yield	Cédez	*say-day*

No U-turn

No passing

Border crossing

Traffic signal ahead

Speed limit
(km/h)

Traffic circle
(roundabout) ahead

No parking

End of no passing
zone

All traffic must go
straight ahead

Danger ahead

Entrance to
expressway

Expressway ends

**Railroad crossing/
Level crossing**

**Oncoming traffic
has right of way**

Yield

No entry

Stop

Height limit

**Gasoline (petrol)
ahead**

Parking

No vehicles

Pedestrian crossing

No left turn

No right turn

e. THE CAR

air bag	sac (*m*) gonflable	*sak gOH-flabl*
air conditioner	climatiseur (*m*)	*klee-ma-tee-zuhr*
battery	batterie (*f*)	*bat-ree*
	les accumulateurs (*m, pl*)	*lay-za-kew-mew-la-tur*
brake	frein (*m*)	*frEH*
bumper	pare-chocs (*m*)	*par-shuk*
car body	carrosserie (*f*)	*ka-russ-ree*
car window	vitre (*f*)	*veet-re*
clutch (pedal)	pédale (*f*) d'embrayage	*pay-dal dAH-breh-ya-zh*
dashboard	tableau (*m*) de bord	*tab-loh de bor*
door	portière (*f*)	*port-yehr*
engine	moteur (*m*)	*mut-ur*
• alternator	alternateur (*m*)	*al-tehr-na-tur*
• fan	ventilateur (*m*) d'aération	*vAH-tee-lat-ur da-ay-ras-yOH*
• fuel pump	pompe (*f*) à essence	*pOHp-a-ay-sAH-ss*
• generator	génératrice (*f*)	*zh-ay-nay-rat-reess*
• piston	piston (*m*)	*peest-OH*
• shaft	arbre-moteur (*m*)	*ar-bre-mut-ur*
	arbre de couche	*ar-bre de koosh*
• spark plug	bougie (*f*)	*boo-zh-ee*
• valve	soupape (*f*)	*soo-pap*
	clapet (*m*)	*klap-eh*
fender	aile (*f*)	*ell*
filter	filtre (*m*)	*feel-tre*
gas pedal (accelerator)	pédale (*f*) d'accélérateur	*pay-dal dak-say-lay-ra-tur*
gas tank	réservoir (*m*) d'essence	*ray-zehr-vwar day-sAH-ss*
gearshift	levier (*m*) de changement de vitesse	*lev-yay de sh-AH-zh-mAH de veet-ehss*
glove compartment	boîte (*f*) à gants	*bwat a gAH*
	vide-poches (*m*)	*veed-pu-sh*
GPS	système (*m*) de navigation	*sees-tehm de nah-vee-ga-syOH*
	GPS (*m*)	*zhay-pay-ess*
handle	poignée (*f*)	*pwan-yay*
hazard lights	feux (*m, pl*) de détresse	*fuh de day-trehss*
heater	système (*m*) de chauffage	*sees-tehm de sh-oh-fazh*
hood	capot (*m*)	*ka-poh*

horn	klaxon (*m*)	*klak-sun*
	avertisseur (*m*)	*a-vehr-tees-ur*
horsepower	cheval-vapeur (*m*)	*sh-val vap-ur*
license plate	plaque (*f*) d'immatriculation	*plak dee-ma-tree-kew-la-syOH*
lights	phares (*m, pl*)	*far*
	projecteurs (*m, pl*)	*pru-zh-ehkt-ur*
• **backup lights**	feux (*m, pl*) de recul	*fuh de re-kewl*
• **parking lights**	feux (*m, pl*) de stationnement	*fuh de stass-yOH-mAH*
muffler	pot (*m*) d'échappement	*poh day-shap-mAH*
oil	huile (*f*)	*ew-eel*
oil filter	filtre (*m*) à huile	*feel-tre-a-ew-eel*
power brake	servofrein (*m*)	*sehr-vu-frEH*
power steering	servodirection (*f*)	*sehr-vu-deer-ehks-yOH*
power window	vitre (*f*) à commande automatique	*veet-re-a-kum-AHd ut-um-at-eek*
radiator	radiateur (*m*)	*rad-yat-ur*
rear window	lunette (*f*) arrière	*lew-neht ar-yehr*
rearview mirror	rétroviseur (*m*) intérieur	*ray-truv-eez-ur EH-tayr-yuhr*
roof	toit (*m*)	*twa*
seat	siège (*m*)	*see-yeh-zh*
seat belt	ceinture (*f*) de sécurité	*sEH-tewr de say-kew-ree-tay*
side mirror	rétroviseur (*m*) extérieur	*ray-truv-eez-ur ehks-tayr-yuhr*
speedometer	compteur (*m*) de vitesse	*kOH-tur de veet-ehss*
steering wheel	volant (*m*)	*vul-AH*
tire	pneu(matique) (*m*)	*pnuh(ma-teek)*
trunk	coffre (*m*)	*kuf-re*
turn signal	clignotant (*m*)	*kleen-yut-AH*
vent	trou (*m*) d'aération (*f*)	*troo-da-ay-ras-yOH*
wheel	roue (*f*)	*roo*
windshield	pare-brise (*m*)	*par-breez*
• **windshield wiper**	essuie-glace (*m*)	*ehs-ew-ee-glahs*

For pictures and words about a vehicle, see page 180.

34. TRAIN, BUS, AND SUBWAY

bus (*long-distance travel*)	autocar (*m*)	*ut-oh-kar*
• **driver**	chauffeur (*m*)	*sh-oh-fur*
• **station, depot**	station (*f*)	*stas-yOH*
	gare (*f*)	*gahr*
coach	voiture (*f*)	*vwa-tewr*
	wagon (*m*)	*vag-OH*
compartment	compartiment (*m*)	*kOH-par-teem-AH*
• **nonsmoking**	non-fumeurs	*nOH fewm-ur*
• **smoking**	fumeurs	*fewm-ur*
conductor	conducteur (*m*)	*kOH-dewk-tur*
	conductrice (*f*)	*kOH-dewk-treess*
connection	correspondance (*f*)	*kor-ehs-pOHd-AH-s*
direct train	train (*m*) direct	*trEH deer-ehkt*
express bus	autocar (*m*) express	*ut-oh-kar ehks-prehss*
express train	train (*m*) express	*trEH ehks-prehss*
get off	descendre (*v*)	*day-sAH-dr*
high speed train	train (*m*) à grande vitesse	*trEH a grAHd vee-tess*
	TGV (*m*)	*tay-zhay-vay*
leave, depart	partir (*v*)	*par-teer*
local train	train (*m*) omnibus	*trEH um-nee-bewss*
miss (*the train, etc.*)	manquer (*v*)	*mAH-kay*
	rater (*v*)	*ra-tay*
newsstand	kiosque (*m*) à journaux	*kee-usk a zh-oor-noh*
porter	porteur (*m*)	*port-ur*
railroad	chemin (*m*) de fer	*shmEHd fehr*
• **station**	gare (*f*)	*gar*
schedule	horaire (*m*)	*or-ehr*
• **early**	tôt (*adv*)	*toh*
	en avance	*AH-nav-AH-s*
• **late**	en retard	*AH re-tar*
• **on time**	à l'heure	*al-ur*
seat	place (*f*)	*plahss*
• **economy**	en classe touriste	*AH klahss toor-eest*
• **first class**	en première classe	*AH prem-yehr klahss*
stop	arrêt (*m*)	*ar-eh*
subway	métro (*m*)	*may-troh*
• **subway station**	station (*f*)	*stas-yOH*
take/catch the train, *etc.*	prendre (*v*)	*prAH-dre*
ticket	billet (*m*)	*bee-yeh*
• **buy a ticket**	acheter (procurer) (*v*) un billet	*ash-tay (pruk-ew-ray) UH bee-yeh*
• **ticket cancelling machine**	composteur (*m*) de billets	*kOH-pust-ur de bee-yeh*
• **ticket counter**	délivrance (*f*) des billets (*m, pl*)	*day-leev-rAH-s day bee-yeh*

track	voie (*f*)	*vwa*
train	train (*m*)	*trEH*
• **All aboard!**	En voiture!	*AH vwa-tewr*
• **coach**	wagon (*m*)	*vagOH*
	voiture (*f*)	*vwa-tewr*
• **train sation**	gare (*f*)	*gahr*
wait for (the train, *etc.*)	attendre (*v*)	*atAH-dre*

35. HOTELS

a. **LODGING**

boarding house	pension (*f*)	*pAHs-yOH*
campground	terrain (*m*) de camping	*tehr-EHd kAH-pin*
chalet	chalet (*m*)	*shal-eh*
hotel	hôtel (*m*)	*oh-tehl*
• **luxury hotel**	hôtel (*m*) de luxe	*oh-tehl de lewks*
motel	motel (*m*)	*mut-ehl*
youth hostel	auberge (*f*) de jeunesse	*oh-behr-zh de zh-uh-nehs*

b. **STAYING IN HOTELS**

bill	compte (*m*)	*kOHt*
• **ask for the bill**	demander (*v*) le compte	*demAH-dayl kOHt*
• **Charge it to my bill.**	Mettez-le sur mon compte.	*meht-ay le sewr mOH kOHt*
bellhop	porteur (*m*)	*port-ur*
breakfast	petit déjeuner (*m*)	*ptee day-zh-un-ay*
• **included (*breakfast*)**	compris (*adj*)	*kOH-pree*
call for a taxi	appeler (*v*) un taxi	*a-play UH tak-see*
complain	se plaindre (*v*)	*se-plEH-dre*
• **complaint**	plainte (*f*)	*plEHt*
doorman	portier (*m*)	*port-yay*
elevator	ascenseur (*m*)	*ass-AH-sur*
entrance	entrée (*f*)	*AH-tray*
exit	sortie (*f*)	*sor-tee*
floor (*level*)	étage (*m*)	*ay-ta-zh*
front desk	réception (*f*)	*rayss-ep-syOH*
garage	garage (*m*)	*gar-azh*
hotel clerk	employé (*m*)	*AH-plwa-yay*
	employée (*f*)	*AH-plwa-yay*
identification card	carte (*f*) d'identité	*kart deed-AH-tee-tay*
key	clef (*f*)	*klay*
• **give back the room key before leaving**	rendre (*v*) la clef de la chambre avant de partir	*rAH-dre la klayd la sh-AH-bre avAH de par-teer*

lobby	foyer (*m*)	*fwa-yay*
• **main door**	porte (*f*) principale	*port prEH-see-pal*
• **main floor**	rez-de-chaussée (*m*)	*rayd-sh-oh-say*
luggage	bagages (*m, pl*)	*ba-ga-zh*
maid	femme (*f*) de chambre	*fam de sh-AH-bre*
manager	gérant (*m*)	*zh-ayrAH*
	gérante (*f*)	*zh-ayrAHt*
	directeur (*m*)	*dee-rehkt-ur*
	directrice (*f*)	*dee-rehkt-reess*
message	message (*m*)	*mehs-azh*
passport	passeport (*m*)	*pahs-por*
pay	payer (*v*)	*pay-ay*
• **cash**	en espèces	*AH-nehs-pehs*
• **check**	chèque (*m*)	*sh-ehk*
• **credit card**	carte (*f*) de crédit	*kart de kray-dee*
• **traveler's check**	chèque (*m*) de voyage	*sh-ehk de vwa-ya-zh*
price, rate	tarif (*m*)	*ta-reef*
• **low season**	basse saison (*f*)	*bahss-sehz-OH*
• **peak season**	haute saison (*f*)	*oht-sehz-OH*
pool	piscine (*f*)	*pee-seen*
porter	portier (*m*)	*por-tyay*
	portière (*f*)	*por-tyehr*
• **give the porter a tip**	donner (*v*) un pourboire au portier	*dun-ay UH poor-bwar oh por-tyay*
receipt	reçu (*m*)	*res-ew*
reservation	réservation (*f*)	*ray-zehr-vas-yOH*
• **reserve**	réserver (*v*)	*ray-zehr-vay*
room	chambre (*f*)	*sh-AH-bre*
• **Do you have a vacant room?**	Avez-vous une chambre libre?	*avay-voo-ewn sh-AH-bre lee-bre*
• **double room**	chambre (*f*) double	*sh-AH-bre dooble*
• **have baggage taken to one's room**	faire (*v*) porter (*v*) les bagages dans la chambre	*fehr por-tay lay ba-ga-zh dAH la sh-AH-bre*
• **bridal suite**	chambre (*f*) matrimoniale	*sh-AH-bre ma-tree-mun-yal*
• **room with bath**	avec bain (*m*)	*a-vehk bEH*
• **room with a shower**	chambre (*f*) avec douche	*sh-AH-bre a-vehk doosh*
• **room with two beds**	à deux lits (*m, pl*)	*a-duh lee*
• **single room**	à un lit (*m*)	*a UH lee*
	pour une personne	*poor ewn pehr-sun*
services	services (*m, pl*)	*sehr-veess*
• **room service**	service (*m*) dans la chambre	*sehr-veess dAH la sh-AH-bre*
• **with Internet**	avec connexion (*f*) Internet	*a-vehk ku-nehk-syOH EH-tehr-neht*
stairs	escalier (*m*)	*ehs-kal-yay*

| view | vue (*f*) | *vew* |
| **wake-up call** | réveil (*m*) par téléphone | *ray-veh-y par tay-lay-fun* |

c. THE HOTEL ROOM

See also Section 23.

armchair	fauteuil (*m*)	*foh-tuh-y*
balcony	balcon (*m*)	*balk-OH*
• **sliding door**	porte (*f*) coulissante	*port kool-ee-sAHt*
bathroom	salle (*f*) de bains	*sal de bEH*
bathtub	baignoire (*f*)	*beh-ny-war*
bed	lit (*m*)	*lee*
• **double bed**	grand lit (*m*)	*grAH lee*
bedside table	table (*f*) de nuit (*f*)	*ta-ble de new-ee*
blanket	couverture (*f*)	*koo-vehr-tewr*
chest of drawers	commode (*f*)	*kum-ud*
closet	armoire (*f*)	*arm-war*
	penderie (*f*)	*pAH-de-ree*
	placard (*m*)	*pla-kahr*
clothes hanger	cintre (*m*)	*sEH-tre*
curtains	rideaux (*m, pl*)	*ree-doh*
dresser	commode (*f*)	*kum-ud*
faucet	robinet (*m*)	*rub-ee-neh*
lamp	lampe (*f*)	*lAHp*
lights	lumières (*f, pl*)	*lewm-yehr*
• **current**	courant (*m*)	*koorAH*
• **switch**	interrupteur (*m*)	*EH-tehr-ewp-tur*
• **turn off**	éteindre (*v*)	*ay-tEH-dr*
• **turn on**	allumer (*v*)	*al-ew-may*
mirror	miroir (*m*)	*meer-war*
	glace (*f*)	*glahss*
pillow	oreiller (*m*)	*or-ay-yay*
radio	radio (*f*)	*rad-yo*
soap	savon (*m*)	*savOH*
shampoo	shampooing (*m*)	*sh-AH-pwEH*
sheets	draps (*m, pl*)	*dra*
shower	douche (*f*)	*doosh*
sink, wash basin	lavabo (*m*)	*la-va-boh*
• **cold water**	eau (*f*) froide	*oh frwad*
• **hot water**	eau (*f*) chaude	*oh sh-ohd*
table	table (*f*)	*ta-bl*
telephone	téléphone (*m*)	*tay-lay-fun*
television set	téléviseur (*m*)	*tay-lay-veez-ur*
thermostat	thermostat (*m*)	*tehrm-us-ta*

toilet	toilette (*f*)	*twa-leht*
	W. C. (*m, pl*)	*doo-ble-vay-say*
• toilet paper	papier (*m*) hygiénique	*pap-yay ee-zh-yay-neek*
towel	serviette (*f*) de bain	*sehrv-yeht de bEH*

36. ON VACATION

a. SIGHTSEEING

amphitheater	amphithéâtre (*m*)	*AH-feet-ay-ah-tre*
art gallery	galerie (*f*) d'art	*gal-ree dar*
avenue	avenue (*f*)	*av-new*
basilica	basilique (*f*)	*ba-zee-leek*
bell tower	campanile (*m*)	*kAH-pa-neel*
	clocher (*m*)	*klush-ay*
bridge	pont (*m*)	*pOH*
castle	château (*m*)	*sh-ah-toh*
cathedral	cathédrale (*f*)	*ka-tay-dral*
church	église (*f*)	*ay-gleez*
city	ville (*f*)	*veel*
city map	plan (*m*) de la ville	*plAHd la veel*
corner	coin (*m*)	*kwEH*
downtown	en ville	*AH veel*
	centre-ville (*m*)	*sAH-tre veel*
garbage can	poubelle (*f*)	*poo-behl*
guide	guide (*m, f*)	*geed*
intersection	croisement (*m*)	*krwaz-mAH*
	carrefour (*m*)	*kar-foor*
kiosk	kiosque (*m*) à journaux	*kee-usk a zh-oor-noh*
monument	monument (*m*)	*mun-ewm-AH*
museum	musée (*m*)	*mew-zay*
park	parc (*m*)	*park*
park bench	banc (*m*)	*bAH*
parking meter	parcmètre (*m*)	*park-meht-r*
	parcomètre (*m*)	*park-uh-meh-tre*
pedestrian crosswalk	passage (*m*) pour piétons	*pahs-azh poor pee-yay-tOH*
public garden	jardin (*m*) public	*zh-ard-EH pew-bleek*
public notices	affiches (*f, pl*) publiques	*a-feesh pew-bleek*
public phone	téléphone (*m*) public	*tay-lay-fun pew-bleek*
• telephone credit card	télécarte (*f*)	*tay-lay-kart*
public washroom	toilettes (*f, pl*) publiques	*twa-leht pew-bleek*
railway crossing	passage (*m*) à niveau	*pahs-azh a nee-voh*
sidewalk	trottoir (*m*)	*trut-war*
square	place (*f*)	*plahss*

street	rue (*f*)	*rew*
• street sign	plaque (*f*) de rue (*f*)	*plak de rew*
take an excursion	faire (*v*) une excursion	*fehr ewn eks-kewrs-yOH*
temple	temple (*m*)	*tAH-ple*
tower	tour (*f*)	*toor*
traffic lights	feux (*m, pl*)	*fuh*
water fountain	fontaine (*f*)	*fOH-tehn*

b. GETTING OUT OF THE CITY

beach	plage (*f*)	*plazh*
• at the beach	à la plage (*f*)	*a la plazh*
• get a suntan	se bronzer (*v*)	*se brOH-zay*
• on vacation	en vacances (*f, pl*)	*AH va-kAH-ss*
• get some sun	prendre (*v*) un peu de soleil	*prAHdr UH puhd sul-ay*
• suntan lotion	crème (*f*) solaire	*krehm sul-ehr*
• take a holiday	avoir (*v*) congé	*avwar kOH-zh-ay*
boat	bateau (*m*)	*ba-toh*
brook	ruisseau (*m*)	*rew-ee-soh*
camping area	camping (*m*)	*kAH-peen*
canoe	canoë (*m*)	*kan-u-ay*
cap	casquette (*f*)	*kas-keht*
cruise	croisière (*f*)	*krwaz-yehr*
fishing	pêche (*f*)	*peh-sh*
in the country	à la campagne	*a-la-kAH-pa-ny*
in the mountains	dans les montagnes (*f, pl*)	*dAH lay mOH-ta-ny*
knapsack	sac (*m*) à dos	*sak a doh*
lake	lac (*m*)	*lak*
mountain boots	chaussures (*f, pl*) de montagne	*sh-oh-sewr de mOH-ta-ny*
mountain climbing	alpinisme (*m*)	*al-pee-nees-me*
on vacation	en vacances (*f, pl*)	*AH vak-AH-ss*
river	fleuve (*m*)	*fluhv*
	rivière (*f*)	*ree-vyehr*
rope	corde (*f*)	*kord*
sea	mer (*f*)	*mehr*
skiing	ski (*m*)	*skee*
• ski resort	station (*f*) de ski	*stas-yOH de skee*
sleeping bag	sac (*m*) de couchage	*sak de koosh-azh*
tent	tente (*f*) de camping (*m*)	*tAHt de kAH-peen*
trip	voyage (*m*)	*vwa-ya-zh*
vacation	vacances (*f, pl*)	*vak-AH-s*

c. ASKING FOR DIRECTIONS

across	à travers (*prep*)	*a-tra-vehr*
ahead	avant (*adv*)	*a-vAH*
at the end of	au bout de	*oh boo de*
	à la fin de	*a la fEH de*
at the top of	au sommet de	*oh sum-eh de*
back	arrière (*adv*)	*ar-yehr*
behind	derrière (*adv*)	*dehr-yehr*
cross (over)	traverser (*v*)	*trav-ehr-say*
• **cross the street**	traverser (*v*) la rue	*trav-ehr-say la rew*
down	bas (*adv*)	*bah*
enter	entrer (*v*) (dans)	*AH-tray (dAH)*
everywhere	partout (*adv*)	*par-too*
exit, go out	sortir (*v*)	*sor-teer*
far (from)	loin (de) (*adv*)	*lwEH (de)*
follow	suivre (*v*)	*sweev-re*
go	aller (*v*)	*al-ay*
go down	descendre (*v*)	*day-sAH-dre*
go up	monter (*v*)	*mOH-tay*
here	ici (*adv*)	*ee-see*
in front of	devant (*prep, adv*)	*de-vAH*
inside	dedans (*prep, adv*)	*de-dAH*
near	près (de) (*adv*)	*preh (de)*
outside	dehors (*adv*)	*de-or*
straight ahead	tout droit (*adv*)	*too-drwa*
there	là (*adv*)	*lah*
through	par (*prep*)	*par*
to the east	à l'est	*al ehst*
to the left	à gauche	*a goh-sh*
to the north	au nord	*oh nor*
to the right	à droite	*a drwat*
to the south	au sud	*oh sewd*
to the west	à l'ouest	*al west*
toward	vers (*prep*)	*vehr*
turn	tourner (*v*)	*toor-nay*

Could you tell me where . . . ?	Pourriez-vous me dire où . . . ?	*poo-ree-yay voom deer oo*
How do you get to . . . ?	Comment va-t-on à . . . ?	*kumAH va-tOH a*
Where is . . . ?	Où est . . . ?	*oo eh*
Turn left . . .	Tournez à gauche . . .	*toor-nay a goh-sh*
Turn right . . .	Tournez à droite . . .	*toor-nay a drwat*
I am looking for . . .	Je cherche . . .	*zhe sh-ehrsh*
How far away . . . ?	À quelle distance . . . ?	*a kehl dee-stAH-s*

LA VOITURE
(L'AUTOMOBILE)
The Car

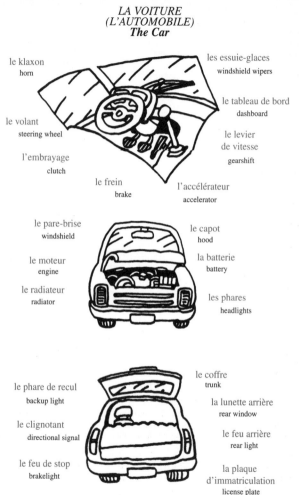

le klaxon
horn

les essuie-glaces
windshield wipers

le tableau de bord
dashboard

le volant
steering wheel

le levier
de vitesse
gearshift

l'embrayage
clutch

le frein
brake

l'accélérateur
accelerator

le pare-brise
windshield

le capot
hood

le moteur
engine

la batterie
battery

le radiateur
radiator

les phares
headlights

le phare de recul
backup light

le coffre
trunk

la lunette arrière
rear window

le clignotant
directional signal

le feu arrière
rear light

le feu de stop
brakelight

la plaque
d'immatriculation
license plate

SCHOOL AND WORK

37. SCHOOL

a. TYPES OF SCHOOLS AND GRADES

coed school	école (*f*) mixte	*ay-kul meekst*
conservatory	conservatoire (*m*)	*kOH-sehr-va-twar*
day care	école (*f*) maternelle	*ay-kul ma-tehr-nehl*
elementary school	école (*f*) primaire élémentaire	*ay-kul pree-mehr ay-lay-mAH-tehr*
evening school	cours (*m*) du soir	*koor dew swar*
(night school)	école du soir	*ay-kul dew swar*
grade	classe (*f*)	*klahss*
grade school	école (*f*) primaire	*ay-kul pree-mehr*
high school	école (*f*) d'enseignement secondaire	*ay-kul dAHseh-ny-mAH se-gOH-dehr*
	lycée (*m*)	*lee-say*
junior high school	école (*f*) d'enseignement secondaire	*ay-kul dAHseh-ny-mAH se-gOH-dehr*
kindergarten	jardin (*m*) d'enfants	*zh-ardEH dAH-fAH*
nursery school	école (*f*) maternelle	*ay-kul ma-tehr-nehl*
private school	école (*f*) privée	*ay-kul pree-vay*
technical/vocational school	institut (*m*) d'enseignement technique	*EHstee-tew dAHseh-ny-mAH tehk-neek*
university	université (*f*)	*ew-nee-vehr-see-tay*
year (*e.g., at university*)	année (*f*)	*a-nay*
• **first year**	première année (*f*)	*prem-yehr a-nay*
• **second year**	deuxième année (*f*)	*duhz-yehm a-nay*

b. THE CLASSROOM

assignment book	carnet (*m*)	*kar-neh*
	calepin (*m*)	*kalpEH*
atlas	atlas (*m*)	*at-lahs*
ballpoint pen	stylo (*m*) à bille	*stee-lo a bee-y*
blackboard	tableau (*m*)	*tab-loh*
blackboard eraser	éponge (*f*) humide	*aypOH-zh uw-meed*
	(vieux) chiffon (*m*)	*(vy-uh) sheef-OH*
book	livre (*m*)	*leev-r*
bookcase	étagère (*f*)	*ay-ta-zh-ehr*
	bibliothèque (*f*)	*beeb-lee-yut-ehk*

chalk	craie (*f*)	*kreh*
compass	compas (*m*)	*kOH-pa*
desk (*pupil's*)	pupitre (*m*)	*pew-peet-re*
• (*teacher's*)	bureau (*m*)	*bew-roh*
dictionary	dictionnaire (*m*)	*deek-see-yun-ehr*
encyclopedia	encyclopédie (*f*)	*AH-see-klup-ay-dee*
eraser	gomme (*f*) à effacer	*gum-a-ay-fa-say*
eyeglasses	lunettes (*f, pl*)	*lew-neht*
film projector	projecteur (*m*) de film	*pruzh-ehk-tur de feelm*
ink	encre (*f*)	*AH-kre*
magazine	magazine (*m*)	*ma-ga-zeen*
	revue (*f*)	*re-vew*
map	carte (*f*) géographique	*kart zh-ay-u-gra-feek*
notebook	cahier (*m*)	*ka-yay*
overhead projector	rétroprojecteur (*m*)	*ray-troh-pruzh-ehk-tur*
paper	papier (*m*)	*pap-yay*
pen	stylo (*m*)	*stee-lo*
pencil	crayon (*m*)	*kreh-yOH*
ruler	règle (*f*)	*reh-gle*
school bag	sac (*m*) d'écolier	*sak day-kul-yay*
slide projector	projecteur (*m*) pour diapositives (*f, pl*)	*pruzh-ehk-tur poor dee-ya-poh-zee-teev*
smart board	tableau (*m*) interactif	*tab-loh EH-tehr-ak-teef*
tack	punaise (*f*)	*pew-nehz*
tape recorder	magnétophone (*m*)	*man-yay-tu-fun*
textbook	livre (*m*) de classe	*leev-re de klahss*
	livre (*m*) de cours	*leev-re de koor*
wall map	carte (*f*) murale	*kart mew-ral*

c. AREAS OF A SCHOOL

campus	campus (*m*)	*kAH-pewss*
classroom	salle (*f*) de classe	*sal de klahss*
gymnasium	gymnase (*m*)	*zh-eem-nahz*
	salle (*f*) de gymnastique	*sal de zh-eem-nas-teek*
hallway	couloir (*m*)	*kool-war*
laboratory	laboratoire (*m*)	*la-bu-rat-war*
language laboratory	laboratoire (*m*) de langues (*f, pl*)	*la-bu-rat-war de lAHg*
library	bibliothèque (*f*)	*beeb-lee-yut-ehk*
main office	direction (*f*)	*deer-ehks-yOH*
professor's office	cabinet (*m*) du professeur	*ka-been-eh dew pruf-ehs-ur*
school yard	cour (*f*)	*koor*
toilets	toilettes (*f, pl*)	*twa-leht*
	W. C. (*m, pl*)	*dooble-vay-say*

d. SCHOOL: PEOPLE

assistant	assistant(e) (*m, f*)	*ass-eest-AH(t)*
class (*of students*)	classe (*f*) d'élèves (d'étudiants)	*klahss day-lehv (day-tewd-yAH)*
janitor	agent(e) (*m, f*) d'entretien	*azh-AH(t) dAH-treh-tyEH*
librarian	bibliothécaire (*m, f*)	*beeb-lee-yut-ay-kehr*
president of a university	recteur (*m*)	*rehk-tur*
	rectrice (*f*)	*rehk-treess*
principal	directeur (*m*)	*dee-rehk-tur*
	directrice (*f*)	*dee-rehk-treess*
professor	professeur (*m*)	*pruf-ehs-ur*
	professeure (*f*)	*pruf-ehs-ur*
pupil	élève (*m, f*)	*ay-lehv*
schoolmate	camarade (*m, f*) d'école	*ka-ma-rad day-kul*
secretary	secrétaire (*m, f*)	*se-kray-tehr*
student	étudiant (*m*)	*ay-tewd-yAH*
	étudiante (*f*)	*ay-tewd-yAHt*
teacher	enseignant(e) (*m, f*)	*AH-sehn-yAH(t)*
• elementary school teacher	maître (*m*)	*meht-re*
	maîtresse (*f*)	*meht-rehss*
• high-school teacher/professor	professeur (*m*)	*pruf-ehs-ur*
	professeure (*f*)	*pruf-ehs-ur*
technician	technicien (*m*)	*tehk-nees-yEH*
	technicienne (*f*)	*tehk-nees-yehn*

e. SCHOOL: SUBJECTS

accounting	comptabilité (*f*)	*kOH-ta-bee-lee-tay*
anatomy	anatomie (*f*)	*a-na-tum-ee*
anthropology	anthropologie (*f*)	*AH-trup-ul-u-zh-ee*
archeology	archéologie (*f*)	*ar-kay-ul-u-zh-ee*
architecture	architecture (*f*)	*ar-shee-tehk-tewr*
art	art (*m*)	*ar*
arts, humanities	lettres (*f, pl*)	*leht-re*
astronomy	astronomie (*f*)	*as-trun-um-ee*
biology	biologie (*f*)	*bee-yul-u-zh-ee*
botany	botanique (*f*)	*but-an-eek*
calculus	calcul (*m*)	*kal-kewl*
chemistry	chimie (*f*)	*shee-mee*
commerce	commerce (*m*)	*kum-ehrs*
economics	économie (*f*)	*ay-kun-um-ee*
engineering	études (*f, pl*) polytechniques	*ay-tewd pul-ee-tehk-neek*
	génie (*m*)	*zhay-nee*
fine arts	beaux-arts (*m, pl*)	*boh-zar*

geography	géographie (*f*)	*zh-ay-ug-rafee*
geometry	géométrie (*f*)	*zh-ay-um-ay-tree*
history	histoire (*f*)	*eess-twar*
languages (foreign)	langues (*f, pl*) étrangères	*lAHg ay-trAH-zh-ehr*
law	études (*f, pl*) de droit	*ay-tewd de drwa*
literature	littérature (*f*)	*lee-tay-ra-tewr*
management	gestion (*f*)	*zh-est-yOH*
mathematics	mathématiques (*f, pl*)	*ma-tay-ma-teek*
medicine	médecine (*f*)	*mayd-seen*
music	musique (*f*)	*mew-zeek*
natural sciences	sciences (*f, pl*) naturelles	*syAHs na-tewr-ehl*
philosophy	philosophie (*f*)	*feel-uz-uf-ee*
physics	physique (*f*)	*fee-zeek*
physiology	physiologie (*f*)	*fee-zee-ul-uzh-ee*
political science	sciences (*f, pl*) politiques	*syAHs pul-ee-teek*
	sciences po	*syAHS-poh*
psychology	psychologie (*f*)	*psee-kul-uzh-ee*
sciences	sciences (*f, pl*)	*syAHs*
sociology	sociologie (*f*)	*suss-yul-uzh-ee*
statistics	statistique (*f*)	*sta-teess-teek*
subject	matière (*f*)	*mat-yehr*
trigonometry	trigonométrie (*f*)	*tree-gun-um-ay-tree*
zoology	zoologie (*f*)	*zu-ul-uzh-ee*

f. ADDITIONAL SCHOOL VOCABULARY

For concepts of thought, see Section 22.

answer	réponse (*f*)	*rayp-OH-s*
• answer	répondre (*v*) (à)	*rayp-OH-dr (a)*
• brief	bref (*adj, m*)	*brehf*
	brève (*f*)	*brehv*
• long	long (*adj, m*)	*lOH*
	longue (*f*)	*lOHg*
• right	correct (*adj, m*)	*kor-ehkt*
	correcte (*f*)	*kor-ehkt*
• short	court (*adj, m*)	*koor*
	courte (*f*)	*koort*
• wrong	faux (*adj, m*)	*foh*
	fausse (*f*)	*foh-ss*
	incorrect (*adj, m*)	*EHkor-ehkt*
	incorrecte (*f*)	*EHkor-ehkt*

assignments, homework	devoirs (*m, pl*)	de-vwar
attend school	assister (*v*) à l'école	ass-ees-tay al ay-kul
be absent	être (*v*) absent(e) (*adj, m, f*)	eh-tre apsAH(t)
be present	être (*v*) présent(e) (*adj, m, f*)	eh-tre prayz-AH(t)
be promoted	être (*v*) reçu(e) (*adj, m, f*)	eh-tre res-ew
class (*students*)	classe (*f*)	klahss
• (*process itself*)	leçon (*f*)	le-sOH
• have a class	avoir (*v*) une leçon	avwar ewn le-sOH
• skip a class	sécher (*v*) un cours	say-shay UH koor
• skip school, play hooky	faire (*v*) l'école buissonnière	fehr lay-kul bew-ee-sun-yehr
• There is no class today.	Il n'y a pas de classe aujourd'hui.	eeln-ya-pahd klahss oh-zh-oor-wee
composition	thème (*m*)	tehm
copy	copie (*f*)	kup-ee
• good, final copy	bonne copie (*f*)	bun kup-ee
• rough copy, draft	brouillon (*m*)	broo-yOH
course	cours (*m*)	koor
• take a course/subject	suivre (*v*) un cours	sweev-re UH koor
degree (*university*)	diplôme (*m*) universitaire	deep-lohm ew-nee-vehr-see-tehr
• Master	licence (*f*)	lee-sAHss
• Doctorate	doctorat (*m*)	duk-tor-a
• get a degree	obtenir (*v*) un diplôme universitaire	up-te-neer UH deep-lohm ew-nee-vehr-see-tehr
dictation	dictée (*f*)	deek-tay
diploma	diplôme (*m*)	deep-lohm
• high school	baccalauréat (*m*)	ba-ka-lor-ay-a
• get a diploma	obtenir (*v*) un diplôme	up-te-neer UH deep-lohm
draw	dessiner (*v*)	day-seen-ay
• drawing	dessin (*m*)	day-sEH
education	éducation (*f*)	ay-dew-kas-yOH
• get an education	recevoir (*v*) une éducation	res-vwar ewn ay-dew-kas-yOH
	recevoir (*v*) une formation	res-vwar ewn formas-yOH
error	erreur (*f*)	ehr-ur
	faute (*f*)	foht
exam	examen (*m*)	ehg-zam-EH
• entrance exam	examen (*m*) d'entrée	ehg-zam-EH dAH-tray

• oral exam	examen (m) oral	*ehg-zam-EH or-al*
• pass an exam	être (v) reçu(e) à un examen	*eh-tre res-ew a UH nehg-zam-EH*
	réussir (v) à un examen	*ray-ew-ssir a UH nehg-zam-EH*
• take an exam	passer (v) un examen	*pah-say UH nehg-zam-EH*
• written exam	examen (m) écrit	*ehg-zam-EH ay-kree*
exercise	exercice (m)	*ehg-zehr-seess*
explanation	explication (f)	*ehks-plee-kas-yOH*
• explain	expliquer (v)	*ehks-plee-kay*
fail an exam	échouer à un examen	*ay-shway a UH nehg-zam-EH*
	être (v) collé(e) à un examen	*eh-tre kul-ay a UH nehg-zam-EH*
field (of study)	champ (m) d'études	*shAH day-tewd*
give/hand back	rendre (v)	*rAH-dr*
grade/mark	note (f)	*nut*
grammar	grammaire (f)	*gram-ehr*
learn	apprendre (v)	*aprAH-dr*
• learn by memory	apprendre (v) par cœur	*aprAH-dr par kur*
lecture	conférence (f)	*kOHfay-rAHs*
• lecture	faire (v) une conférence	*fehr ewn kOHfay-rAHs*
	donner (v) une conférence	*dun-ay ewn kOHfay-rAHs*
listen to	écouter (v)	*ay-koo-tay*
mistake	faute (f)	*foht*
• make mistakes	faire (v) des fautes	*fehr day foht*
note	note (f)	*nut*
• take notes	prendre (v) des notes	*prAH-dr day nut*
problem	problème (m)	*prub-lehm*
• solve a problem	résoudre (v) un problème	*ray-zood-r UH prub-lehm*
question	question (f)	*kehst-yOH*
• ask a question	poser (v) une question	*poh-zay ewn kehst-yOH*
read	lire (v)	*leer*
• reading (passage)	lecture (f)	*lehk-tewr*
registration	inscription (f)	*EH-skreeps-yOH*
• registration fee	droits (m, pl) d'inscription	*drwa dEH-skreeps-yOH*
repeat	répéter (v)	*ray-pay-tay*
review	révision (f)	*ray-veez-yOH*
• review	faire (v) une révision	*fehr ewn ray-veez-yOH*
school	école (f)	*ay-kul*
• finish school	finir (v) la dernière année d'école	*fee-neer la dehrn-yehr a-nay day-kul*
• go to school	aller (v) à l'école	*al-ay al ay-kul*

study	étudier (v)	ay-tewd-yay
take attendance	faire (v) l'appel	fehr lap-ehl
teach	enseigner (v)	AH-sehn-yay
test	épreuve (f)	ay-pruhv
	examen (m)	eg-za-mEH
thesis	thèse (f)	tehz
type	taper (v) à la machine	tap-ay a la mash-een
typewriter	machine (f) à écrire	mash-een a ay-kreer
understand	comprendre (v)	kOH-prAH-dre
write	écrire (v)	ay-kreer

38. WORK

a. JOBS AND PROFESSIONS

accountant	comptable (m, f)	kOH-tabl
actor	acteur (m)	ak-tur
actress	actrice (f)	ak-treess
architect	architecte (m, f)	arsh-ee-tehkt
baker	boulanger (m)	bool-AH-zhay
	boulangère (f)	bool-AH-zh-ehr
barber	coiffeur (m)	kwaf-ur
bricklayer	maçon (m)	mass-OH
bus driver	conducteur (m) d'autobus	kOH-dewk-tur d'uh-toh-bewss
	conductrice (f) d'autobus	kOH-dewk-treess d'uh-toh-bewss
businessman	homme (m) d'affaires	um daf-ehr
businesswoman	femme (f) d'affaires	fahm daf-ehr
butcher	boucher (m)	boosh-ay
	bouchère (f)	boosh-ehr
carpenter	menuisier (m)	me-new-eez-yay
	menuisière (f)	me-new-eez-yehr
	charpentier (m)	shar-pAH-tyay
	charpentière (f)	shar-pAHt-yehr
cook	cuisinier (m)	kew-eez-een-yay
	cuisinière (f)	kew-eez-een-yehr
dentist	dentiste (m, f)	dAH-teest
doctor	médecin (m)	mayd-sEH
	femme (f) médecin	fahm mayd-sEH
	docteur (m)	duk-tur
	femme (f) docteur	fahm duk-tur
• eye doctor	ophtalmologiste (m, f)	uf-tal-mul-uzh-eest
	oculiste (m, f)	uk-ew-leest
editor	rédacteur (m)	rayd-akt-ur
	rédactrice (f)	rayd-ak-treess
electrician	électricien (m)	ay-lehk-tree-syEH
	électricienne (f)	ay-lehk-treess-yehn

engineer	ingénieur (m)	*EH-zhayn-yur*
	ingénieure (f)	*EH-zhayn-yur*
factory worker	ouvrier (m)	*oovr-yay*
	ouvrière (f)	*oovr-yehr*
farmer	fermier (m)	*fehrm-yay*
	fermière (f)	*fehrm-yehr*
fireman	pompier (m)	*pOHp-yay*
graphic artist	graphiste (m, f)	*grah-feest*
hairdresser	coiffeur (m)	*kwaf-ur*
	coiffeuse (f)	*kwaf-uhz*
job	métier (m)	*mayt-yay*
	occupation (f)	*uk-ewp-ass-yOH*
journalist	journaliste (m, f)	*zh-oor-nal-eest*
lawyer	avocat(e) (m, f)	*a-vu-ka(t)*
mechanic	mécanicien (m)	*may-ka-neess-yEH*
	mécanicienne (f)	*may-ka-neess-yehn*
movie director	réalisateur (m)	*ray-al-eez-at-ur*
	réalisatrice (f)	*ray-al-eez-at-reess*
	metteur (m) en scène	*met-ur AH sehn*
	metteuse (f) en scène	*met-uhz AH sehn*
musician	musicien (m)	*mew-zee-syEH*
	musicienne (f)	*mew-zees-yehn*
nurse	infirmier (m)	*EH-feerm-yay*
	infirmière (f)	*EH-feerm-yehr*
occupation	occupation (f)	*uk-ewp-ass-yOH*
painter (*of buildings, rooms*)	peintre (m, f)	*pEH-tre*
• (*artist*)	artiste peintre (m, f)	*ar-teest pEH-tre*
pharmacist	pharmacien (m)	*farm-ass-yEH*
	pharmacienne (f)	*farm-ass-yehn*
pilot	pilote (m, f)	*pee-lut*
plumber	plombier (m)	*plOHb-yay*
police officer	agent (m) de police	*azh-AHd pul-eess*
	policier (m)	*pul-ees-yay*
	policière (f)	*pul-eess-yehr*
professor	professeur (m)	*pruf-ehs-ur*
	professeure (f)	*pruf-ehs-ur*
profession	profession (f)	*pruf-ehs-yOH*
professional	professionnel (m)	*pruf-ehs-yun-ehl*
	professionnelle (f)	*pruf-ehs-yun-ehl*
programmer	programmeur (m)	*prug-ram-ur*
	programmeuse (f)	*prug-ram-uhz*
psychiatrist	psychiatre (m, f)	*psee-kee-atr*
psychologist	psychologue (m, f)	*psee-kul-ug*
researcher	chercheur (m)	*sh-ehr-sh-ur*
	chercheuse (f)	*sh-ehr-sh-uhz*
scientist	scientifique (m, f)	*sy-AH-tee-feek*
secretary	secrétaire (m, f)	*se-kray-tehr*

surgeon	chirurgien (*m*)	*sheer-ewr-zh-y-EH*
	chirurgienne (*f*)	*sheer-ewr-zh-yehn*
tailor	tailleur (*m*)	*tah-y-ur*
	couturière (*f*)	*koo-tewr-yehr*
tattoo	tatouage (*m*)	*ta-too-azh*
	tatouer (*v*)	*ta-too-ay*
• tattoo artist	tatoueur (*m*)	*ta-too-ur*
	tatoueuse (*f*)	*ta-too-uhz*
teacher	professeur (*m*)	*pruf-ehs-ur*
	professeure (*f*)	*pruf-ehs-ur*
trade	métier (*m*)	*may-tee-yay*
typist	dactylographe (*m, f*)	*dak-teel-ug-raf*
webmaster	webmestre (*m, f*)	*web-mehs-tre*
writer	écrivain (*m*)	*ay-kreev-EH*
	écrivaine (*f*)	*ay-kreev-ehn*

b. INTERVIEWING FOR A JOB

> See also Section 11f—Basic Personal Information.

an interview	une entrevue	*ewn AHtre-vew*

<u>Name</u>	<u>Nom</u> (*m*)	*nOH*
first name	prénom (*m*)	*prayn-OH*
surname, family name	nom (*m*) de famille	*nOHd fam-ee*
signature	signature (*f*)	*seen-ya-tewr*
<u>Address</u>	<u>Adresse</u> (*f*)	*ad-rehss*
street	rue (*f*)	*rew*
number	numéro (*m*)	*new-may-roh*
city	ville (*f*)	*veel*
postal code	code (*m*) postal	*kud pus-tal*
<u>Telephone number</u>	<u>Numéro de</u> téléphone (*m*)	*new-may-rohd tay-lay-fun*
area code	code (*m*) régional	*kud ray-zh-yun-al*
<u>Date & place of birth</u>	<u>Date et lieu de</u> naissance	*dat ay ly-uhd nehs-AH-ss*
date	date (*f*)	*dat*
place	lieu (*m*)	*ly-uh*
<u>Age</u>	<u>Âge</u> (*m*)	*ah-zh*
<u>Sex</u>	<u>Sexe</u> (*m*)	*sehks*
male	masculin (*m*)	*mah-skew-lEH*
female	féminin (*f*)	*fay-mee-nEH*

Marital Status	État (*m*) civil	*ay-ta see-veel*
divorced	divorcé(e) (*adj, m, f*)	*dee-vor-say*
married	marié(e) (*adj, m, f*)	*mar-yay*
single	célibataire (*m, f*)	*say-lee-ba-tehr*
widow	veuve (*f*)	*vuv*
widower	veuf (*m*)	*vuhf*
Nationality	Nationalité (*f*)	*nas-yun-al-ee-tay*

See also Section 30d—Nationalities and Languages.

Education	Éducation (*f*)	*ay-dew-kas-yOH*
elementary school	école (*f*) primaire	*ay-kul pree-mehr*
junior high school	école (*f*) d'enseignement secondaire	*ay-kul dAHseh-ny-mAh se-gOH-dehr*
high school	lycée (*m*)	*lee-say*
university	université (*f*)	*ew-nee-vehr-see-tay*
Profession	Profession (*f*)	*pruf-ehss-yOH*
Résumé	Résumé (*m*)	*ray-zewm-ay*

c. THE OFFICE

adhesive tape	ruban (*m*) adhésif	*rewbAH ad-ay-zeef*
appointment book	agenda (*m*) de bureau	*azh-EH-da de bew-roh*
briefcase	serviette (*f*)	*sehrv-yeht*
calendar	calendrier (*m*)	*kal-AH-dr-yay*
chair	siège (*m*) de bureau	*sy-eh-zh de bew-roh*
computer	ordinateur (*m*)	*or-dee-na-tur*
fax	télécopie (*f*)	*tay-lay-cup-ee*
file	classeur (*m*)	*klahs-ur*
	dossier-classeur (*m*)	*duss-yay-klahs-ur*
filing card	fiche (*f*)	*feesh*
intercom	interphone (*m*)	*EH-tehr-fun*
monitor	moniteur (*m*)	*mu-nee-tur*
paper shredder	déchiqueteur (*m*)	*day-sheek-tur*
pen	stylo (*m*)	*stee-lo*
pencil	crayon (*m*)	*kreh-yOH*
photocopier	photocopieur (*m*)	*fu-tu-cup-y-ur*
printer	imprimante (*f*)	*EH-preem-AHt*
ruler	règle (*f*)	*reh-gle*
scissors	ciseaux (*m, pl*)	*see-zo*
sorting	triage (*m*)	*tree-ah-zh*
staple	agrafe (*f*)	*ag-raf*
stapler	agrafeuse (*f*)	*ag-ra-fuhz*
tack	punaise (*f*)	*pew-nehz*
telephone	téléphone (*m*)	*tay-lay-fun*

typewriter	machine (*f*) à écrire	*mash-een a ay-kreer*
video conference	visioconférence (*f*)	*veezee-o-kOH-fay-rAH-ss*
	vidéo-conférence (*f*)	*vee-day-o-kOH-fay-rAH-ss*
wastebasket	corbeille (*f*) à papier (*m*)	*kor-beh-y a pap-yay*

d. ADDITIONAL WORK VOCABULARY

advertising	publicité (*f*)	*pewb-lee-see-tay*
boss (*in an office*)	chef (*m*) de bureau	*sh-ehf de bew-roh*
career	carrière (*f*)	*kar-yehr*
classified ad	petite annonce (*f*)	*pteet anOHs*
commerce	commerce (*m*)	*kum-ehrs*
company	société (*f*) commerciale	*suss-yay-tay kum-ehrs-yal*
contract	contrat (*m*)	*kOH-tra*
earn	gagner (*v*)	*gan-yay*
employ	employer (*v*)	*AH-plwa-yay*
employee	employé(e) (*m, f*)	*AH-plwa-yay*
employer	employeur (*m*)	*AH-plwa-yur*
	employeuse (*f*)	*AH-plwa-yuhz*
employment agency	agence (*f*) d'emploi	*a-zh-AHs dAH-plwa*
factory	usine (*f*)	*ew-zeen*
fire (*dismiss*)	renvoyer (*v*)	*rAH-vwa-yay*
hire	embaucher (*v*)	*AH-boh-shay*
	engager (*v*)	*AH-gazh-ay*
manager	directeur (*m*)	*dee-rehk-tur*
	directrice (*f*)	*dee-rehk-treess*
	gérant(e) (*m, f*)	*zhay-rAH(t)*
market	marché (*m*)	*marsh-ay*
minimum wage	salaire (*m*) minimum	*sal-ehr mee-nee-mum*
	SMIC (*m*)	*smeek*
office	bureau (*m*)	*bew-roh*
retirement, pension	retraite (*f*)	*re-treht*
	pension (*f*)	*pAH-syOH*
• **retire**	se retirer (*v*)	*se-re-tee-ray*
	prendre (*v*) sa retraite	*prAH-dr sa re-treht*
unemployment	chômage (*m*)	*sh-oh-mazh*
wage, salary	paie (*f*)	*peh*
	salaire (*m*)	*sal-ehr*
work	travail (*m*)	*tra-va-y*
• **work**	travailler (*v*)	*tra-va-yay*
• **work associate**	collègue (*m, f*)	*kul-ehg*

EMERGENCIES

39. REPORTING AN EMERGENCY

a. FIRE

alarm	alarme (*f*)	*al-arm*
ambulance	ambulance (*f*)	*AH-bewlAHs*
building	bâtiment (*m*)	*bah-teemAH*
	édifice (*m*)	*ay-dee-feess*
burn	brûlure (*f*)	*brew-lewr*
• burn	brûler (*v*)	*brew-lay*
call the fire department	appeler (*v*) les pompiers	*ap-lay lay pOHp-yay*
	appeler (*v*) les sapeurs-pompiers	*ap-lay lay sap-ur pOHp-yay*
catch fire	prendre (*v*) feu	*prAH-dre fuh*
	s'enflammer (*v*)	*sAH-flam-ay*
CPR	réanimation (*f*) cardio-pulmonaire	*ray-a-nee-mah-syOH kar-dee-yo-pul-mu-nehr*
danger	danger (*m*)	*dAH-zh-ay*
destroy	détruire (*v*)	*day-trew-eer*
emergencies	urgences	*ewr-zh-AH-ss*
emergency exit	sortie (*f*) de secours	*sorteed sekoor*
escape, get out	fuir (*v*)	*few-eer*
	s'échapper (*v*)	*say-sha-pay*
extinguish, put out	éteindre (*v*)	*aytEH-dre*
fire	feu (*m*)	*fuh*
	incendie (*m*)	*EH-sAH-dee*
• be on fire	être (*v*) en feu	*eh-tre AH fuh*
• Fire!	Au feu!	*oh-fuh*
• fire alarm	alarme (*f*) d'incendie	*al-arm dEH-sAH-dee*
• fire extinguisher	extincteur (*m*)	*ehks-tEHkt-ur*
• firefighter	pompier (*m*)	*pOHp-yay*
	sapeur-pompier (*m*)	*sap-ur pOHp-yay*
• fire hose	tuyau (*m*) de pompe	*tew-ee-yo de pOHp*
• fire hydrant	borne (*f*) d'incendie	*born dEH-sAH-dee*
• fire truck	fourgon-pompe (*m*)	*foor-gOH-pOHp*
fireproof	incombustible (*adj*)	*EH-kOH-bews-teebl*
	ignifuge (*adj*)	*eeg-nee-few-zh*
first aid	soins (*m, pl*) d'urgence	*swEH dewr-zh-AH-s*
	premiers soins (*m, pl*)	*prem-yay swEH*
flame	flamme (*f*)	*flahm*
help	aider (*v*)	*ay-day*

• Help!	Au secours!	*oh-skoor*
• give help	donner (*v*) de l'aide	*dun-ay de l-ehd*
ladder	échelle (*f*)	*ay-shell*
out	dehors (*adv*)	*de-or*
• Everybody out!	Tout le monde dehors!	*tool-mOH-d de-or*
protect	protéger (*v*)	*prut-ay-zh-ay*
rescue	sauver (*v*)	*soh-vay*
shout	cri (*m*)	*kree*
• shout	crier (*v*)	*kree-ay*
siren	sirène (*f*)	*seer-ehn*
smoke	fumée (*f*)	*few-may*
spark	étincelle (*f*)	*ayt-EH-sehl*
victim	victime (*f*)	*veek-teem*

b. ROBBERY AND ASSAULT

argue	se disputer (*v*)	*se-dees-pew-tay*
	se quereller (*v*)	*se ke-ray-lay*
arrest	arrêter (*v*)	*ar-ay-tay*
assault	agression (*f*)	*ag-rehss-yOH*
Come quickly!	Venez vite!	*vnay veet*
crime	crime (*m*)	*kreem*
• crime wave	vague (*f*) de criminalité	*vahg de kree-meen-ah-lee-tay*
• criminal	criminel(le) (*m, f*)	*kree-meen-ehl*
description	description (*f*)	*dehs-kreeps-yOH*
fight	se battre (*v*)	*se-bat-re*
firearm	arme (*f*) à feu	*arm-a-fuh*
handcuffs	menottes (*f, pl*)	*me-nut*
handgun	revolver (*m*)	*re-vul-vehr*
	pistolet (*m*)	*pees-tul-eh*
hurry	se dépêcher (*v*)	*se-day-pay-shay*
injure, wound	blesser (*v*)	*bleh-say*
• injury, wound	blessure (*f*)	*blay-sewr*
	plaie (*f*)	*pleh*
kill	tuer (*v*)	*tew-ay*
	assassiner (*v*)	*a-sa-see-nay*
• killer	tueur (*m*)	*tew-ur*
	assassin (*m*)	*a-sas-EH*
knife	couteau (*m*)	*koo-toh*
• pocket knife	couteau (*m*) pliant	*koo-toh plee-yAH*
	couteau (*m*) de poche	*koo-toh de pu-sh*
murder	meurtre (*m*)	*mur-tre*
	homicide (*m*)	*um-ee-seed*
• to murder	assassiner (*v*)	*a-sa-see-nay*
	tuer (*v*)	*tew-ay*

pickpocket	pickpocket (m)	peek-puk-eht
	voleur (m) à la tire	vul-ur a la teer
	voleuse (f) à la tire	vul-uhz a la teer
police	police (f)	pul-eess
• **police officer**	agent (m) de police	azh-AHd pul-eess
	policier (m)	pul-ees-yay
	femme (f) policier	fahm-pul-ees-yay
	policière (f)	pul-eess-yehr
• **call the police**	appeler (v) la police	ap-lay la pul-eess
rape	viol (m)	vee-yul
	violer (v)	vee-yul-ay
rifle	fusil (m)	few-zee
rob	voler (v)	vul-ay
• **robber, thief**	voleur (m)	vul-ur
	voleuse (f)	vul-uhz
• **armed robbery**	vol (m) à main armée	vul-a-mEH arm-ay
• **robbery**	vol (m)	vul
• **Stop thief!**	Au voleur!	oh vul-ur
shoplifting	vol (m) à l'étalage	vul-al-ay-tal-azh
steal	dérober (v)	day-rub-ay
	voler (v)	vul-ay
victim	victime (f)	veek-teem
violence	violence (f)	vee-yul-AHs
weapon	arme (f)	arm
• **shoot**	tirer (v)	tee-ray

Help!	Au secours!	o-skoor
	À l'aide!	a-led
I'm lost!	Je suis perdu(e)!	zhe swee pehr-dew
Someone assaulted me!	On m'a agressé!	OH ma agress-ay
Someone stole my . . .	On m'a volé mon/ma . . .	OH ma vul-ay mOH/ma . . .
Stop thief!	Au voleur!	o vul-ur

c. TRAFFIC ACCIDENTS

accident	accident (m)	aks-eed-AH
• **serious accident**	accident (m) grave	aks-eed-AH grav
• **traffic accident**	accident (m) de voiture	aks-eed-AH de vwa-tewr
ambulance		
• **call an ambulance**	appeler (v) une ambulance	ap-lay ewn AH-bewlAHs

be run over	être (v) renversé(e)	*eh-tre rAH-vehr-say*
	se faire (v) renverser	*se fehr rAH-vehr-say*
bleed	saigner (v)	*sayn-yay*
• **blood**	sang (m)	*sAH*
broken bone	os (m) cassé	*us kah-say*
	os (m) fracturé	*us frak-tew-ray*
bump	heurter (v)	*ur-tay*
collision, smash	collision (f)	*kul-eez-yOH*
• **collide**	entrer (v) en collision	*AH-tray AH kul-eez-yOH*
	se heurter (v)	*se-ur-tay*
doctor	médecin (m)	*mayd-sEH*
	femme (f) médecin	*fahm mayd-sEH*
• **get a doctor**	chercher (v) un médecin	*sh-ehr-shay UH mayd-sEH*
first aid	soins (m, pl) d'urgence	*swEH dewr-zh-AH-s*
• **antiseptic**	antiseptique (m)	*AH-tee-sehp-teek*
• **bandage**	pansement (m)	*pAHs-mAH*
• **CPR**	réanimation (f) cardio-pulmonaire	*ray-a-nee-mah-syOH kar-dee-yo-pul-mu-nehr*
• **gauze**	gaze (f)	*gahz*
• **scissors**	ciseaux (m, pl)	*see-zo*
• **splint**	éclisse (f)	*ay-kleess*
Help!	Au secours!	*oh-skoor*
	À l'aide!	*a-led*
hospital	hôpital (m)	*oh-pee-tal*
• **emergency room**	salle (f) d'urgence	*sal dewr-zh-AH-s*
• **emergency service**	service (m) des urgences	*sehr-veess day-zewr-zh-AHs*
• **X-ray**	radiographie (f)	*rad-yo-grafee*
to have an X-ray	passer (v) une radio(graphie) (f)	*pah-say ewn rad-yo-(grafee)*
pileup	carambolage (m)	*ka-rAH-bu-lazh*
police	police (f)	*pul-eess*
• **call the police**	appeler (v) la police	*ap-lay la pul-eess*
shock	choc (m)	*shuk*
• **in shock**	sous le choc	*sool shuk*
wound, injury	plaie (f)	*pleh*
	blessure (f)	*blay-sewr*

40. MEDICAL CARE

a. THE DOCTOR

> See also Section 12—The Body.

acne	acné (*f*)	*ak-nay*
AIDS	le SIDA	*see-da*
AIDS patient	sidéen (*m*)	*see-day-AH*
	sidéenne (*f*)	*see-day-ehn*
AIDS researcher	sidologue (*m, f*)	*see-du-lug*
allergy	allergie (*f*)	*al-ehrzh-ee*
appendicitis	appendicite (*f*)	*ap-AH-dee-seet*
• **appendix**	appendice (*m*)	*ap-AH-deess*
appointment	rendez-vous (*m*)	*rAH-day-voo*
artery	artère (*f*)	*ar-tehr*
arthritis	arthrite (*f*)	*ar-treet*
aspirin	aspirine (*f*)	*as-pee-reen*
bandage	pansement (*m*)	*pAHs-mAH*
• **bandage**	panser (*v*)	*pAH-say*
blood	sang (*m*)	*sAH*
• **blood pressure**	tension (*f*) artérielle (veineuse)	*tAHs-yOH ar-tayr-yehl (vehn-uhz)*
• **blood test**	analyse (*f*) de sang	*a-na-leez de sAH*
	prise (*f*) de sang	*preez de sAH*
bone	os (*m, sing*)	*us*
	(*pl*) les os	*lay-zo*
brain	cerveau (*m*)	*sehr-vo*
bronchitis	bronchite (*f*)	*brOH-sheet*
cold	rhume (*m*)	*rewm*
convalescence	convalescence (*f*)	*kOH-val-ay-sAHs*
cough	toux (*f*)	*too*
• **cough**	tousser (*v*)	*too-say*
cure	guérison (*f*)	*gay-reez-OH*
• **cure, look after**	guérir (*v*)	*gay-reer*
	soigner (*v*)	*swEHn-ay*
• **get cured, convalesce**	se guérir (*v*)	*se-gay-reer*
	se remettre (*v*)	*se re-meht-re*
dandruff	pellicules (*f, pl*)	*pay-leek-ewl*
digestive system	système (*m*) digestif	*see-stehm dee-zh-ehs-teef*
• **anus**	anus (*m*)	*an-ewss*
• **defecate**	déféquer (*v*)	*day-fay-kay*
• **rectum**	rectum (*m*)	*rehk-tum*
• **stomach**	estomac (*m*)	*ehs-tum-a*
• **have a stomach ache**	avoir (*v*) mal à l'estomac	*av-war mal al ehs-tum-a*

DNA	ADN (*m*)	*ah-day-ehn*
doctor	médecin (*m*)	*mayd-sEH*
	femme (*f*) médecin	*fahm mayd-sEH*
• at the doctor's	chez le médecin	*shayl-mayd-sEH*
doctor's visit	visite (*f*) du médecin	*vee-zeet dew mayd-sEH*
examine (*medically*)	examiner (*v*)	*ehg-zam-ee-nay*
• to get examined	se faire (*v*) examiner	*se-fehr-ehg-zam-ee-nay*
eye doctor	ophtalmologiste (*m*, *f*)	*uf-tal-mul-uzh-eest*
	opticien (*m*)	*up-tee-syEH*
	opticienne (*f*)	*up-tee-syehn*
	oculiste (*m*, *f*)	*uk-ew-leest*
• contact lenses	lentilles (*f*, *pl*) de contact	*lAH-tee-y de kOH-takt*
	verres (*m*, *pl*) de contact	*vehr de kOH-takt*
• eyeglasses	lunettes (*f*, *pl*)	*lew-neht*
• sight	vue (*f*)	*vew*
feel	se sentir (*v*)	*se-sAH-teer*
• feel bad	se sentir (*v*) mal	*se-sAH-teer mal*
• feel well	se sentir (*v*) bien	*se-sAH-teer byEH*
• strong	fort (*adj*, *m*)	*for*
	forte (*f*)	*fort*
• weak	faible (*adj*, *m*, *f*)	*feh-bl*
• How do you feel?	Comment vous sentez-vous?	*kum-AH voo sAH-tay voo*
• I feel . . .	Je me sens . . .	*zhem-sAH*
fever	fièvre (*f*)	*fy-ehvr*
flu	grippe (*f*)	*greep*
headache	mal (*m*) de tête	*mal de teht*
• have a headache	avoir (*m*) mal à la tête	*avwar mal a la teht*
heal	guérir (*v*)	*gay-reer*
health	santé (*f*)	*sAH-tay*
• healthy	sain (*adj*, *m*)	*sEH*
	saine (*adj*, *f*)	*sehn*
• be healthy	être (*v*) en bonne santé	*eht-re AH bun sAH-tay*
heart	cœur (*m*)	*kur*
• heart attack	crise (*f*) cardiaque	*kreez kard-yak*
HIV	VIH (*m*)	*vay-ee-ah-sh*
hurt	avoir (*m*) mal	*avwar mal*
	faire (*v*) mal à	*fehr mal a*
in vitro fertilization	fécondation (*f*) in vitro	*fay-kOH-das-yOH een veetro*
infection	infection (*f*)	*EH-fehks-yOH*
injection	piqûre (*f*)	*peek-ewr*
itch	démangeaison (*f*)	*daym-AH-zh-ehz-OH*

lymphatic system	système (m) lymphatique	see-stehm lEH-fa-teek
measles	rougeole (f)	roozh-ul
medical instruments	instruments (m, pl) médicaux	EH-strewmAH may-dee-ko
• electrocardiograph	électrocardiographe (m)	ay-lehk-tru-kard-yu-graf
• stethoscope	stéthoscope (m)	stay-tus-kup
• syringe	seringue (f)	se-rEHg
• thermometer	thermomètre (m)	tehr-mum-eht-re
medicine (you take)	médicament (m)	may-deek-am-AH
muscle	muscle (m)	mew-sk-le
nerves	nerfs (m, pl)	nehr
• nervous system	système (m) nerveux	see-stehm nehr-vuh
nurse	infirmier (m)	EH-feerm-yay
	infirmière (f)	EH-feerm-yehr
operation	intervention (f) chirurgicale	EH-tehrv-AHs-yOH sheer-ewr-zh-ee-kal
• to have an operation	se faire (v) opérer	se fehr uh-pay-ray
• operating room	salle (f) de chirurgie	sal de sheer-ewr-zh-ee
optician	opticien (m)	up-teess-yEH
	opticienne (f)	up-teess-yehn
pain	douleur (f)	dool-ur
• painful	douloureux (adj, m)	dool-ur-uh
	douloureuse (f)	dool-ur-uhz
patient	patient (m)	pas-yAH
pill	pilule (f)	peel-ewl
pimple	bouton (m)	boot-OH
pneumonia	pneumonie (f)	pnuh-mun-ee
pregnant	enceinte (adj, f)	AH-sEHt
prescription	ordonnance (f)	or-dun-AHs
pulse	pouls (m)	poo
respiratory system	système (m) respiratoire	see-stehm rehs-pee-rat-war
• breath	haleine (f)	al-ehn
• breathe	respirer (v)	rehs-pee-ray
• bad breath	mauvaise haleine (f)	muv-ehz al-ehn
• be out of breath	être hors d'haleine (f)	eh-tre or dal-ehn
	être (v) à bout de souffle	eh-tre a bood-soo-fle
• lung	poumon (m)	poo-mOH
• nostril	narine (f)	na-reen
rheumatism	rhumatisme (m)	rew-ma-teesme
secretary	secrétaire (m, f)	se-kray-tehr
sedative	sédatif (m)	say-da-teef
shot	piqûre (f)	pee-kewr
sick	malade (adj)	mal-ad

• get sick	tomber (v) malade	tOH-bay mal-ad
• sickness, disease	maladie (f)	mal-ad-ee
sneeze	eternuement (m)	ay-tehr-new-mAH
• sneeze	éternuer (v)	ay-tehr-new-ay
sore back, have a	avoir (v) mal au dos	avvar mal oh doh
sore/twisted neck, have a	avoir (v) mal au cou	avvar mal oh koo
	avoir (v) un torticolis	avvar UH tor-tee-kul-ee
specialist	spécialiste (m, f)	spay-sy-al-eest
STD	MST (f)	em-ess-tay
suffer	souffrir (v)	soof-reer
suppository	suppositoire (m)	sew-po-zeet-war
surgeon	chirurgien (m)	sheer-ewr-zh-y-EH
	femme (f) chirurgien	fahm sheer-ewr-zh-y-EH
• surgery	chirurgie (f)	sheer-ewr-zh-ee
swollen	enflé(e) (m, f)	AH-flay
tablet	comprimé (m)	kOH-pree-may
temperature (fever)	fièvre (f)	fee-yehvre
• take one's temperature	prendre (v) la température	prAH-dre la tAH-pay-ra-tewr
throat	gorge (f)	gor-zh
• sore throat	mal (m) de gorge	mal-de-gor-zh
• have a sore throat	avoir (v) mal à la gorge	avvar mal a la gor-zh
throw up	rendre (v)	rAH-dr
• vomit	vomir (v)	vum-eer
tonsillitis	amygdalite (f)	ameeg-da-leet
tonsils	amygdales (f, pl)	a-meeg-dal
urinary system	système urinaire	see-stehm ew-ree-nehr
• kidney	rein (m)	rEH
• urinate	uriner (v)	ew-ree-nay
vein	veine (f)	vehn
wheelchair	fauteuil (m) roulant	fo-tu-y rool-AH

b. THE DENTIST

anesthetic	anesthésique (m)	a-nehs-tay-zeek
appointment	rendez-vous (m)	rAH-day-voo
cavity, tooth decay	carie (f) dentaire	ka-ree dAH-tehr
brush (teeth)	se brosser (v) les dents	se-bruss-ay lay dAH
crown	couronne (f) dentaire	koor-un dAH-tehr
dentist	dentiste (m, f)	dAH-teest
• at the dentist's	chez le (la) dentiste	shayl (la) dAH-teest
• dentist's chair	fauteuil (m)	fo-tu-y
• dentist's office	cabinet (m) du (de la) dentiste	kab-ee-neh dew (de la) dAH-teest
denture, false teeth	dentier (m)	dAHt-yay
drill	fraise (f)	frehz

examine	examiner (*v*)	*ehg-zam-ee-nay*
extract, pull (a tooth)	extraire (*v*) une dent	*ehks-trehr ewn dAH*
• **extraction**	extraction (*f*)	*ehks-traks-yOH*
filling	obturation (*f*) dentaire	*up-tew-rahss-yOH dAH-tehr*
	plombage (*m*)	*plum-bazh*
mouth	bouche (*f*)	*boosh*
• **gums**	gencives (*f, pl*)	*zh-AH-seev*
• **jaw**	mâchoire (*f*)	*mah-sh-war*
• **lip**	lèvre (*f*)	*lehv-re*
• **Open your mouth, please.**	Ouvrez la bouche, s'il vous plaît.	*oov-ray la boosh seel-voo-pleh*
• **palate**	palais (*m*)	*pal-eh*
• **tongue**	langue (*f*)	*lAHg*
needle	aiguille (*f*)	*ehg-ew-ee-y*
novocaine	novocaïne (*f*)	*nu-vu-ka-een*
office hours	heures de bureau (*m*)	*ur de bew-ro*
	heures d'ouverture	*ur doo-vehr-tewr*
rinse	(se) rinser (*v*)	*(se) rEH-say*
tooth	dent (*f*)	*dAH*
• **canine**	la (dent) canine	*la (dAH) kan-een*
• **incisor**	dents (*f, pl*) incisives	*dAH EH-see-seev*
• **molar**	dents (*f, pl*) molaires	*dAH mul-ehr*
• **root**	racine (*f*)	*ra-seen*
• **wisdom tooth**	dent (*f*) de sagesse	*dAH de sazh-ehss*
toothache	mal (*m*) aux dents	*mal oh dAH*
• **have a toothache**	avoir (*v*) mal aux dents	*avwar mal oh dAH*
• **My tooth hurts!**	J'ai mal à la dent!	*zhay mal a la dAH*
toothbrush	brosse (*f*) à dents	*bruss a dAH*
toothpaste	dentifrice (*m*)	*dAH-tee-freess*
X-ray	radiographie (*f*)	*rad-yo-grafee*
• **have an X-ray**	passer (*v*) une radio(graphie) (*f*)	*pah-say ewn rad-yo-(grafee)*

41. LEGAL MATTERS

accusation	accusation (*f*)	*ak-ew-zas-yOH*
• **accuse**	accuser (*v*)	*ak-ew-zay*
• **accused (person)**	accusé(e) (*m, f*)	*ak-ew-zay*
address oneself to	s'adresser (*v*) à	*sad-rehss-ay a*
admit	admettre (*v*)	*ad-meht-re*
	avouer (*v*)	*a-voo-ay*
agree	être (*v*) d'accord	*eh-tre dak-or*
capital punishment	peine (*f*) capitale	*pehn ka-pee-tal*
chief of police	préfet (*m*) de police	*pray-feh de pul-eess*
controversy	controverse (*f*)	*kOH-truv-ehrss*

convince	convaincre (v)	kOH-vEH-kre
court	tribunal (m)	tree-bewn-al
	cour (f)	koor
• court of appeal	cour (f) d'appel	koor dap-ehl
courtroom	salle (f) du tribunal	sal dew tree-bewn-al
	salle (f) d'audience	sal du-dyAHss
curfew	couvre-feu (m)	koovr-fuh
debate	débat (m)	day-ba
• debate	débattre (v)	day-ba-tre
defend oneself	se défendre (v)	se-dayf-AH-dre
disagree	se disputer (v)	se-deess-pew-tay
discuss	discuter (v)	deess-kew-tay
DNA	ADN (m)	ah-day-ehn
guilt	culpabilité (f)	kewl-pa-bee-lee-tay
• guilty	coupable (adj, m, f)	koop-abl
innocence	innocence (f)	een-us-AH-s
• innocent	innocent(e) (adj, m, f)	een-us-AH(t)
judge	juge (m, f)	zh-ew-zh
• judge	juger (v)	zh-ew-zhay
jury	jury (m)	zh-ew-ree
justice	justice (f)	zh-ew-steess
law	loi (f)	lwa
• lawful, legal	légal(e) (adj, m, f)	lay-gal
• unlawful, illegal	illégal(e) (adj, m, f)	ee-lay-gal
• civil law	loi (f) civile	lwa see-veel
	droit (m) civil	drwa see-veel
• criminal law	droit (m) pénal	drwa pay-nal
lawsuit, charge	action (f) en justice	ak-syOH AN zh-ew-steess
lawyer	avocat (m)	a-vuk-a
	avocate (f)	a-vuk-aht
• trial lawyer	avoué (m)	av-way
	femme (f) avoué	fahm av-way
litigation	litige (m)	lee-tee-zh
• litigate	intenter (v) une action en justice	EH-tAH-tay ewn ak-syOH AH zh-ew-steess
magistrate	magistrat (m)	mazh-ees-tra
persuade	persuader (v)	pehr-sew-ad-ay
plea	plaidoirie (f)	plehd-war-ee
• plea for mercy	supplication (f) pour clémence	sewp-lee-kas-yOH poor klaym-AH-s
plead	plaider (v)	pleh-day
• to plead guilty	plaider coupable	pleh-day koop-abl
• to plead innocent	plaider non coupable	pleh-day nOH koop-abl
police station	commissariat (m) de police	kum-ee-sar-ya de pul-eess

prison, jail	prison (*f*)	*preez-OH*
• **imprison**	emprisonner (*v*)	*AH-pree-zun-ay*
• **life imprisonment**	emprisonnement (*m*) à perpétuité	*AH-pree-zun-mAH a pehr-pay-tew-ee-tay*
public prosecutor	procureur (*m*) de la République	*pruk-ewr-ur de la ray-pew-bleek*
right, privilege	droit (*m*)	*drwa*
sentence	jugement (*m*)	*zh-ew-zh-mAH*
• **life sentence**	condamnation (*f*) à vie	*kOH-dam-na-syOH a vee*
• **prison sentence**	peine (*f*) de prison	*pen de preez-OH*
• **pass a sentence**	prononcer (*v*) un jugement	*prun-OH-say UH zh-ew-zh-mAH*
• **serve a sentence**	purger (*v*) une peine de prison	*pewr-zhay ewn pen de preez-OH*
sue	poursuivre (*v*) en justice	*poor-swee-vre AH zh-ew-steess*
summons	citation (*f*)	*see-tahs-yOH*
trial	procès (*m*)	*pruss-eh*
• **be on trial**	être (*v*) en procès	*eh-tre AH pruss-eh*
• **put someone on trial**	faire (*v*) passer en justice	*fehr pah-ssay AH zh-ew-steess*
verdict	verdict (*m*)	*vehr-deekt*
• **guilty**	coupable (*adj*)	*koop-abl*
• **not guilty**	non coupable (*adj*)	*nOH koop-abl*
witness	témoin (*m*)	*taym-wEH*
• **eyewitness**	témoin (*m*) oculaire	*taym-wEH uk-ew-lehr*
• **for the defense**	témoin (*m*) à décharge	*taym-wEH a day-shar-zh*
• **for the prosecution**	témoin (*m*) à charge	*taym-wEH a shar-zh*

THE CONTEMPORARY WORLD

42. SCIENCE AND TECHNOLOGY

> For more vocabulary on basic matter, see Section 13.

antenna	antenne (*f*)	*AH-tehn*
• **dish antenna**	antenne (*f*) parabolique	*AH-tehn pa-ra-bul-eek*
astronaut	astronaute (*m, f*)	*as-tru-noht*
	cosmonaute (*m, f*)	*kus-mu-noht*
atom	atome (*m*)	*at-ohm*
• **electron**	électron (*m*)	*ay-lehk-trOH*
• **neutron**	neutron (*m*)	*nuh-trOH*
• **proton**	proton (*m*)	*prut-OH*
clone	cloner (*v*)	*kloh-nay*
compact disk	disque compact (*m*)	*deesk-kOH-pakt*
fax machine	télécopieur (*m*)	*tay-lay-kup-yur*
	émetteur-récepteur (*m*) de fac-similé	*ay-meht-ur-ray-sehp-tur-de-fak-see-mee-lay*
	fax (*m*)	*fahks*
GPS	GPS (*m*)	*zhay-pay-ess*
iPod	iPod (*m*)	*ee-puhd*
laser	laser (*m*)	*la-zehr*
• **light beam**	rayon (*m*) de lumière	*reh-yOH d lewm-yehr*
microwave	micro-onde (*f*)	*meek-ru-OHd*
missile	missile (*m*)	*mee-seel*
• **launch pad**	rampe (*f*) de lancement	*rAHp de lAHs-mAH*
molecule	molécule (*f*)	*mul-ay-kewl*
monorail vehicle	monorail (*m*)	*mu-nu-rah-y*
nuclear industry	industrie (*f*) nucléaire	*EH-dews-tree new-klay-ehr*
• **fission reactor**	réacteur (*m*) à fission	*ray-akt-u a feess-yOH*
• **fusion reactor**	réacteur (*m*) à fusion	*ray-akt-u a fewz-yOH*
• **nuclear energy**	énergie (*f*) nucléaire	*ay-nehr-zh-ee new-klay-ehr*
• **nuclear fuel**	combustible (*m*) nucléaire	*kOH-bews-teebl new-klay-her*
• **nuclear reactor**	réacteur (*m*) nucléaire	*ray-akt-ur new-klay-ehr*

robot	robot (*m*)	*rub-oh*
satellite	satellite (*m*)	*sa-tay-leet*
• **artificial satellite**	satellite (*m*) artificiel	*sa-tay-leet ar-tee-fee-syehl*
scientific research	recherche (*f*) scientifique	*re-sh-ehrsh sy-AH-tee-feek*
spacecraft	vaisseau (*m*) spatial	*veh-so spas-yal*
• **lunar module**	module (*m*) lunaire	*mud-ewl lew-nehr*
• **space shuttle**	navette (*f*) spatiale	*na-veht spas-yal*
technology	technologie (*f*)	*tehk-nu-lu-zhee*
telecommunications	télécommunications (*f, pl*)	*tay-lay-kum-ewn-ee-kahs-yOH*
• **teleconference**	télé-conférence (*f*)	*tay-lay-kOH-fay-rAHs*
theory of relativity	théorie (*f*) de la relativité	*tay-or-ee de la re-la-tee-vee-tay*
• **quantum theory**	théorie (*f*) des quanta	*tay-or-ee day kwAH-ta*
video conference	visioconférence (*f*)	*veezee-o-kOH-fay-rAH-ss*

43. COMPUTERS

artificial intelligence	intelligence (*f*) artificielle	*EH-tehl-ee-zh-AHs ar-tee-fee-syehl*
byte	multiplet (*m*)	*mewl-teep-leh*
compatible	compatible (*adj*)	*kOH-pa-tee-bl*
computer	ordinateur (*m*)	*or-dee-na-tur*
• **computer-assisted instruction**	instructions (*f, pl*) automatisées	*EH-strewk-syOH ut-um-a-teez-ay*
• **computer language**	langage-machine (*m*)	*lAHg-azh-ma-sheen*
	langage (*m*) de programmation	*lAHg-azh de prug-ram-ahs-yOH*
• **computer science**	informatique (*f*)	*EH-form-at-eek*
crash	tomber (*v*) en panne (*f*)	*tOH-bay AH pahn*
	planter (*v*)	*plAH-tay*
data	données (*f, pl*)	*dun-ay*
	information (*f*)	*EH-form-ass-yOH*
• **data processing**	traitement (*m*) de l'information	*trehtmAH de lEH-form-ass-yOH*
desktop computer	ordinateur (*m*) de bureau	*or-dee-na-tur de bewr-oh*
disk	disque (*m*)	*deesk*
• **floppy disk**	disquette (*f*)	*deesk-eht*
	disque (*m*) souple	*deesk-soop-le*
download	télécharger (*v*)	*tay-lay-shar-zh-ay*

e-mail	courrier (m) électronique	*koo-ree-yay-aylehk-trun-eek*
	courriel (m)	*koo-ree-yel*
e-mail address	adresse (f) électronique	*ad-rehss aylehk-trun-eek*
file	fichier (m)	*feesh-yay*
firewall	pare-feu (m)	*pahr-fuh*
flash drive	clé (f) USB	*klay ew-ess-bay*
flow chart	schéma (m) fonctionnel	*shay-ma fOH-ks-yun-ehl*
function	fonction (f)	*fOH-ks-yOH*
hard drive	disque (m) dur	*deesk dewr*
hardware	matériel (m)	*ma-tayr-yehl*
	hardware (m)	*ard-wehr*
integrated circuit	circuit (m) intégré	*seer-kew-ee EH-tay-gray*
interface	interface (f)	*EH-tehr-fahss*
Internet	Internet (m)	*EH-tehr-net*
Internet café	cybercafé (m)	*see-behr-ka-fay*
keyboard	clavier (m)	*klav-yay*
• **keyboard operator**	claviste (m, f)	*klav-eest*
laptop (computer)	portable (m)	*por-ta-ble*
	portatif (m)	*por-ta-teef*
link	lien (m)	*lyEH*
memory	mémoire (f)	*may-mwar*
• **random access memory**	RAM (f)	*rahm*
microcomputer	micro-ordinateur (m)	*meek-ro-or-dee-na-tur*
microprocessor	microprocesseur (m)	*meek-ro-pru-say-sur*
modem	modem (m)	*mud-ehm*
monitor	moniteur (m)	*mu-nee-tur*
mouse	souris (f)	*soo-ree*
office automation	automatisation (f) de bureau	*ut-um-a-teez-ah-syOH de bew-roh*
	bureautique (f)	*bew-roh-teek*
optical reader	lecteur optique (m)	*lehk-tur up-teek*
peripherals	périphériques (m, pl)	*pay-reef-ay-reek*
personal computer	ordinateur (m) personnel	*or-dee-na-tur pehr-sun-ehl*
printer	imprimante (f)	*EHpreem-AHt*
program	programme (m) d'ordinateur	*prug-ram dor-dee-na-tur*
• **programmer (person)**	programmeur (m)	*prug-ram-ur*
	programmeuse (f)	*prug-ram-uhz*
• **programmer (machine)**	programmateur (m)	*prug-ram-at-ur*
• **programming**	programmation (f)	*prug-ram-ahs-yOH*

screen	écran (*m*) de visualisation	*ay-krAH d veez-ew-al-eez-as-yOH*
software	logiciel (*m*)	*luzh-ee-syehl*
	software (*m*)	*suf-wehr*
spam	pourriel (*m*)	*poor-ee-yel*
terminal	terminal (*m*)	*tehr-mee-nal*
user-friendly	facile (*adj*) à utiliser	*fa-seel a ew-tee-lee-zay*
virus	virus (*m*)	*vee-rews*
• **antivirus program**	programme (*m*) antivirus	*pru-grahm AH-tee-vee-rews*
webcam	webcam (*f*)	*web-kahm*
window	fenêtre (*f*)	*fneh-tre*
word processing	traitement (*m*) de texte	*treht-mAH de tekst*
word processor	machine (*f*) de traitement de texte	*ma-sheen de treht-mAH de tekst*
World Wide Web	web (*m*)	*wehb*

44. POLITICS

See also Sections 16, 17, 21, and 22.

---

arms race	course (*f*) aux armements	*koors oh zar-me-mAH*
arms reduction	réduction (*f*) des armements	*ray-dewks-yOH day-zar-me-mAH*
assembly	assemblée (*f*)	*as-AH-blay*
association	association (*f*)	*as-us-yah-syOH*
communism	communisme (*m*)	*kum-ew-neesme*
• **communist**	communiste (*m, f*)	*kum-ew-neest*
conservative party	parti (*m*) conservateur	*par-tee kOH-sehr-va-tur*
council	conseil (*m*)	*kOH-seh-y*
democracy	démocratie (*f*)	*day-muk-ra-see*
• **democrat**	démocrate (*m, f*)	*day-muk-rat*
• **democratic**	démocratique (*adj*)	*day-muk-ra-teek*
demonstration	manifestation (*f*)	*ma-nee-fehs-tas-yOH*
	manif (*f*)	*man-eef*
disarmament	désarmement (*m*)	*day-zar-me-mAH*
economy	économie (*f*)	*ay-kun-um-ee*
elect	élire (*v*)	*ay-leer*
• **elections**	élections (*f, pl*)	*ay-lehk-syOH*
globalization	mondialisation (*f*)	*mOHd-yal-ee-zas-yOH*
govern	gouverner (*v*)	*goo-vehr-nay*
• **government**	gouvernement (*m*)	*goo-vehrn-mAH*
ideology	idéologie (*f*)	*ee-day-ul-uzh-ee*

inflation	inflation (*f*)	*EH-flah-syOH*
labor/trade union	syndicat (*m*)	*sEH-dee-ka*
legislation	législation (*f*)	*lay-zhee-slah-syOH*
liberal party	parti (*m*) libéral	*par-tee lee-bay-ral*
minister	ministre (*m*)	*mee-nee-stre*
monarchy	monarchie (*f*)	*mun-ar-shee*
• **king**	roi (*m*)	*rwa*
• **queen**	reine (*f*)	*rehn*
• **prince**	prince (*m*)	*prEHs*
• **princess**	princesse (*f*)	*prEHs-ehs*
parliament	parlement (*m*)	*parl-emAH*
• **elected**	député (*m*)	*day-pew-tay*
politician,	députée (*f*)	*day-pew-tay*
representative	représentant(e) (*m, f*)	*re-prayz-AH-tAH(t)*
• **house/chamber of**	la Chambre des Députés	*la sh-AH-bre day day-pew-tay*
representatives	(Assemblée Nationale)	*assAH-blay nas-yun-al*
• **President of the French Republic**	Président(e) (*m, f*) de la République Française	*pray-zeedAH(t) de la ray-pew-bleek frAH-sehz*
• **Senate**	Sénat (*m*)	*say-na*
• **senator**	sénateur (*m*)	*say-na-tur*
	sénatrice (*f*)	*say-na-treess*
• **universal suffrage/right to vote**	suffrage (*m*) universel	*sewf-razh ew-nee-vehr-sehl*
peace	paix (*f*)	*peh*
policy	politique (*f*)	*pul-ee-teek*
politician	homme (*m*) politique	*um pul-ee-teek*
	femme (*f*) politique	*fahm pul-ee-teek*
• **left wing**	gauche (*f*)	*go-sh*
• **right wing**	droite (*f*)	*drwat*
politics	politique (*f, sing*)	*pul-ee-teek*
• **political party**	parti (*m*) politique	*par-tee pul-ee-teek*
• **political power**	pouvoir (*m*) politique	*poov-war pul-ee-teek*
president	président (*m*)	*pray-zee-dAH*
	présidente (*f*)	*pray-zee-dAHt*
prime minister	premier ministre (*m*)	*prem-yay mee-nee-str*
protest	protestation (*f*)	*prut-ehs-tah-syOH*
reform	réforme (*f*)	*ray-form*
republic	république (*f*)	*ray-pew-bleek*
revolt	révolte (*f*)	*ray-vult*
• **revolution**	révolution (*f*)	*ray-vul-ew-syOH*
riot	émeute (*f*)	*ay-muht*

socialism	socialisme (*m*)	*suss-yal-eesme*
• **socialist**	socialiste (*m, f*)	*suss-yal-eest*
• **socialist party**	parti (*m*) socialiste	*pahr-tee suss-yal-eest*
state	état (*m*)	*ay-ta*
• **head of state**	chef (*m*) d'état	*sh-ehf day-ta*
strike	grève (*f*)	*grehv*
• **go on strike**	être (*v*) en grève	*eh-tre AH grehv*
	faire (*v*) grève	*fehr grehv*
Third World	Tiers Monde (*m*)	*tyehr mOHd*
underdeveloped countries	pays (*m, pl*) sous-développés	*peh-ee soo-day-vlup-ay*
unilateral	unilatéral(e) (*adj*)	*ew-nee-la-tehr-al*
vote	vote (*m*)	*vut*
• **vote**	voter (*v*)	*vut-ay*
war	guerre (*f*)	*gehr*
welfare	assistance (*f*) sociale	*a-seest-AHs sus-yal*

45. CONTROVERSIAL ISSUES

a. THE ENVIRONMENT

For more vocabulary, see Sections 13 and 42.

air pollution	pollution (*f*) atmosphérique	*pul-ew-syOH at-mus-fay-reek*
conservation	préservation (*f*)	*pray-zehr-va-syOH*
consumption	consommation (*f*)	*kOH-sum-ass-yOH*
ecology	écologie (*f*)	*ay-kul-uzh-ee*
ecosystem	écosystème (*m*)	*ay-ku-see-stehm*
energy	énergie (*f*)	*ay-nehr-zhee*
• **energy crisis**	crise (*f*) d'énergie	*kreez day-nehr-zhee*
• **energy needs**	besoins (*m, pl*) d'énergie	*be-zwEH day-nehr-zhee*
• **energy source**	source (*f*) d'énergie	*soors day-nehr-zhee*
environment	environnement (*m*)	*AH-veer-un-mAH*
fossil fuels	combustibles (*m, pl*) fossiles	*kOH-bews-teebl fuss-eel*
geothermal energy	énergie (*f*) géothermique	*ay-nehr-zhee zh-ay-u-tehrm-eek*
global warming	réchauffage (*m*) de la planète	*ray-shoh-fazh de la plan-eht*
greenhouse effect	effet (*m*) de serre	*ay-feh de sehr*
natural resources	ressources (*f, pl*) naturelles	*re-soors na-tewr-ehl*
nuclear energy	énergie (*f*) nucléaire	*ay-nehr-zhee new-klay-ehr*

petroleum	pétrole (*m*)	*pay-trul*
pollution	pollution (*f*)	*pul-ew-syOH*
radiation	radiation (*f*)	*rad-yah-syOH*
• **radioactive waste**	déchets (*m, pl*) radioactifs	*day-sh-eh rad-yo-akteef*
solar cell	cellule (*f*) solaire	*sehl-ewl sul-ehr*
solar energy	énergie (*f*) solaire	*ay-nehr-zhee sul-ehr*
thermal energy	énergie (*f*) thermique	*ay-nehr-zhee tehr-meek*
water pollution	pollution (*f*) des eaux	*pul-ew-syOH day-zoh*
wind energy	énergie (*f*) éolienne	*ay-nehr-zhee ay-ul-yehn*
wind farm	champ (*m*) d'éoliennes	*shAH day-o-lee-yen*

b. SOCIETY

abortion	avortement (*m*)	*av-ort-mAH*
• **fetus**	fœtus (*m*)	*fay-tewss*
AIDS	SIDA (*m*)	*see-da*
AIDS patient	sidéen (*m*)	*see-day-AH*
	sidéenne (*f*)	*see-day-ehn*
AIDS researcher	sidologue (*m, f*)	*see-du-lug*
capital punishment	peine (*f*) capitale	*pehn ka-pee-tal*
censorship	censure (*f*)	*sAH-sewr*
drugs	drogue (*f*)	*drug*
• **drug addiction**	toxicomanie (*f*)	*tuks-ee-kum-an-ee*
• **drug pusher**	trafiquant(e) (*m, f*) des stupéfiants	*tra-feek-AH(t) day stew-pay-fyAH*
• **take drugs**	prendre (*v*) de la drogue	*prAH-dre de la drug*
	se droguer (*v*)	*se-drug-ay*
• **drug trafficking**	trafic (*m*) des stupéfiants	*tra-feek day stew-pay-fyAH*
feminism	féminisme (*m*)	*fay-meen-eesme*
• **feminist**	féministe (*m, f*)	*fay-meen-eest*
HIV	VIH (*m*)	*vay-ee-ah-sh*
homosexual	homosexuel(le) (*m, f*)	*um-u-sehks-ew-ehl*
• **homosexuality**	homosexualité (*f*)	*um-u-sehks-ew-al-ee-tay*
• **gay**	gai(e) (*adj, m, f*)	*gay*
• **lesbian**	lesbienne (*f*)	*lehs-by-ehn*
• **lesbianism**	lesb(ian)isme (*m*)	*lehs-b(y-an)-ee-sme*
morality	moralité (*f*)	*mu-ra-lee-tay*
nuclear war	guerre (*f*) nucléaire	*gehr new-klay-ehr*
nuclear weapon	arme (*f*) nucléaire	*arm new-klay-ehr*
• **antinuclear protest**	protestation (*f*) anti-nucléaire	*prut-ehs-tah-syOH AH-tee-new-klay-ehr*

• **atomic bomb**	bombe (*f*) atomique	*bOHb a-tum-eek*
biological weapon	arme (*f*) bactériologique	*arm bak-tay-ree-yul-uzh-eek*
• **chemical weapon**	arme (*f*) chimique	*arm shee-meek*
passive resistance	résistance (*f*) passive	*ray-zeess-tAHss pahss-eev*
pornography	pornographie (*f*)	*por-nug-ra-fee*
prostitution	prostitution (*f*)	*prus-tee-tew-syOH*
racism	racisme (*m*)	*ra-see-sme*
terrorism	terrorisme (*m*)	*tehr-ur-eesme*

c. EXPRESSING YOUR OPINION

according to me	selon moi	*slOH mwa*
as a matter of fact	à vrai dire	*a vreh deer*
by the way	à propos	*a pro-po*
for example	par exemple	*par-ehg-zAH-ple*
I believe that . . .	Je crois que . . .	*zhe krwa ke*
I don't know if . . .	Je ne sais pas si . . .	*zhen seh pah see*
I doubt that . . .	Je doute que . . .	*zhe doot ke*
I think that . . .	Je pense que . . .	*zhe pAHs ke*
I'd like to say . . .	Je voudrais dire . . .	*zhe vood-reh deer*
I'm not sure that . . .	Je ne suis pas sûr(e) que . . .	*zhen swee pah sewr ke*
I'm sure that . . .	Je suis sûr(e) que . . .	*zhe swee sewr ke*
in conclusion	en conclusion	*AH kOH-klew-zyOH*
in my opinion	à mon avis	*a-mun-avee*
in my view	à mon avis	*a mOH na-vee*
It seems to me that . . .	Il me semble que . . .	*eel me sAHble ke*
It's clear that . . .	Il est clair que . . .	*eel eh klehr ke*
	Il est évident que . . .	*eel eh tay-veed-AH ke*
that is to say	c'est-à-dire	*seh-ta-deer*
There's no doubt that . . .	Il n'y a pas de doute que . . .	*eel ny-a-pah de doot ke*
therefore	donc (*conj*)	*dOHk*

ENGLISH-FRENCH WORDFINDER

This alphabetical listing of all the English words in *French Vocabulary* will enable you to find the information you need quickly and efficiently. If all you want is the French equivalent of an entry word, you will find it here. If you also want pronunciation and usage aids, or closely associated words and phrases, use the reference number(s) and letter(s) to locate the section(s) in which the entry appears. This is especially important for words that have more than one meaning.

Remember that numbers refer to sections, not page numbers, in this book.

A

a un *(m, s)*; une *(f, s)* 8c

abbreviation l'abréviation *(f)* 19c

able to (be) pouvoir *(v)* 21a

abortion l'avortement *(m)* 45b

above au-dessus *(adv)* 3d; en haut 3d

abroad à l'étranger 19e, 30a

absent absent(e) *(adj, m, f)* 37f

accelerator pedal la pédale d'accélérateur 33e

accent l'accent *(m)* 8a, 19c

accept accepter *(v)* 21b

acceptable acceptable *(adj)* 21b

accident l'accident *(m)* 33c, 39c

according to me selon moi 45c

accordion l'accordéon *(m)* 28c

account le compte 26; *(bill)* le compte 35b

accountant le (la) comptable 38a

accounting la comptabilité 37e

accusation l'accusation *(f)* 41

accuse accuser *(v)* 41

accused accusé(e) *(adj, m, f)* 41

ace l'as *(m)* 27a; **ace of spades** *(cards)* l'as de pique 27a

acid l'acide *(m)* 13c

acne l'acné *(f)* 40a

acquaintance la connaissance 10b, 16b

across à travers *(prep)* 3d, 36c

act l'acte *(m)* 28e; **to act** jouer *(v)* dans une pièce 28e

active actif *(adj, m)*, active *(adj, f)* 8a, 11e

activity l'activité *(f)* 11e

actor l'acteur *(m)* 28a, 38a

actress l'actrice *(f)* 28a, 38a

actually effectivement *(adv)* 17b

acute aigu, aiguë *(adj)* 2b

adapt adapter *(v)* 11e

adaptable adaptable *(adj)* 11e

add (on) ajouter *(v)* 1e

addition l'addition *(f)* 1e

address l'adresse *(f)* 11f, 19e, 38b

address oneself to s'adresser *(v)* à 41

addressee le destinataire 19e

adhesive strip 1e sparadrap 25h

adhesive tape le ruban adhésif transparent 19d, 25c, 38c

adjacent *(angle)* adjacent *(adj)* 2b

adjective l'adjectif *(m)* 8a, 8e, 8f

admit admettre *(v)*, avouer *(v)* 41

adolescence l'adolescence *(f)* 11b

adolescent adolescent(e) *(n, adj)* 11b

adult l'adulte *(m/f)* 11b

adventure novel le roman d'aventure *(f)* 20a

adverb l'adverbe *(m)* 8a

advertising la publicité 20a, 38d

advice   le conseil   17a

advise   conseiller   *(v)*   17a

affection   l'affection   *(f)*   11e

affectionate   affectueux, affectueuse
(adj, m, f)   11e, 21a

affectionately   affectueusement
(adv)   19b

Africa   l'Afrique   *(f)*   30b

after   après   *(adv)*   4e

afternoon   l'après-midi   *(m)*   4a

again   de nouveau   *(adv)*, encore
une fois   4e

age   l'âge   *(m)*   11b, 38b

aggressive   agressif, agressive   *(adj,
m, f)*   11e

aggressiveness   l'agressivité   *(f)*
11e

agnostic   agnostique   *(adj, m, f)*
11d

ago   il y a   *(adv)*   4e

agree   être   *(v)* d'accord   *(m)*
21a, 22b, 41

agriculture   l'agriculture   *(f)*   14a

ahead   avant   *(adv)*   3d, 36c

AIDS   le SIDA   40a, 45b

AIDS patient   le sidéen, la sidéenne
40a, 45b

AIDS researcher   le, la sidologue
40a, 45b

aikido   l'aïkido   *(m)*   27b

air   l'air   *(m)*   6a, 13c

air bag   le sac gonflable   33e

air conditioner   le climatiseur   23e,
33e

air conditioning   la climatisation
23e

air pollution   la pollution
atmosphérique   45a

airline   la ligne aérienne   32a

airmail   par avion   19e

airplane   l'avion   *(m)*   32c

airport   l'aéroport   *(m)*   32a

aisle   l'allée   *(f)*, le passage   28a,
32c

aisle seat   le siège côté allée   32c

alarm   l'alarme   *(f)*   39a

alarm clock   le réveil, le réveille-
matin   4d, 25i

albatross   l'albatros   *(m)*   15b

Alberta   l'Alberta   *(f)*   30b

alcoholic beverage   la boisson
alcoolique   24k

algebra   l'algèbre   *(f)*   1f

algebraic   algébrique   *(adj)*   1f

Algeria   l'Algérie   *(f)*   30b

Algiers   Alger   30c

all   tout   *(adj)*, toute chose   3c

All aboard!   En voiture!   34

all day   toute   *(adj)* la journée
4a

All Saints' Day   La Toussaint   29a

allegory   l'allégorie   17a

allergy   l'allergie   *(f)*   40a

allude   faire   *(v)* allusion   17a

almost   presque   *(adv)*   3c

almost never   presque   *(adv)*
jamais   *(adv)*   4e

alphabet   l'alphabet   *(m)*   8a

already   déjà   *(adv)*   4e

alternator   l'alternateur   *(m)*   33e

although   bien que   *(conj)*, quoique
(conj)   8p

altruism   l'altruisme   *(m)*   11e

altruist   l'altruiste   *(m, f)*   11e

altruistic   altruiste   *(adj, m, f)*   11e

always   toujours   *(adv)*   4e

amateur   l'amateur   *(m)*   27b

ambition   l'ambition   *(f)*   11e

ambitious   ambitieux, ambitieuse
(adj, m, f)   11e

ambulance   l'ambulance   *(f)*   33a,
39a, 39c

America   l'Amérique   *(f)*   30b

American *(nationality)*   Américain
(m), Américaine   *(f)*   30d;
(language) américain   *(m)*,
anglais   *(m)*   30d

ammonia   l'ammoniaque   *(f)*   13c

among   parmi   *(prep)*   3d, 8g

amphitheater   l'amphithéâtre   *(m)*
36a

an   un   *(m, s)*, une   *(f, s)*   8c

analogy   l'analogie   *(f)*   17a

anatomy   l'anatomie   *(f)*   37e

anchovy   l'anchois   *(m)*   24d

and   et   *(conj)*   8p

anesthetic l'anesthésique *(m)*
40b

anger la colère 11e, 21a

angle l'angle *(m)* 2b

angry en colère 11e; fâché(e)
(adj, m, f) 21a

animal l'animal *(m)* 15a

ankle la cheville 12a

anniversary l'anniversaire *(m)*
11c, 29a

announce annoncer *(v)* 17a

announcement l'annonce *(f)*
17a; le faire-part 19e

annually annuel, annuelle *(adj)*,
annuellement *(adv)* 4c

answer la réponse 9, 17a, 37f;
répondre *(v)* 9, 17a, 18b, 37f

answering machine le répondeur
téléphonique, le téléphone-
répondeur 18a

ant la fourmi 15d

Antarctic Antarctique *(adj, m, f)*
13b

Antarctic Circle le Cercle
antarctique 13e

antenna l'antenne *(f)* 20b, 42

anterior antérieur(e) *(adj)* 4e

anthropology l'anthropologie *(f)*
37e

antibiotic l'antibiotique *(m)* 25h

antidepressant l'antidépresseur
(m) 25h

antihistamine l'antihistaminique
(m) 25h

antinuclear protest la protestation
antinucléaire 45b

antiseptic l'antiseptique *(m)* 39c

antivirus program le programme
antivirus 43

anus l'anus *(m)* 40a

anxiety l'anxiété *(f)* 21a

anxious anxieux, anxieuse *(adj,
m, f)* 11e, 21a

anxiousness l'anxiété *(f)* 11e,
21a

any *(partitive)* *see* **Partitive** 8d

apartment l'appartement *(m)*
23g

apartment building l'immeuble
(m) 23g

aperitif l'apéritif *(m)* 24g

apostrophe l'apostrophe *(f)* 19c

appeal court la cour d'appel 41

appendicitis l'appendicite *(f)*
40a

appendix l'appendice *(m)* 20a,
28d, 40a

appetizer les hors-d'oeuvre variés
(m, pl) 24g

appetizing appétissant(e) *(adj, m,
f)* 24p

applaud applaudir *(v)* 28e

applause l'applaudissement *(m)*
28e

apple la pomme 14d, 24f

apple pie la tarte aux pommes
24g

apple tree le pommier 14c

appointment le rendez-vous 40a,
40b

appointment book l'agenda de
bureau 38c

approval l'approbation *(f)* 21b

approve approuver *(v)* 21b

approximately à peu près *(adv)*
3c; environ *(adv)* 3c

apricot l'abricot *(m)* 14d, 24f

April l'avril *(m)* 5b

Aquarius le Verseau 5d

Arab *(nationality)* Arabe *(m/f)*
30d; *(language)* l'arabe *(m)*
30d

Arabic numerals chiffres *(m)*
arabes 1d

archbishop l'archevêque *(m, f)*
11d

archeology l'archéologie *(f)* 37e

archipelago l'archipel *(m)* 13b

architect l'architecte *(m, f)* 38a

architecture l'architecture *(f)*
28b, 37e

Arctic Arctique *(adj, m, f)* 13b

Arctic Circle le Cercle arctique
13e

area la superficie 3a, 13e; la
surface 3a, 13e

area code le code régional 18b, 38b

argue se disputer *(v)* 17a; se disputer *(v)*, se quereller *(v)* 39b

argument l'argument *(m)*, la dispute 17a

Aries le Bélier 5d

arithmetic l'arithmétique *(f)* 1f

arithmetical arithmétique *(adj)* 1f

arithmetical operations les opérations fondamentales 1e

arm le bras 12a

armchair le fauteuil 23c, 35c

armed robbery le vol à main armée 39b

arms race *(politics)* la course aux armements 44

arms reduction la réduction des armements 44

around autour de 3d

arrest arrêter *(v)* 39b

arrival l'arrivée *(f)* 32a

arrive arriver *(v)* 3e

arrogant arrogant(e) *(adj, m, f)* 11e

art l'art *(m)* 11e, 28b, 37e

art gallery la galerie d'art 36a

artery l'artère *(f)* 40a

arthritis l'arthrite *(f)* 40a

artichoke l'artichaut *(m)* 14e, 24e

article l'article *(m)* 8a, 8b, 8c, 20a

articulate articuler *(v)* 17a

artificial artificiel(le) *(adj, m, f)* 13d, 25i

artificial intelligence l'intelligence *(f)* artificielle 42b

artificial satellite le satellite artificiel 42

artist l'artiste *(m, f)* 28b

artistic artistique *(adj)* 11e

arts *(humanities)* les lettres *(f, pl)* 37e

as *(since)* comme *(conj)* 8p

as a matter of fact en fait 17b; à vrai dire 45c

as if comme si *(conj)* 8p

as much as tant que 3c; autant que 3c

as soon as aussitôt que *(conj)*, dès que *(conj)* 4e, 8p

Asia l'Asie *(f)* 30b

ask *(for)* demander *(v)* 9, 17a

ask a question poser *(v)* une question 37f

ask for the bill demander *(v)* le compte 35b

ask to do (something) demander *(v)* de faire quelque chose 17a

asparagus l'asperge *(f)* 14e, 24e

aspirin l'aspirine *(f)* 25h, 40a

assassin l'assassin *(m)* 39b

assault l'agression *(f)* 39b

assembly l'assemblée *(f)* 44

assignment book le calepin, le carnet 37b

assignments les devoirs *(m, pl)* 37f

assistant l'assistant(e) *(m, f)* 37d

association l'association *(f)* 44

Assumption *(August 15, National French Holiday)* l'Assomption *(f)* 5f, 29a

assure assurer *(v)* 21a

asterisk l'astérisque *(m)* 19c

asteroid l'astéroïde *(m)* 13a

astronaut l'astronaute *(m, f)*, le (la) cosmonaute 42

astronomy l'astronomie *(f)* 13a, 37e

astute astucieux, astucieuse *(adj, m, f)* 11e

astuteness l'astuce *(f)* 11e

at à *(prep)* 3d, 8g

at home à la maison, chez soi 23f

at midnight à minuit *(m)* 4a

at night dans la nuit 4a; de nuit 4a

at noon à midi *(m)* 4a

at one o'clock à une heure 4b

at someone's place chez quelqu'un 3d

at the beach   à la plage   36b

at the bottom   au fond, en bas   3d

at the dentist's   chez le (la) dentiste   40b

at the doctor's   chez le docteur   40a

at the edge of   au bord de   3d

at the end of   au bout de, à la fin de   36c

at the present time   à l'heure actuelle   4a

at the same time   en même temps, à la fois   4e

at the tip of one's tongue   au bout de la langue   12a

at the top of   au sommet de   36c

at three o'clock   à trois heures   4b

at two o'clock   à deux heures   4b

At what time?   A quelle heure?   4b

atheism   l'athéisme *(m)*   11d

atheist   l'athée *(m, f)*   11d

athlete   l'athlète *(m, f)*   27b

Atlantic   Atlantique *(adj, m, f)*   13b

atlas   l'atlas *(m)*   20a, 37b

ATM   le guichet automatique   26

atmosphere   l'atmosphère *(f)*   13b

atmospheric   atmosphérique *(adj)*   13b

atmospheric conditions   les conditions *(f, pl)* atmosphériques   6a

atom   l'atome *(m)*   13c, 42

atomic bomb   la bombe atomique   45b

atomic clock   l'horloge *(f)* atomique   4d

attend school   assister *(v)* à l'école *(f)*   37f

attic   le grenier   23a

attitude   l'attitude *(f)*   21a

attractive   attrayant, beau, bel *(adj, m)*; attrayante, belle *(f)*   11a, 11e

attractiveness   la fascination   11e

audience   le public, les spectateurs *(m, pl)*   28e

audio-visual equipment   les appareils audio-visuels *(m, pl)*   20b

August   l'août *(m)*   5b

aunt   la tante   10a

Australia   l'Australie *(f)*   30b

Australian *(nationality)*   Australien *(m)*, Australienne *(f)*   30d

Austria   l'Autriche *(f)*   30b

Austrian *(nationality)*   Autrichien *(m)*, Autrichienne *(f)*   30d

authentic   authentique *(adj)*   13d

author   l'auteur *(m)*, l'auteure *(f)*   20a

autobiography   l'autobiographie *(f)*   28d

automobile   l'auto(mobile) *(f)*   33a

automobile fuel   l'essence *(f)*   13c

autumn   l'automne *(m)*   5c

avarice   l'avarice *(f)*   11e

avaricious   avare *(adj)*   11e

avenue   l'avenue *(f)*   11f, 36a

average   moyen(ne) *(adj, m, f)*   1f

average height   la taille moyenne   11a

away   au loin *(adv)*   3d

awful   mauvais(e) *(adj, m, f)*   6a

awful weather   un temps mauvais   6a

axis   l'axe *(m)*   2b

B

baby   le bébé   11b

bachelor   célibataire *(n/adj, m, f)*   11c

back *(backward)*   en arrière *(adv)*   3d; arrière *(adv)*   36c

back up   reculer *(v)*   33c

backup lights   les feux *(m, pl)* de recul   33e

bacon   le bacon   24c

bad *(mean, nasty)*   méchant(e) *(adj, m, f)*   11e

bad *(quality)*   mauvais(e) *(adj, m, f)*   24p

Bad(ly)!   Mal! *(adv)*   16a

bad breath la mauvaise haleine 40a

bad mood la mauvaise humeur; **in a bad mood** de mauvaise humeur 21a

bag le sac 23d; **shopping bag** le sac à provisions 25a

baggage les bagages *(m, pl)* 31

baggage claim la délivrance des bagages 32a

bagpipes la cornemuse 28c

baked au four 24p

baker le boulanger, la boulangère 38a

bakery la boulangerie 24n

balcony le balcon 35c

ball la balle 27b; *(in basketball, football, volleyball)* le ballon 27b

ballet le ballet 28c

ballpoint pen le stylo à bille 7c, 19d, 25c, 37f

banana la banane 14d, 24f

bandage le pansement 25h, 39c, 40a; panser *(v)* 40a

bank la banque 26

bank draft la traite bancaire 26

bank book le carnet de banque 26

bank rate le taux bancaire 26

banknote *(bill, currency)* le billet de banque 26

baptism le baptême 11d

barber le coiffeur 12d, 38a

barber shop le salon de coiffure *(f)* pour hommes 12d

Barcelona Barcelone 30c

bark *(cry of a dog)* aboyer *(v)* 15a

barley l'orge *(f)* 24i

barn la grange 15a

barometer le baromètre 6c

barometric pressure la pression barométrique 6c

bartender le barman 24m

base *(sports)* la base, le but 27b

baseball le base-ball 27b

basement le sous-sol 23a

basil le basilic 14e, 24j

basilica la basilique 36a

basin le bassin 13b

basket la corbeille 23d; le panier 23d

basket *(in basketball)* le panier 27b

basketball le basket(ball) 27b

bass drum la grosse caisse 28c

bassoon le basson 28c

Bastille Day *(July 14)* la Fête Nationale 5f; la Prise de la Bastille, le quatorze juillet 29a

bat *(animal)* la chauve-souris, la pipistrelle 15a

bat *(sports)* la batte 27b

bath oil l'huile *(f)* de bain 25f

bathing suit le maillot de bain *(m)* 25k

bathroom la salle de bains *(m, pl)* 23b, 35c

bathtub la baignoire 23a, 35c

batter *(sports)* le batteur 27b

battery la pile 25b; *(of car)* la batterie, les accumulateurs, les accus *(m, pl)* 33e

bay la baie 13b

be able pouvoir *(v)* 21a

be about to être *(v)* sur le point de 4

be absent être *(v)* absent(e) *(adj, m, f)* 37f

be absent-minded être *(v)* dans la lune 13a

be afraid avoir *(v)* peur *(f)* 21a

be against être *(v)* contre *(prep)* 21a

be ashamed avoir *(v)* honte *(f)* 21a

be at the tip of one's tongue être *(v)* sur le bout de la langue 12a

be awful *(weather)* faire *(v)* un temps mauvais 6a

be beautiful *(weather)* faire *(v)* beau temps 6a

be born naître *(v)* 11c

be called s'appeler *(v)* 11f

Be careful! Attention! 21c

be cold *(persons)* avoir *(v)* froid *(m)* 6b, 12b

be cold *(weather)* faire *(v)* froid 6a

be cool *(weather)* faire *(v)* frais 6a

be damp *(weather)* faire *(v)* humide 6a

be down *(mood)* avoir *(v)* le cafard 21a

be early être *(v)* de bonne heure 4e; être *(v)* tôt 4e

be enough suffire *(v)*, être *(v)* assez 3c

be fond of avoir *(v)* une passion pour, aimer *(v)* beaucoup 21b

be from . . . être *(v)* de . . . 11f

be healthy être *(v)* en bonne santé 40a

be hot *(persons)* avoir *(v)* chaud *(m)* 6b, 12b

be humid *(weather)* faire *(v)* humide 6a

be hungry avoir *(v)* faim *(f)* 12b, 24o

be in a bad mood être *(v)* de mauvaise humeur 11e

be in a good mood être *(v)* de bonne humeur 11e

be in orbit être *(v)* en orbite 13a

be in the clouds *(distracted)* être *(v)* dans les nuages *(m, pl)* 6a

be interested in s'intéresser *(v)* à 22b

be late être *(v)* tard (en retard) 4e

be located se trouver *(v)* 13e

be mild *(weather)* faire *(v)* doux 6a

be muggy *(weather)* faire *(v)* un temps lourd 6a

be on a familiar *(first-name)* **basis** tutoyer *(v)* 16b

be on a formal basis vouvoyer *(v)* 16b

be on fire être *(v)* en feu 39a

be on strike être *(v)* en grève 44

be on the point/verge of être *(v)* sur le point de 4e

be on time être *(v)* à l'heure *(f)* 4a, 4e

be on trial être *(v)* en procès 41

be out of breath être *(v)* hors d'haleine, être *(v)* à bout de souffle 40a

be pregnant être *(v)* enceinte *(adj, f)* 11c

be present être *(v)* présent(e) *(adj, m, f)* 37f

be promoted être *(v)* reçu(e) *(adj, m, f)* 37f

be right *(persons)* avoir *(v)* raison *(f)* 22b

be run over être *(v)* renversé(e), se faire *(v)* renverser 39c

be seated s'asseoir *(v)* 16b

Be seated, please. Asseyez-vous, s'il vous plaît 16b; Assieds-toi, s'il te plaît 16b

be sleepy avoir *(v)* sommeil *(m)* 12b

be the fool in an affair être *(v)* le pigeon dans une affaire 15b

be thirsty avoir *(v)* soif *(f)* 12b, 24o

be tired être *(v)* fatigué(e) *(adj)* 12b

be up *(good mood)* être *(v)* remonté(e) *(adj, m, f)*, être *(v)* heureux(-euse) 21a

be white with fear être *(v)* vert de peur 7a

be windy faire *(v)* du vent *(m)* 6a

be wrong *(persons)* avoir *(v)* tort *(m)* 22b

beach la plage 13b, 36b

beak le bec 15b

beam of light le rayon de lumière 42

bean le haricot, les fèves *(f, pl)* de haricot 14e, 24e

bear l'ours *(m)* 15a
beard la barbe 12a
beast la bête 15a
beautician l'esthéticien, l'esthéticienne 12d
beautiful beau, bel, beaux, belle, belles *(adj)* 11a, 25l
beautiful weather beau temps 6a
beauty la beauté 11a
because parce que *(conj)* 8p
become devenir *(v)* 4e, 25a
become angry se fâcher *(v)*, se mettre en colère 11e
become big grandir *(v)* 3c, 11a; agrandir *(v)* 3c; grossir *(v)* 3c
become bored s'ennuyer *(v)* 21a
become engaged se fiancer *(v)* 11c
become fat grossir *(v)* 11a
become friends devenir *(v)* amis *(m, pl)*; faire *(v)* l'amitié *(f)* 10b
become old vieillir *(v)* 11b
become red with anger devenir *(v)* rouge de colère 7a
become sick tomber *(v)* malade *(adj)* 11a
become small rendre *(v)* plus petit 3c; rapetisser *(v)* 3c
become thin maigrir *(v)* 11a
become weak s'affaiblir *(v)* 11a
bed le lit 23c, 35c
bed sheet le drap 23d
bedbug la punaise 15d
bedroom la chambre à coucher *(v)* 23b
bedside table la table de nuit *(f)*, la table de chevet 23c, 35c
bedspread le couvre-lit 23d
bee l'abeille *(f)* 15d
beech tree le hêtre 14c
beef le boeuf 24c
beer la bière 24k
beet la betterave 14e, 24e
before avant *(adv)*, auparavant *(adv)* 4e
begin commencer *(v)* 4e

beginning le commencement 4e; le début 3e
behind derrière *(adv)* 36c
Beijing/Peking Bèijīng/Pékin 30c
Belgian *(nationality)* Belge *(m/f)* 30d
Belgium la Belgique 30b
belief la crédence, la croyance 11d
believe croire *(v)* 11d, 22b
believe in croire en 11d
believer le (la) croyant(e) 11d
bell tower le campanile, le clocher 36a
bellhop le porteur 35b
below zero dessous zéro 6c
belt la ceinture 25k
Berlin Berlin 30c
beside *(next to)* à côté (de) 3d
best-seller le best-seller 20a, 25o
Best wishes! Meilleurs voeux! 16c, 29c
Better late than never! Mieux vaut tard que jamais! 4e
between entre 3d, 8g
between friends entre amis 10b
beverage la boisson 24k
beyond au-delà (de) 3d
Bible la Bible 11d
bicycle la bicyclette 33a
Bicycle Lane Piste cyclable 33d
bicycle racing les courses cyclistes 27b
big grand(e) *(adj)* 3c, 11a, 25l; gros *(adj, m)*, grosse *(f)* 3c
bigness la grandeur 11a
bike le vélo 33a
bill *(banknote, currency)* le billet de banque 26
bill *(cash register tape)* la fiche de caisse 25a; le compte 35b
bill *(invoice)* la facture 25a; **check** *(to pay in a restaurant)* l'addition *(f)* 24m
billiard ball la bille 27a
billiard table la table de billard *(m)* 27a
billiards, to play jouer *(v)* au billard *(m)* 27a

billionth milliardième 1b

binary binaire *(adj)* 1d

bingo le bingo 27a

bingo card la fiche 27a

biography la biographie 28d

biological weapon l'arme *(f)* bactériologique 45b

biology la biologie 37e

bird l'oiseau *(m)* 15b

birth la naissance 11c

birthday l'anniversaire *(m)* de naissance *(f)* 11c, 29a

bisector la bissectrice 2b

bishop l'évêque 11d; *(in chess)* le fou 27a

bitter amer *(adj, m)*, amère *(adj, f)* 24p

black le noir 7a; **black coffee** le café noir 24k

blackbird le merle 15b

blackboard le tableau 37b

blackboard eraser l'éponge *(f)* humide; le (vieux) chiffon 37b

black ice le verglas 6a

blade la lame 23d, 25f

blank cassette la cassette vierge 20b

blanket la couverture 23d, 35c

bleat bêler *(v)* 15a

bleed saigner *(v)* 39c

Bless you! *(after a sneeze)* A vos (tes) souhaits! 16c

blind aveugle *(n/adj, m, f)* 12c

blindness la cécité 12c

blog le blog 17a

blond blond(e) *(adj)* 11a

blonde blonde *(f)* 11a

blood le sang 12a, 39c, 40a

blood pressure la tension artérielle (veineuse) 40a

blood test l'analyse *(f)* de sang, la prise de sang 40a

bloom fleurir *(v)* 14a

blouse le chemisier 25k

blue le bleu 7a

blueberry la myrtille, le bleuet (Québec) 24f

blueprint le bleu 28b

bluetooth la technologie bluetooth 20b

boarding *(travel)* l'embarquement *(m)* 32a

boarding house la pension 35a

boarding pass la carte d'embarquement *(m)* 32a

boat le bateau 36b

bodily physique le physique 11a

body le corps 11a, 12a; *(of a letter)* le contenu, le corps 19c

body building le culturisme 27b

boiling point le point d'ébullition *(f)* 6c

bold *(brash)* effronté(e) *(adj)* 11e

bolt of lightning un coup d'éclair 6a

bond *(banking, commerce)* l'obligation *(f)* 26

bone l'os *(m)* 12a, 40a

book le livre 20a, 25o, 37b

book of adventure le livre d'aventure *(f)* 25o

bookcase l'étagère *(f)*, la bibliothèque 23c, 37b

bookshelf l'étagère *(f)* à livres 23c

bookstore la librairie 25o

boot la botte 25n

border la frontière 13e, 31; borner *(v)* 13e; toucher *(v)* 13e

bore ennuyer *(v)* 21a

bored *see* **become bored, feel bored**

boredom l'ennui *(m)* 21a

boss in an office le chef de bureau 38d

botanical botanique *(adj)* 14a

botany la botanique 14a, 37e

both les deux, tous les deux, toutes les deux 3c

bottle la bouteille 23d, 24l

bottom le fond 3d; au fond 3d

bouquet of flowers la botte de fleurs *(f)* 14b

bow *(of a stringed instrument)* l'archet *(m)* de violon 28c

bowl le bol, l'assiette *(f)* creuse 24l; **to bowl** jouer *(v)* au bowling 27b

bowling le bowling 27b

bowling alley la piste 27b

bowling ball la boule 27b

bowling pin la quille 27b

box la boîte 23d

box office le guichet 28a

boxing la boxe 27b

boxing glove le gant de boxe 27b

boxing ring *(sport)* le ring 27b

boy le garçon 11a, 11b

boyfriend l'ami, le petit ami 10b

bra le soutien-gorge 25k

bracelet le bracelet 25i

bracket le crochet 19c

brain le cerveau 12a, 40a

brake le frein 33a, 33e; freiner *(v)* 33c

brakelight le feu de stop 36c

branch la branche 14a

brash effronté(e) *(adj)* 11e

brass instruments les cuivres *(m, pl)* 28c

Brazil le Brésil 30b

Brazilian *(nationality)* Brésilien *(m)*, Brésilienne *(f)* 30d

bread le pain 24i

break down *(vehicle)* tomber *(v)* en panne 33c

break off a friendship rompre *(v)* une amitié 10b

breakdown *(machine, vehicle)* la panne 33c

breakfast le petit déjeuner 24a, 35b

breakfast included le petit déjeuner compris 35b

breath l'haleine 40a

breathe respirer *(v)* 12b, 40a

bricklayer le maçon 38a

bridal suite la chambre matrimoniale 35b

bride la mariée 11c

bridegroom le marié 11c

bridge le pont 33c, 36a

brief bref, brève *(adj, m, f)* 4e, 37f

briefcase la serviette 25c, 38a

briefly brièvement *(adv)*, en bref 4e, 17b

bright éclatant(e) *(adj)* 7b

brilliant brillant(e) *(adj)* 11e

bring apporter *(v)* 25a

brioche la brioche 24i

British Columbia la Colombie Britannique 30b

broccoli le brocoli 14e, 24e

brochure la brochure, le dépliant 20a, 30a

broiled grillé(e) *(adj, m, f)* 24b

broken bone l'os cassé (fracturé) 39c

broken line la ligne brisée 2b

bronchitis la bronchite 40a

bronze le bronze 13c

brooch la broche 25i

brook le ruisseau 36b

broom le balai 23d

broth le bouillon 24g

brother le frère 10a

brother-in-law le beau-frère 10a

brown le brun, le marron 7a

brush la brosse 12d, 25f; *(artist's)* le pinceau 28b

brush oneself se brosser *(v)* 12d

brush teeth se brosser *(v)* les dents 40b

buckle *(fasten)* **seat belt** boucler *(v)* la ceinture de sécurité 32c

bud bourgeonner *(v)* 14a; le bourgeon 14a

Buddhism le bouddhisme 11d

Buddhist bouddhiste *(m/f)* 11d

budget le budget 26

buffalo le buffle 15a

build construire *(v)* 23f

building l'édifice *(m)*; le bâtiment 23g, 39a

bulb *(plant)* le bulbe 14a

bull le taureau 15a

bump heurter *(v)* 39c

bumper *(car)* le pare-chocs 33e

burn brûler *(v)* 39a; la brûlure 39a

bus l'autobus *(m)* 33a; *(long-distance travel)* l'autocar *(m)* 34

bus driver le chauffeur 34; le conducteur (la conductrice) d'autobus 38a

bus station la gare, la station 34

business card la carte de visite 16b

business class la classe affaires 30a

business letter la lettre commerciale *(adj)* 19e

businessman l'homme d'affaires 38a

businesswoman la femme d'affaires 38a

busy occupé(e) *(adj)* 18b

but mais *(conj)* 8p

butcher le boucher, la bouchère 38a

butcher shop la boucherie 24n

butter le beurre 24h

butterfly le papillon 15d

buttermilk le babeurre, le lait de beurre 24h

button le bouton 25g

buy acheter *(v)* 23f, 25a

buy a ticket acheter *(v)* un billet 30a, 34; procurer *(v)* un billet 34

by boat en bateau *(m)* 30a

by plane en avion *(m)* 30a

by the way à propos 17b, 45c

by train par le train 30a

byte le multiplet 42b

C

cabbage le chou 14e, 24e

cabin *(travel)* la cabine 32c

cable le câble (téléphonique) 18a; *(hardware)* le câble 25b

cable television la télévision par câble 20b

cafeteria la cafétéria, le restaurant self-service 24m

cake le gâteau 24g

calculate calculer *(v)* 1f

calculation le calcul 1f

calculus le calcul 37e

calendar le calendrier 5b, 38c

call appeler *(v)* 17a

call a taxi appeler *(v)* un taxi 35b

call an ambulance appeler *(v)* une ambulance 39c

call collect téléphoner *(v)* en P.C.V. 18b

call the fire department appeler *(v)* les pompiers, appeler *(v)* les sapeurs-pompiers 39a

call the police appeler *(v)* la police 39b, 39c

caller ID l'afficheur *(m)* 18a

calling/business card la carte de visite 16b

calm calme *(adj)* 11e

calmness le calme 11e

camel le chameau 15a

camera l'appareil *(m)* photo (l'appareil photographique) 25d

camera shop le magasin de photo 25d

camping area le camping 36b

campus le campus 37c

Can you tell me . . . ? Pourriez-vous me dire . . . ? *(pol)*; Peux-tu me dire . . . ? *(fam)* 9

Canada le Canada 30b

Canadian *(nationality)* Canadien *(m)*, Canadienne *(f)* 30d

canceled flight le vol annulé 32b

Cancer *(sign of the zodiac)* le Cancer 5d

canine *(tooth)* la (dent) canine 40b

canoe le canoë 36b

cap la casquette 36b

capacity la capacité 3c

capital *(finance)* le capital

capital city la capitale 13e, 30a

capital letter la lettre majuscule 19c

capital punishment la peine
capitale 41, 45b
Capricorn *(sign of the zodiac)* le
Capricorne 5d
car l'auto *(f)*, la voiture 33a
car body la carrosserie 33e
car gas l'essence *(f)* 13c
car racing la course automobile
27b
car radio l'autoradio *(m)* 20b
car window la vitre 33e
caramel pudding la crème au
caramel 24h
carat le carat 25i
carbon *(element)* le carbone 13c;
le charbon 13c
card la carte 25e
cardigan le cardigan 25k
cardinal cardinal(e) *(adj, m, f)*
1a, 1d
career la carrière 11f, 38d; la
profession 11f
carnation l'oeillet *(m)* 14b
carpenter le menuisier, la
menuisière, le charpentier, la
charpentière 38a
carpet le tapis 23c; **wall-to-wall
carpeting** la moquette 23c
carriage *(of a typewriter)* le chariot
19d
carrot la carotte 14e, 24e
carry porter *(v)* 31
carry-on baggage les bagages *(m,
pl)* à main 31
cash *(money in currency and coins)*
to pay in cash payer *(v)* en
espèces 25a, 26, 35b
cash a check toucher *(v)* un
chèque 26
cash desk la caisse 26
cash register la caisse 25a, 26
cash register tape receipt la fiche
de caisse 25a
cashier le caissier, la caissière
25a, 26
cassette la cassette 20b, 25j;
cassette tape la bande
magnétique 20b

castle le château 36a
cat le chat, la chatte 15a
catch attraper *(v)* 27b; **catch
*(the train, etc.)*** prendre *(v)* 34
catch fire prendre *(v)* feu,
s'enflammer *(v)* 39a
catcher's mask le masque du
receveur 27b
catechism le catéchisme 11d
caterpillar la chenille 15d
catfish le poisson-chat 15c
cathedral la cathédrale 36a
Catholic catholique *(m, f)* 11d
Catholicism le catholicisme 11d
cauliflower le chou-fleur, les
choux-fleurs *(m, pl)* 14e, 24e
cavity la carie dentaire 40b
CD le CD 25j
ceiling le plafond 23a
celebrate one's birthday fêter *(v)*
l'anniversaire *(m)* de naissance
(f) 11c
celery le céleri 14e, 24e
cell la cellule 14a
cell phone le téléphone cellulaire, le
portable 18a
cello le violoncelle 28c
cellular phone le téléphone
cellulaire, le téléphone portable, le
portable 18a
Celsius Celsius 6c
censorship la censure 45b
center le centre 2a
centigrade centigrade *(n/adj, m)*
6c
centimeter le centimètre 3a
Central America l'Amérique
centrale *(f)* 30b
central heating le chauffage central
23e
century le siècle 4c
chain la chaîne 25i
chain guard *(bicycle)* le couvre-
chaîne 33a
chair la chaise 23c; le siège de
bureau 38c
chalet le chalet 35a
chalk la craie 37b

Chamber of Representatives (deputies) la Chambre des Députés 44

chamomile la camomille 24k

change changer (v) 4e, 25a

change (money return in a transaction) la monnaie 25a

change gears changer (v) de vitesse 33c

change subject changer (v) de sujet (m) 17a

channel (television) la chaîne, le canal 20b

channel (water) le chenal 13b

chapter le chapitre 28d

character le caractère 11e; (in literature) le personnage 28d

characteristic caractéristique (n/adj, f) 11e

characterize caractériser (v) 11e

charge (law) la cause 41

charge (atom) la charge 13c

Charge it to my bill. Mettez-le sur mon compte. 35b

charter flight le vol charter 30a

chat causer (v) 17a

cheap bon marché (adj, m, f) 24p

check (in a restaurant) l'addition (f) 24m

check (to pay with a) payer (v) par chèque 25a, 26, 35b

check the oil vérifier (v) l'huile 33c

checkbook le carnet de chèques 26

checkerboard le damier 27a

checker piece le pion 27a

checkers, to play jouer (v) aux dames 27a

checkmate l'échec et mat (m) 27a

cheek la joue 12a

Cheers! A votre santé! A la vôtre! 16c, 24l

cheese le fromage 24h; **grated** râpé; **melted** fondu; **puffed** soufflé 24h

cheesecake le gâteau au fromage 24i

chemical chimique (adj) 13c; le produit chimique 13c

chemical formula la formule chimique 13c

chemical weapon l'arme (f) chimique 45b

chemistry la chimie 13c, 37e

cherry la cerise 14d, 24f

cherry pie la tarte aux cerises 24g

cherry tree le cerisier 14c

chess, to play jouer (v) aux échecs 27a

chessboard l'échiquier (m) 27a

chest la poitrine 12a

chest of drawers la commode 23c, 35c

chestnut la châtaigne, le marron 14d

chestnut tree le châtaignier 14c

chick le poussin 15b

chicken le poulet 15b, 24c

chief of police le préfet de police 41

child l'enfant (m, f) 11b

children les enfants 11b

chimney la cheminée 23a

chin le menton 12a

China la Chine 30b

Chinese (nationality) Chinois (m), Chinoise (f) 30d; (language) le chinois 30d

chlorine le chlore 13c

chlorophyll la chlorophylle 14a

chocolate le chocolat 24g

chocolate ice cream la glace au chocolat 24h

chocolate pie la tarte au chocolat 24g

Christian chrétien (n/adj, m), chrétienne (n/adj, f) 11d

Christianity le christianisme 11d

Christmas le Noël 5f, 29a

chum le copain, la copine 10b

church l'église (f) 11d, 36a

cigar le cigare 25e

cigarette la cigarette 25e

cinema le cinéma, le ciné 28a

circle le cercle 2a

circumference la circonférence 2a

citric citrique *(adj)* 14d

citrus (fruit) les agrumes *(m, pl)* 14d, 24f

city la ville 11f, 13e, 30a, 36a, 38b

city map le plan de la ville 36a

civil law le droit civil, la loi civile 41

clam la palourde 24d

clamp *(hardware)* le serre-joint 25b

clap of thunder le tonnerre, le coup de tonnerre 6a

clarinet la clarinette 28c

class la classe 30a, 37f

class of students la classe d'étudiants (d'élèves) 37d

classical music la musique classique 25j, 28c

classified ad la petite annonce 38d

classroom la salle de classe 37c

clause la proposition 8a

clean propre *(adj)* 11a, 12d, 25g; nettoyer *(v)* 23f

clean oneself se débarbouiller *(v)* 12d

clear clair(e) *(adj)* 6a; **clear picture** la photo nette 25d

clear sky le ciel clair 6a

clear the table desservir *(v)* la table, débarrasser *(v)* la table 23f, 24o

clerk l'employé(e) *(m, f)*, le commis 19e

clerk's window le guichet 19e

clever ingénieux, ingénieuse *(adj, m, f)* 11e

cleverness l'ingénuité *(f)* 11e

climate le climat 6a

climb monter *(v)* 3e

clip *(paper)* le trombone 19d

clock l'horloge *(f)* 4d, 25i; **atomic clock** une horloge atomique 4d

clone cloner *(v)* 42

close an account arrêter *(v)* un compte, clore *(v)* un compte 26

close friend l'ami(e) intime 10b

closed fermé(e) *(adj, m, f)* 25a

closed circuit le circuit fermé 20b

closet la penderie, le placard 23b, 35c

closing *(of a letter)* la formule de politesse, la salutation (finale) 19c

closing time *(store)* l'heure *(f)* de fermeture 25a

clothes les vêtements *(m, pl)* 25g

clothes basket le panier à linge 25g

clothes hanger le cintre 23d, 35c

clothespin la pince à linge 25g

clothing les vêtements *(m, pl)*, l'habillement *(m)* 25k

clothing store le magasin d'habillement 25k

cloud le nuage 6a, 13b

cloudy nuageux *(adj, m)*, nuageuse *(adj, f)*, couvert *(adj, m)* 6a

clove of garlic la gousse d'ail 24g

clown le clown 11e

clubs *(cards)* le trèfle 27a

clutch pedal *(car)* la pédale d'embrayage 33e

coach *(sports)* l'entraîneur *(m/f)* 27b; *(of a train)* la voiture, le wagon 34

coal le charbon 13c

coal mine la mine de charbon 13c

coal mining la houille 13c

coast la côte 13b

coat le manteau 25k; **fur coat** le manteau de fourrure 25k

cockroach la blatte, le cafard 15d

coconut macaroon le macaron 24i

codfish la morue 15c, 24d

coed school l'école *(f)* mixte 37a

coffee le café 24k; **black coffee** le café noir 24k; **coffee pudding**

la crème au café   24h; **coffee with cream** un café-crème   24k; **light coffee** (half-and-half) le café au lait   24k

coffee machine la cafetière électrique, le percolateur   23d

coffee pot la cafetière   23d

coin la pièce de monnaie (f)   27a; **coin token** le jeton   18a

coin collecting la numismatique   27a

cold le froid, froid(e) (adj, m, f)   6a, 6b, 24p; (illness) le rhume   40a

cold cuts les viandes (f, pl) froides   24c

cold water l'eau (f) froide   35c

colleague le (la) collègue   10b

collide entrer (v) en collision, se heurter (v)   39c

collision la collision   39c

cologne l'eau (f) de cologne   25f

colon deux points (m, pl)   19c

color la couleur   7a–7c; colorer (v)   7c

color photo la photo en couleur   25d

colored coloré(e) (adj, m, f)   7c

coloring le colorant   7c

comb le peigne   12d, 25f

comb (one's hair) se peigner (v)   12d

come venir (v)   3e
I'm coming! J'arrive!   3e
Come here! Venez (pol) ici! Viens (fam) ici!   17b

come in entrer (v) (dans)   16b; **Come in!** Entrez! (pol); Entre! (fam)   16b

Come on! Allons! Allons donc!   20b

Come quickly! Venez (Viens) vite!   39b

come to light mettre (v) en lumière (f)   13a

comedian l'acteur (l'actrice) comique   28e

comedy la comédie   20a, 28e

comet la comète   13a

comic book le magazine de bandes dessinées   20a, 25o

comic strip la bande dessinée   20a

comma la virgule   19c

commerce le commerce   37e, 38d

commercial (advertising) la publicité   20b

communicate communiquer (v)   17a

communication la communication   17a

communism le communisme   44

communist le (la) communiste   44

compact car la voiture compacte   33a

compact disk le disque compact   20b, 25j, 42

company (business) la société commerciale   38d

compare comparer (v)   17a

comparison la comparaison   8a, 17a

compartment (of a train) le compartiment   34

compass le compas   2b, 37b; la boussole   3d

compatible compatible (adj, m, f)   42b

competition le concours   27b

complain se plaindre (v)   21a, 35b

complaint la plainte   21a, 35b

complementary complémentaire (adj, m, f)   2b

complex complexe (adj)   1d

complicated compliqué(e) (adj, m, f)   22a

Compliments! Mes compliments! (m, pl)   29c

composer le compositeur, la compositrice   25j, 28c

composition la composition   28c; le thème   37f

compound le composé   13c

computer l'ordinateur (m)   38c, 42b

computer-assisted instruction les instructions *(f, pl)* automatisées 42b

computer keyboard le clavier d'ordinateur 19d

computer language le langage-machine, le langage de programmation 42b

computer printer l'imprimante *(f)* d'ordinateur 42b

computer science l'informatique *(f)* 42b

concave concave *(adj)* 2b

concept le concept 22a

concert le concert 28c

conclude conclure *(v)* 17a

conclusion la conclusion 17a

conditional conditionnel(le) *(adj, m, f)* 8a

condominium l'immeuble *(m)* en copropriété *(f)* 23g

conductor *(of a public vehicle)* le conducteur, la conductrice 34

cone *(geometry)* le cône 2a; **ice cream cone** le cornet 24h

confirmation la confirmation 11d

conformist le (la) conformiste 11e

congratulate féliciter *(v)* 17a

Congratulations! Félicitations! *(f, pl)* 16c, 29c

conjugation la conjugaison 8a

conjunction la conjonction 8a, 8p

connection *(travel)* la correspondance 32a, 34

conscience la conscience 11e, 22a

conscientious consciencieux *(adj, m)*, consciencieuse *(f)* 11e, 22a

consecutive consécutif, consécutive *(adj)* 2b

consequently donc *(conj)* 8p

conservation la préservation 45a

conservative conservateur, conservatrice *(adj, m, f)* 11e

conservative party *(politics)* le parti conservateur 44

conservatory le conservatoire 37a

consonant la consonne 8a

constant constant(e) *(adj, m, f)* 1f

consumption la consommation 45a

contact lenses les lentilles *(f, pl)* de contact, les verres *(m, pl)* de contact 40a

contents le contenu 19c

continent le continent 13e, 30a

continental continental(e) *(adj, m, f)* 6a, 13e

continental drift la dérive des continents 13b

continually continuellement *(adv)* 4e

continue continuer *(v)* 4e

contract le contrat 38d

controversy la controverse 41

convalesce se remettre *(v)* 40a

convalescence la convalescence 40a

conversation la conversation 17a

convertible la décapotable 33a

convex convexe *(adj, m, f)* 2b

convince convaincre *(v)* 22b, 41

cook le cuisinier, la cuisinière 38a; cuire *(v)*, faire *(v)* la cuisine, cuisiner *(v)* 24o

cookbook le livre de cuisine 25o

cookie le sablé, le petit-beurre, le gâteau sec, le biscuit 24i

cooking la cuisine 24b

cool frais *(adj, m)*, fraîche *(adj, f)* 6a

cool weather faire *(v)* frais 6a

coordinate la coordonnée 2b

co-pilot le (la) copilote 32c

copper le cuivre 13c

copy la copie 37f

Cordially yours Salutations amicales 19a

cordless phone le téléphone sans fil 18a

corn le maïs 14e, 24i

corner le coin 36a

corner *(street)* le coin de la rue 33c

correspondence la correspondance 19e

corridor le couloir 23a

cortisone la cortisone 25h

cosecant la cosécante 2b

cosine le cosinus 2b

cosmetics/perfume shop la parfumerie 25f

cosmos le cosmos 13a

cost coûter (v) 24o, 25a; **price** le prix, le coût 25a

cost of living le coût de la vie 26

cotangent la cotangente 2b

cotton le coton 13c, 251

cough la toux; tousser (v) 40a

Could you tell me . . . ? Pourriez-vous me dire . . . ? 36c

council le conseil 44

count compter (v) 1f

countable comptable (adj) 1f

counter le comptoir 25a

country le pays 11f, 13e, 30a

courage le courage 11e

courageous courageux, courageuse (adj) 11e

course le cours 37f

court (of law) le tribunal, la cour 41

court of appeal la cour d'appel 41

courtesy la courtoisie 11e

courteous courtois(e) (adj) 11e

courtroom la salle du tribunal 41

cousin le cousin, la cousine 10a

cover la couverture 20a

cover charge (dining out) le couvert 24m

cow la vache 15a

CPR la réanimation cardio-pulmonaire 39a, 39c

crash (computer) tomber (v) en panne (f) 42b; planter (v) 43

crayon le crayon gras 7c

crazy fou, fol, folle (adj) 11e

cream la crème 24h, 25f

cream cake (pie) le gâteau à la crème 24i

cream puff le chou à la crème 24i

creamed horn le cornet feuilleté à la crème 24i

creative créatif (adj, m), créative (adj, f) 11e

credit le crédit 26

credit card (to pay with a credit card) payer (v) avec carte (f) de crédit 25a; la carte de crédit 26, 35b

crime le crime 39b

crime wave la vague de criminalité 39b

criminal le criminel, la criminelle 39b

criminal law le droit pénal 41

critical critique (adj) 11e

criticism la critique 20a, 28d

crocodile le crocodile 15c

cross-country skiing le ski de fond 27b

cross over traverser (v) 36c

cross the street traverser (v) la rue 36c

crouton le croûton 24i

crow le corbeau 15b

crown la couronne dentaire 40b

cruise la croisière 36b

crumb la miette 24i

crust la croûte 24i

cry (weep) pleurer (v) 11e, 21a

crying en larmes (f, pl) 11e

cube le cube 2a

cube root la racine cubique 1e

cubed au cube 1e

cubic centimeter le centimètre cubique 3a

cubic kilometer le kilomètre cubique 3a

cubic meter le mètre cubique 3a

cubic millimeter le millimètre cubique 3a

cucumber le concombre 14e, 24e

cue (billiards) la queue de billard (m) 27a

cultivate cultiver (v) 14a

cultivation la culture 14a

cultured cultivé(e) (adj) 11e

cup la tasse 23d, 241

cure la guérison; guérir (v) 40a

curfew le couvre-feu 41

curiosity la curiosité 11e

curious curieux, curieuse *(adj)*
11e

curler le bigoudi 12d, 25f

curls les boucles *(f)* de cheveux
12d; les cheveux *(m, pl)* frisés
12d

curly-haired les cheveux *(m, pl)*
bouclés, les cheveux frisés 11a

currency *(bill, banknote)* le billet
de banque 26

current le courant 35c

current account le compte courant
26

curtains les rideaux *(m, pl)* 23c,
28e, 35c

curve la courbe 2b; le virage
33c

curved line la ligne courbe 2b

cushion *(billiard table)* la bande
27a

custard le flan 24h

customer le client, la cliente 25a,
26

customs la douane 31

customs officer le douanier, la
douanière 31

cut couper *(v)* 24o

Cut it out! Arrêtez! Arrêtez donc!
20b

cut one's hair se faire *(v)*
couper *(v)* les cheveux *(m, pl)*
12d

cutlet la côtelette 24g

cyclamen le cyclamen 14b

cylinder le cylindre 2a

cymbals les cymbales *(f, pl)* 28c

cypress tree le cyprès 14c

D

dad le papa 10a

dahlia le dahlia 14b

daily quotidien, quotidienne *(adj)*,
quotidiennement *(adv)* 4c, 20a

daily newspaper le journal
quotidien 20a

dairy product le produit laitier
24h

dairy shop la laiterie 24n

daisy la marguerite 14b

damp humide *(adj)* 6a

dance danser *(v)* 28c, 29b; le bal
28c, 29b

dance music la musique de danse
25j

dancer le danseur, la danseuse
28c

dandruff les pellicules *(f, pl)* 40a

danger le danger 39a

Danish *(nationality)* Danois *(m)*,
Danoise *(f)* 30d; *(language)* le
danois 30d

dark *(color)* sombre, foncé *(adj)*
7b

dark *(weather)* faire *(v)* sombre
(adj) 6a

dark blue le bleu foncé 7a

dark-haired les cheveux *(m, pl)*
bruns 11a

dark matter la matière noire 13a

Darn it! Zut! 20b

dashboard le tableau de bord 33e

data les données *(f, pl)*,
l'information *(f)* 42b

data processing le traitement de
l'information 42b

date la date 5e, 11f, 19c; *(fruit)*
la datte 14d, 24f

date of birth la date de naissance
(f) 11f, 38b

daughter la fille 10a

daughter-in-law la belle-fille 10a;
la bru 10a

dawn l'aube *(f)* 4a

day le jour 4a, 4c
  the next day le lendemain 4a

day after tomorrow après-demain
4a

day before yesterday avant-hier
(adv) 4a

day care l'école maternelle 37a

day of the week le jour de la
semaine 5a

deaf sourd, sourde *(adj, m, f)* 12c

deafness la surdité 12c

Dear ... Cher, Chère, Chers,
Chères ... 19b

dear friend cher ami, chère amie 10b

Dear Madam . . . Madame, Chère Madame . . . 19a

Dear Sir . . . Monsieur, Cher Monsieur . . . 19a

death la mort 11c

debate le débat; débattre *(v)* 17a, 41

debit le débit 26

debit card la carte de retrait 26

debt la dette 26

decade la décennie 4c

decagon le décagone 2a

December le décembre 5b

decimal décimal(e) *(adj, m, f)* 1f

declarative déclaratif *(adj, m),* déclarative *(adj, f)* 8a, 8n

declare déclarer *(v)* 17a, 31

decorating la décoration 23c

decrease diminuer *(v),* la diminution 3c

deer le cerf 15a

defecate déféquer *(v)* 40a

defend oneself se défendre *(v)* 41

definite défini(e) *(adj, m, f)* 8a, 8b

definition la définition 20a

degree le degré 2b, 6c

degree *(university)* la licence 11f, 37f; le doctorat 11f, 37f; le diplôme universitaire 37f

delicate délicat(e) *(adj)* 11e

delicatessen l'épicerie *(f)* fine 24n

Delighted! Heureux! Heureuse! 16b

democracy la démocratie 44

democrat le (la) démocrate 44

democratic démocratique *(adj, m, f)* 44

demonstrate démontrer *(v)* 22b

demonstration *(politics)* la manifestation, la manif 44

demonstrative démonstratif *(adj, m),* démonstrative *(adj, f)* 8a, 8e, 8m

Denmark le Danemark 30b

dense dense *(adj)* 3b

density la densité 3b, 13d

dentist le (la) dentiste 38a, 40b

dentist's chair le fauteuil 40b

dentist's office le cabinet du (de la) dentiste 40b

denture le dentier 40b

deny nier *(v)* 17a

deodorant le déodorant 25f

depart partir *(v)* 3e, 34

department *(of a store)* le rayon 25a

department store le grand magasin 25a

departure le départ 32a

deposit le versement 26; verser *(v)* 26

deposit slip la fiche de versement 26

depot *(station)* la gare, la station 34

depressed déprimé(e) *(adj, m, f)* 21a

depression la dépression 21a

descend descendre *(v)* 3e

describe décrire *(v)* 17a

description la description 17a, 39b

descriptive descriptif *(adj, m),* descriptive *(adj, f)* 8a

desert le désert 13b

desk *(pupil's)* le pupitre; *(teacher's)* le bureau 37b; le bureau 38c

desktop computer l'ordinateur *(m)* de bureau 43

desperate désespéré(e) *(adj, m, f)* 21a

desperation le désespoir 21a

dessert le dessert 24g

destroy détruire *(v)* 39a

detest détester *(v)* 21b

dial *(of a timepiece)* le cadran 4d, 25i

dial a telephone number composer le numéro 18b

diameter le diamètre 2a

diamond le diamant 25i; *(cards)* le carreau 27a

diamond anniversary les noces *(f)* de diamant 11c

dice *(to play)* jouer *(v)* aux dés *(m, pl)* 27a

dictate dicter *(v)* 17a

dictation la dictée 37f

dictionary le dictionnaire 20a, 25o, 37b

die mourir *(v)* 11c

diesel le gazole 13c

difference la différence 1f

difficult difficile *(adj, m, f)* 22a

dig creuser *(v)* 14a

digestive system le système digestif 40a

digit le chiffre 1d

digress faire *(v)* une digression 17a

diligence la diligence 11e

diligent assidu(e) *(adj)*, travailleur, travailleuse *(adj)* 11e

dimension la dimension 2b, 3b
two-dimensional (2D) à deux dimensions *(f, pl)* 2b
three-dimensional (3D) à trois dimensions *(f, pl)* 2b

dining room la salle à manger *(v)* 23b

dinner le dîner 24a

diploma le diplôme 11f, 37f

diplomatic diplomatique *(adj)* 11e

direct direct(e) *(adj, m, f)* 8a, 8i

direct dialing téléphoner *(v)* en direct 18b

direct train le train direct 34

direction la direction 3d

dirty sale *(adj)* 11a, 12d, 25g

dirty word le mot grossier 20b

disagree être *(v)* en désaccord *(m)* 21a; se disputer *(v)* 41

disagreement le désaccord 21a

disappoint décevoir *(v)* 21a

disappointed déçu(e) *(adj, m, f)* 21a

disappointment la déception 21a

disarmament le désarmement 44

disco la discothèque 29b

discount le rabais, la remise 25a

discourse le discours 8a

discourteous discourtois(e) *(adj)* 11e

discuss discuter *(v)* 17a, 41

discussion la discussion 17a

disease la maladie 40a

disgust le dégoût 21b

disgusted dégoûté(e) *(adj, m, f)* 21b

dish antenna l'antenne *(f)* parabolique 42

dishonest malhonnête *(adj)* 11e

dishonesty la malhonnêteté 11e

dishwasher le lave-vaisselle 23d

disk le disque 42b; **floppy disk** la disquette, le disque souple 42b

dislike (not to like) ne pas aimer *(v)* 21b

disorganized désorganisé(e) *(adj, m, f)* 11e

dissatisfaction l'insatisfaction *(f)*, le mécontentement 21a

dissatisfied insatisfait(e) *(adj, m, f)*, mécontent(e) *(adj, m, f)* 21a

distance la distance 3d, 33c

divide diviser *(v)* 1e

divided by divisé par 1e

division la division 1e

divorce le divorce; divorcer *(v)* 11c

divorced divorcé(e) *(adj)* 11c, 38b

DNA ADN *(m)* 40a, 41

do faire *(v)* 18b; **do the dishes** faire *(v)* la vaisselle 23f

Do you have a vacant room? Avez-vous une chambre libre? 35b

doctor le médecin, la femme médecin, le docteur, la femme docteur 38a, 39c, 40a

doctorate degree le doctorat 37f

doctor's visit la visite du médecin 40a

documentary documentaire *(adj, m, f)* 20b

documents les documents *(m, pl)* 31

dodecahedron le dodécaèdre 2a

does not equal n'est pas égal à 1f

dog le chien, la chienne 15a

dollar le dollar 26

dolphin le dauphin 15c

donkey l'âne *(m)* 15a

Don't mention it! Il n'y a pas de quoi! De rien! 16c

door la porte 23a; *(of car)* la portière 33e

doorbell la sonnette *(f)* 23a

doorman le portier 35b

double double *(n/adj, m, f)* 3c

double bass la contrebasse 28c

double bed le grand lit 35c

double roll *(of bread)* le petit pain double 24i

double room une chambre double 35b

doubt le doute 22a; douter *(v)* 22b

dove la colombe 15b

down bas *(adv)* 3d, 36c; en bas 3d

downhill skiing le ski alpin 27b

download télécharger *(v)* 25j, 42b

downtown en ville *(f)*, le centre-ville 30a, 36a

Dr. *(M.D. degree)* Dr., le docteur 11f; le docteur, la docteure 16b; *(Ph.D. degree)* Dr., le docteur 16b

draft *(rough copy)* le brouillon 37f

drama le drame 20a, 28e

draw dessiner *(v)* 2b, 37f

draw *(score in sports)* le match nul 27b; terminer *(v)* à match nul (à égalité) 27b

drawer le tiroir 23c

drawing le dessin 37f

drawing instruments les instruments *(m)* de dessin *(m)* 2b

dress la robe 25k

dresser la commode 23c, 35c

dressing room la cabine d'essayage 25k

dried cod la merluche 24d

drill *(dentist's)* la fraise 40b

drill *(hardware)* la foreuse, la perceuse 25b

drink boire *(v)* 12b, 24o; la boisson 24k

drive conduire *(v)* 3e, 33b, 33c

driver *(of a car)* le chauffeur, l'automobiliste *(m/f)* 33b

driver's license le permis de conduire 33b

drop *(e.g., of rain)* la goutte 6a

drug addiction la toxicomanie 45b

drug pusher le (la) trafiquant(e) des stupéfiants 45b

drug trafficking le trafic des stupéfiants 45b

drugs la drogue 45b

drugstore la pharmacie 25h

drum *(music)* le tambour 28c

dry sec *(adj, m)*, sèche *(adj, f)* 6a

dry cleaning le nettoyage à sec 25g

dry oneself se sécher *(v)* 12d

dryer *(clothes)* la sécheuse, le sèche-linge 23d

duck le canard 15b, 24c

dull *(color)* terne *(adj)* 7b

dumpling la boulette 24g

dump truck le camion-benne 33a

during pendant *(prep)* 4e

Dutch *(nationality)* Hollandais *(m)*, Hollandaise *(f)* 30d; *(language)* le hollandais 30d

duty tax le tarif douanier 31

DVD D.V.D. *(m)* 20b

dwarf planet une planète naine 13a

dynamic dynamique *(adj)* 11e

E

e-ticket (electronic ticket) le billet électronique 32a

each chaque *(adj)* 3c
eagle l'aigle *(m)* 15b
ear l'oreille *(f)* 12a
early de bonne heure *(adv)*, tôt *(adv)* 4e, 32b, 34; *(arrival/ departure time)* en avance 32b, 34
earn gagner *(v)* 38d
earphone l'écouteur *(m)* 18a
earring la boucle d'oreille 25i
Earth la Terre 13a
earthquake le tremblement de terre, le séisme 13b
easel le chevalet 28b
east l'est *(m)* 3d; **to the east** à l'est 3d
Easter les Pâques *(f)* 5f, 29a
eastern oriental(e) *(adj)* 3d
easy facile *(adj, m, f)* 22a
eat manger *(v)* 12b, 24o
eccentric excentrique *(adj)* 11e
eclair l'éclair *(m)* 24i
eclipse l'éclipse *(f)* 13a
ecology l'écologie *(f)* 45a
economics l'économie *(f)* 37e
economy l'économie *(f)* 44
economy class *(travel)* la classe touriste 30a, 32a, 34
ecosystem l'écosystème *(m)* 45a
edge le bord 3d
editor le rédacteur, la rédactrice 20a, 38a
editor (correcting) le correcteur, la correctrice 20a
editor (writing) rédacteur *(m)* 20a
editorial éditorial(e) *(adj, m, f)* 20a
education l'éducation *(f)* 11f, 37f, 38b
eel l'anguille *(f)* 15c, 24d
egg l'oeuf *(m)* 24h
eggplant l'aubergine *(f)* 14e, 24e
egoism l'égoïsme *(m)* 11e
egoist l'égoïste *(m, f)* 11e
egoistic égoïste *(adj)* 11e
Egypt l'Egypte *(f)* 30b

eight huit 1a
eighteen dix-huit 1a
eighth huitième 1b
eighty quatre-vingts 1a
eighty-one quatre-vingt-un 1a
elastic élastique *(n, m/adj)* 13d
elbow le coude 12a
elderly person une personne âgée 11b
elect élire *(v)* 44
elected politician le député, la députée 44
elections les élections *(f, pl)* 44
electric razor le rasoir électrique 12d, 25f
electric stove la cuisinière électrique 23d
electrical électrique *(adj, m, f)* 13c, 25b
electrician l'électricien *(m)*, l'électricienne *(f)* 38a
electricity l'électricité *(f)* 13c, 23e
electrocardiograph l'électrocardiographe *(m)* 40a
electron l'électron *(m)* 13c, 42
elegance l'élégance *(f)* 11a
elegant élégant(e) *(adj)* 11a, 251
elegantly élégamment *(adv)* 11a
element l'élément *(m)* 13c
elementary school l'école *(f)* primaire 37a, 38b
elementary school teacher le maître, la maîtresse 37d
elephant l'éléphant *(m)* 15a
elevator l'ascenseur *(m)* 23g, 35b
eleven onze 1a
eleventh onzième 1b
eloquence l'éloquence *(f)* 11e
eloquent éloquent(e) *(adj)* 11e
e-mail le courrier électronique, le courriel 43
e-mail address l'adresse *(f)* électronique 42b
emerald l'émeraude *(f)* 25i
emergencies les urgences *(f, pl)* 39

emergency exit la sortie de secours 32c, 39a

emergency lane la piste d'urgence (f) 33d

emergency room la salle d'urgence 39c

emphasis l'accent (m) 17a

emphasize mettre (v) l'accent sur 17a

employ employer (v) 38d

employee l'employé(e) (m, f) 11f, 26, 38d

employer l'employeur, l'employeuse 11f, 38d

employment l'emploi (m) 11f

employment agency l'agence (f) d'emploi (m) 38d

empty vide (adj), vider (v) 3c

encourage encourager (v) 21a

encouragement l'encouragement (m) 21a

encyclopedia l'encyclopédie (f) 20a, 25o, 37b

end la fin 4e; finir (v) 4e

endorse endosser (v) 26

endorsement l'endossement (m), l'endos (m) 26

enemy l'ennemi(e) 10b

energetic énergique (adj) 11e

energy l'énergie (f) 11e, 13c, 45a

energy crisis la crise d'énergie (f) 45a

energy needs les besoins (m) d'énergie (f) 45a

energy source la source d'énergie (f) 45a

engaged fiancé(e) (adj) 11c

engagement les fiançailles (f, pl) 11c, 29a

engine le moteur 33e, 36c

engineer l'ingénieur, l'ingénieure (f) 38a

engineering les études (f, pl) polytechniques, le génie 37e

England l'Angleterre (f) 30b

English (nationality) Anglais (m), Anglaise (f) 30d; (language) l'anglais (m) 30d

enjoy oneself s'amuser (v) 21a

Enjoy your meal! Bon appétit! 16c, 24l

enjoyment l'amusement (m) 21a

enough assez (adv) 3c; suffisant(e) (adj) 3c

Enough! Assez! 21c

enter entrer (v) (dans) 3e, 16b, 36c

entire entier, entière (adj) 3c

entrance l'entrée (f) 23a, 25a, 35b

entrance exam l'examen (m) d'entrée 37f

entry (dictionary) l'entrée (f) 20a

entry (encyclopedia) l'article (m) 20a

envelope l'enveloppe (f) 19d, 19e, 25c

envious envieux, envieuse (adj) 11e

environment l'environnement (m) 13b, 45a

envy l'envie (f) 11e

equality l'égalité (f) 1f

equals est égal à 1f

equation l'équation (f) 1f

equator l'équateur 13e

equilateral équilatéral (adj) 2a

equinox l'équinoxe (m) 5c

eraser (for pencil) la gomme 2b, 19d; la gomme à effacer 37b

error l'erreur (f), la faute 37f

eruption l'éruption (f) 13b

escape, get out fuir (v), s'échapper (v) 39a

essay l'essai (m) 20a

euro un euro 26

Eurocurrency eurodevise (f) 26

Eurodollar eurodollar (m) 26

Europe l'Europe (f) 30b

even pair (adj, m) 1d

even though même si (conj) 8p

evening le soir 4a

evening school le cours du soir, l'école du soir 37a

every tout, toute, tous, toutes *(adj)* 3c; chaque *(adj, m/f)* 3c

everybody, everyone tout le monde 3c, 8o

Everybody out! Tout le monde dehors! 39a

everything tout, toute, toute chose, toutes les choses 3c, 8o

everywhere partout *(adv)* 36c

exam l'examen *(m)* 37f

examine examiner *(v)* 40a, 40b

exchange échanger *(v)* 25a; le change, changer *(v)* 26

exchange rate le taux du change 26

exclamation point le point d'exclamation *(f)* 19c

excursion l'excursion *(f)* 30a

excuse l'excuse *(f)* 17a

Excuse me! Excusez-moi! *(pol)*, Excuse-moi! *(fam)*, Pardonnez-moi! *(pol)*, Pardonne-moi! *(fam)* 16c

excuse oneself s'excuser *(v)* 17a

exercise l'exercice *(m)* 37f

exhibition l'exposition *(f)* 28b

existence l'existence *(f)* 22a

exit sortir *(v)* 3e, 25a, 36c; la sortie 35b

expensive cher *(adj, m, s)*, chère *(adj, f, s)*; chers *(adj, m, pl)*, chères *(adj, f, pl)* 24p; coûteux *(adj, m)*, coûteuse *(adj, f)* 24p, 25a

expiration *(date)* l'échéance *(f)* 26

explain expliquer *(v)* 17a, 37f

explanation l'explication *(f)* 17a, 37f

express exprimer *(v)* 17a

express bus l'autocar express 34

express oneself s'exprimer *(v)* 17a

express train le train express 34

expression l'expression *(f)* 17a

extension l'extension *(f)* 3b

extinguish éteindre *(v)* 39a

extract extraire *(v)* 40b

extract a root *(numbers)* extraire *(v)* la racine 1e

extraction l'extraction *(f)* 40b

eye l'oeil *(m)* 12a; les yeux *(m, pl)* 12a

eye doctor l'ophtalmologiste *(m/f)*, l'oculiste *(m/f)*, l'opticien *(m)*, l'opticienne *(f)* 38a, 40a

eyebrow le sourcil 12a

eyeglasses les lunettes *(f)* 37b, 40a

eyelash le cil 12a

eyelid la paupière 12a

eyewitness le témoin oculaire 41

F

fable la fable 28d

fabric le tissu 25l

face le visage, la figure 12a

face powder la poudre 25f

factor le facteur 1f; mettre *(v)* en facteurs *(m, pl)* 1f

factorial factoriel *(adj)* 1f; la factorielle 1f

factorization la mise en facteurs 1f

factory l'usine *(f)* 38d

factory worker l'ouvrier, l'ouvrière 38a

Fahrenheit Fahrenheit 6c

fail an exam échouer *(v)* à un examen, être collé(e) à un examen 37f

fairy tale le conte de fées *(f)* 28d

faith la foi 11d; la confiance 21a

faithful fidèle *(adj)* 11d, 11e

fake faux, fausse *(adj)* 13d, 25i

falcon le faucon 15b

fall tomber *(v)* 3e

fall *(season)* l'automne 5c

fall asleep s'endormir *(v)* 12b

fall in love tomber *(v)* amoureux 11c

false faux *(adj, m)*, fausse *(adj, f)* 25i

false teeth le dentier 40b

family la famille 10a

family friend l'ami(e) de la famille (f) 10b

family name le nom de famille (f) 11f, 38b

family relationship la parenté 10a

fan (of a vehicle) le ventilateur d'aération 33e

far loin (adv) 3d; **far from** loin de 36c; lointain(e) (adj) 3d

Farewell! Adieu! 16a

farm la ferme 15a

farmer le fermier, la fermière 15a, 38a

farmland le terrain agricole 13b

fascinate fasciner (v) 11e

fascinating fascinant(e) (adj) 11e

fascination la fascination 11e

fashion la mode 25k, 251

fast vite (adj/adv) 3d; rapide 3d

fast food le fast-food 24m

fasten (buckle) **seat belt** boucler (v) la ceinture de sécurité 32c

fat gros, grosse (adj) 11a

father le père 10a

father-in-law le beau-père 10a

faucet le robinet 23a, 35c

fax le fax 18b; la télécopie 18b, 38c

fax machine le télécopieur, l'émetteur-récepteur de fac-similé, le fax 18a, 42

fear la peur; avoir (v) peur 21a

Feast of the Assumption (National French Holiday) l'Assomption (f) 5f, 29a

feather la plume 15b

February le février 5b

feel sentir (v) 12c, 21a; se sentir (v) 40a

feel bad avoir (v) mal (m) 12b; se sentir (v) mal (m) 12b, 40a

feel bored crever (v) d'ennui (m) 21a

feel like avoir (v) envie de 21a

feel well aller (v) bien (adv) 12b; se sentir (v) bien (adv) 12b, 40a

feeling see mood

felt-tip pen le stylo-feutre 7c, 19d

female la femelle 11a, 38b

feminine féminin(e) (adj, m, f) 8a, 11a, 38b

feminism le féminisme 45b

feminist le (la) féministe 45b

fence la barrière, la clôture 15a

fencing (sport) l'escrime (f) 27b; **to fence** faire (v) de l'escrime 27b

fender (of vehicle) l'aile (f) 33e

fennel le fenouil 14e

fetus le foetus 45b

fever la fièvre 40a

fiance le fiancé 10b, 11c

fiancee la fiancée 10b, 11c

fiber la fibre 13c

fiction l'ouvrage (m) de fiction 20a; le livre de fiction (f) 28d

field le champ 13b, 27b

field of study le champ d'études 37f

fifteen quinze 1a; **about fifteen** une quinzaine 1c

fifth cinquième 1b

fifty cinquante 1a; **about fifty** une cinquantaine 1c

fifty-one cinquante et un 1a

fifty-two cinquante-deux 1a

fig la figue 14d, 24f

fig tree le figuier 14c

fight se battre (v) 39d

figure of speech la figure de rhétorique 17a

file (computers) le fichier 43

file (hardware) la lime 25b

file (office) le classeur, le dossier-classeur 38c

filet le filet 24g

filing card la fiche 38c

fill remplir (v) 3c

fill up (gasoline, petrol tank) faire (v) le plein 33c

filling *(tooth)* l'obturation *(f)*, le plombage 40b

film le film 25d, 28a

film projector le projecteur de film 37b

filter *(of vehicle)* le filtre 33e

fin la nageoire 15c

fine *(traffic ticket)* la contravention 33c

Fine! Bien! *(adv)* 16a

fine arts les beaux-arts *(m, pl)* 37e

finger le doigt 12a

fingernail l'ongle *(m)* 12a

finish finir *(v)* 4e

finish school finir *(v)* l'école *(f)* 11f; finir la dernière année d'école 37f

fir tree le sapin 14c

fire le feu, l'incendie *(m)* 13c, 39a

Fire! Au feu! 39a

fire *(to discharge an employee)* renvoyer *(v)* 38d

fire alarm l'alarme *(f)* d'incendie 39a

fire extinguisher l'extincteur *(m)* 39a

fire hose le tuyau de pompe 39a

fire hydrant la borne d'incendie 39a

fire truck le fourgon-pompe 33a, 39a

firearm l'arme *(f)* à feu 39b

firefighter le pompier, le sapeur-pompier 39a

fireman le pompier 38a

fireplace la cheminée 23a

fireproof ignifuge *(adj)*, incombustible *(adj)* 39a

firewall *(computer)* le pare-feu 43

first premier *(adj, m)*, première *(adj, f)* 1b, 8a

first aid les soins *(m, pl)* d'urgence, les premiers soins *(m, pl)* 39a, 39c

first class *(travel)* la première classe *(f)* 30a, 32a, 34

first floor (U.S.) le rez-de-chaussée 23a

first name le prénom 11f, 38f

first showing *(entertainment)* la première représentation 28a

fish le poisson 15c, 24d; pêcher *(v)*, aller *(v)* à la pêche 15c

fish stew la bouillabaisse 24g

fish store la poissonnerie 24n

fishbone l'arête *(f)* 15c

fisherman le pêcheur, la pêcheuse 15c

fishing la pêche 15c, 36b

fishing rod la canne à pêche 15c

fission reactor le réacteur à fission 42

fit *(size)* la mesure, la taille 3b, 25k

five cinq 1a

fix ajuster *(v)*, réparer *(v)* 25i, 33c; **fix, do it yourself** bricoler 23f

fixed bank rate le taux fixe 26

fixed price le prix fixe 24m, 25a

flame la flamme 39a

flash le flash 25d

flash drive la clé USB 43

flash of lightning le coup d'éclair, faire *(v)* des éclairs 6a

flashlight la lampe de poche 25b

flatter flatter *(v)* 21a

flattery la flatterie 21a

flavor la saveur 12c

flea la puce 15d

Flemish *(language)* le flamand 30d

flight le vol 32a; **canceled flight** le vol annulé 32b

flight attendant le steward, l'hôtesse de l'air 32c

floor le plancher, le parquet 23a

floor *(level, story of a building)* l'étage *(m)* 23a, 35b; **first floor (U.S.)** le rez-de-chaussée 23a

floppy disk la disquette, le disque souple 42b

Florence Florence 30c

flour la farine 24i

flow couler *(v)* 13b

flow chart le schéma fonctionnel 42b

flower fleurir *(v)* 14a; la fleur 14b

flower bed le parterre de fleurs 14b

flu la grippe 40a

fluorescent fluorescent(e) *(adj, m, f)* 25b

flute la flûte 28c

fly *(insect)* la mouche 15d

focus mettre *(v)* au point 25d

fog le brouillard 6a

foggy brumeux *(adj, m)*, brumeuse *(adj, f)* 6a

foil *(fencing)* le fleuret français 27b

foliage le feuillage 14a

folk music la musique folklorique 28c

follow suivre *(v)* 3e, 36c

fond of, to be avoir *(v)* une passion pour, aimer *(v)* beaucoup 21b

food la nourriture 24a

food coloring le colorant alimentaire 7c

fool le bouffon 11e

foolish bête *(adj, m, f)* 11e

foot le pied 12a

football le football américain 27b

footnote la note en bas de page 20a

for pour 8g

for example par exemple 45c

for now pour le moment 4e

for sale à vendre *(v)* 25a

for (since) three days depuis trois jours 4e

for the first time pour la première fois 16b

force an uneasy smile sourire *(v)* jaune 7a

forehead le front 12a

foreign currency la monnaie étrangère 31

foreign languages les langues *(f, pl)* étrangères 37e

foreigner l'étranger *(m)*, l'étrangère *(f)* 31

forest la forêt 13b

forget oublier *(v)* 22b

fork la fourchette 23d, 241

form *(to fill out)* la formule 31

Fortunately! Heureusement! *(adv)* 21c

forty quarante la; **about forty** une quarantaine 1c

forty-one quarante et un 1a

forty-two quarante-deux 1a

forward avant *(adv)* 3d

fossil le fossile 13c

fossil fuels les combustibles *(m)* fossiles 13c, 45a

foul line *(sports)* la ligne de jeu 27b

four quatre 1a

four-sided figures les figures *(f)* à quatre côtés 2a

four thousand quatre mille 1a

fourteen quatorze 1a

fourth quatrième 1b

fox le renard 15a

fraction la fraction 1d

fractional fractionnaire *(adj, m, f)* 1d

France la France 30b

Frankfurt Francfort 30c

free *(not occupied)* libre *(adj, m, f)* 18b

freeze geler *(v)* 6a

freezer le congélateur 23d

French *(nationality)* Français *(m)*, Française *(f)* 30d; *(language)* le français 30d

French foil *(fencing)* le fleuret français 27b

French fries les frites *(f, pl)* 24g

French National Holiday la Fête Nationale (le 14 juillet) 29a

French Polynesia la Polynésie française 30b

frequent fréquent(e) *(adj, m, f)* 4e

frequently fréquemment *(adv)* 4e

fresco painting la fresque 28b

Friday le vendredi 5a

fried frit(e) *(adj, m, f)* 24p

fried egg (sunny side up) l'oeuf *(m)* sur le plat 24h

friend l'ami(e) 10b

friendly amical(e) *(adj)* 11e

friendship l'amitié *(f)* 10b

frog la grenouille 15c

from de *(prep)* 3d, 8g

from now on dès maintenant 4e

From what country are you? De quel pays êtes-vous? 13e

front desk (hotel) la réception 35b

front page *(of newspaper)* la une, la première page 20a

frozen gelé(e) *(adj, m, f)* 6a

fruit le fruit 14d, 24f

fruit flan le flan aux fruits 24i

fruit market le marché aux fruits 24n

fruit tartlet la tartelette aux fruits 24g

fruit tree le fruitier 14c

fuel le carburant 13c

fuel, automobile l'essence *(f)* 13c

fuel pump la pompe à essence 33e

full plein *(adj/m)*, pleine *(f)* 3c

full moon la pleine lune 13a

fun l'amusement *(m)*; **to have fun** s'amuser *(v)* 21a

function la fonction 1f, 42b

funny amusant(e) *(adj)* 11e; comique *(adj)* 11e; drôle *(adj)* 11e; marrant(e) *(adj, m, f)* 11e

fur coat le manteau de fourrure 25k

furnace la chaudière 23e

furniture le meuble 23c

fuse *(hardware)* le fusible, le plomb fusible 25b

fusion reactor le réacteur à fusion 42

fussy méticuleux, méticuleuse *(adj, m, f)* 11e

future le futur, l'avenir *(m)* 4e, 8a

G

Gaelic *(language)* le gaélique 30d

gain weight prendre *(v)* du poids 11a

galaxy la galaxie 13a

game le jeu, le match, la partie 27a, 27b

garage le garage 23a, 35b

garbage bin la poubelle 36a

garbage truck le camion de collecte 33a

garden le jardin 14e, 23a

garlic l'ail *(m)* 24g, 24j; **clove of garlic** la gousse d'ail 24g

gas le gaz 13c, 23e

gas pedal (accelerator) la pédale d'accélérateur 33e

gas stove la cuisinière à gaz 23d

gasoline l'essence *(f)* 13c, 33c

gasoline pump la pompe à essence 33e

gasoline service station la station-service 33c

gasoline tank le réservoir d'essence 33e

gate *(travel)* la porte 32a

gather récolter *(v)*, cueillir *(v)* 14a

gauze la gaze 39c

gay *(homosexual)* gai(e) *(adj, m, f)* 45b

gearshift le levier de vitesse 33e, 36c

Gemini les Gémeaux *(m, pl)* 5d

gender le genre 8a

general delivery *(post office)* la poste restante 19c

generator la génératrice 33e

generosity la générosité 11e

generous généreux, généreuse *(adj)* 11e

genre le genre 28d

gentle doux *(adj, m)*, douce *(adj, f)* 11e

gentleman le monsieur 11a

geographical géographique *(adj)* 13e

geography la géographie 13e, 37e

geometrical géométrique *(adj)* 2b

geometry la géométrie 2b, 37e

geothermal energy l'énergie *(f)* géothermique 45a

geranium le géranium 14b

German *(nationality)* Allemand *(m),* Allemande *(f)* 30d; *(language)* l'allemand *(m)* 30d

Germany l'Allemagne *(f)* 30b

gerund le gérondif 8a

get a degree obtenir *(v)* un diplôme universitaire 37f

get a diploma obtenir *(v)* un diplôme 37f

get a doctor chercher *(v)* un médecin 39c

get a loan obtenir *(v)* un prêt 26

get a suntan se bronzer *(v)* 36b

get an education recevoir *(v)* une éducation; recevoir *(v)* une formation 37f

get cured se guérir *(v)* 40a

get dressed s'habiller *(v)* 25m

get examined se faire *(v)* examiner 40a

Get lost! Allez-vous en! Va-t'en! 20b

get off *(train, bus)* descendre *(v)* 34

get out *(to escape a danger)* fuir *(v),* s'échapper *(v)* 39a

get sick tomber *(v)* malade 40a

get some sun prendre *(v)* un peu de soleil *(m)* 36b

get up se lever *(v)* 3e, 12b

get used to s'habituer à *(v)* 11c

gift le cadeau 11c, 25a

gingerbread le pain d'épices 24i

giraffe la girafe 15a

girl la jeune fille 11a, 11b

girlfriend l'amie, la petite amie 10b

give a gift donner *(v)* un cadeau 11c

give a tip *(gratuity)* donner *(v)* un pourboire 24m

give back rendre *(v)* 37f

give back the key ... rendre *(v)* la clef ... 35b

give birth accoucher *(v)* 11c

give help donner *(v)* de l'aide 39a

Give my regards to ... Un bon souvenir à ... 19b

give the porter a tip *(in hotel)* donner *(v)* un pourboire au portier 35b

glacier le glacier 13b

gladiolus le glaïeul 14b

glass *(drinking)* le verre 23d, 241

glazed, iced, icing glacé(e) *(adj, m, f)* 24i

global warming le réchauffage de la planète 45a

globalization la mondialisation 44

globe le globe 13e

glove le gant 25k, 27b

glove compartment *(of a car)* la boîte à gants, le vide-poches 33e

glue la colle 19d

go aller *(v)* 3e, 36c

Go ahead! Allez-y! *(pol),* Vas-y! *(fam)* 17b

go away s'en aller *(v)* 3e

go down descendre *(v)* 3e, 36c

go forward avancer *(v)* 33c

go on a trip *see* take a trip

go on board monter *(v)* à bord 32a

go on foot aller *(v)* à pied *(m)* 3e

go on strike faire *(v)* la grève, être *(v)* en grève 44

go out sortir *(v)* 3e, 29b, 36c

go to bed se coucher *(v)* 12b

go to school aller *(v)* à l'école *(f)* 11c, 11f, 37f

go up monter *(v)* 3e, 36c

goal le but 27b

goalie le gardien (la gardienne) de but 27b

goat la chèvre 15a

God le Dieu 11d

gold l'or *(m)* 13c, 25i

gold *(color)* or de couleur 7a

golden anniversary les noces *(f)* d'or 11c

goldfish le poisson rouge 15c

golf, to play jouer *(v)* au golf *(m)* 27b

good bon *(adj, m)*, bonne *(adj, f)* 11e, 24p

good *(at something)* habile *(adj)* 11e

Good afternoon! Bonjour! 16a

Good evening! Bonsoir! 16a

good, final copy la bonne copie 37f

Good heavens! Oh! là! là! 21c

Good luck! Bonne chance! 16c

good mood la bonne humeur; **in a good mood** de bonne humeur 21c

Good morning! Bonjour! 16a

Good night! Bonsoir! Bonne nuit! *(when going to bed)* 16a

Good-bye! Au revoir! 16a

goodness la bonté 11e

goose l'oie *(f)* 15b

gossip le bavardage, les potins *(m, pl)*; potiner *(v)* 17a

govern gouverner *(v)* 44

government le gouvernement 44

GPS le système de navigation, le GPS 33e, 42

graceful gracieux, gracieuse *(adj, m, f)* 11e

grade la classe 37a

grade *(mark)* la note 37f

grade school l'école *(f)* primaire 37a

graduate obtenir *(v)* un diplôme 11f

graduate *(from a university)* obtenir *(v)* sa licence (sa maîtrise, son doctorat) 11f

grain le froment, le blé 14a

gram le gramme 3a

grammar la grammaire 8a, 37f

grand piano le piano à queue *(f)* 28c

grandchildren les petits-enfants *(m)* 10a

grandfather le grand-père 10a

grandfather clock l'horloge *(f)* à pendule *(f)*, l'horloge *(f)* normande 4d

grandmother la grand-mère 10a

grapefruit le (la) pamplemousse 14d, 24f

grapes le raisin 14d, 24f

graphic artist le graphiste, la graphiste 38a

graphic novel la bande dessinée 28d

grass l'herbe *(f)* 13b, 14e

grated cheese le fromage râpé 24h

gratuity *(tip)* le pourboire 24m

gravitation la gravitation 13a

gravity la gravité 13a

gravy au jus 24b

gray le gris 7a

Greece la Grèce 30b

greed l'avarice *(f)* 11e

greedy avare *(adj)* 11e

Greek *(nationality)* Grec *(m)*, Grecque *(f)* 30d; *(language)* le grec 30d

green le vert 7a

green bean le haricot vert 14e

green pepper le poivron vert 14e

greenhouse la serre 14a

greenhouse effect l'effet *(m)* de serre 45a

greet saluer *(v)* 16a

greeting le salut, la salutation 16a

Greetings! Sincères salutations! 19b

grilled grillé(e) *(adj, m, f)* 24b

grocery store l'épicerie *(f)* 24n

groom *(bridegroom)* le marié 11c

grooming la toilette 12d

ground floor *(main floor)* le rez-de-chaussée 23a, 23g

groundhog la marmotte (d'Amérique) 15a

grow croître *(v)* 3c

grow up grandir *(v)* 11b

growth la croissance 3c

guide le (la) guide 36a

guidebook le guide 25o

guilt la culpabilité 41

guilty coupable *(adj, m, f)*;
  plead guilty plaider *(v)*
  coupable 41

guitar la guitare 28c

guitarist le (la) guitariste 28c

gulf le golfe 13b

gums *(mouth)* les gencives *(f, pl)*
  40b

gymnasium le gymnase 27b; la
  salle de gymnastique 37c

gymnastics la gymnastique 27b

H

habit *(custom)* l'habitude *(f)* 11e

hail *(weather)* la grêle 6a; grêler
  (v) 6a

hair *(on head)* les cheveux *(m, pl)*
  12a

hair dryer le séchoir à cheveux
  25f

hairdresser le coiffeur, la coiffeuse
  12d, 38a

hair spray la laque (le spray) pour
  les cheveux 12d

Haiti le Haïti 30b

Haitian le Haïtien, la Haïtienne
  30b

half demi *(m)*, demie *(f)* 1c, 3c

hallway le couloir 37c

ham le jambon 24c

hammer le marteau 25b

hand la main 12a

hand *(of a timepiece)* l'aiguille *(f)*
  4d, 25i

hand back rendre *(v)* 37f

hand luggage les bagages *(m, pl)*
  à main 31

handcloth la serviette de toilette
  (f) 12d

handcuffs les menottes *(f, pl)*
  39b

handgun le revolver, le pistolet
  39b

handkerchief le mouchoir 25k

handle le manche 23d; *(car door)*
  la poignée 33e

handlebar *(bicycle)* le guidon 33a

hands free mains *(f, pl)* libres
  18b

handshake la poignée de main
  16a

handsome beau, bel, beaux 11a

hang up *(telephone)* raccrocher
  (v) 18b

happen arriver *(v)*, se produire
  (v) 4e

happiness le bonheur 11e, 21a

happy content(e) *(adj)* 11e, 21a;
  heureux, heureuse *(adj)* 11e,
  21a

Happy birthday! Bon anniversaire!
  (m) 11c, 16c, 29c

Happy Easter! Bonnes Pâques!
  Joyeuses Pâques! *(f, pl)* 16c,
  29c

Happy New Year! Bonne (et
  heureuse) année! *(f)* 16c, 29c

Happy to make your acquaintance!
  Heureux (Heureuse) de faire votre
  (ta) connaissance! 16b

hard dur(e) *(adj, m, f)* 13d

hard-boiled egg l'oeuf *(m)* dur
  24h

hard drive le disque dur 42b

hardware la quincaillerie 25b

hardware *(computers)* le matériel,
  le hardware 42b

hardware store la quincaillerie
  25b

hard-working diligent(e) *(adj)*
  11e

hare le lièvre 15a

harmony l'harmonie *(f)* 28c

harp la harpe 28c

harpsichord le clavecin 28c

hat le chapeau 25k

hate la haine 11e, 21b; haïr *(v)*
  11e, 21b

hateful détestable *(adj)* 11e

hatred la haine 11e, 21b

have a baby avoir *(v)* un enfant 11c

have a class avoir *(v)* une leçon 37f

Have a good vacation! Bonnes vacances! *(f, pl)* 16c, 29c

Have a good time! Amusez-vous bien! *(pol)*, Amuse-toi bien! *(fam)* 16c

Have a good trip! Bon voyage! *(m)* 16c

have a headache avoir *(v)* mal à la tête 40a

Have a nice day! Bonne journée *(f)* 29c

Have a nice trip! Bon voyage! *(m)* 30a

have a snack prendre *(v)* un goûter 24o

have a sore back avoir *(v)* mal au dos 40a

have a sore neck avoir *(v)* mal au cou 40a

have a sore throat avoir *(v)* mal à la gorge 40a

have a stomach ache avoir *(v)* mal à l'estomac 40a

have a toothache avoir *(v)* mal aux dents 40b

have a twisted neck avoir *(v)* mal au cou (un torticolis) 40a

have an operation se faire *(v)* opérer 40a

have an X-ray passer *(v)* une radio(graphie) 39c, 40b

have baggage taken to one's room faire *(v)* porter les bagages dans la chambre 35b

have chills être *(v)* frileux *(adj, m)*, frileuse *(adj, f)* 6b

have dinner dîner *(v)* 24o

have fun s'amuser *(v)* 29b; **Have fun!** Amusez-vous! *(pol)*, Amuse-toi! *(fam)* 29c

have lunch déjeuner *(v)* 24o

have one's head in the clouds être *(v)* dans les nuages *(m, pl)* 6a

have patience avoir *(v)* de la patience 21a

have reason to be worried avoir de quoi s'inquiéter 21a

have to (must) devoir *(v)* 21a

have white hair avoir *(v)* les cheveux blancs *(m, pl)* 11b

hazard lights *(of a vehicle)* les feux *(m, pl)* de détresse 33e

he il 8h; lui 8l

He/She is a pain in the neck! C'est un casse-pieds! 12a

head la tête 12a

head of state le chef d'état 44

head office le siège social 26

headache le mal de tête 40a

heading *(newspaper)* la rubrique 20a

heading *(of a letter)* l'en-tête *(f)* 19c

headline la manchette 20a

headlights *(of a vehicle)* les phares *(m, pl)*, les projecteurs *(m, pl)* 33e

headphones le casque (à écouteurs) 20b; *(on a plane)* le casque d'écoute 32c

heal guérir *(v)* 40a

health la santé 11a, 40a

healthy sain(e) *(adj)* 11a, 40a; en bonne santé *(f)* 11a, 40a

hear entendre *(v)* 12c

hearing l'ouïe *(f)* 12c

heart le coeur 12a, 27a, 40a

heart attack la crise cardiaque 40a

heat la chaleur 13c

heater *(of a vehicle)* le système de chauffage 33e

heating le chauffage 23e; **central heating** le chauffage central 23e

heavy lourd(e) *(adj, m, f)* 3b, 11a, 13d, 31

Hebrew *(language)* le hébreu 30d

hectare l'hectare *(m)* 3a

hectogram l'hectogramme *(m)* 3a

hedge la haie 14a

height la taille, la stature 11a

Hello! Bonjour! *(during daytime)*; Bonsoir! *(during evening hours)* 16a, 17b; *(answering a telephone call)* Allô! 18b

helmet le casque 27b

help aider *(v)* 39a

Help! Au secours! 39a, 39b 39c; À l'aide! 39b, 39c

hemisphere l'hémisphère *(m)* 13e

hen la poule 15b

heptagon l'heptagone *(m)* 2a

her *(possessive)* sa *(f, s)*, ses *(m/f, pl)* 8f; la 8i; elle 8l

herb l'herbe *(f)* 24j; **herbs** les fines herbes *(f, pl)* 14e

here ici *(adv)* 3d, 36c

heredity l'hérédité *(f)* 11c

hero le héros 28e

heroine l'héroïne *(f)* 28e

herring le hareng 24d

herself *(reflexive)* se 8k

hesitate hésiter *(v)* 17a

hesitation l'hésitation 17a

hexagon l'hexagone *(m)* 2a

Hi! Salut! 16a, 17b

high school l'école *(f)* d'enseignement secondaire, le lycée 37a, 38b

high school diploma le baccalauréat 37f

high school teacher/professor le professeur, la professeure 37d

high speed train le train à grande vitesse, le TGV 34

high temperature la température élevée 6c

highway l'autoroute *(f)* 33c

highway police l'agent *(m)* de police routier 33b

hill la colline 13b

him le 8i; lui 8l

himself *(reflexive)* se 8k

Hindu hindou(e) *(n/adj, m, f)* 11d

hip la hanche 12a

hip-hop le hip-hop 28c

hippopotamus l'hippopotame *(m)* 15a

hire *(to employ)* embaucher *(v)*, engager *(v)* 38d

his son *(m, s)*, ses *(m/f, pl)* 8f

history l'histoire *(f)* 37e

hit *(ball)* battre *(v)* 27b

HIV VIH *(m)* 40a, 45b

hobby le passe-temps 27a

hockey le hockey 27b; **ice hockey** le hockey sur glace 27b

hockey player le joueur (la joueuse) de hockey 27b

hockey stick la crosse, le stick 27b

hole le trou 25g

holiday *(official)* le jour férié 5a, 29a

holidays les jours *(m, pl)* de fête *(f)* 29a

Holland la Hollande 30b

home, at someone's chez *(prep)* 3d

home plate *(baseball)* la plaque 27b

homework les devoirs *(m, pl)* 37f

homosexual homosexuel(le) *(m, f)* 45b

homosexuality l'homosexualité *(f)* 45b

honest honnête *(adj)* 11e

honesty l'honnêteté *(f)* 11e

honey le miel 24j

honeymoon la lune de miel *(m)* 11c, 13a

hood *(of a vehicle)* le capot 33e

hook *(fishing)* l'hameçon *(m)* 15c

hope l'espoir 21a; espérer *(v)* 21a

horizontal horizontal(e) *(adj)* 3d

horn *(musical instrument)* le cor 28c

horn *(of a vehicle)* le klaxon, l'avertisseur *(m)* 33e

horoscope l'horoscope *(m)* 5d

horse le cheval 15a

horsepower le cheval-vapeur 33e

horse racing les courses *(f)* de chevaux, la course au galop 27b

horseradish sauce la sauce au raifort 24j

horticulture l'horticulture *(f)* 14a

hospital l'hôpital *(m)* 39c

hostel (youth) l'auberge *(f)* de jeunesse 35a

hot chaud(e) *(adj, m, f)* 6a, 6b, 24p

hot water l'eau *(f)* chaude 35c

hotel l'hôtel *(m)* 35a; **luxury hotel** l'hôtel de luxe 35a

hotel clerk l'employé *(m)*, l'employée *(f)* 35b

hour l'heure *(f)* 4c

hourly à l'heure 4c

house la maison 23a

House/Chamber of Representatives (Deputies) la Chambre des Députés 44

house number le numéro de la maison 11f

how comment *(adv)* 9

How are you? Comment allez-vous? *(pol)* 16a; Comment vas-tu? *(fam)* 16a

How come? Mais comment? 9

How do you feel? Comment vous sentez-vous? 40a

How do you get to . . . ? Comment va-t-on à . . . ? 36c

How do you say . . . ? Comment dit-on . . . ? 9

How do you say . . . in French? Comment dit-on . . . en français? 17b

How do you spell your name? Comment s'écrit votre (ton) nom? 11f

How does one say . . . ? Comment dit-on . . . ? 9

How far away . . . ? À quelle distance . . . ? 36c

how much/many combien *(adv)* 3c, 9

How much do you weigh? Combien pesez-vous? 11a

How much does it come to? Ça fait combien? 25a

How much does it cost? Ça coûte combien? 25a

How much is it? C'est combien? 25a

How old are you? Quel âge avez-vous (as-tu)? 11b

How tall are you? Combien mesurez-vous?; Quelle taille avez-vous? 11a

How's it going? Comment ça va? Ça va? 16a

How's the weather? Quel temps fait-il? 6a

however cependant *(conj)*, pourtant *(conj)*, toutefois *(conj)* 8p

howl hurler *(v)* 15a

human humain(e) *(adj, m, f)* 11d, 15a

human being l'être *(m)*, l'être *(m)* humain 11d, 15a

humanitarian humanitaire *(adj)* 11e

humanities (arts) les lettres *(f, pl)* 37e

humanity l'humanité *(f)* 11d

humble humble *(adj)* 11e

humid humide *(adj)* 6a

humidity l'humidité *(f)* 6a

humility l'humilité *(f)* 11e

humor l'humour *(m)* 11e

hundredth centième 1b

hunger la faim 12b

hunter le chasseur, la chasseuse 15a

hunting la chasse 15a

hurricane l'ouragan *(m)* 6a

hurry se dépêcher *(v)* 39b

hurt avoir *(v)* mal, faire *(v)* mal à 40a

husband le mari   10a, 11c; l'époux
10a, 11c
hydrogen l'hydrogène *(m)*   13c
hyena l'hyène *(f)*   15a
hygiene l'hygiène *(f)*   12d
hygienic hygiénique *(adj, m, f)*
12d
hyphen le tiret, le trait d'union
19c
hypothesis l'hypothèse *(f)*   22a

I

I je   8h
I am . . . (+ *name*) Je suis . . .   16b
I am looking for . . . Je cherche . . .
36c
I am . . . old J'ai . . . ans   11b
I am . . . tall J'ai la taille . . .; Je
fais . . . pieds.   11a
I believe that . . . Je crois que
. . .   45c
I can't stand him (her)! Je ne peux
pas le (la) supporter!   21b
I can't stand the cold! Je ne
supporte pas le froid!   6b
I can't stand the heat! Je ne
supporte pas la chaleur!   6b
I don't believe it! Je ne le crois pas!
21c
I don't feel like . . . Je n'ai pas
envie de . . .   21c
I don't know if . . . Je ne sais pas
si . . .   45c
I don't understand. Je ne
comprends pas.   9, 17b
I doubt that . . . Je doute que
. . .   45c
I feel . . . Je me sens . . .   40a
I have some of it (them). J'en ai.
3c
I live on . . . Street Je demeure
rue . . .   11f
I love the cold! J'aime le froid!
6b
I love the heat! J'aime la chaleur!
6b
I think that . . . Je pense que . . .
45c

I was born in . . . (year) Je suis
né(e) *(m, f)* en . . .   5e
I was born on . . . Je suis né(e)
le . . .   11c
I weigh . . . Je pèse . . .   11a
I wish! (If only . . . !) Si
seulement . . . !   21c
I would like to say that . . . Je
voudrais dire que . . .   45c
ice la glace   6a, 13b; **ice chips**
les glaçons   *(m, pl)*   24p; **black
ice** le verglas   6a
ice cap la calotte glaciaire   13b
ice cream la glace, la crème glacée
24h; **cone** le cornet   24h
ice hockey le hockey sur glace
27b
ice skate patiner *(v)* sur glace
(f)   27b
icing, iced, glazed glacé(e) *(adj,
m, f)*   24i
icosahedron l'icosaèdre *(m)*   2a
idea l'idée *(f)*   22a
idealism l'idéalisme *(m)*   11e
idealist, idealistic idéaliste
(m, f)   11e
identification l'identification *(f)*
11f
identification card (papers) la
carte d'identité   31, 35b
identify identifier *(v)*   17a
ideology l'idéologie *(f)*   44
if si *(conj)*   8p
ignorant ignorant(e) *(adj, m, f)*
22a
illegal illégal(e) *(adj, m, f)*   41
illustration l'illustration *(f)*   20a
I'm lost! Je suis perdu(e)!   39b
I'm not sure that . . . Je ne suis pas
sûr(e) que . . .   45c
I'm serious! Je suis sérieux *(adj,
m)*, sérieuse *(adj, f)*!   21c
I'm sorry! Je regrette! Je suis
désolé!   21c
I'm sure that . . . Je suis sûr(e) que
. . .   17b, 45c; Je suis certain(e)
que . . .   17b

imaginary imaginaire *(adj, m, f)* 1d

imagination l'imagination *(f)* 11e, 22a

imaginative imaginatif, imaginative *(adj, m, f)* 11e

imagine imaginer *(v)* 22b

immediately immédiatement *(adv)*, tout de suite 4e

impatient impatient(e) *(adj, m, f)* 11e

imperative impératif *(adj, m)*, impérative *(adj, f)* 8a, 8n

imperfect imparfait(e) *(adj, m, f)* 8a

import importer *(v)* 31

Impossible! Pas possible! 21c

imprison emprisonner *(v)* 41

impudence l'impudence *(f)* 11e

impudent impudent(e) *(adj, m, f)* 11e

impulse l'impulsion *(f)* 11e

impulsive impulsif, impulsive *(adj, m, f)* 11e

in dans *(prep)* 3d, 8g

in an hour's time dans une heure 4e

in black and white en noir et blanc 25d

in conclusion en conclusion 45c

in front of devant *(adv/prep)* 3d, 36c

in love amoureux *(adj)* 11c

in my opinion à mon avis 22a, 45c

in my view à mon avis 45c

in order that afin que *(conj)*, pour que *(conj)* 8p

in shock sous le choc 39c

In short En somme 17b

in the afternoon dans (de) l'après-midi *(m)* 4a

in the country(side) à la campagne 36b

in the evening dans le soir, du soir 4a

in the fall en automne 5c

in the latest style/fashion à la mode, au dernier cri 251

in the meantime entre-temps 4e

in the middle au centre, au milieu 3d

in the morning dans le matin 4a; du matin 4a

in the mountains dans les montagnes 36b

in the spring au printemps 5c

in the summer en été 5c

in the winter en hiver 5c

in time à temps *(m)* 4e

in two minutes' time dans deux minutes 4e

in vitro fertilization la fécondation in vitro 40a

incisor *(tooth)* les dents *(f, pl)* incisives 40b

income le revenu 26

increase l'augmentation *(f)* augmenter *(v)* 3c

indecisive indécis(e) *(adj, m, f)* 11e

indefinite indéfini(e) *(adj, m, f)* 8a, 8c

independent indépendant(e) *(adj, m, f)* 11e

index l'index *(m)* 20a

index finger l'index *(m)* 12a

India l'Inde *(f)* 30b

indicate indiquer *(v)* 17a

indication l'indication *(f)* 17a

indicative indicatif *(adj, m)*, indicative *(adj, f)* 8a

indifference l'indifférence *(f)* 21a

indifferent indifférent(e) *(adj, m, f)* 21a

indirect indirect(e) *(adj, m, f)* 8a, 8j

individualist individualiste *(adj)* 11e

industrial industriel(le) *(adj, m, f)* 13c

industry l'industrie *(f)* 13c

inelegant inélégant(e) *(adj)* 11a

inexpensive bon marché *(adj, m, f)* 25a

infection l'infection *(f)* 40a

infinitive l'infinitif *(m)* 8a

inflation l'inflation *(f)* 44

inform informer *(v)*, faire savoir *(v)* 17a

informal restaurant le bistro (bistrot) 24m

information le renseignement 18b

information desk le bureau de renseignements 32a

infrared light la lumière infrarouge 13a

ingenious ingénieux, ingénieuse *(adj, m, f)* 11e

ingenuity l'ingénuité *(f)* 11e

ingenuous ingénu(e) *(adj, m, f)* 11e

inherit hériter *(v)* 11c

injection l'injection *(f)*, la piqûre 25h, 40a

injure blesser *(v)* 39b

injury la blessure, la plaie 39b, 39c

ink l'encre *(f)* 19d, 37b

innocence l'innocence *(f)* 11e, 41

innocent innocent(e) *(adj, m, f)* 11e, 41; **plead innocent** plaider *(v)* non coupable 41

inorganic inorganique *(adj, m, f)* 13c

insect l'insecte *(m)* 15d

inside dedans *(prep/adv)* 3d, 36c

insolence l'insolence *(f)* 11e

insolent insolent(e) *(adj, m, f)* 11e

instant l'instant *(m)* 4c

instrument l'instrument *(m)* 28c; **to play an instrument** jouer *(v)* de (du, de l', de la) 28c

insulation l'isolant *(m)* 25b

insulin l'insuline *(f)* 25b

insurance l'assurance *(f)* 26, 30a

insurance card la carte d'assurance 33b

integer le nombre entier 1d

integrated circuit le circuit intégré 42b

intelligence l'intelligence *(f)* 11e

intelligent intelligent(e) *(adj, m, f)* 11e

intercom l'interphone *(m)* 18a, 38c

interest l'intérêt *(m)* 26

interest rate le taux d'intérêt 26

interesting intéressant(e) *(adj, m, f)* 22a

interface *(computers)* l'interface *(f)* 42b

intermission l'entracte *(m)* 28e

Internet l'Internet *(m)* 43

Internet (with, in hotel) avec connexion *(f)* Internet 35b

Internet café le cybercafé 43

interrogative interrogatif *(adj, m)*, interrogative *(f)* 8a

interrupt interrompre *(v)* 17a

interruption l'interruption *(f)* 17a

intersection le carrefour, le croisement 33c, 33d, 36a

interview l'interview *(f)* 20a, 20b; l'entrevue *(f)* 38b

intransitive intransitif *(adj, m)*, intransitive *(adj, f)* 8a

introduce someone présenter *(v)* quelqu'un 16b

introduction la présentation 16b

invertebrate invertébré(e) *(adj, m, f)* 15a

invest investir *(v)* 26

investment l'investissement *(m)* 26

invitation l'invitation *(f)*, le faire-part 19e

invite inviter *(v)* 17a

iodine l'iode *(m)* 13c

iPod l'iPod *(m)* 42

irascible irascible *(adj)* 11e

Ireland l'Irlande *(f)* 30b

Irish *(nationality)* Irlandais *(m)*, Irlandaise *(f)* 30d

iron (*metal*) le fer 13c; (*for ironing, pressing*) le fer à repasser 25g; repasser (*v*) 25g
ironical ironique (*adj*) 11e
irony l'ironie (*f*) 11e
irrational irrationnel(le) (*adj, m, f*) 1d
irregular irrégulier (*adj, m*), irrégulière (*adj, f*) 8a
irritable irritable (*adj*) 11e
Is ... (*name of person*) **in?** Est-ce que ... est là? 18b
is equivalent to est équivalent à 1f
is greater than est supérieur à 1f
is less than est inférieur à 1f
is similar to est pareil à 1f
Islamic islamique (*adj*) 11d
island l'île (*f*) 13b
Isn't it so? N'est-ce pas? 17b
isosceles isocèle (*adj*) 2a
Israel l'Israël (*m*) 30b
Israeli (*nationality*) Israélite (*m, f*) 30d
it (*subject pro*) il (*m, s*), elle (*f, s*) 8h; (*direct obj pro*) le (*m*), la (*f*) 8i
It costs an arm and a leg! Cela coûte les yeux de la tête! (*lit.,* **It costs both eyes of your head!**) 25a
It doesn't matter! Peu importe! 21c
It seems to me that ... Il me semble que ... 17b, 45c
It's ... C'est ... 7a
It's a bit cold (*weather*). Il fait un peu froid. 6a
It's a bit hot (*weather*). Il fait un peu chaud. 6a
It's a quarter to three. Il est trois heures moins le quart. 4b; Il est deux heures quarante-cinq. 4b
It's awful (*weather*)! Il fait un temps affreux! 6a
It's beautiful (*weather*). Il fait beau temps. 6a
It's clear that ... Il est clair que ..., Il est évident que ... 45c

It's cloudy. Il fait un temps couvert. 6a
It's cold (*weather*). Il fait froid. 6a
It's cool (*weather*). Il fait frais. 6a
It's dark (*weather*) **today.** Il fait sombre aujourd'hui. 6a
It's exactly three o'clock. Il est trois heures précises. 4b
It's five o'clock (AM). Il est cinq heures. 4b
It's five o'clock (PM). Il est dix-sept heures. 4b
It's foul weather. Il fait un temps pourri. 6a
It's four twenty-five. Il est quatre heures vingt-cinq. 4b
It's hot (*weather*). Il fait chaud. 6a
It's humid (*weather*). Il fait humide. 6a
It's January second. C'est le deux janvier. 5e
It's July. C'est juillet. 5b
It's mild (*weather*). Il fait doux. 6a
It's Monday. C'est lundi *or* Nous sommes lundi. 5a
It's muggy (*weather*). Il fait un temps lourd. 6a
It's my pleasure! C'est mon plaisir! 16b
It's necessary that ... Il est nécessaire que ...; Il faut que ... 17b
It's 2012. C'est 2012. 5e
It's not true. Ce n'est pas vrai. 17b
It's obvious that ... Il est évident que ... 17b
It's October first. C'est le premier octobre. 5e
It's one o'clock. Il est une heure. 4b
It's one fifteen. Il est une heure et quart. 4b
It's one ten. Il est une heure dix. 4b

It's pleasant *(weather).* Il fait un temps agréable. 6a

It's raining. Il pleut. 6a

It's raining buckets. Il pleut à seaux. 6a

It's rainy. Il fait un temps pluvieux. 6a

It's snowing. Il neige. 6a

It's sunny Il fait (du) soleil. 6a

It's ten minutes to six. Il est six heures moins dix. 4b

It's ten o'clock (AM). Il est dix heures. 4b

It's ten o'clock (PM). Il est vingt-deux heures. 4b

It's three fifteen. Il est trois heures et quart. 4b

It's three o'clock. Il est trois heures. 4b

It's three o'clock on the dot. Il est trois heures juste (pile). 4b

It's three thirty. Il est trois heures et demie. 4b

It's thundering! Il tonne! 6a

It's true! C'est vrai! 17b

It's two o'clock. Il est deux heures. 4b

It's very cold *(weather).* Il fait très froid. 6a

It's very good! C'est très bon! 17b

It's very hot *(weather).* Il fait très chaud. 6a

It's windy! Il fait du vent! 6a

itself *(reflexive)* se 8k

Italian *(nationality)* Italien *(m),* Italienne *(f)* 30d; *(language)* l'italien *(m)* 30d

italics en italique *(m)* 19c

Italy l'Italie *(f)* 30b

itch la démangeaison 40a

J

jacket la veste, le veston 25k

jail la prison 4l

jam (preserves) la confiture 24j

janitor l'agent(e) *(m, f)* d'entretien 37d

January le janvier 5b

Japan le Japon 30b

Japanese *(nationality)* Japonais *(m),* Japonaise *(f)* 30d; *(language)* le japonais 30d

jaw la mâchoire 12a, 40b

jazz le jazz 25j, 28c

jealous jaloux, jalouse *(adj, m, f)* 11e

jelly la gelée 24j

jelly roll le roulé 24i

jest plaisanter *(v)* 17a

jewel le bijou 25i

jewelry store la bijouterie, la joaillerie 25i

Jewish Juif, Juive 11d

job le travail 11f; le métier, l'occupation *(f)* 38a

jog faire *(v)* du jogging *(m)* 27b

jogging le jogging 27b

joke la plaisanterie 17a

joker *(cards)* le joker 27a

journalist le (la) journaliste 20a, 38a

journey le voyage 30a

joy la joie 21a

judge le juge; juger *(v)* 41

judgment le jugement 22a

judo le judo 27b

juice le jus 24k

July le juillet 5b

June le juin 5b

junior high school l'école *(f)* d'enseignement secondaire 37a, 38a

Jupiter Jupiter *(m)* 13a

jury le jury 41

just now à l'instant *(m)* 4e

justice la justice 22a, 41

K

karate le karaté 27b

Keep quiet! Taisez-vous!/ Tais-toi! 21c

kettle la bouilloire 23d

key la clef 23d, 35b

keyboard le clavier 19d, 42b;
computer keyboard le clavier
d'ordinateur 19d

keyboard instruments les
instruments *(m/pl)* à clavier
(m) 28c

keyboard operator le (la) claviste
42b

kick donner *(v)* un coup de pied
27c

kidney le rein 40a

kill tuer *(v)*, assassiner *(v)* 39b

killer le tueur, l'assassin *(m)* 39b

kilogram le kilogramme 3a

kilometer le kilomètre 3a

kind *(person)* gentil *(adj, m)*,
gentille *(adj, f)* 11e

kindergarten le jardin d'enfants
37a

kindness la bonté 11e

king le roi 27a, 44

kiosk le kiosque à journaux 36a

kiss le baiser, la bise 11c, 19b;
embrasser *(v)* 11c, 21b

kitchen la cuisine 23b

knapsack le sac à dos *(m)* 27b,
31, 36b

knee le genou 12a

knife le couteau 23d, 24l, 39b;
blade la lame 23d; **handle** le
manche 23d

knight *(in chess)* le cavalier 27a

know *(a fact)* savoir *(v)* 22b

know *(a person)* connaître *(v)*
22b

know *(be acquainted with)*
connaître 22b

know someone connaître quelqu'un
16b, 22b

knowledge la connaissance, le
savoir 22a

knowledgeable connaisseur *(adj,
m)*, connaisseuse *(f)* 22a

Knucklehead! Tête de noeud! 12a

knuckles les articulations *(f)*, les
jointures *(f)* des doigts *(m, pl)*
12a

Koran le Coran 11d

L

label l'étiquette *(f)* 25a

labor/trade union le syndicat 44

laboratory le laboratoire 13c, 37c

lack manquer (à) *(v)* 25a

ladder l'échelle *(f)* 25b, 39a

ladle la louche 23d

lady la dame 11a

laity la laïcité 11d

lake le lac 13b, 36b

lamb l'agneau *(m)* 15a, 24c

lamp la lampe 23c, 35c

land la terre 13b; le terrain 13b;
(airplane) atterrir *(v)* 32c

landing *(airplane)* l'atterrissage
(m) 32c

landing gear *(airplane)* le train
d'atterrissage 32c

landlord le (la) propriétaire 23g

landscape le paysage 13b

lane *(traffic)* la voie 33c

language laboratory le laboratoire
de langues 37c

languages *(foreign)* les langues *(f,
pl)* étrangères 37e

laptop *(computer)* le portable, le
portatif 42b

large grand(e) *(adj)* 3c, 11a;
gros *(adj, m)*, grosse *(f)* 3c

large bill *(banknote, currency)* le
gros billet 26

laser le laser 42

last *(previous)* dernier *(adj, m)*,
dernière *(f)*, passé(e) *(adj)* 4e

last durer *(v)* 4e

last a long time durer *(v)*
longtemps *(adv)* 4e

last a short time durer *(v)* peu
de temps 4e

last month le mois dernier (passé)
4e

last night cette nuit *(actual night)*,
hier soir *(actual evening)* 4a

last year l'an *(m)* dernier *(m)*,
l'année *(f)* dernière *(f)* 4e

late tard *(adv)*, en retard *(adv)*
4e, 34; *(arrival/departure)* en
retard 32b, 34

Latin America l'Amérique *(f)* Latine 30b
latitude la latitude 13e
laugh rire *(v)* 11e, 21a
laugh halfheartedly, reluctantly rire *(v)* jaune, rire *(v)* à contrecoeur 21a
laughter le rire 11e, 21a
launch pad la rampe de lancement 42
laundry la lessive, le linge 25g
lava la lave 13b
law les études *(f, pl)* de droit 37e; la loi 41
lawful légal(e) *(adj, m, f)* 41
lawn la pelouse 13b
lawnmower la tondeuse 25b
lawsuit l'action *(f)* en justice 41
lawyer l'avocat *(m)*, l'avocate *(f)* 38a, 41; **trial lawyer** l'avoué *(m)*, la femme avoué 41
layer la couche 13b
layperson laïc, laïque *(adj, m, f)* 11d
laziness la paresse 11e
lazy paresseux, paresseuse *(adj, m, f)* 11e
lead le plomb 13c
leaf la feuille 14a
leaf through *(a book, magazine, etc.)* feuilleter *(v)* 20a
leap year l'année *(f)* bissextile 5b
learn apprendre *(v)* 22b, 37f
learn by memory apprendre *(v)* par coeur 37f
lease le bail 23g
leather le cuir 13c, 25l
leave partir *(v)*, quitter *(v)* 3e, 34
lecture la conférence; donner *(v)* une conférence 17a; faire une conférence 37f
left *(location)* gauche *(adj)* 3d; **to the left** à gauche 3d, 33c
left wing *(politics)* la gauche 44
leg la jambe 12a

legal légal(e) *(adj, m, f)* 41
legislation la législation 44
lemon le citron 14d, 24f
lemon tree le citronnier 14c
length la longueur 3a
lengthen *(clothing)* faire *(v)* allonger *(v)* 25m
lens *(camera)* l'objectif *(m)* 25d
lentil la lentille 14e
Leo *(sign of the zodiac)* le Lion 5d
leopard le léopard 15a
lesbian la lesbienne 45b
lesbianism le lesbianisme, le lesbisme 45b
less moins *(adv)* 3c
let out *(clothing)* faire *(v)* élargir *(v)* 25m
letter la lettre 8a, 19c, 19d
letter carrier le facteur, la factrice 19e
letterhead le papier à en-tête 19d
lettuce la laitue 14e, 24e
level le niveau 3d; *(story, floor of a building)* l'étage *(m)* 35b
Level Crossing le Passage à niveau 33d
liar le menteur, la menteuse 17a
liberal libéral(e) *(adj)* 11e
liberal party *(politics)* le parti libéral 44
Libra la Balance 5d
librarian le (la) bibliothécaire 37d
library la bibliothèque 37c
license plate la plaque d'immatriculation 33e, 36c
lid le couvercle 23d
lie *(falsehood)* le mensonge 17a; *(to tell a lie)* mentir *(v)* 17a
lie down se coucher *(v)* 3e
life la vie 11c
life imprisonment l'emprisonnement *(m)* à perpétuité 41
life sentence la condamnation à vie 41
lifejacket le gilet de sauvetage 32c

lift lever *(v)* 3e

lift *(elevator)* l'ascenseur 23g

light *(color)* clair *(adj)* 7b

light *(weight)* léger, légère *(adj, m, f)* 3b, 11a, 13d, 31; la lumière 6a, 13a; *(power)* l'éclairage *(m)* 23e

light beam le rayon de lumière 42

light blue le bleu clair 7a

light bulb l'ampoule *(f)* 25b, 25d

light music la musique légère 28c

light year l'année *(f)* lumière 13a

lighter *(cigar, cigarette)* le briquet 25e

lightning l'éclair *(m)* 6a

lights *(electric)* les lumières 35c

lights *(headlights of a vehicle)* les phares *(m, pl)*, les projecteurs *(m, pl)* 33e

like aimer *(v)* bien 11e, 21b

likeable *(person)* aimable *(adj, m, f)*, sympathique *(adj, m, f)* 11e

liking *(taste for)* le penchant 21b

lily le lis (lys) 14b

lima bean la fève 14e

lime le citron vert 14d

line la ligne 2b, 19c; la queue 26

line of work le genre de travail *(m)* 11f

line up faire *(v)* la queue 15a, 26

link *(computer)* le lien 42b

lion le lion 15a

lip la lèvre 12a, 40b

lipstick le rouge à lèvres 25f

liqueur la liqueur 24k

liquid le liquide 13c

listen *(to)* écouter *(v)* 12c, 17a, 20b, 37f

Listen! Ecoutez! *(pol)*, Ecoute! *(fam)* 17b

liter le litre 3a

literal litéral(e) *(adj, m, f)* 17a

literary work l'ouvrage *(m)* 28d

literature la littérature 28d, 37e

litigate intenter *(v)* une action en justice 41

litigation le litige 41

little *(size)* petit(e) *(adj)* 3c, 11a; *(quantity)* peu *(adv)* 3c

little finger le petit doigt 12a

live vivre *(v)* 11c

live somewhere demeurer *(v)* 11f; habiter *(v)* 11f, 23f

lively vif, vive *(adj, m, f)* 7b, 11e

liver le foie 24c

living room le salon, la salle de séjour *(m)* 23b

loan le prêt 26; **get a loan** obtenir *(v)* un prêt 26

lobby le foyer 28a, 35b

lobster le homard, la langouste 24d

local train le train omnibus 34

locate localiser *(v)* 13e; situer *(v)* 13e

located (be) se trouver *(v)* 13e

location la localité 13e

logarithm le logarithme 1f

logarithmic logarithmique *(adj)* 1f

London Londres 30c

long long *(adj, m)*, longue *(f)* 3b, 37f

long-distance (telephone) call l'appel *(m)* interurbain 18b

long loaf of bread le pain long 24i

long stick of bread la baguette, la flûte 24i

long-term à long terme 4e

longitude la longitude 13e

look (at) regarder 12c, 20b

look for something (or someone) chercher *(v)* 25a

look forward to s'attendre à *(v)* 4e

loose *(clothing)* ample *(adj, m, f)*, non-ajusté(e) *(adj, m, f)*, vague *(adj, m, f)* 25l

loose change la monnaie 26

lose perdre *(v)* 27b

lose weight perdre *(v)* du poids 11a

loss la perte 27b

lost and found les objets *(m, pl)* perdus 32a

lotion la lotion 25f

lots of beaucoup (de) *(adv)* 3c

loudspeaker le haut-parleur 20b

louse le pou, les poux 15d

lovable adorable *(adj, m, f)* 11e

love l'amour *(m)* 11c, 11e, 21b; aimer *(v)* 11c, 11e, 21b

love affair l'affaire *(f)* d'amour *(m)*, une liaison 10b

love and kisses grosses bises *(f, pl)* 19b

lover l'amant(e) *(m, f)* 10b

low season *(tourism)* la basse saison 35b

low temperature la température basse 6c

luggage les bagages *(m, pl)* 31, 35b

lunar eclipse l'éclipse *(f)* lunaire 13a

lunar module le module lunaire 42

lunch le déjeuner 24a

lung le poumon 12a, 40a

Luxembourg le Luxembourg 30b

luxury hotel l'hôtel *(m)* de luxe 35a

lymphatic system le système lymphatique 40a

M

macaroon le macaron 24i

mackintosh (raincoat) l'imperméable *(m)* 25k

mad (crazy) fou, fol, folle *(adj)* 11e

madness la folie 11e

magazine le magazine, la revue 20a, 25o, 37b

maggot l'asticot *(m)* 15d

magistrate le magistrat 41

maid la femme de chambre 35b

mail le courrier, la poste 19e; mettre *(v)* une lettre à la poste 19e

mail delivery la distribution du courrier *(m)* 19e

mailbox la boîte à lettres *(f, pl)* 19e, 23a

mailman *see* **letter carrier**

main principal(e) *(adj, m, f)* 8a

main door la porte principale 35b

main floor le rez-de-chaussée 35b

main office la direction 37c

make faire *(v)* 18b, 23f

make a movie tourner *(v)* un film 28a

make a request faire *(v)* une demande 9

make a telephone call faire *(v)* un appel téléphonique 18b

make mistakes faire *(v)* des fautes 37f

make the bed faire *(v)* le lit 23f

make-up le fard 12d; le maquillage 12d, 25f

male le mâle, masculin(e) *(adj, m, f)* 11a, 38b

malicious malicieux, malicieuse *(adj, m, f)* 11e

malign diffamer *(v)* 17a

malleable malléable *(adj, m, f)* 13d

mammal le mammifère 15a

management la gestion 37e

manager le directeur, la directrice 26, 35b, 38d; le gérant, la gérante 35b, 38d

mandarin orange la mandarine 14d, 24f

mandolin la mandoline 28c

manicure les soins *(m, pl)* esthétiques des mains *(f, pl)* 12d

Manitoba le Manitoba 30b

Many thanks! Merci mille fois! Merci infiniment! 16c

map la carte 13e; **map (of city)** le plan 13e; **map of France** la carte de France 13e; la carte géographique 37b

maple tree l'érable *(m)* 14c

March le mars 5b

margin la marge 19c

marinated mariné(e) *(adj, m, f)* 24b

marital status l'état *(m)* civil 11c, 38b

mark (grade) la note 37f

marker (for writing) le marqueur, le crayon-feutre 19d, 25c

market le marché 24n, 38d

marmalade la confiture d'oranges, la marmalade d'oranges 24j

marriage le mariage 11c

married marié(e) *(n/adj, m, f)* 11c, 38b

marry (someone) épouser *(v),* se marier *(v)* avec 11c

Mars Mars *(m)* 13a

Marseilles Marseille 30c

mascara le mascara 12d , 25f

masculine masculin(e) *(adj, m, f)* 8a, 11a

mask le masque 27b

masking tape le papier cache 25b

Mass la messe 11d

mass la masse 3b

massage le massage 12d

masterpiece (art) le chef d'oeuvre 28b

master's degree la licence 37f

match (sports) le jeu, le match, la partie 27b

matches les allumettes *(f)* 25e

material le matériel 13c

mathematics les mathématiques *(f, pl)* 37e

matter la matière 13c; **to matter (be of importance)** importer *(v)* 21a

matrimony le mariage 11c

maximum le maximum 3b, 31; **maximum temperature** la température maximum 6c

May (month) le mai 5b

May I . . . ? Puis-je . . . ? 16c

May I come in? Puis-je entrer? 16c

May I help you? Vous désirez? Puis-je vous aider? 16c

me me 8i; moi 8l

meal le repas 24a

mean (nasty) méchant(e) *(adj, m, f)* 11e

mean (signify, have in mind) signifier *(v),* vouloir dire *(v)* 17a

meaning la signification, le sens 17a

meanness la méchanceté 11e

measles la rougeole 40a

measure mesurer *(v)* 3b

measuring tape le mètre à ruban 3b

meat la viande 24c

mechanic le mécanicien, la mécanicienne 33c, 38a

mechanical mécanique *(adj, m, f)* 25b

medical instruments les instruments *(m, pl)* médicaux 40a

medicine (field of study) la médecine 37e

medicine (medication) le médicament 25h, 40a

mediocre médiocre *(adj, m, f)* 21b

Mediterranean méditerranéen *(adj, m),* méditerranéenne *(f)* 6a

medium moyen *(adj)* 3b

medium (average) height la taille moyenne 11a

medium (cooked food) à point 24b

meet rencontrer *(v)* 16b

Melba toast la biscotte 24i

melon le melon 14d, 24f

melted cheese le fromage fondu 24h

melting point le point de fusion *(f)* 6c

membrane la membrane 14a

memory la mémoire 42b

memory card la carte d'extension mémoire 25d

mend raccommoder *(v)* 25g

men's shop/clothing le magasin d'habillement masculin 25k

mention mentionner *(v)*, faire *(v)* mention de 17a

menu la carte, le menu 24g

meow miauler *(v)* 15a

mercury le mercure 6c, 13c

Mercury Mercure *(m)* 13a

Merge Confluence 33d

meridian le méridien 13e

meringue la meringue 24i

Merry Christmas! Joyeux Noël! *(m)* 16c, 29c

message le message 18b, 35b

metal le métal 13c

metamorphosis la métamorphose 15d

metaphor la métaphore 17a

meteor le météore 13a

meteorite la météorite 13a

meter le mètre 3a

meter postage la vignette 19e

methane le méthane 13c

Mexico le Mexique 30b

microcomputer le micro-ordinateur 42b

microphone le microphone 20b

microprocessor *(computer)* le microprocesseur 42b

microscope le microscope 13c

microwave la micro-onde 42

microwave oven le four à micro-ondes *(f, pl)* 23d

middle finger le majeur, le médius 12a

midnight le minuit 4a

Milan Milan 30c

mild *(weather)* doux *(adj, m)*, douce *(adj, f)* 6a

mild pas très épicé(e) 24p

milk le lait 24h

millennium le millénaire 4c

millimeter le millimètre 3a

millionth millionième 1b

mime le (la) mime 28e

mind l'esprit *(m)* 22a

mineral le minéral 13c

mineral water l'eau *(f)* minérale 24k

minimum le minimum 3b; **minimum temperature** la température minimum 6c

minimum wage le salaire minimum, le SMIC 38d

miniskirt la minijupe 25k

minister le ministre, la femme ministre 11d, 44

mini-van la fourgonnette 33b

mint la menthe 14e, 24j

minus moins *(adv)* 1e, 6c

minute la minute 4c

mirror le miroir 23c, 35c; la glace 35c

mischievous espiègle *(adj, m, f)* 11e

miser avare *(adj, m/f)* 11e

Miss Mademoiselle 11f, 16b

miss *(the train, etc.)* manquer *(v)*, rater *(v)* 34

missile le missile 42

mistake la faute 37f; **to make mistakes** faire *(v)* des fautes 37f

modal modal(e) *(adj, m, f)* 8a

model *(molecule)* le modèle 13c

modem *(computers)* le modem 42b

molar *(tooth)* les dents *(f, pl)* molaires 40b

mole la taupe 15a

molecular formula la formule moléculaire 13c

molecule la molécule 42

mom la maman 10a

moment le moment 4c, 4e **at the moment** en ce moment 4e

monarchy la monarchie 44

Monday le lundi 5a

money l'argent *(m)* 26

money order le mandat *(m)* 19e, 26

monitor le moniteur 38c, 43

monk le moine 11d

monkey le singe 15a

monorail vehicle le monorail 42

month le mois 4c

month of the year le mois de l'année 5b

monthly mensuel *(adj)*, mensuellement *(adv)* 4c, 5b

Montreal Montréal 30c

monument le monument 36a

mood *(grammar)* le mode 8a

mood *(feeling)* l'humeur *(f)* 11e, 21a; **in a bad mood** de mauvaise humeur 21b; **in a good mood** de bonne humeur 21b

moon la lune 5c, 6a, 13a

moonray/moonbeam le rayon de lune *(f)* 13a

moose l'orignal *(m)* 15a

moped la Mobylette 33a

morality la moralité 45b

more plus *(adv)* 3c

morning le matin 4a

mortgage l'hypothèque *(f)* 26

Moscow Moscou 30c

mosque la mosquée 11d

mosquito le moustique 15d

motel le motel 35a

moth le papillon (nocturne) 15d

mother la mère 10a

mother-in-law la belle-mère 10a

motion la motion 3e

motorcycle la motocyclette, la moto 33a

motorcycle driver le (la) motocycliste 33a

mountain la montagne 13b

mountain boot la chaussure d'escalade *(f)* 27b; la chaussure de montagne 36b

mountain chain la chaîne de montagnes *(f, pl)* 13b

mountain climbing l'alpinisme *(m)* 27b, 36b

mountainous montagneux, montagneuse *(adj, m, f)* 13b

mouse *(animal)* la souris 15a; *(computer)* la souris 42b

moustache la moustache 12a

mouth la bouche 12a, 40b

move bouger *(v)*, remuer *(v)* 3e

move oneself bouger *(v)*, se déplacer *(v)* 3e

move *(out of a house)* déménager *(v)* 23f

movement le mouvement 3e

movie *(film, motion picture)* le film 28a

movie camera la caméra 25d

movie director le réalisateur, la réalisatrice, le metteur en scène, la metteuse en scène 28a, 38a

movies *(cinema)* le cinéma, le ciné 28a

Mr. M., Monsieur 11f, 16b

Mrs. Mme, Madame 11f, 16b

Ms. Mlle, Mademoiselle 11f, 16b

much beaucoup *(adv)* 3c

muffler *(of a vehicle)* le pot d'échappement 33e

mug une chope 23d

mugginess *(weather)* la lourdeur 6a

muggy *(weather)* lourd *(adj, m)*, lourde *(adj, f)* 6a

mule le mulet 15a

multiple le multiple 1f

multiplication la multiplication 1e

multiplication table la table de multiplication *(f)* 1e

multiplied by multiplié par 1e

multiply multiplier *(v)* 1e

mumble grommeler *(v)* 17a

murder le meurtre, l'homicide 39b; assassiner *(v)*, tuer *(v)* 39b

murmur murmurer *(v)* 17a

muscle le muscle 12a, 40a

museum le musée 36a

mushroom le champignon 14e, 24e

music la musique 25j, 28c, 37e

musical la comédie musicale 20a

musician le musicien, la musicienne 28c, 38a

Muslim musulman(e) *(m, f)* 11d

mussels les moules *(f, pl)* 24d

must *see* **have to**

mute *(person)* muet, muette *(adj, m, f)* 12c

my mon *(m, s)*, ma *(f, s)*, mes *(m/f, pl)* 8f

My God! Mon Dieu! 21c

My name is . . . Mon nom est . . . 11f; Je m'appelle . . . 11f, 16b; **I am . . .** Je suis . . . 16b

My tooth hurts! J'ai mal à la dent! 40b

myself *(reflexive)* me 8k

mystery novel le roman policier 20a, 25o

myth le mythe 11d, 28d

mythology la mythologie 28d

N

nag (torment, pester) harceler *(v)* 17a

nail *(hardware)* le clou 25b

nail polish le vernis à ongles *(m, pl)* 25f

naive naïf, naïve *(adj, m, f)* 11e

name le nom 11f, 38b

napkin la serviette 23d, 24l

Naples Naples 30c

napoleon *(pastry)* le millefeuille 24i

narrow étroit *(adj, m)*, étroite *(f)* 3b

nation la nation 13e, 30a

national national(e) *(adj, m, f)* 13e

National Assembly l'Assemblée *(f)* Nationale 44

nationality la nationalité 11f, 38b

natural naturel(le) *(adj, m, f)* 1d, 13b

natural gas le gaz naturel 13c

natural resources les ressources *(f)* naturelles 13c, 45a

natural sciences les sciences *(f, pl)* naturelles 37e

nature la nature 13b

near près (de) *(adv)* 3d, 36c

nearly presque *(adv)* 3c

neat soigné(e) *(adj, m, f)* 11e

neck le cou 12a; **stiff (twisted) neck** le torticolis 40a; **sore neck** le mal au cou 40a

necklace le collier 25i

necktie la cravate 25k

need le besoin; avoir *(v)* besoin de 21a

needle l'aiguille *(f)* 40b

negative négatif; négative *(adj, m, f)* 1d, 8n

neigh hennir *(v)* 15a

neon au néon 25b

nephew le neveu 10a

Neptune Neptune *(m)* 13a

nerves les nerfs *(m, pl)* 40a

nervous system le système nerveux 40a

net *(sports)* le but 27b

network le réseau 20b

neutrino le neutrino 13c

neutron le neutron 13c, 42

never jamais *(adv)* 4e

nevertheless néanmoins 9p

New Brunswick le Nouveau-Brunswick 30b

new moon la nouvelle lune 13a

New Testament le Nouveau Testament 11d

New Year le Nouvel An 5f

New Year's Day le Jour de l'An 5f, 29a

New Year's Eve la Nuit de la Saint-Sylvestre 5f, 29a

New Zealand la Nouvelle-Zélande 30b

Newfoundland la Terre-Neuve 30b

newlyweds les nouveaux-mariés *(m, pl)* 11c

news les actualités 20a

news report les nouvelles, les actualités 20b

newscast *(on radio)* les informations *(f, pl)*, les infos *(f, pl)* 20b; *(on television)* le journal télévisé 20b

newspaper le journal 20a, 25o

newsstand le kiosque à journaux 34

next to à côté (de) *(prep)* 3d

nice *(person)* sympathique *(adj, m, f)* 11e

niece la nièce 10a

night la nuit 4a

night club la boîte de nuit 29b

night school le cours du soir, l'école du soir 37a

nightingale le rossignol 15b

nine neuf 1a

nineteen dix-neuf 1a

ninety quatre-vingt-dix 1a

ninety-one quatre-vingt-onze 1a

ninth neuvième 1b

nitrogen l'azote *(m)*, le nitrogène 13c

No! Non! 16c

No Entry Défense d'entrer 33d

No Left Turn Virage à gauche interdit 33d

no one personne 3c, 8o

No Parking Stationnement interdit 33d

No Passing Interdiction de dépasser 33d

No Problem! Pas de problème! 22a

No Right Turn Virage à droite interdit 33d

No Smoking Défense de fumer 32a

No Stopping Arrêt interdit 33d

No Thoroughfare Circulation interdite 33d

No U-Turn Demi-tour interdit 33d

No way! Pas de moyen! Pas possible! Pas question! 17b, 20b

noise le bruit 12c

noisy bruyant(e) *(adj, m, f)* 12c

nonconformist le (la) non-conformiste 11e

nonfiction l'ouvrage *(m)* non romanesque 20a

nonsmoking compartment non-fumeurs 34

noon le midi 4a

north le nord 3d; **to the north** au nord 3d

North America l'Amérique *(f)* du Nord 30b

North Pole le Pôle Nord 13e

northern septentrional(e) *(adj)* 3d

Norway la Norvège 30b

Norwegian *(nationality)* Norvégien *(m)*, Norvégienne *(f)* 30d; *(language)* le norvégien 30d

nose le nez 12a

nostril la narine 12a, 40a

Not bad! Pas mal! *(adv)* 16a

not guilty non coupable 41

not nice antipathique *(adj, m, f)* 11e

note la note 20a, 37f; **to take notes** prendre *(v)* des notes 37f; *(music)* la note 28c

note pad le bloc-notes 25c

notebook le cahier 37b

nothing rien *(adv/pro)*, nul *(adj/pro, m)*, nulle *(f)* 3c

nothing to declare rien à déclarer 31

noun le nom 8a

Nova Scotia la Nouvelle-Écosse 30b

novel le roman 20a, 25o, 28b

November le novembre 5b

novocaine la novocaïne 40b

now maintenant *(adv)* 4e, 17b; à présent 4e

nowadays de nos jours 4e

nowhere nulle part *(adv)* 3d

n-sided figures les figures *(f)* à côtés *(n)* 2a

nth root à la racine *(n)* 1e

nuclear energy l'énergie *(f)* nucléaire 13c, 42, 45a

nuclear fuel le combustible nucléaire 42

nuclear industry l'industrie *(f)* nucléaire 42

nuclear reactor　le réacteur nucléaire　42

nuclear war　la guerre nucléaire 45b

nuclear weapon　l'arme (f) nucléaire　45b

nucleus　le noyau　13c, 14a

number　le nombre　1d, 8a; le numéro　1d, 38b; numéroter (v)　1d; le chiffre　1d

numeral　le numéral　1d

numeral, Roman　le chiffre romain 1d

numerical　numérique (adj)　1d

nun　la religieuse　11d

nurse　l'infirmier (m), l'infirmière (f)　38a, 40a

nursery school　l'école (f) maternelle　37a

nylon　le nylon　251

O

oak tree　le chêne　14c

oat　l'avoine (f)　24i

obesity　l'obésité (f)　11a

obituary　la notice nécrologique, la nécrologie　20a

object (grammar)　le complément d'objet (m)　8a, 8i, 8j, 8l

oboe　le hautbois　28c

obstinate　obstiné(e) (adj, m, f) 11e

obtuse　obtus (adj)　2b

obtuse-angled　obtusangle (adj) 2a

occasionally　de temps en temps (adv)　4e

occupation　l'occupation (f)　38a

occur　arriver (v), se produire (v) 4e

ocean　l'océan (m)　13b

octagon　l'octogone (m)　2a

octahedron　l'octaèdre (m)　2a

October　l'octobre (m)　5b

octopus　la pieuvre, le poulpe　15c

odd　impair (adj, m)　1d

odious　antipathique (adj, m, f) 11e

of　de　8g

of it　en (pron)　3c, 8o

of the day　du jour　24g

of them　en (pron)　8o

offend　offenser (v)　17a

office　le bureau　38d

office automation　l'automatisation (f) de bureau, la bureautique 43

office hours　les heures (f, pl) de bureau, les heures (f, pl) d'ouverture　40b

often　souvent (adv)　4e

Oh, my!　Oh! là! là!　21c

oil　l'huile (f)　13c, 24j, 33e

oil filter　le filtre à huile　33e

ointment　la pommade　25h

OK!　D'accord! Entendu!　16c

old　vieux (m), vieille (f)　11b

old age　la vieillesse　11b

older brother　le frère aîné　11b

older sister　la soeur aînée　11b

Old Testament　l'Ancien Testament (m)　11d

olive　l'olive (f)　14d, 24e

olive tree　l'olivier (m)　14c

omelette　l'omelette (f)　24h; **with cheese** au fromage; **with ham** au jambon; **with whipped cream** mousseline　24h

on　sur (prep)　3d, 8g

On guard! (fencing)　En garde! (f) 27b

on Mondays　le lundi　5a

on sale　en vente (f)　25a

on Saturdays　le samedi　5a

on Sundays　le dimanche　5a

on the air (radio and television)　à l'antenne (f)　20b

on the dot (telling time)　juste (pile)　4b

on time　à l'heure　32b, 34

on vacation　en vacances (f, pl) 36b

once　une fois　4e

once in a while　de temps à autre 4e

once upon a time　il était une fois 4a, 4e

one un *(m)*, une *(f)* la; on 8h, 8o
one billion un milliard 1a
one-fifth un cinquième 1c
one-fourth un quart 1c
one-half un demi 1c
one hundred cent la; **about one hundred** une centaine 1c
one hundred and one cent un 1a
one hundred million cent millions 1a
one hundred thousand cent mille 1a
one million un million 1a
one million and one un million un 1a
one-third un tiers 1c
one thousand mille 1a; **about a thousand** un millier 1c
one thousand and one mille un 1a
one turn (360°) le tour 2b
oneself *(reflexive pron)* se 8k; soi 8l
One-Way Street Sens Unique 33d
one-way ticket l'aller-simple *(m)* 30a
onion l'oignon *(m)* 14e, 24e
onion soup la soupe à l'oignon 24g
only seulement *(adv)* 4e
Ontario l'Ontario *(m)* 30b
opal l'opale *(f)* 25i
opaque opaque 7b, 13d
open ouvert(e) *(adj, m, f)* 25a
open an account ouvrir *(v)* un compte 26
Open your mouth, please. Ouvrez la bouche, s'il vous plaît. 40b
opening hours *(store)* les heures d'ouverture 25a
opera l'opéra *(m)* 28c
operating room la salle de chirurgie 40a
operation *(surgery)* l'intervention *(f)* chirurgicale; **to have an operation** se faire *(v)* opérer 40a

operator *(telephone)* le (la) téléphoniste 18b
opinion l'opinion *(f)* 22a; **in my opinion** à mon avis 22a
opposite opposé(e) *(adj, m, f)* 2b
optic fiber la fibre optique 18a
optical reader le lecteur optique 42b
optician l'opticien, l'opticienne 40a
optimism l'optimisme *(m)* 11e
optimist l'optimiste *(m, f)* 11e
optimistic optimiste *(adj, m, f)* 11e
or ou *(conj)* 8p
oral oral(e) *(adj, m, f)* 17a
oral exam l'examen *(m)* oral 37f
orally oralement *(adv)* 17a
orange l'orange *(f)* 14d, 24f
orange *(color)* orange *(adj, invariable)*, orangé *(adj)* 7a
orange tree l'oranger *(m)* 14c
orbit l'orbite *(f)* 13a; être *(v)* en orbite, mettre *(v)* en orbite, placer *(v)* sur orbite 13a
orchestra l'orchestre *(m)* 28c
orchestra conductor le chef d'orchestre *(m)* 28c
orchid l'orchidée *(f)* 14b
order l'ordre *(m)*, ordonner *(v)* 17a; *(food)* commander *(v)* 17a, 24o
ordinal ordinal(e) *(adj, m, f)* 1b, 1d
organ *(music)* l'orgue *(m)* 28c
organic organique *(adj, m, f)* 13c
organism l'organisme *(m)* 14a, 15d
oriental oriental(e) *(m, f)* 11d
original original(e) *(adj, m, f)* 11e
Orthodox orthodoxe *(m, f)* 11d
ostrich l'autruche *(f)* 15b
others autrui *(indef pron)*, les autres 8o

our notre *(m/f, s)*, nos *(m/f, pl)* 8f

ourselves *(reflexive pron)* nous 8k

out dehors *(adv)* 39a

out of focus *(photo)* la photo floue 25d

outlet la prise 18a, 25b

outside dehors *(adv)* 3d, 36c; en dehors *(adv)* 3d

outskirts *(suburbs)* la banlieue, les environs *(m, pl)* 30a

outspokenly franchement *(adv)* 17a

oven le four 23d; **microwave oven** le four à micro-ondes *(f, pl)* 23d

overhead projector le rétroprojecteur 37b

overnight bag le sac de voyage 31

owl la chouette, le hibou 15b

ownership papers les documents *(m)* de propriété 33b

ox le bœuf, les bœufs 15a

oxygen l'oxygène *(m)* 13c

oyster l'huître *(f)* 24d

P

Pacific Pacifique *(adj, m, f)* 13b

pack *(one's bags/luggage)* faire *(v)* les bagages 31

package le colis, le paquet 19e, 25a

pad le bloc-notes 19d

pagan païen, païenne *(n/adj, m, f)* 11d

page la page 19d, 20a

pager le pager 18a

pail le seau 23d

pain la douleur 40a

painful douloureux *(adj, m)*, douloureuse *(adj, f)* 40a

paint peindre *(v)* 7c, 23f, 28b

painter le peintre, la peintre 7c, 38a; l'artiste-peintre *(m/f)* 28b, 38a

painting *(picture)* le tableau 23c; la peinture 28b

pair la paire 3c, 25n

pajamas le pyjama 25k

palate le palais 40b

pale pâle *(adj)* 7b

palette la palette 28b

palm tree le palmier 14c

pamphlet le dépliant, la brochure 20a

pan la casserole, la sauteuse 23d

pancake la crêpe 24g

panties *(underpants)* le slip 25k

pantomime la pantomime 28e

pants *(slacks)* le pantalon 25k

paper le papier 19d, 25c, 37b

paper clip le trombone 19d

paper shredder le déchiqueteur 38c

paragraph le paragraphe 19c

parakeet la perruche 15b

parallel line la ligne parallèle 2b

parallelogram le parallélogramme 2a

parenthesis la parenthèse 19c; **in parenthesis** entre parenthèses 19c

parents les parents *(m)* 10a

Paris Paris 30c

park *(a vehicle)* stationner *(v)* 33c

park le parc 36a; **park bench** le banc 36a

parking le stationnement 33c

parking lights les feux *(m, pl)* de stationnement 33e

parking meter le parcmètre, le parcomètre 36a

Parliament le Parlement 44

parrot le perroquet 15b

parsley le persil 14e, 24j

part la part, la partie 3c

participle le participe 8a

particle la particule 13c

partitive le partitif 8a, 8d

party la fête 29b

pass passer *(v)* 27b

pass a sentence *(judgment)* prononcer *(v)* un jugement 41

pass a vehicle dépasser *(v)* 33c

pass an exam être *(v)* reçu(e) à un examen, réussir à un examen 37f

pass by passer *(v)* 3e

passenger le passager, la passagère 32c, 33b

passenger van le fourgon automobile 33a

Passing Lane la voie de dépassement 33d

passive passif *(adj, m)*, passive *(adj, f)* 8a

passive resistance la résistance passive 45b

Passover la Pâque 5f, 29a

passport le passeport 31, 35b

passport control le contrôle de passeports 31

past le passé 4e; passé(e) *(adj, m, f)* 8a

past *(grammar)* le passé composé 8a, 8n

past definite *(grammar)* le passé simple 8a

past participle le participe passé 8a

pasta les pâtes *(f, pl)* 24g

pastel le pastel 28b

pastries les pâtisseries *(f, pl)* 24i

pastry shop la pâtisserie 24n

patience la patience 11e, 21a; **to have patience** avoir *(v)* de la patience 21a

patient patient(e) *(adj, m, f)* 11e

paw la patte 15a

pawn *(in chess)* le pion 27a

pay payer *(v)* 25a, 26, 35b

pay customs/duty payer *(v)* les droits de douane 31

pay off acquitter *(v)* 26

pay phone le téléphone public 18a

pay through the nose payer *(v)* un oeil 12a

payment le paiement 26

peace la paix 44

peach la pêche 14d, 24f

peach pie la tarte aux pêches 24g

peach tree le pêcher 14c

peak le sommet 13b

peak season *(tourism)* la haute saison 35b

peanut l'arachide *(f)*, la cacahouète 24f

pear la poire 14d

pear tree le poirier 14c

pearl la perle 25i

peas les (petits) pois *(m)* 14e, 24e

pedal la pédale 33a

pedestrian le piéton, la piétonne 33b

pedestrian crossing le passage pour piétons, le passage piétonnier, le passage clouté 33c, 36a

peel éplucher *(v)* 24o

Peking/Beijing Pékin/Béjing 30c

pelican le pélican 15b

pen le stylo 2b, 7c, 19d, 25c, 37b, 38c

penalty *(sports)* la pénalité 27b

pencil le crayon 2b, 19d, 25c, 37b, 38c

penguin le manchot 15b

penicillin la pénicilline 25h

peninsula la péninsule, la presqu'île 13b

penis le pénis 12a

pension (retirement) la retraite, la pension 38d

pentagon le pentagone 2a

people les gens *(m & f, pl)* 11d; *(of a nation)* le peuple 44

pepper le poivre 24j

per hour à l'heure *(f)* 3a

per minute à la minute 3a

per second à la seconde 3a

perceive percevoir *(v)* 12c

percent pour cent 1f

percentage le pourcentage 1f

perception la perception 12c

percussion instruments les instruments *(m, pl)* à percussion *(f)* 28c

perfect parfait(e) *(adj, m, f)* 8a

perfection la perfection 11e

perfectionist perfectionniste *(m, f)* 11e

perfume le parfum 12d, 25f

perfume/cosmetics shop la parfumerie 25f

period *(punctuation)* le point 19c

periodical *(weekly)* hebdomadaire *(adj/n, m, f)* 20a

peripherals les périphériques *(m, pl)* 42b

permanent *(wave)* la permanente 12d

perpendicular line la ligne perpendiculaire 2b

person la personne 8a, 11d

personal personnel(le) *(adj, m, f)* 8a

personal computer l'ordinatuer *(m)* personnel 42b

personality la personnalité 11e

perspire transpirer *(v)* 6b

persuade convaincre *(v)* 22b; persuader *(v)* 22b, 41

pessimism le pessimisme 11e

pessimist le (la) pessimiste 11e

pessimistic pessimiste *(adj, m, f)* 11e

pet l'animal *(m)* domestique 15a

petal le pétale 14b

petrol *see* gasoline

petroleum le pétrole 13c, 45a

petunia le pétunia 14b

pharmaceutical drug le médicament 25h

pharmacist le pharmacien, la pharmacienne 25h, 38a

pharmacy la pharmacie 25h

Ph.D. (Dr.) le docteur, la doctoresse 16b

philosophy la philosophie 37e

phone (to telephone) téléphoner *(v)* 18b

phone bill la facture 18b

phone book l'annuaire *(m)* téléphonique, le Bottin 18a

phone booth la cabine téléphonique 18a

phone call l'appel *(m)* téléphonique 18b

phone line la ligne téléphonique 18b

phone number le numéro de téléphone 11f, 18b

phone *see also* telephone

phonetics la phonétique 8a

photo la photo(graphie) 20a, 25d

photocopier le photocopieur 38c

photosynthesis la photosynthèse 14a

phrase la phrase 19c

physical physique *(adj, m, f)* 13c

physics la physique 13c, 37e

physiology la physiologie 37e

physique *(appearance)* l'aspect *(m)* physique 11a

pianist le (la) pianiste 28c

piano le piano 28c

pick *(hardware)* le pic, la pioche 25b

pick flowers cueillir *(v)* des fleurs 14b

pick up *(the phone)* décrocher *(v)* 18b

pickup truck la camionnette 33a

pickpocket le pickpocket, le voleur (la voleuse) à la tire 39b

picky *(person)* tatillon, tatillonne *(adj, m, f)*, difficile *(adj, m, f)* 11e

picnic le pique-nique 29a

picture *(photo)* la photo(graphie) 20a, 25d

pie la tarte 24g

piece la pièce 3c

piece of furniture le meuble 23c

piece of luggage la valise 31

pig le cochon 15a

pigeon le pigeon 15b

pileup le carambolage 39c

pill la pilule 25h, 40a

pillow l'oreiller 23d, 35c

pillowcase la taie d'oreiller 23d

pilot le (la) pilote 38a

pimple le bouton 40a

pine tree le pin 14c

pineapple l'ananas *(m)* 14d, 24f

pink le rose 7a; **to see life through rose-colored glasses** voir (v) la vie en rose 7a

pipe (*smoking*) la pipe 25e

Pisces les Poissons (m) 5d

piston le piston 33e

pitcher (*sports*) le lanceur 27b

pizza parlor la pizzeria 24m

place l'endroit (m) 3d; le lieu 3d, 19c

place of birth le lieu de naissance (f) 11f, 38b

place of employment le lieu d'emploi (m) 11f

plain (*terrain*) la plaine 13b

plane (*hardware*) le rabot 25b

plane figures les figures (f) planes 2a

planet la planète 13a

plant la plante, planter (v) 14a

plastic le plastique (adj, m, f) 13c

plate (dish) l'assiette (f) 23d, 24l

platinum le platine 13c

play jouer (v) 27a; le jeu 27b

play (*theater*) la pièce de théâtre 20a, 28e

play a musical instrument jouer (v) de (du, de l', de la) 28c

play a record passer (v) un disque 20b

play cards jouer (v) aux cartes (f, pl) 27a

play hooky faire (v) l'école buissonnière 37f

player le joueur, la joueuse 27b, 28c

playwright le (la) dramaturge, l'auteur (m) dramatique, l'auteure (f) dramatique 28e

plea la plaidoirie 41

plea for mercy la supplication pour clémence 41

plead plaider (v); **to plead guilty** plaider (v) coupable; **to plead innocent** plaider (v) non coupable 41

pleasant (*person*) aimable (adj, m, f) 11e; sympathique (adj, m, f) 11e; agréable (adj, m, f) 21b

Please! S'il vous plaît! (pol), S'il te plaît! (fam) 16c

Please accept . . . (*in a business letter*) Veuillez accepter, Veuillez agréer . . . 19a

Please give my regards/greetings to . . . Mon bon souvenir à . . . 16a

pleasure plaisir (m) 16b; **The pleasure is mine!** C'est mon plaisir! 16b

pliers les pinces (f, pl) 25b

plot (*of a novel*) l'intrigue (f) 20a, 28d, 28e

plug (*hardware*) la fiche de prise de courant 25b

plug (*telephone*) la fiche téléphonique 18a

plum la prune 14d, 24f

plumber le plombier 38a

plumbing la plomberie 25b

pluperfect (*grammar*) le plus-que-parfait 8a

plural le pluriel, pluriel(le) (adj, m, f) 8a

plus plus (adv) le, 6c; et (conj) 1e

Pluto Pluton (m) 13a

pneumonia la pneumonie 40a

poached egg l'oeuf (m) poché 24h

pocket la poche 25g; **billiard table pocket** la poche 27a

pocket book/paperback le livre de poche 20a

pocket knife le couteau pliant, le couteau de poche 39b

poem le poème 20a

poet le poète, la femme poète, la poétesse 28d

poetry la poésie 20a, 25o, 28d

point le point 2b; (*sports*) la marque 27b

point out indiquer (v) 17a

Poland la Pologne 30b

pole le pôle 13e; **North Pole** le Pôle Nord; **South Pole** le Pôle Sud 13e

police la police 33b, 39b, 39c

police officer l'agent (m) de police, le policier, la femme policier, la policière 33b, 38a, 39b

police station le commissariat de police 41

policy (politics) la politique 44

Polish (nationality) Polonais (m), Polonaise (f) 30d; (language) le polonais 30d

polite poli(e) (adj, m, f) 11e

political party le parti politique 44

political power le pouvoir politique 44

political science les sciences (f, pl) politiques, les sciences (f, pl) po 37e

politician l'homme (m) politique, la femme politique 44

politics la politique 44

pollen le pollen 14a

pollution la pollution 13c, 45a

polyester le polyester 251

polyhedron le polyèdre 2a

pony le poney 15a

pool (swimming) la piscine 27b, 35b

poor pauvre (adj, m, f) 11e

Poor man! Pauvre homme! 21c

Poor woman! Pauvre femme! 21c

poplar tree le peuplier 14c

poppy le pavot, le coquelicot 14b

porch le porche, la véranda 23a

pork le porc 24c

pornography la pornographie 45b

porpoise le marsouin 15c

portable phone le téléphone portatif 18a

portable radio la radio portative 20b

porter le porteur 32a, 34; (in hotel) le portier, la portière 35b

portion le morceau, la portion 3c

portrait le portrait 28b

Portugal le Portugal 30b

Portuguese (nationality) Portugais (m), Portugaise (f) 30d; (language) le portugais 30d

position la position 3d

positive positif, positive (adj, m, f) 1d

possessive possessif, possessive (adj, m, f) 8a, 8f, 8n, 11e

post office le bureau de poste 19e

post office box la case postale, la boîte postale 19e

postage l'affranchissement (m) 19e

postage stamp le timbre-poste 19e

postal code le code postal 19e, 38b

postal rate le tarif 19e

postcard la carte postale 19e

postdate postdater (v) 26

posterior postérieur(e) (adj) 4e

postman see letter carrier

pot (cooking) le faitout, la marmite 23d

pots and pans la batterie de cuisine 23d

potato la pomme de terre 14e, 24e

potato salad la salade de pommes de terre 24e

poultry la volaille 24c

pour verser (v) 24o

powder la poudre 25f, 25h

power brake le servofrein 33e

power steering la servodirection 33e

power window la vitre à commande automatique 33e

practice a sport faire (v) du sport (m) 27b

praise louer (v) 17a

prawn la crevette, la langoustine 24d

pray prier (v) 11d, 17a

prayer la prière 11d, 17a

preach prêcher (v) 17a

precious précieux (adj, m), précieuse (adj, f) 25i

predicate le prédicat *(m)* 8a
predicate adjective l'attribut *(m)* 8a
preface la préface 28d
prefer préférer *(v)* 21b
pregnancy la grossesse 11c
pregnant enceinte *(adj, f)* 11c, 40a
premier showing la première représentation 28a
preposition la préposition 8a, 8g, 8l
prescription l'ordonnance *(f)* 25h, 40a
present le présent 4e; présent(e) *(adj, m, f)* 4e, 8a, 8n, 37f; actuel(le) *(adj, m, f)* 4e
present participle le participe présent 8a
presently actuellement *(adv)*, à présent 4e
president le président, la présidente 44
president of a university le recteur, la rectrice 37d
President of the French Republic le (la) Président(e) de la République Française 44
presumptuous présomptueux, présomptueuse *(adj, m, f)* 11e
pretentious prétentieux, prétentieuse *(adj, m, f)* 11e
pretzel le bretzel 24i
previous précédent(e) *(adj, m, f)* 4e
previously précédemment *(adv)*, auparavant *(adv)* 4e
price le prix 24m, 25a; **rate** le tarif 35b
price tag l'étiquette *(f)* 25a
priest le prêtre 11d
primate le primate 15a
prime le nombre premier 1d
prime meridian le méridien origine 13e
prime minister le premier ministre 44

prime number le nombre premier 1d
prince le prince 44
Prince Edward Island l'Île-du-Prince-Édouard *(f)* 30b
princess la princesse 44
principal le directeur, la directrice 37d
print imprimer *(v)* 20a
Print your name Ecrivez votre nom (Ecris ton nom) en caractères d'imprimerie 11f
printed matter les imprimés *(m, pl)* 19e
printer *(computer)* l'imprimante *(f)* 19d, 38c, 43
printing la typographie 20a
printing edition *(in publishing)* le tirage 20a
prism le prisme 2a
prison la prison 41
prison sentence la peine de prison 41
private school l'école *(f)* privée 37a
privilege le droit 41
problem le problème 1f, 22a, 37f
problem to solve le problème à résoudre *(v)* 1f, 37f
produce market le marché aux légumes et fruits 24n
product le produit 1f
production *(theater)* la mise en scène 28e
Prof. le Prof., le professeur, la femme professeur 11f
profession la profession 11f, 27b, 38a, 38b
professional professionnel(le) *(adj, m, f)* 11f, 38a
professor le professeur, la professeure 11f, 37d, 38a
professor's office le cabinet du professeur 37c
program le programme, l'émission *(f)* 20b, 28e

program *(computer)* le programme d'ordinateur 43

programmer *(person)* le programmeur, la programmeuse 38a, 42b; *(machine)* le programmateur 42b

programming *(computer)* la programmation 42b

projector le projecteur 20b

promise la promesse; promettre *(v)* 17a

promissory note le billet à ordre 26

promoted reçu(e) *(adj, m, f)* 37f

pronoun le pronom 8a, 8h–8o

pronounce prononcer *(v)* 17a

pronunciation la prononciation 8a, 17a

proofreader correcteur *(m)* 20a

propose proposer *(v)* 17a

prostitution la prostitution 45b

protect protéger *(v)* 39a

protest la protestation 44

Protestant protestant(e) *(m, f)* 11d

Protestantism le protestantisme 11d

proton le proton 13c, 42

protractor le goniomètre 2b

proud fier, fière *(adj, m, f)* 11e

provided that pourvu que *(conj)* 8p

province la province 13e

prudent prudent(e) *(adj, m, f)* 11e

prune le pruneau 14d, 24f

P. S. P.-S., le post-scriptum 19c

psychiatrist le (la) psychiatre 38a

psychologist le (la) psychologue 38a

psychology la psychologie 37e

public garden le jardin public 36a

public notices les affiches *(f, pl)* publiques 36a

public parking le stationnement public 33c

public phone le téléphone public 36a

public prosecutor le procureur de la République 41

public washrooms les toilettes *(f, pl)* publiques 36a

publish publier *(v)* 20a

publisher l'éditeur *(m)* 20a

publishing house la maison d'édition 20a

puck le palet, le puck 27b

pudding la crème 24h

puffed cheese le fromage soufflé 24h

pull tirer *(v)* 3e

pull out a tooth extraire *(v)* une dent 40b

pulse le pouls 40a

pumpernickel bread le pain noir 24i

pumpkin la citrouille 14e

punch *(hardware)* le poinçon 25b

punctuation la ponctuation 19c

pupil l'élève *(m/f)* 37d

purchase l'achat *(m)*, acheter *(v)* 25a

pure pur(e) *(adj)* 7b, 13d

purple le pourpre, le violet 7a

put mettre *(v)*, placer *(v)* 3e

put a room in order mettre *(v)* une pièce en ordre 23f

put down poser *(v)* 3e

put in orbit mettre *(v)* en orbite; placer *(v)* sur orbite 13a

put on (se) mettre *(v)* 25m

put on make-up se farder *(v)*, se maquiller *(v)* 12d

put on perfume se parfumer *(v)* 12d

put out (extinguish) éteindre *(v)* 39a

put someone on trial faire *(v)* passer en justice 41

pyramid la pyramide 2a

Q

quantity la quantité 3c

quantum theory la théorie des quanta 42

quark le quark 13c

quart le quart de gallon *(m)* 3a
Quebec le Québec 30b
queen la reine 27a, 44; *(in chess)* la dame 27a
question la question 37f; **to ask a question** poser *(v)* une question 37f
question mark le point d'interrogation *(f)* 19c
queue up faire *(v)* la queue 15a
quiche la quiche 24g; **with cheese** au fromage; **with ham** au jambon 24g
quickly rapidement *(adv)*, vite *(adv)* 3e
Quiet! Silence! 21c
Quite well! Très bien! *(adv)* 16a
quotation mark le guillemet 19c
quotient le quotient 1f

R
rabbi le rabbin 11d
rabbit le lapin 15a
race *(population)* la race 11d; *(sports)* la course 27b
racism le racisme 45b
radiation la radiation 13c, 45a
radiator le radiateur 33e
radio la radio 20b, 23d, 35c
radioactive waste les déchets *(m)* radioactifs 13c, 45a
radish le radis 14e
radius le rayon 2a
railroad le chemin de fer 34; **station** la gare 34
railway crossing le passage à niveau 36a
rain la pluie; pleuvoir *(v)* 6a
raincoat l'imperméable *(m)* 25k
rainforest la forêt pluviale 13b
rainy weather un temps pluvieux 6a
raise *(someone)* élever *(v)* 11c
raise to a power élever *(v)* à une puissance 1e
raisin le raisin sec 14d, 24f
rake le râteau 25b

Ramadan le ramadan 5f, 29a
ramp la rampe, la bretelle d'accès 33c
random access memory *(computers)* la RAM 43
rap le rap 25j, 28a
rape le viol; violer 39b
rare rare *(adj)* 4e
rare *(cooked food)* saignant(e) *(adj, m, f)* 24b
rarely rarement *(adv)* 4e
raspberry la framboise 14d, 24f
rat le rat 15a
rate le tarif 35b
ratio la proportion 1e
rational rationnel(le) *(adj, m, f)* 1d
razor le rasoir 12d, 25f; le rasoir électrique 12d, 25f
razor blade la lame 12d
read lire *(v)* 20a, 37f
reader *(person)* le lecteur, la lectrice 20a
reading *(passage, selection)* la lecture 37f
real réel(le) *(adj, m, f)* 1d
Really? Vraiment? 21c
reap récolter *(v)*, cueillir *(v)* 14a
rear window *(vehicle)* la lunette arrière 33e
rear-view mirror *(vehicle)* le rétroviseur intérieur 33e
reason la raison 22a; raisonner *(v)* 22b
rebellious rebelle *(adj, m, f)* 11e
receipt l'acquit *(m)*, le récépissé, le reçu 25a, 26, 35b
receive recevoir *(v)* 19e
receiver *(telephone handset)* le combiné 18a
recent récent(e) *(adj)* 4e
recently récemment *(adv)* 4e
reception la réception 11c
reciprocal réciproque *(adj)* 1d
recommend recommander *(v)* 17a

record (recording) le disque 20b, 25j; **to record** enregistrer *(v)* 20b; **to play a record** passer *(v)* un disque 20b

record player le tourne-disque 20b

rectangle le rectangle 2a

rectum le rectum 40a

red le rouge 7a; **to become red with anger** devenir *(v)* rouge de colère 7a

red-haired roux, rousse *(adj, m, f)* 11a

reduced price le prix réduit 25a

referee l'arbitre *(m/f)* 27b

reference book l'ouvrage *(m)* de référence 20a, 25o

refined raffiné(e) *(adj, m, f)* 11e

reflect (think) réfléchir *(v)* 22b

reflexive pronoun le pronom personnel réfléchi 8a, 8k

reflexive verb le verbe pronominal 8a

reform la réforme 44

refrigerator le réfrigérateur, le frigo 23d

reggae le reggae 28c

region la région 13e

registered letter la lettre recommandée 19e

registration l'inscription *(f)* 37f; **fee** les droits *(m, pl)* d'inscription 37f

registration papers *(vehicle)* la carte grise 33b

regular régulier *(adj, m)*, régulière *(adj, f)* 4e, 8a

regularly régulièrement *(adv)* 4e

rehearsal la répétition 28e

relate raconter *(v)* 17a

relative relatif *(adj, m)*, relative *(adj, f)* 8a

relatives les proches parents *(m)* 10a

relax se relaxer *(v)* 12b

relief le soulagement 21a; **sigh of relief** le soupir de soulagement 21a

religion la religion 11d

religious pieux, pieuse *(adj, m, f)* 11d

remain rester *(v)* 29b

remember se rappeler *(v)*, se souvenir *(v)* de 22b

remote control *(television)* la télécommande 20b

rent le loyer; louer *(v)* 23g

rental car la voiture de location 33a

repair réparer *(v)* 25i

repeat répéter *(v)* 17a, 37f

repetition la répétition 17a

reply la réponse; répondre *(v)* 19e

report le compte rendu, faire *(v)* un compte rendu, faire *(v)* un rapport sur 17a

reporter le (la) journaliste, le (la) reporter 20a

representative le (la) représentant(e) 44

reproach reprocher *(v)* 17a

reproduce reproduire *(v)* 14a

reproduction la reproduction 14a

reptile le reptile 15c

republic la république 44

request la demande; demander *(v)* 17a

rescue sauver *(v)* 39a

researcher le chercheur, la chercheuse 38a

reservation la réservation 24m, 32a, 35b

reserve réserver *(v)* 35b

reserved réservé(e) *(adj, m, f)* 11e, 24m

residence le domicile 11f

resistant résistant(e) *(adj, m, f)* 13d

respiratory system le système respiratoire 40a

rest se reposer *(v)* 12b

restaurant le restaurant 24m; **informal restaurant** le bistro (bistrot) 24m

restless agité(e) *(adj, m, f)* 11e

restore restaurer *(v)* 23f

résumé le résumé 38b

retire se retirer *(v)*, prendre sa retraite 38d

retirement *(pension)* la retraite, la pension 38d

return retourner *(v)* 3e, 29b; revenir *(v)* 29b

return an item rendre *(v)* 25a

return address l'adresse *(f)* de l'expéditeur 19e

review la révision; faire *(v)* une révision 37f

review *(on media)* la critique 20a

revolt la révolte 44

revolution la révolution 44

rhetoric la rhétorique 17a, 28d

rhetorical rhétorique *(adj, m, f)* 17a

rhetorical question la question rhétorique 17a

rheumatism le rhumatisme 40a

rhinoceros le rhinocéros 15a

rhombus le rhombe 2a

rhythm le rythme 28c

rice le riz 24i

rice pudding la crème de riz 24h

rice with vegetables le riz aux légumes *(m, f, pl)* 24g

rich riche *(adj, m, f)* 11e

rifle le fusil 39b

right *(privilege)* le droit 41

right *(location)* droit(e) *(adj, m, f)* 3d; **to the right** à droite 3d, 33c

right *(angle)* droit(e) *(adj, m, f)* 2b

right *(accurate)* correct(e) *(adj, m, f)* 37f

right away tout de suite *(adv)* 4e

right prism le prisme droit 2a

right wing *(politics)* la droite 44

right-angled rectangle *(adj)* 2a

right to vote le suffrage universel 44

right *(jewelry)* la bague, l'anneau *(m)* 25i

ring *(telephone)* sonner *(v)* 18b

ring finger l'annulaire *(m)* 12a

rink *(hockey)* la patinoire 27c

rinse (se) rinser *(v)* 40b

riot l'émeute *(f)* 44

ripe mûr(e) *(adj, m, f)* 14a

rise se lever *(v)* 3e

rite le rite 11d

river le fleuve 13b, 36b; *(small)* la rivière 13b, 36b

road le chemin, la route 33c

road map la carte routière 33b

Road Work (in Progress) Travaux 33d

roar rugir *(v)* 15a

roast rôti(e) *(adj, m, f)* 24b

roast beef le rosbif 24g

rob voler *(v)* 39b

robber le voleur, la voleuse 39b

robbery le vol 39b

robin le rouge-gorge 15b

robot le robot 42

robust robuste *(adj)* 13d

rock la roche, le rocher 13b

rock music la musique rock 25j

roll *(of bread)* le petit pain chapelet 24i

roll *(of film)* le rouleau de film (pellicule), la pellicule 25d

roll *(sweet)* la brioche 24i

roller skate patiner *(v)* à roulettes *(f, pl)* 27b

Roman numeral le chiffre romain 1d

romance novel le roman d'amour 20a, 25o

romantic romantique *(adj, m, f)* 11e

Rome Rome 30c

roof le toit 23a, 33e

rook *(chess)* la tour 27a

room la pièce 23b; la chambre 35b

room service le service dans la chambre 35b

room with bath la chambre avec bain 35b

room with a shower la chambre avec douche 35b

room with two beds la chambre à deux lits 35b

rooster le coq 15b

root la racine 14a, 40b

rope la corde 27b, 36b; **ropes** *(boxing)* les cordes *(f, pl)* 27b

rose la rose 14b

rosemary le romarin 14e, 24j

Rosh Hashana le Roch ha-Shana 29a

rotten pourri(e) *(adj, m, f)* 14a

rough brut, brute *(adj, m, f)* 11e; rude *(adj)* 13d

rough copy, draft le brouillon 37f

round bread le pain rond 24i

round-trip ticket l' aller-retour *(m)* 30a

row le rang 28a

ruby le rubis 25i

rude impoli(e) *(adj, m, f)*, grossier, grossière *(adj, m, f)* 11e

rug le tapis 23c; **wall-to-wall carpeting** la moquette 23c

ruler la règle 2b, 19d, 37b, 38c

rumor le bruit 17a

run courir *(v)* 3e, 12b, 27b

run (baseball) le point 27b

Run for your life! Sauve qui peut! 39b

run into someone rencontrer *(v)* quelqu'un 16b

runway *(airplane)* la piste 32c

rush hour les heures *(f, pl)* d'affluence, les heures de pointe 33c

rusk *(Melba toast)* la biscotte 24i

Russia la Russie 30b

Russian *(nationality)* Russe *(m/f)* 30d; *(language)* le russe 30d

rye and wheat bread le pain de campagne 24i

rye bread le pain au seigle 24i

S

saber *(fencing)* le sabre d'escrime *(f)* 27b

sad triste *(adj, m, f)* 11e, 21a

sadness la tristesse 11e, 21a

safe *(for valuables)* le coffre-fort 26

safe deposit box le coffre (de sécurité) 26

Sagittarius le Sagittaire 5d

salad la salade 24g

salamander la salamandre 15c

salami le salami 24c

salary le salaire 26, 38d

sale la vente 25a; **for sale** à vendre *(v)* 25a; **on sale** en vente *(f)* 25a

sales (lower prices) les soldes *(m, pl)* 25a

salmon le saumon 24d

salt le sel 13c, 24j

salty salé(e) *(adj, m, f)* 24p

salutation *(of a letter)* la formule (la salutation) initiale 19c

sand le sable 13b

sandwich le sandwich 24g; **with cheese** au fromage; **with ham** au jambon 24g

sap *(plants)* la sève 14a

sapphire le saphir 25i

sarcasm le sarcasme 11e

sarcastic sarcastique *(adj, m, f)* 11e

sardine la sardine 15c, 24d

Saskatchewan le Saskatchewan 30b

satellite le satellite 13a, 42

satellite radio la radio par satellite 20b

satellite television la télévision par satellite 20b

satisfaction la satisfaction 21a

satisfied satisfait(e) *(adj, m, f)* 21a

Saturday le samedi 5a

Saturn Saturne *(m)* 13a

saucer la soucoupe 23d, 24l

sausage la saucisse 24c

save économiser *(v)*, épargner *(v)* 26

savings l'épargne *(f)* 26

saw *(hardware)* la scie 25b

saxophone le saxophone 28c

say dire *(v)* 17a

scalene scalène *(adj)* 2a

scarf l'écharpe *(f)* 25k

scene la scène 28e

scenery *(theater)* le décor 28e

schedule l'horaire *(m)* 4e, 34

school l'école *(f)* 37f

school yard la cour 37c

school year l'année *(f)* scolaire 5b

schoolbag le sac d'écolier 37b

schoolmate le (la) camarade d'école 37d

science fiction la science-fiction 20a, 25o

sciences les sciences *(f, pl)* 37e

scientific research la recherche scientifique 42

scientist le (la) scientifique 38a

scissors les ciseaux *(m, pl)* 12d, 19d, 38c, 39c

scooter le scooter 33a

score *(sports)* la marque 27b

Scorpio le Scorpion 5d

scorpion le scorpion 15d

screen l'écran *(m)* 25d, 28a

screen *(computer)* l'écran de visualisation 42b

screw la vis 25b

screwdriver le tournevis 25b

sculpt sculpter *(v)* 28b

sculptor le sculpteur 28b

sculptress la femme sculpteur 28b

sculpture la sculpture 28b

sea la mer 6a, 13b, 36b

seafood les fruits de mer 24d

seagull la mouette 15b

seal *(animal)* le phoque 15c

season la saison 5c

Season's Greetings Meilleurs voeux 16c

seat la place 28a, 34; le siège 28a, 32c, 33e

seat *(bicycle)* la selle 33a

seat belt la ceinture de sécurité 32c, 33e

secant la sécante 2b

second deuxième, second(e) *(adj, m, f)* 1b, 8a; *(time)* la seconde 3a, 4c

second floor (U.S.) le premier étage 23a

secretary le (la) secrétaire 37d, 38a, 40a

secularism la laïcité 11d

security *(airport)* le contrôle de sécurité 32a

sedative le sédatif 40a

seduction la séduction 11e

seductive séduisant(e) *(adj, m, f)* 11e

see voir *(v)* 12c, 30a

see life through rose-colored glasses voir la vie en rose 7a

See you! Salut! 16a

See you later! A tout à l'heure! 16a

See you soon! A bientôt! 16a

See you Sunday! A dimanche! 16a

seed la semence; semer *(v)* 14a

segment *(line)* la ligne segmentée 2b

self-service le self-service 33c

self-sufficient indépendant(e) *(adj, m, f)* 11e

sell vendre *(v)* 23f, 25a

semicolon le point virgule 19c

Senate le Sénat 44

senator le sénateur, la sénatrice 44

send envoyer *(v)*, expédier *(v)* 3e, 19e

sender le destinateur, l'expéditeur 19d, 19e

sense le sens; sentir *(v)* 12c

sense of humor le sens de l'humour 11e

sensitive sensible *(adj, m, f)* 11e

sentence *(grammar)* la phrase 8a, 8n, 19c

sentence *(law)* le jugement 41

sentimental sentimental(e) *(adj, m, f)* 11e

separate (se) séparer *(v)* 11c

separated séparé(e) *(adj, m, f)* 11c

separation la séparation 11c

September le septembre 5b

series *(television)* la série télévisée 20b

serious sérieux *(adj, m)*, sérieuse *(f)* 11e

serious accident l'accident *(m)* grave 39c

sermon le sermon 17a

serve servir *(v)* 24o

serve a prison sentence purger *(v)* une peine de prison 41

server *(restaurant)* le serveur, la serveuse 24m

service le service 24m; **services** les services 35b

set *(numbers)* l'ensemble *(m)* 1f

set of drums *(music)* la batterie 28c

set the table mettre *(v)* le couvert 23f; mettre la table 24o

seven sept 1a

seventeen dix-sept 1a

seventh septième 1b

seventy soixante-dix 1a

several plusieurs *(adj/adv)* 3c

sew coudre *(v)* 25g

sewing machine la machine à coudre 23d

sex le sexe 11a, 38b

shade l'ombre *(f)* 6a

shadow l'ombre *(f)* 6a

shaft *(of motor)* l'arbre-moteur *(m)*, l'arbre de couche 33e

shake hands serrer *(v)* la main à quelqu'un, donner *(v)* la main à quelqu'un 16a

shame la honte 21a

shampoo le shampooing 12d, 25f, 35c

shave *(oneself)* (se) raser *(v)* 12d

shaving cream la crème à raser, la mousse à raser 25f

she elle 8h

shed light on tirer *(v)* quelque chose au clair 13a

sheep le mouton 15a

sheet *(bed)* le drap 23d; les draps 35c

sheet *(of paper)* la feuille de papier 25c

shelf l'étagère *(f)* 23a

shellfish les crustacés *(m, pl)* 24d

sherbet le sorbet 24g

shirt la chemise 25k

shock le choc; **in shock** sous le choc 39c

shoe la chaussure 25n

shoe horn le chausse-pied 25n

shoe repair store la cordonnerie 25n

shoe store le magasin de chaussures 25n

shoelace le lacet 25n

shoot tirer *(v)* 39b

shop la boutique 25a; **to shop** faire *(v)* des achats, faire des emplettes, faire du shopping 25a

shop for food faire *(v)* les courses 24o

shop window la vitrine 25a

shoplifting le vol à l'étalage 39b

shopping bag le sac à provisions 23d

shopping mall le centre commercial, la grande surface 25a

short *(height)* petit(e) *(adj, m, f)* 3c, 11a, 25l

short *(thing)* court(e) *(adj, m, f)* 3b, 37f

short story le conte, la nouvelle 20a, 28d

shorten *(clothing)* raccourcir *(v)* 25m

short-term à court terme 4e

shot *(injection)* la piqûre, l'injection *(f)* 25h, 40a

shoulder l'épaule *(f)* 12a

shout le cri; crier *(v)* 17a, 39a

shovel la pelle 25b

show (*entertainment*) le spectacle 28c

show (*television*) l'émission (*f*) 20b

shower la douche 23a, 35c

shredder, paper le déchiqueteur 38c

shrewd rusé(e) (*adj, m, f*) 11e

shrewdness la ruse 11e

shrimp la crevette 24d

shrink rétrécir (*v*) 25m

Shut up! Ferme-la! Tais-toi! 17a

shy timide (*adj, m, f*) 11e

sick malade (*adj*) 11a, 40a

sickness la maladie 11a, 40a

side (*angle*) côté (*adj*) 2b

sideburns les favoris (*m, pl*), les pattes (*f, pl*) 12a

side-view mirror (*vehicle*) le rétroviseur extérieur 33e

sidewalk le trottoir 36a

sigh of relief le soupir de soulagement (*m*) 21a

sight la vision 12c, 40a; la vue 12c, 40a

sign (*one's name*) signer (*v*) 11f, 19c, 26

signature la signature 11f, 19c, 26, 38b

signs of the zodiac les signes (*m*) du zodiaque 5d

silence le silence 17a

silent silencieux (*adj, m*), silencieuse (*adj, f*) 17a; **to be silent** se taire (*v*) 17a

silk la soie 13c, 25l

silkworm le ver à soie 15d

silly bête (*adj, m, f*) 11e

silver l'argent (*m*) 13c, 25i

silver (*color*) argent (*adj, invariable*), argenté (*adj*) 7a

silver anniversary les noces (*f*) d'argent 11c

simple simple (*adj, m, f*) 11e, 22a

simultaneous simultané(e) (*adj*) 4e

simultaneously simultanément (*adv*) 4e

since depuis (*prep*) 4e; comme (*conj*) 8p; depuis que (*conj*) 8p

since Monday depuis lundi 4e

since yesterday depuis hier 4e

sincere sincère (*adj, m, f*) 11e

sincerity la sincérité 11e

sine le sinus 2b

sing chanter (*v*) 28c

singer le chanteur, la chanteuse 25j, 28c

single (*unmarried*) célibataire 38b

single room une chambre à un lit, pour une personne 35b

singular le singulier (*adj, m*), singulière (*adj, f*) 8a

sink (*kitchen*) l'évier (*m*) 23a; (*bathroom*) le lavabo 23a, 35c

siren la sirène 39a

sister la soeur 10a

sister-in-law la belle-soeur 10a

sit down s'asseoir (*v*) 3e, 32c

six six 1a

sixteen seize 1a

sixth sixième 1b

sixty soixante 1a; **about sixty** une soixantaine 1c

size la grandeur 3b; la mesure, la taille 3b, 25k; (*of shoe*) la pointure 25n

skate patiner (*v*) 27b; (**ice skate**) le patin à glace 27b

skateboard le skateboard, la planche à roulettes 27b

ski faire (*v*) du ski, skier (*v*) 27b

ski resort la station de ski 36b

skier le skieur, la skieuse 27b

skiing le ski 27b, 36b

skimmed milk le lait écrémé 24h

skin la peau 12a

skinny maigre (*adj*) 11a

skip a class sécher (*v*) un cours 37f

skip school faire (*v*) l'école buissonnière 37f

skirt la jupe 25k

sky le ciel 6a, 13b

sleep dormir (v) 12b

sleeping bag le sac de couchage 36b

sleeve la manche 25g

slice la tranche 24i; trancher (v) 24o

slice of cream cake la tranche de gâteau à la crème 24i

slide la diapositive 20b, 25d

slide projector le projecteur pour diapositives (f, pl) 20b, 37b

sliding door la porte coulissante 35c

slim maigre (adj) 11a

slip *(undergarment)* la combinaison, le fond de robe, le jupon 25k

slipper le chausson, la pantoufle 25n

Slippery When Wet Chaussée glissante 33d

sloppy désorganisé(e) (adj, m, f); négligé(e) (adj, m, f) 11e

slot *(for tokens)* la fente 18a

slow lent(e) (adj) 3e, 4e

slow down ralentir (v) 33c

slowly lentement (adv) 3e, 4e

small *(size)* petit(e) (adj, m, f) 3c, 11a, 25l

small bill *(banknote, currency)* le petit billet 26

small letter *(lower case letter)* la lettre minuscule 19c

small round loaf of bread la petite boule 24i

smart intelligent(e) (adj, m, f) 11e

smart board le tableau interactif 37b

smash *(auto collision)* la collision 39c

smell l'odeur (f) 12c; la senteur 12c; sentir (v) 12c

smile le sourire; sourire (v) 11e, 21a; **to force an uneasy smile** sourire (v) jaune 7a

smock la blouse 25k

smoke la fumée 13c, 39a

smoke shop le bureau de tabac 25e

smoking compartment fumeurs 34

smooth lisse (adj) 13d

snack le casse-croûte, le goûter 24a

snack bar le buffet 24m

snails les escargots (m, pl) 24g

snake le serpent 15c

sneeze l'éternuement (m); éternuer (v) 40a

snob snob (n/adj, m, f) 11e

snobbish hautain(e) (adj, m, f) 11e

snow la neige; neiger (v) 6a

snow goggles les lunettes (f, pl) de glacier (m) 27b

snowboarding le surf des neiges 27b

So? Et alors? 9

So, so! Comme-ci, comme-ça! (adv) 16a

so that afin que (conj), pour que (conj) 8p

soap le savon 12d, 25f, 35c

soap opera *(radio and television)* le feuilleton, le soap 20b

soap powder la lessive en poudre 25g

soccer le foot 27b; **to play soccer** jouer (v) au foot 27b

soccer ball le ballon 27b

Social Welfare l'Assistance (f) sociale 44

socialism le socialisme 44

socialist le (la) socialiste 44

socialist party le parti socialiste 44

sociology la sociologie 37e

sock *(clothing)* la chaussette 25n

sodium le sodium 13c

sodium bicarbonate le bicarbonate de soude 25h

sodium citrate le citrate de soude 25h

sofa le canapé, le sofa 23c

soft mou *(adj, m)*, doux *(adj, m)* 13d

soft-boiled egg l'oeuf *(m)* à la coque 24h

soft drink la gazeuse 24k

software *(computers)* le logiciel, le software 42b

solar cell la cellule solaire 45a

solar eclipse l'éclipse *(f)* solaire 13a

solar energy l'énergie *(f)* solaire 13c, 45a

solar system le système solaire 13a

sole *(fish)* la sole 15c, 24d

solid le solide 13c

solid figures les figures *(f)* solides 2a

solstice le solstice 5c

soluble soluble *(adj)* 13d

solution la solution 1f

solve résoudre *(v)* 1f

solve a problem résoudre *(v)* un problème 1f, 37f

some quelque(s) *(adj)* 3c; *see also* **partitive** 8d

some of it (them) en *(pron)* 3c, 8o

some (people) des gens 8o

someone quelqu'un *(m)*, quelqu'une *(f)* *(pron)* 8o

Someone assaulted me! On m'a agressé(e)! 39b

Someone stole my . . . On m'a volé mon / ma . . . 39b

something quelque chose *(pron)* 8o

something to declare quelque chose à déclarer 31

somewhere quelque part *(adv)* 3d

son le fils 10a

son-in-law le gendre 10a

song la chanson 25j, 28c

soon bientôt *(adv)* 4e

sooner or later tôt ou tard 4e

sore back le mal au dos 40a

sore throat le mal de gorge 40a

sore/twisted neck le mal au cou, un torticolis 40a

sorrow le chagrin 21a

sorting le triage 38c

soul l'âme *(f)* 11d

sound le bruit, le son 12c

soundtrack la bande sonore 28a

soup la soupe, le potage 24g; **of the day** du jour 24g

sour aigre *(adj, m, f)* 24p

south le sud 3d; **to the south** au sud 3d

South America l'Amérique *(f)* du Sud 30b

South Pole le Pôle Sud 13e

southern méridional(e) *(adj)* 3d

space l'espace *(m)* 2b, 13a

space shuttle la navette spatiale 42

spacecraft le vaisseau spatial 42

spades *(cards)* la pique 27a

Spain l'Espagne *(f)* 30b

spam le spam, le pourriel 20b, 43

Spanish *(nationality)* Espagnol *(m)*, Espagnole *(f)* 30d; *(language)* l'espagnol *(m)* 30d

spark l'étincelle *(f)* 39a

spark plug *(vehicle)* la bougie 33e

sparrow le moineau 15b

speak parler *(v)* 17a

speak badly of someone diffamer *(v)* quelqu'un 17a

speaker *(audio apparatus)* la caisse acoustique 20b

special delivery l'expédition express 19e

specialist le (la) spécialiste 40a

species l'espèce *(f)* 14a

speech le discours 17a

speed la vitesse 3a, 33c

Speed Limit Vitesse maximum, la limitation de vitesse 33d

speed up accélérer *(v)* 33c

speedometer le compteur de vitesse 33e

spelling l'orthographe *(f)* 19c

spend *(money)* dépenser *(v)* 4e, 25a

spend *(time)* passer *(v)* 4e

sphere la sphère 2a

spice l'épice *(f)* 24j

spicy épicé(e) *(adj, m, f)* 24p

spider l'araignée *(f)* 15d

spinach les épinards *(m, pl)* 14e, 24e

spirit l'esprit *(m)* 11d

spiritual spirituel(le) *(adj, m, f)* 11d

splint l'éclisse *(f)* 39c

spoke *(bicycle)* le rayon 33a

spoon la cuiller (la cuillère) 23d, 24l

sporadic sporadique *(adj)* 4e

sporadically sporadiquement *(adv)* 4e

sport le sport 27b

sport utility vehicle le véhicule sport utilitaire 33a

sports car la voiture de sport 33a

sports fan l'enthousiaste *(m/f)* du sport, le fan, le (la) fanatique du sport 27b

spot *(stain)* la tache 25g

spouse l'époux, l'épouse 11c

spring *(metal coil)* le ressort 25i

spring *(season)* le printemps 5c

square la place 11f, 36a; le carré 2a

square bracket le crochet 19c

square centimeter le centimètre carré 3a

square kilometer le kilomètre carré 3a

square meter le mètre carré 3a

square millimeter le millimètre carré 3a

square root la racine au carré 1e

squared au carré 1e

squid le calmar 24d

stable stable *(adj, m, f)* 13d

stadium le stade 27b

stage *(theater)* la scène 28e

stain la tache 25g

stainless steel l'acier *(m)* inoxydable 13c

stairs l'escalier 23a, 35b

stamp *(postage)* le timbre-poste 19e, 27a

stamp collecting la collection de timbres, la philatélie 27a

stand in line faire *(v)* la queue 15a

staple l'agrafe *(f)* 19d, 25c, 38c

stapler l'agrafeuse *(f)* 19d, 25c, 38c

star l'étoile *(f)* 6a, 13a

starch l'amidon *(m)* 25g

start *(car)* mettre *(v)* en marche, démarrer *(v)* 33c

state l'état *(m)* 13e, 44

state (to make a statement) affirmer *(v)* 17a

statement l'affirmation *(f)* 17a

station *(radio)* la station de radio 20b

station *(train, bus, subway)* la gare, la station 34

station wagon le break 33b

stationery store la papeterie 25c

statistical statistique *(adj)* 1f

statistics la statistique 1f, 37e

STD la MST 40a

steak le bifteck 24g

steal dérober *(v)*, voler *(v)* 39b

steel l'acier *(m)* 13c

steering wheel le volant 33e

stem la tige 14a

stereo la chaîne-stéréo, stéréo(phonique) *(adj)* 20b

stethoscope le stéthoscope 40a

stiff (twisted) neck le torticolis 40a

still (as yet) encore *(adv)*, toujours *(adv)* 4e

stingy radin *(m)*, radine *(f)* 11e

stitch le point 25g

stock (share) l'action *(f)* 26

stock market / exchange la Bourse 26

stocking le bas 25n

stomach l'estomac *(m)* 12a, 40a

stone la pierre 13b

stool (*furniture*) le tabouret 23c

stop arrêter (*v*) 3e

Stop Arrêt 33d, 34

stop oneself s'arrêter (*v*) 3e

Stop thief! Au voleur! 39b

store le magasin 25a

store clerk l'employé(e) (*m/f*) 25a

store hours les heures (*f, pl*) 25a

store window la vitrine 25a

stork la cigogne 15b

storm la tempête 6a

story (*literature*) le conte, l'histoire (*f*) 17a

stove la cuisinière électrique (à gaz) 23d

straight (*angle*) droit (*adj*) 2b

straight ahead tout droit (*adv*) 36c

straight line la ligne droite 2b

strawberry la fraise 14d, 24f

strawberry ice cream la glace aux fraises 24h

street la rue 11f, 36a, 38b

street corner le coin de la rue 33c

street sign la plaque de rue 36a

streetcar le tram, le tramway 33a

strength la force 11a

strike (*labor*) la grève 44

string la ficelle 19d, 25c; (*of a musical instrument*) la corde 28c

string bean le haricot vert 14e, 24e

stringed instruments les instruments (*m, pl*) à cordes (*f*) 28c

striped rayé(e) (*adj, m, f*) 25l

strong fort(e) (*adj*) 11a, 11e, 13d, 40a

structure la structure 13c

stubborn têtu(e) (*adj, m, f*) 11e; entêté(e) (*adj, m, f*) 11e

student l'étudiant(e) (*m/f*) 37d

study étudier (*v*) 22b, 37f

stuff l'étoffe (*f*), le tissu 13c

stuffed egg l'oeuf (*m*) dur farci 24h

stupid bête, stupide (*adj, m, f*) 11e

style (*fashion*) la mode, à la mode, au dernier cri 25k, 25l; (*writing*) le style 28d

subject le sujet 8a, 8h

subject (*learning matter*) la matière 37e

subjunctive subjonctif (*adj, m*), subjonctive (*adj, f*) 8a

subordinate subordonné(e) (*adj, m, f*) 8a

substance la substance 13c

subtract soustraire (*v*) 1e

subtraction la soustraction 1e

suburbs la banlieue, les environs (*m, pl*) 30a

subway le métro(politain) 34

subway station la station de métro 34

sue poursuivre (*v*) en justice 41

suffer souffrir (*v*) 40a

suffice suffire (*v*) 3c

sufficient suffisant(e) (*adj*) 3c

sugar le sucre 24j

suggest suggérer (*v*) 17a

suit (*clothing*) le complet, le costume 25k

suit jacket la veste, le veston 25k

suitcase la valise 31

sulfide le sulfure 13c

sulfur le soufre 13c

sulfuric acid l'acide (*m*) sulfurique 13c

sum le calcul 1f

sum up additionner (*v*) 1f; sommer (*v*) 1f

summarize résumer (*v*), faire un résumé 17a

summary le sommaire, le résumé 17a

summer l'été (*m*) 5c

summons la citation 41

sun le soleil 5c, 6a, 13a

Sunday le dimanche 5a

sunlight la lumière solaire, la lumière du soleil 13a

sunray le rayon de soleil *(m)* 13a

sunrise le lever du soleil 4a

sunset le coucher du soleil 4a

suntan lotion la crème solaire 36b

superintendent *(of apartment building)* le (la) concierge 23g

supermarket le supermarché 24n

superstitious superstitieux, superstitieuse *(adj, m, f)* 11e

supplementary supplémentaire *(adj)* 2b

suppository le suppositoire 40a

surgeon le chirurgien, la chirurgienne 38a, 40a

surgery la chirurgie 40a

surname le nom de famille *(f)* 11f, 38b

surprise la surprise; surprendre *(v)* 21a

surprised surpris(e) *(adj, m, f)* 21a

SUV le SUV, le véhicule sport utilitaire 33b

swallow (bird) l'hirondelle 15b

swan le cygne 15b

swear *(e.g., in court)* jurer *(v)* 17a; *(e.g., profanity)* dire *(v)* des jurons 17a

swear word le juron 17a

sweater le pull-over, le sweater, le tricot 25k

Sweden la Suède 30b

Swedish *(nationality)* Suédois *(m)*, Suédoise *(f)* 30d; *(language)* le suédois 30d

sweet doux *(adj, m)*, douce *(f)* 11e, 24p

swim nager *(v)* 27b

swimming la natation 27b

swimming pool la piscine 27b, 35b

Swiss *(nationality)* Suisse *(m/f)* 30d

switch *(light)* l'interrupteur *(m)* 23a, 35c

switchboard telephone operator le (la) standardiste 18b

Switzerland la Suisse 30b

swollen enflé *(m)*, enflée *(f)* 40a

swordfish l'espadon *(m)* 15c

symbol le symbole 1f, 17a

sympathetic compatissant(e) *(adj, m, f)* 21a

sympathy la compassion 21a

symphony la symphonie 28c

synagogue la synagogue 11d

synthesizer le synthétiseur 28c

synthetic synthétique *(adj, m, f)* 13d

syringe la seringue 40a

syrup le sirop 25h

T

T-shirt le T-shirt 25k

tab *(of a typewriter)* le tabulateur 19d

table la table 23a, 24l, 35c

table of contents la table des matières 20a

tablecloth la nappe 23d, 24l

tablespoon la cuiller à soupe 23d

tablet *(medication)* le comprimé 25h, 40a

tableware les ustensiles *(m, pl)* à (de) table 23d, 24l; le couvert 24l

tack la punaise 37b, 38c

tail la queue 15a

tailor le tailleur, la couturière 38a

tailored suit *(woman's)* le tailleur 25k

take prendre *(v)* 25a, 34

take a holiday avoir *(v)* congé *(m)* 36b

take a picture *(photo)* prendre *(v)* une photo 25d

take a subject/course suivre *(v)* un cours 37f

take a trip faire *(v)* un voyage 30a

take a walk faire *(v)* une promenade 3e

take an exam passer *(v)* un examen 37f

take an excursion faire *(v)* une excursion 36a

take attendance faire *(v)* l'appel 37f

take back *(return an item)* rendre *(v)* 25a

take drugs prendre *(v)* de la drogue, se droguer *(v)* 45b

take in (clothing) reprendre *(v)* 25m

take notes prendre *(v)* des notes 37f

take off *(remove)* enlever *(v)* 25m; *(airplane)* le décollage 32c; décoller *(v)* 32c

take one's temperature prendre *(v)* la température 40a

take-out *(food)* à emporter *(v)* 24m, 24o

take place avoir lieu 4e

talcum powder le talc 25f

talented artistique *(adj)* 11e

talk parler *(v)* 17a; le discours 17a

tall grand(e) *(adj)* 3b, 11a; haut(e) *(adj)* 3b

tangent la tangente 2a, 2b

tanker *(truck)* le camion-citerne 33a

tape *(magnetic)* la bande magnétique 20b

tape recorder le magnétophone 20b, 37b

tapioca pudding le tapioca au lait 24h

tariff le tarif 31

tarot le tarot 27a

tartlet la tartelette 24i

taste goûter *(v)* 12c

tasty savoureux *(adj, m)*, savoureuse *(f)* 24p

tattoo le tatouage, tatouer *(v)* 38a

tattoo artist le tatoueur, la tatoueuse 38a

Taurus le Taureau 5d

taxi le taxi 33a

tea le thé 24k

teach enseigner *(v)* 37f

teacher l'enseignant(e) *(m/f)* 37d; le professeur, la professeure 37d, 38a

teacher's desk le bureau, la chaire 37b

team l'équipe *(f)* 27b

teapot la théière 23d

tears *(weeping)* les larmes *(f, pl)* 21a

teaspoon la cuiller à café 23d, 24l

technical book le livre de technologie 25o

technical school l'institut *(m)* d'enseignement technique 37a

technician le technicien, la technicienne 37d

technology la technologie 42

teenager adolescent(e) *(n, adj)* 11b

telecommunication la télécommunication 18a, 42

telecommunications satellite le satellite de télécommunications 18a

teleconference la télé-conférence 42

telephone le téléphone, téléphoner *(v)* 18a, 18b, 23e, 35c, 38c; l'appareil *(m)* téléphonique 18a

telephone credit card la télécarte 18a, 36a

telephone number le numéro de téléphone *(m)* 11f, 18b, 38b

telephone operator le (la) téléphoniste 18b

telephone switchboard operator le (la) standardiste 18b

telephone see also phone

television la télévision 20b

television set le téléviseur 20b, 23d, 35c

tell dire *(v)* 17a

tell a joke dire (raconter) *(v)* une plaisanterie, une blague 17a

tell a story raconter *(v)* une histoire, conter 17a

teller (cashier) le caissier, la caissière 26

teller's window le guichet 26

telly (TV) la télé 20b

temperature la température 6c; *(fever)* la fièvre 40a

template le gabarit 2b

temple le temple 11d, 36a

temporarily temporairement *(adv)* 4e

temporary temporaire *(adj)* 4e

ten dix 1a; **about ten** une dizaine 1c

tenant le (la) locataire 23g

tennis (to play) jouer *(v)* au tennis 27b; *(the sport)* le tennis 27b

tennis racket la raquette 27b

tense (verb) le temps 8a, 8n

tent la tente de camping 36b

tenth dixième 1b

terminal l'aérogare *(f)* 32a, le terminal 32a, 42b

termite le termite 15d

terrace la terrasse 23a

territory le territoire 13e

terrorism le terrorisme 45b

tetrahedron le tétraèdre 2a

test l'épreuve *(f)*, l'examen 37f

Testament, New le Nouveau Testament 11d

Testament, Old l'Ancien Testament *(m)* 11d

text le texte 19c, 20a; le texto 18b, 20b; le SMS 18b; envoyer *(v)* un texto 18b

textbook le livre de classe *(f)*, le livre d'étude *(f)*, 25o, le livre de cours 37b

textile le textile 13c

Thailand la Thaïlande 30b

thank remercier *(v)* 17a, 21a

Thank goodness! Dieu merci! Grâce à Dieu! 21a

Thank you! Merci! 16c

thankful reconnaissant(e) *(adj, m, f)* 21a

thankfulness la gratitude, la reconnaissance 21a

that ce *(m, s)*, cet *(m, s)*, cette *(f, s)* 8e

that is to say . . . c'est-à-dire . . . 45c

the le *(m, s)*, la *(f, s)*, l' *(m/f, s)*, les *(m/f, pl)* 8b

the one celui *(m)*, celle *(f)* 8m

the ones ceux *(m)*, celles *(f)* 8m

theater le théâtre 28e

their leur *(m/f, s)*, leurs *(m/f, pl)* 8f

them les 8i; eux *(m)*, elles *(f)* 8l

theme le thème 28d

themselves se 8k

then alors *(adv)*, lors *(adv)* 4e; ensuite *(adv)* 4e

theory of relativity la théorie de la relativité 42

there là *(adv)* 3d, 36c

There's lightning! Il fait des éclairs! 6a

therefore donc *(conj)* 8p, 45c

thermal energy l'énergie *(f)* thermique 45a

thermometer le thermomètre 6c, 25h, 40a

thermostat le thermostat 6c, 35c

these ces *(m/f, pl)* 8e

thesis la thèse 37f

they ils *(m)*, elles *(f)* 8h; eux *(m)*, elles *(f)* 8l

thick épais *(adj, m)*, épaisse *(f)* 3b

thick puree la purée 24g

thick soup le potage 24g

thief le voleur, la voleuse 39b

thigh la cuisse 12a

thin maigre *(adj)* 3b, 11a; mince *(adj)* 3b

think penser *(v)* 22b

third troisième *(adj, m, f)* 1b, 8a

Third World le Tiers Monde 44

thirst la soif 12b

thirteen treize 1a

thirteenth treizième 1b

thirty trente 1a; **about thirty** une trentaine 1c

thirty-one trente et un 1a

thirty-two trente-deux 1a

this ce *(m, s),* cet *(m, s),* cette *(f, s)* 8e

this afternoon cet *(adj, m)* après-midi *(m)* 4a

this evening ce *(adj, m)* soir *(m)* 4a

This is . . . (+ *name in telephone call*) Ici . . . 18b

This looks bad on me. Ceci ne me va pas bien. 25l

This looks nice on me. Ceci me va bien. 25l

this morning ce *(adj, m)* matin *(m)* 4a

this night cette nuit 4a

thorn l'épine *(f)* 14b

those ces *(m/f, pl)* 8e

thought la pensée 22a

thousandth millième 1b

threat la menace 17a

threaten menacer *(v)* 17a

three trois 1a

three-D (3D) goggles les lunettes *(f, pl)* 3D 28a

three-D (3D) movie le film en relief 28a

three-dimensional à trois dimensions *(f, pl)* 2b

three-dimensional space l'espace *(m)* tridimensionnel 13a

three hundred trois cents 1a

three million trois millions 1a

three thousand trois mille 1a

three-year-old de trois ans 11b

threshold le seuil 23a

throat la gorge 12a, 40a

through à travers, par *(prep)* 3d, 36c

throw lancer *(v)* 27b

throw up (vomit) rendre *(v)* 40a

thumb le pouce 12a

thunder le tonnerre, le coup de tonnerre 6a; faire *(v)* un bruit de tonnerre, tonner 6a

Thursday le jeudi 5a

tick *(insect)* la tique 15d

ticket le billet, le ticket 27b, 30a, 32a, 34

ticket *(traffic fine)* la contravention 33c

ticket cancelling machine le composteur de billets 34

ticket counter la délivrance des billets 34

ticket window le guichet 32a

tide la marée 13b

tide, high la marée haute 13b

tide, low la marée basse 13b

tie *(necktie)* la cravate 25k

tie *(score in sports)* le match nul 27b

tiger le tigre 15a

tight serré(e) *(adj, m, f)* 25l

time *(hour)* l'heure *(f);* **every time** la fois; *(in general)* le temps 4a

Time flies! Le temps fuit! 4a

timetable *(schedule)* l'horaire *(m)* 4e, 34

time zone le fuseau horaire 13e

timpani les timbales *(f, pl)* 28c

tint teindre *(v),* la teinte 7c

tip le pourboire 24m; donner *(v)* un pourboire 24m

tire *(of wheel)* le pneu(matique) 33a, 33e

tissue le mouchoir de papier 25h

title le titre 11f, 16b, 20a

to à *(prep)* 3d, 8g

to clone cloner *(v)* 42

to go + à + city; to go to Paris aller *(v)* à Paris 30c

to go + prep. + country; to go to France aller *(v)* en France 30c

to have reason to be worried avoir de quoi s'inquiéter 21a

to her lui (à elle) 8j

to him lui (à lui) 8j

to laugh halfheartedly, reluctantly
rire *(v)* jaune, rire *(v)* à
contrecoeur 21a

to me me (à moi) 8j

to someone's place chez quelqu'un
3d

to the east à l'est 36c

to the fourth power à la quatrième
puissance 1e

to the left à gauche 3d, 33c, 36c

to the north au nord 36c

to the nth power à la puissance n
1e

to the power of à la puissance de
1e

to the right à droite 3d, 33c, 36c

to the south au sud 36c

to the west à l'ouest 36c

to them leur 8j

to this day jusqu'à ce jour *(adv)*
4e

to us nous 8j

To whom it may concern A qui de
droit 19a

to you *(s, fam)*, vous *(pl)* 8j

toad le crapaud 15c

toast *(in honor of someone)* porter
(v) un toast 17a

toast griller *(v)* 24o; **Melba
toast** la biscotte 24i

toaster le grille-pain 23d

tobacco le tabac 25e

tobacconist le buraliste 25e

today aujourd'hui *(adv)* 4a

toe l'orteil *(m)* 12a

toilet les toilettes *(f, pl)* 32c,
35c; W. C. *(m, pl)* 35c, 37c

toilet paper le papier hygiénique
35c

tolerance la tolérance 21a

tolerate tolérer *(v)* 21a

Toll Péage 33d

toll booth le poste de péage 33c

tomato la tomate 14d, 24f

tomorrow demain *(adv)* 4a

day after tomorrow après-
demain *(adv)* 4a (See note.)

tomorrow afternoon demain après-
midi *(m)* 4a

tomorrow evening demain soir
(m) 4a

tomorrow morning demain matin
(m) 4a

tomorrow night demain pendant la
nuit 4a; demain soir *(m)* 4a

toner le toner 19d

tongue la langue 12a, 40b

tonight ce soir *(evening)*, cette
nuit *(actual night)* 4a

tonsillitis l'amygdalite *(f)* 40a

tonsils les amygdales *(f, pl)* 40a

Too bad! Dommage! 21b

too much trop *(adv)* 3c

tool l'outil *(m)* 25b

tools les outils *(m, pl)* 23d, 33c

tooth la dent 12a, 40b

tooth decay la carie dentaire 40b

toothache le mal aux dents 40b

toothbrush la brosse à dents *(f,
pl)* 12d, 25h, 40b

toothpaste la pâte dentifrice 12d,
25h; le dentifrice 12d, 40b

toothpick le cure-dent 24l

top le sommet 3d; **at (to) the top**
au sommet 3d

topaz la topaze 25i

Torah la Torah 11d

tornado la tornade 6a

touch le toucher 12c; toucher *(v)*
12c

tour *(travel)* le voyage organisé
30a

tour bus l'autocar *(m)* de
tourisme (d'excursion) 30a

tour guide le (la) guide 30a

tourist le (la) touriste 30a, 36c

Tow-Away Zone Zone de
remorquage 33d

tow truck la dépanneuse 33c

toward vers *(prep)* 3d

towel la serviette de toilette 12d;
la serviette de bain 35c

tower la tour 36a

town la ville 11f

track la piste 27b; *(of a train)* la voie 34

tractor truck le camion-tracteur 33a

trade le métier 38a

trade/labor union le syndicat 44

traditional traditionnel(le) *(adj, m, f)* 11e

traffic la circulation 33c

traffic accident l'accident *(m)* de voiture 39c

traffic jam l'embouteillage *(m)* le bouchon 33c

traffic lane la voie 33c

traffic lights les feux *(m, pl)* 33c, 36a

traffic police l'agent *(m)* de patrouille 33b

traffic signal le feu de signalisation 33c

tragedy la tragédie 20a, 28e

trailer la remorque 33a

train le train 34; **direct train** le train direct 34; **express train** le train express 34

train station la gare 34

transformer *(hardware)* le transformateur 25b

transitive transitif *(adj, m)*, transitive *(adj, f)* 8a

translate traduire *(v)* 17a

translation la traduction 17a

transmission *(radio, television)* l'émission 20b

transparent transparent(e) *(adj, m, f)* 7b, 13d

transplant transplanter *(v)* 14a

transplantation la transplantation 14a

transport truck le camion des marchandises 33a

trapezoid le trapèze 2a

trash can la poubelle 23d

travel voyager *(v)* 30a

travel agency l'agence *(f)* de voyages *(m, pl)* 30a

traveler's check le chèque de voyage *(m)* 26, 35b

tray le plateau à servir 23d, 241, 32c

tree l'arbre *(m)* 14c

trial le procès 41; **trial lawyer** l'avoué *(m)*, la femme avoué 41; **to be on trial** être *(v)* en procès 41

triangle le triangle 2a

trigonometric trigonométrique *(adj)* 2b

trigonometry la trigonométrie 2b, 37e

trip le voyage 30a, 36b

triple triple *(n/adj, m, f)* 3c

tripod *(easel)* le chevalet 28b

trolley le trolley 33a

trombone le trombone 28c

tropic le tropique 13e

Tropic of Cancer le Tropique du Cancer 13e

Tropic of Capricorn le Tropique du Capricorne 13e

tropical tropique *(adj)* 13e; tropical(e) *(adj, m, f)* 6a

troublemaker provocateur, provocatrice *(adj, m, f)* 11e

trout la truite 15c, 24d

truck le camion 33a

truck, pickup la camionnette 33a

trumpet la trompette 28c

trunk *(of tree)* le tronc 14a; *(of a vehicle)* le coffre 33e

trust la confiance 21a; avoir *(v)* confiance en 21a

try on *(clothing)* essayer *(v)* 25m

tuba le tuba 28c

Tuesday le mardi 5a

tulip la tulipe 14b

tuna fish le thon 15c, 24d

tunnel le tunnel 33c

turbulence la turbulence 32c

turkey la dinde 15b, 24c

turn tourner *(v)* 3e, 36c; *(vehicle)* virer *(v)* 33c

turn left tournez à gauche 36c

turn off éteindre *(v)* 20b, 35c

turn on allumer *(v)* 20b, 35c

turn pages, leaf through tourner *(v)* les pages, feuilleter *(v)* 20a

turn right tournez à droite 36c

turn signal *(vehicle)* le clignotant *(m)* 33e

turned out badly *(photo, picture)* la photo mal réussie 25d

turned out well *(photo, picture)* la photo bien réussie 25d

turtle la tortue 15c

TV la télé 20b

TV movie le téléfilm 20b

twelfth douzième 1b

twelve douze 1a

twenty vingt 1a; **about twenty** une vingtaine 1c

twenty-one vingt et un 1a

twenty-two vingt-deux 1a

twin le jumeau, la jumelle 10a

twisted neck le torticolis 40a

two deux 1a

two billion deux milliards 1a

two-dimensional à deux dimensions *(f, pl)* 2b

two hundred deux cents 1a

two hundred and one deux cent un 1a

two hundred thousand deux cent mille 1a

two million deux millions 1a

two thousand deux mille 1a

two thousand and one deux mille un 1a

two-year-old de deux ans 11b

type taper *(v)* (à la machine) 19d, 37f

typewriter la machine à écrire *(v)* 19d, 37f, 38c

typist le dactylographe, la dactylographe 38a

typography la typographie 20a

U

Ugh! Pouah! 21c

ugliness la laideur 11a

ugly laid(e) *(adj, m, f)* 11a, 25l

ultraviolet light la lumière ultraviolette 13a

unacceptable inacceptable *(adj)* 21b

Unbelievable! Incroyable! 21c

uncle l'oncle 10a

under sous *(prep)* 3d

underdeveloped countries les pays *(m, pl)* sous-développés 44

underlining le soulignement 19c

underpants (panties) le slip 25k

understand comprendre *(v)* 22b, 37f

underwear les sous-vêtements *(m, pl)* 25k

undress se déshabiller *(v)* 25m

unemployment le chômage 38d

Unfortunately! Malheureusement! 21c

unilateral unilatéral(e) *(adj, m, f)* 44

United States of America les Etats-Unis *(m, pl)* d'Amérique 30b

universal suffrage le suffrage universel 44

universe l'univers *(m)* 13a

university l'université *(f)* 37a, 38b

university degree la licence 11f; le doctorat 11f

unlawful illégal(e) *(adj, m, f)* 41

unleaded gasoline l'essence *(f)* sans plomb 33c

unless à moins que *(conj)* 8p

unmarried célibataire *(adj)* 11c

unpleasant désagréable *(adj, m, f)* 21b

until jusque(s) *(prep)* 4e; jusqu'à ce que *(conj)* 8p

up haut *(adv)*, en haut 3d

upright piano le piano droit 28c

Uranus Uranus *(m)* 13a

urinary system le système urinaire 40a

urinate uriner *(v)* 40a

us nous 8i, 8l

used to, to get s'habituer à 11c

user-friendly *(computers)* facile *(adj, m, f)* à utiliser 43

usually d'habitude *(adv)* 4e

V

vacation les vacances *(f, pl)* 29a, 36b

vaccine le vaccin 25h

vacuum cleaner l'aspirateur 23d

vagina le vagin 12a

vain vaniteux, vaniteuse *(adj, m, f)* 11e

valley le val, la vallée 13b

valve *(a vehicle)* la soupape, le clapet 33e

van le fourgon 33a

vanilla la vanille 24h

vanilla ice cream la glace à la vanille 24h

vapor la vapeur 13c

variable *(numbers)* la variable 1f

variable bank rate le taux variable 26

VCR le VCR, le magnétoscope, le système d'enregistrement *(m)* à vidéocassettes 20b

veal le veau 24c

vector le vecteur 2b

vegetable le (la) légume 14e, 24e

vegetable garden le potager 14e

vegetable market le marché aux légumes 24n

vegetation la végétation 13b

vehicle le véhicule 33a

vein la veine 40a

velocity la vélocité 3a

Venice Venise 30c

vent *(vehicle)* le trou d'aération *(f)* 33e

Venus Vénus *(f)* 13a

verb le verbe 8a, 8n

verdict le verdict 41

versatile versatile *(adj, m, f)* 11e

vertebrate vertébré(e) *(adj, m, f)* 15a

vertex (angle) le sommet 2b

vertical vertical(e) *(adj)* 3d

vest le gilet 25k

Very well! Très bien! *(adv)* 16a

VHS/SECAM/TV le VHS/SECAM/TV 20b

vibrant vibrant(e) *(adj)* 7b

victim la victime 39a, 39b

video camera la caméra vidéo 25d

video conference la visioconférence, la vidéo-conférence 38c, 42

video game le jeu-vidéo 20b

videocassette recorder la vidéocassette 20b

videorock le vidéorock 20b

videotape la bande magnétique 20b

view la vue 35b

village le village 11f

vinegar le vinaigre 24j

viola la viole 28c

violence la violence 39b

violet la violette 14b

violin le violon 28c

violinist le (la) violoniste 28c

Virgo la Vierge 5d

virile viril(e) *(adj)* 11a

virus le virus 42b

visa le visa 31

visit *(a person)* rendre *(v)* visite à 29b

visit *(a place)* visiter *(v)* 30a

vitamin la vitamine 25h

vocabulary le vocabulaire 17a

vocational school l'institut *(m)* d'enseignement technique 37a

volcano le volcan 13b

volleyball le volley-ball 27b

volume le volume 3a

volume control le réglage de volume 20b

vomit vomir *(v)* 40a

vote le vote; voter *(v)* 44

vowel la voyelle 8a

vulnerable vulnérable *(adj, m, f)* 11e

W

wafer la gaufrette 24i

waffle la gaufre 24i

wage la paie, le salaire 38d

waist la taille 12, 12a

wait *(for)* attendre *(v)* 4e, 19e, 34

waiting room la salle d'attente *(f)* 32a

wake up se réveiller *(v)* 12b

wake-up call le réveil par téléphone 35b

walk marcher *(v)* 3e, 12b; aller *(v)* à pied *(m)* 3e; la promenade 3e

walkie-talkie le talkie-walkie 20b

wall le mur 23a

wall map la carte murale 37b

wall-to-wall carpeting la moquette 23c

walnut la noix 14d, 24f

walnut tree le noyer 14c

want to désirer *(v)*, vouloir *(v)* 21a

war la guerre 44

warm up se chauffer *(v)* 6b

warn avertir *(v)*, prévenir *(v)* 17a

warning l'avertissement *(m)* 17a

wash laver *(v)* 23f, 25g

wash basin *(sink)* le lavabo 23a, 35c

wash one's hair se laver *(v)* les cheveux *(m, pl)* 12d

wash oneself se laver *(v)* 12d

wash the clothes faire *(v)* la lessive 23f

wash the dishes faire *(v)* la vaisselle 23f

washable lavable *(adj, m, f)* 25g

washcloth le gant de bain, le gant de toilette 12d

washing machine le lave-linge, la machine à laver *(v)* 23d

wasp la guêpe 15d

wastebasket la corbeille à papier 23d, 38c

watch regarder *(v)* 20b

watch *(timepiece)* la montre 4d, 25i; **The watch is fast.** La montre avance. 4d; **The watch is slow.** La montre retarde. 4d

watchband le bracelet d'une montre 4d, 25i

watch battery la pile d'une montre 4d

water l'eau *(f)* 13c, 23e, 24k; arroser *(v)* 14a

water fountain la fontaine 36a

water pollution la pollution des eaux 45a

water polo le water-polo 27b

water skiing le ski nautique 27b

watercolor l'aquarelle *(f)* 28b

watermelon le melon d'eau, la pastèque 14d, 24f

wave l'onde *(f)*, le flot, la vague 13b

we nous 8h, 8l

weak faible *(adj, m, f)* 11a, 11e, 13d, 40a

weakness la faiblesse 11a

weapon l'arme *(f)* 39b

wear porter *(v)* 25m

weather le temps 6a; **The weather is beautiful.** Il fait beau temps. 6a; **The weather is rotten.** Il fait un temps pourri. 6a

weather forecast la prévision scientifique du temps, la météo 6c

weather report le bulletin météorologique 6c

webcam la webcam 43

webmaster le webmestre, la webmestre 38a

website le site web 20b

wedding le mariage 11c, 29a; la noce 11c; les noces *(f, pl)* 29a

wedding announcement le faire-part de mariage 19e

wedding invitation l'invitation 19e

wedding ring l'anneau *(m)* d'alliance, l'anneau *(m)* de mariage, l'alliance *(f)* 11c

Wednesday le mercredi 5a

week la semaine 4a, 4c

a week from . . . . . . en huit 4a

in a week d'ici une semaine 4a

next week la semaine prochaine 4a

weekend le week-end, la fin de semaine 5a

weekly hebdomadaire *(adj)*, hebdomadairement *(adv)* 4c; *(periodical)* hebdomadaire *(adj, n, m, f)* 20a

weigh peser *(v)* 3b, 24o

weigh oneself se peser *(v)* 11a

weight le poids 3a, 11a, 31

weight (due to gravity) la pesanteur 3a

weight lifting l'haltérophilie *(f)* 27b

Welfare l'Assistance *(f)* sociale 44

well-done (*cooked food*) bien cuit(e) *(adj, m, f)* 24b

well-mannered bien élevé(e) *(adj, m, f)* 11e

west l'ouest *(m)* 3d; **to the west** à l'ouest 3d

western occidental(e) *(adj, m, f)* 3d, 11d

whale la baleine 15c

What? Comment? Pardon? Quoi? 9

What a bore! (*person*) Quel raseur! *(m)*; Quelle raseuse! *(f)*; Quelle barbe! 21c

What color is it? De quelle couleur est-ce? 7a

What day is it? Quel jour est-ce? 5a

What do you call this (that) in French? Comment appelle-t-on ceci (cela) en français? 9

What do you think of it? Qu'en pensez-vous? *(pol)*, Qu'en penses-tu? *(fam)* 22b

What does it mean? Que veut dire cela? Que signifie cela? 9

What month are we in? Quel mois sommes-nous? 5b

What month is it? Quel mois est-ce? 5b

What time is it? Quelle heure est-il? 4b

What was I saying? Qu'est-ce que je disais? 17b

What year is it? Quelle année est-ce? 5e

What's the weather like? (How's the weather?) Quel temps fait-il? 6a

What's today's date? Quelle est la date aujourd'hui? 5e

What's your name? Quel est votre nom (ton nom)? 11f; Comment vous appelez-vous? *(pol)*, Comment t'appelles-tu? *(fam)* 16b

wheat le froment, le blé 14a, 24i

wheel la roue 33e

wheelchair le fauteuil roulant 40a

wheel, landing gear (*airplane*) le train d'atterrissage 32c

when quand *(adv)* 4e, 8p, 9

When were you born? Quand êtes-vous né(e)? *(m, f, pol)* 5e

where où *(adv)* 3d, 9

Where do you live? Où demeurez-vous (demeures-tu)? 11f

Where is . . .? Où est . . . ? 36c

whereas tandis que *(conj)* 8p

which (*one*) lequel *(m)*, laquelle *(f)* 9

which (*ones*) lesquels *(m, pl)*, lesquelles *(f, pl)* 9

while pendant que *(conj)* 4e; tandis que *(conj)* 8p

whipped cream la crème Chantilly 24h; **omelette with whipped cream** l'omelette *(f)* mousseline 24h

whisper chuchoter *(v)* 17a

white le blanc *(m)*; la blanche *(f)* 7a; **to be white with fear** être *(v)* vert de peur 7a

who qui *(pron)* 9

Who knows? Qui sait? 17b

whole wheat bread le pain complet 24i

why pourquoi *(adv, conj)* 9

wide large *(adj)* 3b
widow la veuve 11c, 38b
widower le veuf 11c, 38b
width la largeur 3b
wife la femme, l'épouse 10a, 11c
wild animal l'animal *(m)* sauvage 15a
wildflower la fleur sauvage 14b
willingly volontiers *(adv)* 11e
wilted flower la fleur fanée 14b
win gagner *(v)*, le gain 27b
wind *(a timepiece)* remonter *(v)* 4d, 25i
wind *(weather)* le vent 6a; **It's windy.** Il fait du vent. 6a
wind energy l'énergie *(f)* éolienne 45a
wind farm le champ d'éoliennes 45a
wind instruments les instruments *(m, pl)* à vent 28c
windbreaker *(clothing)* le blouson 25k
window la fenêtre 23a; **store/shop window** la vitrine 25a
window *(airplane)* le hublot 32c
window *(computer)* la fenêtre 42b
window seat le siège côté fenêtre, le siège côté hublot 32c
window sill le rebord de la fenêtre 23a
windshield *(vehicle)* le pare-brise 33e
windshield wiper l'essuie-glace *(m)* 33e
windy weather faire *(v)* du vent 6a
wine le vin 24k
wine cellar la cave à vin *(m)* 23b
wineglass le verre à vin 24l
wing l'aile *(f)* 15b, 32c
winter l'hiver *(m)* 5c
wire le fil métallique 25b
wisdom la sagesse 11e, 22a
wisdom tooth la dent de sagesse 40b
wise sage *(adj, m, f)* 11e

with avec 8g
with ice chips avec glaçons *(m, pl)* 24p
with Internet *(in hotel)* avec connexion *(f)* Internet 35b
with sauce *(gravy)* au jus 24b
withdraw *(banking)* prélever *(v)* 26
withdrawal *(banking)* le prélèvement 26
withdrawal slip la fiche de prélèvement *(m)* 26
within *(a certain time)* en *(prep)* 4e
witness le témoin 41; **for the defense** à décharge; **for the prosecution** à charge 41
wolf le loup, la louve 15a
woman la femme 11a
women's shop/clothing le magasin d'habillement féminin 25k
woods le (les) bois *(m)* 13b
wool la laine 13c; en laine 25l
word le mot *(written)*, la parole *(spoken)* 17a, 19c
word processing *(computer)* le traitement de texte 42b
word processor *(computer)* la machine de traitement de texte 42b
work travailler *(v)* 11f, 38d; le travail 11f, 38d; *(literary)* l'ouvrage *(m)* 28d
workday le jour de travail 5a
work out *(body exercises)* faire *(v)* de l'exercice 27b
world le monde 13a, 30a
World Wide Web le web 42b
worm le ver 15d
wound la blessure, la plaie 39b, 39c; blesser *(v)* 39b
wrench *(adjustable)* la clé anglaise 25b
wrestling la lutte 27b
wrist le poignet 12a
wristwatch le bracelet-montre 4d, 25i; la montre 4d; la montre-bracelet 25i

write écrire *(v)* 19e, 20a, 37f
writer l'écrivain *(m)*, l'écrivaine *(f)* 37f
wrong incorrect(e) *(adj, m, f)*, faux *(adj, m)*, fausse *(adj, f)* 37f
Wrong number! *(telephone)* Mauvais numéro! 18b

X, Y, Z

X-ray une radiographie 39c, 40b

yawn le bâillement, bâiller *(v)* 17a
year l'an *(m)*, l'année *(f)* 4c
year two thousand l'an *(m)* deux mille 4c
yell le cri; crier *(v)* 17a
yellow le jaune 7a
yellow pages les pages jaunes *(f, pl)* 18a
Yes! Oui! 16c
yesterday hier *(adv)* 4a
yesterday afternoon hier après-midi 4a
yesterday morning hier matin 4a
yet encore *(adv)* 4e
Yield Cédez 33d
yogurt le yaourt 24h
you tu *(s, fam)*, vous *(s, pl, pol)*, te *(s, fam)* 8h, 8i; toi 8l; vous 8l
young jeune *(adj)* 11b
young lady la demoiselle 11a
young man le jeune homme 11a
younger plus jeune 11b
younger brother le frère cadet 11b

younger sister la soeur cadette 11b
your *(pol)* votre *(m/f, s)*, vos *(m/f, pl)* 8f; *(fam)* ton *(m, s)*, ta *(f, s)*, tes *(m/f, pl)* 8f
You're welcome! Je vous en prie! *(pol)*, Je t'en prie! *(fam)* De rien! Il n'y a pas de quoi! 16c
Yours . . . *(closing of a letter)* Bien à toi *(fam)* 19b
Yours truly . . . *(in a business letter)* Veuillez agréer mes salutations distinguées 19a
yourself *(reflexive)* te *(s, fam)*, vous *(s, pol)* 8k
yourselves *(reflexive)* vous 8k
youth la jeunesse 11b
youth hostel l'auberge *(f)* de jeunesse 35a
youthful juvénile *(adj)*, jeune *(adj, m, f)* 11b
Yuch! Berk! 20b

zebra le zèbre 15a
zenith le zénith 13e
zero zéro 1a, 6c
zipper la fermeture à glissière, la fermeture éclair 25g
zodiac le zodiaque 5d
zone la zone 13e; **time zone** le fuseau horaire 13e
zoo le zoo, le jardin zoologique 15a
zoology la zoologie 15a, 37e
zoom le zoom 25d
zucchini la courgette 14e